# *the* Human Project

## THIRD EDITION

Readings on

the Individual,

Society,

and Culture

*Edited by*
## Clive Cockerton
*Humber College of Applied Arts and Technology*

## Melanie Chaparian
*Humber College of Applied Arts and Technology*

StudyDesk Program
George Byrnes
Humber College of Applied Arts and Technology

Consulting Editor
William R. Hanna
Humber College of Applied Arts and Technology

Editorial Committee
Lynda Archer, George Byrnes, John Elias, Jason MacLean,
Greg Narbey, Declan Neary, Wendy O'Brien,
Colin Pearce, Jerry Persaud, Morton Ritts,
David Stamos, John Steckley, Brian Wetstein

Prentice
Hall

Toronto

**Canadian Cataloguing in Publication Data**

Main entry under title:

The human project : readings on the individual, society, and culture

3rd ed.
Second edition edited by William R. Hanna, Clive Cockerton.
Includes index.
ISBN 0-13-031913-9

1. Humanities.  I. Cockerton, Clive.  II. Chaparian, Melanie, 1958–

AZ221.H85 2002                    001.3      C2001-930694-6

ISBN 0-13-031913-9

Vice-President, Editorial Director: Michael Young
Editor-in-Chief: David Stover
Acquisitions Editor: Andrew Wellner
Executive Marketing Manager: Christine Cozens
Associate Editor: Tammy Scherer
Production Editor: Joe Zingrone
Copy Editor: Madeline Koch
Production Coordinator: Wendy Moran
Page Layout: Arlene Edgar
Photo Research: Patricia Buckley
Permissions Research: Jane McWhinney
Art Director: Mary Opper
Cover/Interior Design: Amy Harnden
Cover Image: Caspar David Friedrich, *The Wanderer*. Hamburger Kunsthalle,
photographed by Elke Walford, Fotowerkstatt.


2 3 4 5     05 04 03 02


Printed and bound in Canada.

# CONTENTS

# UNIT 3
# THE INDIVIDUAL AND THE COLLECTIVE: CONFLICT AND COOPERATION     129

# UNIT 4
# SCIENCE AND THE NATURAL WORLD     201

# UNIT 5
# ARTS AND CULTURE     259

# APPENDIX A    331

# APPENDIX B    343

# PREFACE FOR INSTRUCTORS

*The Human Project* is an issues-based reader for colleges, designed to introduce students to the Humanities and Social Sciences. It is organized around the fundamental questions asked by a liberal education—questions of social change, politics, science and the arts. The complexity of our world is examined with competing answers to questions such as the following: Are we free or determined? Do we have the sense to cooperate with each other or are we doomed to perpetual conflict? Can science provide solutions to the problems it creates? Students are challenged to grapple with issues that don't have easy answers, to develop the higher level thinking skills that such complex questions require, and to acquire a tolerance for the fundamental ambiguities that many of life's basic problems engender. Students who meet this challenge not only become more valuable, flexible and reflective workers and citizens, but they have also started down the path of discovery, making them wiser and more fully rounded individuals.

**Features:** The text includes a number of features designed to make the book both approachable for students and useful to instructors. The readings included in this text present a nice balance between commissioned articles written by experienced college teachers that are specifically geared toward the college audience, and previously published articles written by professional and academic authors, that are geared toward the wider Canadian community. There are *review boxes* throughout the text, as well as *boldfaced key terms* with marginal definitions. *Quotations* related to text discussion are sprinkled throughout.

**StudyDesk Disk:** StudyDesk is a computer-based companion guide to the text, for use with any WINDOWS 95 or higher system in both online and offline modes. In its offline mode, this program uses an easy-to-understand Web page format to provide definitions and commentary on more than 200 terms and biographical background on more than 100 historical figures. Point-form summaries of each textbook article and a selection of representative works and reference materials are also featured. In its online mode, StudyDesk has been extensively revised to link to key online resources for each of the five units, as well as to online reference materials such as encyclopedias, dictionaries and newspapers.

**New to the Third Edition:** In the third edition of *The Human Project*, we have continued to present multidimensional issues that encourage students to explore different perspectives and compare theoretical views with their own experience. New articles have been included to ensure that current issues are addressed and an array of views represented.

Wendy O'Brien's article, "From Biology to Biography: A Brief History of the Self," weighs the contributions made by behaviourists and biologists to our understanding and explores the ideas of thinkers such as Descartes, Freud and Nietzsche. Ellen Ullman's "The Museum of Me" joins Neil Postman's "The Judgment of Thamus" in a critical analysis of the glowing promise of technology. Jason MacLean, in "The New Capitalism—and What It Means for You," turns his attention to corporate culture in the new economy. W.H. Auden illuminates the struggle between pleasure and reality in "Work, Labor and Play." Two short stories—"The Grown-up," by Booker Prize–winning author Ian McEwan, and "The Disclaimer," by Ron Carlson—deal with our experience of time and the quality of life that various times afford us. As well, two exceptional poems—"I Go Back to May 1937," by Sharon Olds, and "The Voice You Hear When You Read Silently," by Thomas Lux—further strengthen the literary component of the text. New articles to this edition of the text attempt to add fresh insights to the discussions in each unit.

**Organization:** The perspectives are drawn from various disciplines, including psychology, philosophy, sociology, anthropology, political theory, science, medicine and the arts. They are organized into units that begin with the individual and extend to the social, political, physical and cultural realms where the individual operates. This organization, going from the individual outwards, allows the student to approach the complexities of the world from familiar ground. Students are encouraged to arrive at an appreciation of the inter-connectedness of things and of how the world is inter-related by starting with themselves.

We have been eager to show that contemporary problems have their roots in the past and their solutions in a rich diversity of theoretical perspectives. At least in some measure, the text reflects the following goals of general education: aesthetic appreciation, civic life, cultural understanding, personal development, science, technology, work and the economy. It is only when students become engaged with such issues that real intellectual stretching occurs and they are able to arrive at their own, unique conclusions. We hope that our book, based on classroom experience and inspired by much of the animated debate on general education that has taken place over the last decade, contributes in a real and practical way to the ongoing discussion about what students need to know to face an ever-changing, complex reality.

**Acknowledgements:** The editors wish to thank the team that gave their time and effort so generously to the task of creating a new text. Our editorial committee—Lynda Archer, George Byrnes, John Elias, Jason MacLean, Greg Narbey, Declan Neary, Wendy O'Brien, Colin Pearce, Jerry Persaud, Morton Ritts, David Stamos, John Steckley, and Brian Wetstein—made the evolution of this text an object lesson in collaborative effort.

The editors would like to thank the hard-working folks at Pearson Education Canada—including editor-in-chief, David Stover; acquisitions editor, Andrew Wellner; associate editor, Tammy Scherer; and production editor, Joe Zingrone; and also Madeline Koch, our excellent copy editor. Special thanks go to contributing writers who used their understanding of students to translate difficult issues in a way that has relevance to students' lives. Above all, we would like to thank all of the instructors who field-tested materials used in this text, and all of the students who have responded with such insight and enthusiasm.

# INTRODUCTION FOR THE STUDENT

Everyone, it seems, wants to be an individual, to be recognized as a unique and special person. Most people also relish the notion of freedom, the idea that they hold the reins, at least some of the time, in determining the course of their lives. Yet, as desirable as individuality and freedom are, very few of us want to live alone. Indeed, most of us need a community of others if we are to live well and flourish. However, the cost of living in a community is usually some sacrifice (in theory anyway) of our individuality and freedom.

Our family expects us to behave in certain ways, our friends demand a code of behaviour, and all the institutions of society, our schools, businesses, churches and government, influence and control our behaviour on many levels. So to live with others is to live with constraint, and yet if we submit to everyone's expectations of us, we run the danger of losing ourselves, our sense of who we are. A natural tension exists in every healthy life and this tension between individual and larger goals doesn't ever finally resolve itself. It is not something you grow out of; it doesn't go away. Just when you're being most dutiful, you can be haunted by the temptation to be wild. Just when you think that indulging your every whim is the answer, the heart responds to a larger call and a need greater than the self.

What do you do with a tension that cannot be resolved, that resists easy answers? You can pretend it doesn't exist and be blown about by the forces of change in an unconscious way. Or you can seek to understand the great tensions and problems of our day and hopefully gain not only awareness, but also some influence on how your life evolves.

This book attempts to grapple with some of the difficult problems that confront everyone, from questions of our basic human nature, to social change, to politics, to technology, and to arts and culture. This is frequently a dark and complex world, and modern students need all the information, all the understanding, and all the light they can get if they are to find their own way in this world. Grappling with these questions will most probably give your grey cells a good workout, and thinking skills can be developed that will be useful in all your courses at college and, even more importantly, in your place of work. The possibility of developing your high-level thinking skills through the study of this text is of real and obvious practical benefit. But along the way, not in every section, but perhaps in some area, we hope you find some personal revelation and acquire some understanding that is unique to you.

# *the* Human Project

THIRD EDITION

# UNIT 1

# The Individual: Reflections on the Self

After all, mind is such an odd predicament for matter to get into. I often marvel how something like hydrogen, the simplest atom, forged in some early chaos of the universe, could lead to us and the gorgeous fever we call consciousness. If a mind is just a few pounds of blood, dream, and electric, how does it manage to contemplate itself, worry about its soul, do time-and-motion studies, admire the shy hooves of a goat, know that it will die, enjoy all the grand and lesser mayhems of the heart? What is mind, that one can be *out of one's*? How can a neuron feel compassion? What is a self? Why did automatic, hand-me-down mammals like our ancestors somehow evolve brains with the ability to consider, imagine, project, compare, abstract, think of the future? If our experience of mind is really just the simmering of an easily alterable chemical stew, then what does it mean to know something, to want something, *to be*? How do you begin with hydrogen and end up with prom dresses, jealousy, chamber music?

*Diane Ackerman*

The gods do not die, only take new forms, new names. There is something in us that will not let them go, not a longing for redemption, though we do long for it, or even a fear of the dark though we do go in terror of it, but an unquenchable need to have ourselves and our mundane doings reflected and exalted, to see the saga of ourselves written across the sky.

*John Banville*

# Introduction

# Toward the Examined Life

You have likely already noticed that the scope of *The Human Project* is quite broad—encompassing issues drawn from the entire spectrum of the liberal arts, including the humanities, social sciences and natural sciences. But unless you are preparing for a career that draws heavily upon one or more of these academic areas, you may have also questioned the value of this textbook and the course for which it is required reading. In other words, you might have asked yourself the question: *Why should I care about all this?*

As you will read later, in Unit 3, "Whether we care or not, politics matters." The same may be said of all the disciplines introduced in this text: Whether we care or not, developments in psychology, sociology, biology, medicine, art, philosophy—as well as politics—matter. Why? Because they shape the world in which we live, study, love, hate, work, play, buy, parent, socialize, vote, worship, etc. The latest theories in psychology, for example, may very well influence the way teachers teach—via lectures, or group work, or experiential exercises—in our college or university courses as well as in our children's elementary-school and high-school classes. And the conditions in which we work—at the office or at home, full time or part time, long term or by contract—may be significantly affected by the current views of those sociologists, political scientists and economists who study and comment on the business world. On an even more personal level, high-tech solutions to medical problems such as infertility may entice us with hope but also force us to reexamine our most basic ethical assumptions. So to truly understand our world and have some real control over our lives, it is necessary to have a familiarity with the ideas that matter. As the old adage says, "The unexamined life is not worth living." A study of the ideas introduced in this reader is a good beginning for an examination of timely issues in contemporary life. This is precisely why you should care about all this!

And the "this" that we should, must and actually do (although perhaps unwittingly) care about is nothing less than the "human project"—the world as it has been and continues to be constructed, transformed and explained by the accumulated efforts of humankind. This may sound like too lofty a subject of study until we recognize that this "project" is manifest in the various spheres of the everyday world in which we live today. A selected survey of the issues presented in *The Human Project* reflects this perspective: Is the human mind nothing more than a naturally occurring, albeit very sophisticated, computer? What might this mean about the personal decisions we make in life? Are big changes in society best understood as a step forward, or as a step backward, or as adaptively necessary, or as whimsically fashionable, or as none of the above? What might this imply about the growing incidence of alternative family structures or the increasingly multicultural composition of contemporary society? Is conflict among individuals and violence between nations inevitable? How might this affect the way federal governments and international coalitions are best structured? Do the conclusions of the physical sciences always trump explanations drawn from social science, philosophy, art and religion? How might this influence the working relationship between scientists and others? Do the arts offer nothing more than pleasant entertainment or do they also contain a special kind of serious insight? What impact might this have on the required curriculum not only in elementary schools and high schools but also in professional and technical programs in colleges and universities?

As this list of issues reveals, the human project is—and always has been and always will be—a work in progress. As such, it can be seen as the largest public works project ever, since every individual, in every society, in every era—including you, in Canada, during the first decade of the twenty-first century—plays a part in modifying, maintaining and interpreting this project. The part we play as individuals depends on the responses we make to the timely issues of our day. And our responses, in turn, are greatly enhanced by a familiarity with some of the theories proposed by those thinkers who have wrestled with similar, and even different, issues in the past. It is for this reason that *The Human Project* invites us to think through contemporary issues in consultation with works constructed in the near-to-distant past in the fields of psychology, sociology, politics, science, art and philosophy.

Ultimately, all theories about the world—even scientific theories seemingly unconcerned with humanity—make assumptions, if not statements, about human nature. (The very idea that we are capable of transcending our human perspective and understanding the world objectively is in itself a bold assumption about human nature.) Thus we are led to the question of questions: What is human nature? What makes humans human? Any answer to these questions must account both for the qualities that make us all human as well as the characteristics that make each of us different.

# "Know Thyself"

Every man bears the whole stamp of the human condition.

*Michel de Montaigne,* Essays, Bk. II, Ch. 12.

Since the abstract concept of "human nature" is brought to life in each individual human being, perhaps this is the best place to begin our investigation. In other words, the first step toward the examined life may be to "know thyself." As such, Unit 1 in *The Human Project* is entitled "The Individual."

So what is the "individual"? Is it the same as the "self"? And what is the "self"? When you refer to "your*self*," who is the "you" that speaks? Is it the same as your "soul" or "mind"? Clearly, these are important to your understanding of "self" if you take pride in your spirituality or your intellect. But is not your body also essential to your understanding of "self"? It certainly seems so if you take any pride in your physical appearance and abilities. If so, does the body—in particular, the brain—have a significance equal to that of the mind? Contemporary neurology suggests that the brain is essential to all mental processes. That said, what is the relationship between the mental and physical qualities of the individual?

These are but a few of the difficult questions that arise when a serious attempt is made to understand the meaning of our life experience as human beings, as individuals, as minds, as bodies. This quest is even more difficult because our subjective experience may stand in the way of a fully objective self-investigation. But unless we accept the prospect of living the *un*examined life, we are compelled at least to attempt such an investigation.

Fortunately, we can benefit from the previous investigations of others. In the first article in Unit 1—"From Biology to Biography: A Brief History of the Self"—Wendy O'Brien explores the theories of self offered in turn by the French philosopher René Descartes (1596–1650), the Austrian psychologist Sigmund Freud (1856–1939) and the German philosopher Friedrich Nietzsche (1844–1900) as well as the contemporary approaches informed by the practice of behaviourism and the research of the Human Genome Project. In her discussion of these different theories and views, O'Brien touches upon three issues fundamental to the study of self: 1) the mind-body problem, 2) the nature-nurture question and 3) the free will-determinism debate. In "Personality and Science: The Assumptions of Materialism," Peter Morea discovers the same themes in his analysis of the response of contemporary cognitive psychology to more traditional theories of self such as that of the American philosopher and psychologist William James (1842–1910).

# The Mind-Body Problem

The mind-body problem stems from the "dualism" proposed by Descartes. This is the theory that human beings consist of two essentially different and distinct "substances": mind—a thinking entity that is purely mental in nature, and body—a physical thing that is completely material in nature. Although both of these substances are important to human nature, Descartes argues that the mind is not only the more knowable but also the more essential of the two. Most of us find that common sense confirms the Cartesian view of the dualistic self: We tend to think of ourselves as mind—our true, lasting, "inner" self—on the one hand, and body—our less true, changing, "outer" self—on the other. This everyday experience notwithstanding, Descartes and those, such as James, who agree with him have yet to come up with a convincing answer to a tough question: How is it possible for a purely mental, nonphysical mind to interact with an entirely material, physical body? In other words, is it really possible to move physical objects with your (purely mental) mind alone? When put this way, it is less obvious that dualism conforms to common sense.

Of course, not everyone agrees with Descartes and James that the mind is distinct from, and more significant than, the body. As O'Brien explains, the scientists involved in the Human Genome Project take a very different approach to the study of human nature; in fact, this impressive research project is limited in scope to a physical investigation of human beings through study of our genetic makeup. This does not mean that geneticists necessarily deny the existence of the mind. But when they propose, as O'Brien notes some do, that personality traits are determined by genetics, they are in effect claiming that the mind is at most the creation of, and, as such, less essential than, the body.

This is also the position, as Morea explains, of contemporary cognitive psychology, which attempts to explain this puzzling proposal—that the mental workings of the mind are the creations of the physical workings of the body—by analogy to how computers "think." According to this perspective, the brain is the hardware and the mind is the software that together constitute the human self. Intriguing as this model may be, Morea is quick to point out that the human mind does not really seem to operate like a computer at all: while the human mind may use its conscious understanding to exhibit "rule-following behaviour" even the most sophisticated computer really only displays automatic "law-like behaviour."

Perhaps Richard Restak has the most convincing solution to the mind-body problem. In "My Brain and I Are One," Restak, a practising neurologist, states in no uncertain terms that the brain's "temporal lobe is responsible for . . . our personal identity. . . . " But he also acknowledges how difficult it is, even for him, to really believe that who he is—an individual, a mind, a self—is determined by his brain. So Restak proposes an interesting compromise: namely, that mind and body really reflect different perspectives of the same reality—with mind existing in time and body existing in space. Both perspectives are real, but we can't understand one in terms of the other. So the mind-body problem remains just that—an unsolved problem.

## The Nature-Nurture Question

Behaviourists such as B. F. Skinner (1904–1990) skirt the mind-body problem either by ignoring the mind—since it is not an observable entity and, therefore, is not amenable to scientific study—or by simply denying its existence. Nonetheless, the behaviourists do have a very clear position on another big issue in the study of human nature: the nature-nurture question. This question asks whether the self is more the result of nature—qualities we are born with, such as genetics or instincts or even innate "drives"—or more the result of nurture—influences stemming from our environment, such as upbringing, schooling, socioeconomic status, culture, etc. Behaviourism is the theory that we are not what we think but what we do, i.e., how we behave, and that what we do is determined by rewards and punishments in our environment. But, as O'Brien argues, these environmental influences do not seem to have the lasting effect that behaviourists claim they do.

The Human Genome Project will provide evidence for the nature side of this debate if it does indeed discover that personality traits are determined by genetic makeup. But, as O'Brien notes, our understanding of genetics to date only points to probabilities, not certainties. Environmental factors may ultimately explain why certain genetic dispositions develop into realities while others do not.

Indeed, most if not all serious thinkers acknowledge that both nature and nurture are significant factors in understanding human nature. And this is the position of Sigmund Freud: while the *id* consists of irresistible innate instincts, the *superego* contains socially constructed rules and expectations, forcing the *ego* to try to mediate between the two in a realistic way. For Freud, nature (id) has a greater impact on the self than nurture (superego and ego), but both are strong and essential forces in human nature.

# The Free Will-Determinism Debate

The id has the stronger hand in Freud's model of the self because it is part of the unconscious mind; after all, it is hard to control something if we are not aware of it. This leads us to the debate over whether or not we are truly free to make choices between alternative courses of action. This issue, summarized in "Am I Free or Determined?" by Melanie Chaparian, hinges on the debate between determinists—those who argue that all our actions are caused by forces beyond our control—and libertarians—those who argue that at least some of our actions are the result of our free will.

This debate is informed by the previous investigation into the nature of self. In other words, our view of the nature of the individual has a direct bearing on our position on free will. If you agree with Freud, for example, that the self is inalterably created by natural and environmental forces over which we have no control, you will have little hope that human beings can exercise true freedom. Or if, on the other hand, you are persuaded by the behaviourist thesis that we are unendingly shaped by rewards and punishments in our environment, you will see no trace of free will in human behaviour.

If, however, you are convinced by Nietzsche's understanding of the self as a personally styled work of art, you will find James' theory of libertarianism not only probable but likely evident as well. Indeed, James invites us to view both the determinist and the libertarian positions through introspective lenses to discern which makes the most sense of reality as we experience it in our daily lives. He suggests that although objective explanations of reality may be useful at times, they do not successfully account for our subjective experience of our lived lives in which we frequently feel free to make choices and often regret the choices we and others make. Restak's medical understanding of his epileptic patients helps him to treat them effectively, for instance, but at the same time he finds it difficult to convince himself that his patients as well as he, himself, are ultimately determined by the (mis)functions of the body and the brain—a "three-pound mass of protoplasm with the consistency of an overripe avocado."

# From Biology to Biography: A Brief History of the Self

## Wendy O'Brien

René Descartes

What do you mean when you say: "I'm so sorry, I'm just not myself today." Do you mean that somehow you have inadvertently deviated from your essential core of being? Perhaps you're hinting that you're more complicated than even you had thought. Who or what is this self that we refer to, this presence that provides continuity and perspective to our experience? Many great minds have asked themselves similar questions. Thinkers as diverse as Descartes, Freud, Skinner and Nietzsche have attempted to explore this notion of the self, and while they have all contributed to our understanding, they would also probably admit that even after careful reflection and analysis there are still unanswered questions.

The modern search to understand the self finds its basis in the writings of the 17th-century philosopher René Descartes. Often regarded as the father of modern philosophy, Descartes' reputation is grounded on how he taught us to think about the self as much as on the theory of identity that he developed. Descartes was writing during the scientific revolution, a time of great hope and belief in the possibility of progress. It was, as well, a time marked by insecurity as science began to challenge existing theories about the natural world and consequently put into question long-held beliefs about human beings—about their innate qualities and characteristics, their place in nature and their relationship to God.

In forcing us to address these questions, the new science not only dispelled many myths about the world and about ourselves, but it also changed the way we think. No longer could we rely on authority figures to explain how the world worked and how we should act. Now we were left on our own to discover for ourselves the answers to these questions. Reason replaced faith as the source of knowledge and we were forever changed as a result.

While many of his contemporaries such as Galileo were busy applying the principles of science to the natural world, Descartes applied these principles to the study of human beings. His methodology consisted of four basic rules:

"From Biology to Biography: A Brief History of the Self" is by Wendy O'Brien of Humber College. Used by permission.

1. Do not accept any statement as true without evidence.
2. Divide every problem into its simplest parts.
3. Start with what is simple and build your way up to more complex ideas.
4. Be thorough: carefully record and analyze data in order to ensure that nothing is left out.

Why try to study human beings, the self, from a scientific perspective rather than accept the teachings of the church or rely upon tradition? As noted earlier, Descartes lived in a time when it seemed that the whole world was being turned upon its head. In this regard, perhaps he has a lot in common with people like us living at the dawn of the 21st century. Even if you are as young as 20 or 25, you know how many things have changed throughout your lifetime. And with the current advances in science and the development of technology, you know that things aren't likely to slow down any time soon. Descartes must have felt much the same way as the scientific revolution began to take hold and change the lives of those living in the 1600s. Like many of us, Descartes responded to this change by trying to find one thing, just one thing that he could hold onto, one thing that he could know was true and would always be so. If he could find just one thing that he could know for certain, then he believed that maybe he could make sense of the changes that were taking place.

In order to accomplish this goal, Descartes adopted the method of "radical doubt." If he was going to discover something that he could know for certain, it would have to be something that was literally beyond doubt. So he began doubting everything that he had once taken for granted as true. He doubted the teachings of authority. Descartes was a rebel in his time. He dared to ask if politicians, religious leaders, teachers and other experts could be relied upon to tell the truth. He quickly realized that while authorities often knew a lot about one thing, they tended to extend their claims beyond their expertise.

Well, if we can't rely on others to tell us what is true, surely we can rely on our own experiences, our own sense perceptions to provide us with knowledge. As I sit here writing this, I see the screen on my computer. I feel the keys on the keyboard. I smell the coffee that sits in the cup beside my computer. Given what my senses tell me, I can claim that these things—the computer and my cup—are real. Or can I? You only have to think for a minute about how even great food can taste so flavourless when you have a cold or how a high fever can make you feel so chilly to understand why Descartes concluded that even our own experiences could not be trusted to lead us to the truth.

Descartes continued his quest for certainty by thinking about all those things that he considered real. While he sat by the fire, writing his meditations, he knew that the pen in his hand and the fire in the hearth were real, just as you know that the book that you are holding and the chair you are sitting on are real. But, how do you know they are real? How do you know that you aren't dreaming that you are reading this page? Haven't you ever had a dream that was so real that you thought that you had really lived it? If you have, then you can understand Descartes' point. How can you prove that what you are experiencing now isn't the same sort of a dream? Descartes questioned whether everything that we have known to date is part of a long and elaborate dream and thus put into question all those things that we readily take for granted.

But even if the claims of authorities, the knowledge gained from sense perceptions and our assumptions about what is real are all possibly false, certainly such abstract truths as mathematical formulas must be true. It is true, Descartes argued, that it seems that 2+2 has always been and will always be 4. But how do we know that this is the right answer? How do we know that there is not a supreme being who enjoys playing with our minds? What if this supreme being, rather than being benevolent as portrayed in many religious teachings, is, in fact, an evil demon who gets his/her/its kicks out of playing mind games with us and has indeed tricked us into believing that 2+2 is 4 when in reality it is 27? True, this argument may be farfetched; however, if you have seen the movie *The Matrix*, you have a good idea of what Descartes had in mind here. In this film, robotic bugs have tricked the humans into believing that their everyday lives are real. They think that they live in New York City, that they work and that they fall in love, when, in fact, they are living inside pods and having their energy sucked out of them to fuel a complex computer system known as the Matrix. How can you prove that even the most abstract truths aren't, in fact, illusions? Can you conclusively put aside any and all doubt that Descartes' evil demon or the Matrix may be real? If even the smallest doubt remains in your mind, you are left to conclude that you can't even be certain of the principles of mathematics.

It seemed like Descartes' search for one thing to believe in, for one thing that he could know for certain, failed. It seemed like there was nothing in the world that one could unquestioningly accept as true. But his search really just began. For it was at this point that the realization came to him—there *was* one thing that he could know for certain. In order for him to be sitting there doubting everything that exists, there was one thing that he was unable to doubt: He couldn't doubt that he was doubting, for if he doubted that he was doubting, he would nonetheless be doubting. (Don't worry if this sounds confusing the first time you read it. Read the sentence over a few times. Now sit back and doubt whether the book in front of you is real. Now doubt that you are doubting that the book is real. It is impossible, for in doubting that you are doubting you are still doubting.) But proving the existence of doubting alone didn't make much sense to Descartes. How can doubting exist on its own? It was impossible. In order for there to be doubting, there must be some thing that is doing the doubting.

If it is true that the one thing that we cannot doubt is that we are doubting, and if doubting cannot exist on its own but rather there must be some "thing" that is doing the doubting, what is this thing that, according to the logic of the argument, we can know is true? Descartes concluded that it was the self. But what is the self? For him the self was nothing more than "a thing that thinks"—a thing that understands, affirms, knows, imagines and doubts. In other words, the self was synonymous with what many of us would describe as the mind. This means that the minute we begin to doubt that we exist, we prove our own existence—for to doubt our existence is to think and thus to affirm the reality of the self. *"Cogito ergo sum,"* Descartes concluded: "I think, therefore I am."

In making this claim, Descartes made the self the grounding point of modern philosophy. The one thing that we can know for certain, the one thing that will provide a foundation for the knowledge that we gain about the world around us, about other people, about the existence of God, is our knowledge of the self. But in making this claim, Descartes only really began his investigation into identity. For, while he had proven the existence of the mind, he found himself with a new problem.

Recall that in his method of radical doubt Descartes had placed in question the **veracity** of information that we gain using the body. In discrediting the body as a source of knowledge and locating the self in the mind, Descartes advanced the theory of "dualism." According to him, each of us is composed of two different kinds of substances, mind and body. The mind has an immaterial and internal existence that only the mind can know. It is not available for public scrutiny. It cannot be located in space nor is it divisible. The body, on the other hand, exists in space and therefore is divisible. I can clearly distinguish between its various parts. This is my hand, while this is my finger and my thumb.

**veracity**
truth

Moreover, the body exists in the external world and is, as such, open to public appraisal. For Descartes, it was critical to distance the mind from the body in such a manner, for this ensured that the uncertainty associated with bodily perceptions would not infect the perfect knowledge that we could have of the mind.

These descriptions of the mind and the body that Descartes offered seem fairly accurate. But if he is right, how is it that the two can be reconciled? We don't think of our selves as being pure mind. We don't experience ourselves as disembodied, dislocated and lonely minds. Most of the time when we talk about our "selves," we are referring to our bodies too. Descartes himself seemed to recognize this fact when he defined the self as a "*thing* that thinks." But how is this possible? How can the self be two such different kinds of things at one and the same time?

Descartes resolved this dilemma by acknowledging the existence of the body but giving it a secondary role. The mind was the "pilot of the vessel" that controlled and directed the body. Indeed, this is the view that many of us continue to hold regarding the self. How many times have you heard people say that looks aren't everything and that what really matters is what kind of person they are? In doing so, they are claiming, along with Descartes, that when push comes to shove, the body really isn't all that important.

This account of the self has raised as many questions as it has provided answers. Can we be so certain that the self exists? Descartes thought that it was impossible to disprove the existence of the self, but it seems that for some of us, it isn't all that clear that there is something inside of us directing and guiding our actions. How many times have you been asked "what are you thinking?" and your response has been "I dunno"? It seems like the mind is not the easiest thing for us to access but instead is the hardest thing for us to know. Furthermore, it seems that there is more to me than just my mind. What I think, what I imagine and what I hope for are all important aspects of who I am, but so too are my body and my family and my friends. And these factors are not isolated aspects of my self. Somehow they manage to work together to create my identity. Consider, for example, how the body affects the mind just as the mind affects the body. If you have ever been drunk or have been with someone who is drunk, you have first- or at least second-hand experience of how powerful this influence can be. The question of who is the "pilot of the vessel" is not all that clear.

It was just such questions that led Sigmund Freud to believe that there was more to the self than his predecessors appreciated. Theories that

Sigmund Freud

grounded the self in the mind seemed to him too simplistic. They attempted to make the self a thing that was, at least potentially, ultimately in control and relatively easy to understand. Listening to people describe their experiences of the self, he realized that the self was mysterious, messy and complicated. And it seemed to be divided against itself—pulled and pushed in different directions by unknown forces.

Consider, for example, what happens when you attempt to do something as simple as buy a pair of shoes. You get to the shoe department and immediately notice how cute the sales clerk is. You are there to buy shoes, not to look for a date. You begin looking through the displays. You see one pair that seems perfect. And you know you would look good in those shoes. The only thing is, they cost about three times more than you had planned to spend. There are other shoes more in keeping with your budget, but, well, they just aren't *those* shoes. As you are standing there still checking out the clerk, a debate rages on in your head: "Buy them." "Don't buy them." "Buy them." "Go for a walk and think about it." "Buy them." "No, don't."

How many times a day do you find yourself engaged in such conversations in your head? Sometimes the debate rages on about buying shoes, but other times it is about whether or not to ask the clerk out or what to watch on television. We seem divided against ourselves. Why? Why can't we be clear and decisive? Why is it so hard to make decisions about even the simplest things? What is it that pulls and pushes us in so many directions? Freud abandoned Descartes' project of trying to find one thing to believe in and, instead, tried to explain why the self seemed unable to be certain about anything—including its own workings.

The self, as described by Freud, could be compared to an iceberg. If you saw *Titanic* you know that the ice formations that you see looming above the water compose only a small portion of the complete size of the iceberg. The same holds true for human beings. What we see is definitely not the whole of what we are. The self, for Freud, was an intricate web of conflicting desires, dictates and attempts to be rational that, to a great extent, remains unexplored. His goal was to chart this unknown territory, to provide a map of the psyche. His analysis divided the self into three parts: the id, the superego and the ego.

Go back to the shoe example. Why is it that you want the expensive shoes? Is it really because they are comfortable or do you have some ulterior motive? Why shoes of all things? To answer these questions, Freud would suggest that we have to explore the id. The *id* contains two instincts—thanatos and eros—that constantly nag at us, wanting immediate satisfaction, and pressuring us to act irrationally. And they are successful. In our behaviour we often find direct but, even more often, subtle expressions of these inborn desires.

*Thanatos* is our drive toward death, aggression and violence. It is that part of the self that is willing to pull your pair of shoes out of the hands of another customer if they dare to pick them up. Most often, however, it takes more subtle forms and is expressed in feelings of envy and arrogance. While thanatos directs our feelings of aggression, *eros* concerns our desire for pleasure. According to Freud, the id operates according to the pleasure principle: it constantly desires to maximize pleasure, particularly those pleasures associated with our bodily desires such as sex and food. If it feels good, it is good. Think about the shoes. Why is it that you want the shoes and you want those shoes now? Isn't it because they are a source of pleasure? They are not only comfortable; they also might serve to attract attention from others, which could lead to a date or even more. Well, if eros and thanatos are always trying to get us to act on our desires even though we remain mostly unaware of their workings, why aren't our closets full of shoes and our credit card bills permanently at their limits?

While it is true that the unconscious contains our basic instincts and desires, it also must wrestle with that part of our self that is constantly telling us "Don't." Think of all the lists of dos and don'ts that you have been subjected to throughout your lifetime. Our friends, religious leaders, politicians, the media and, above all, others in our family are constantly telling us what we should do and how we should do it. An integral part of our psyche, the *superego*, has been internalizing all these lists to make sure that we obey them when we find ourselves in similar situations. Remember going to the store with your parents and being told "NO" you can't have a new toy? Don't you hear that same "NO" reverberating in your head when you go to buy a new pair of shoes? And when you ask yourself why you can't have them, you get the line that you heard a million times as a teenager: "Don't waste your money." The superego demands that we adhere to each and every social rule: it demands perfect and complete obedience at all times.

But it doesn't get such obedience, and a battle rages within you. Both the id and the superego attempt to alter the structure of the self by denying the reality or the importance of the other. It is the role of the *ego*, of the conscious part of the self, to try to referee between our multitude of desires and our storehouse of social rules. None of us can live according to the pleasure principle alone. If we tried, we would quickly find ourselves in jail. Similarly, those who try to live according to every existing social rule would quickly find themselves immobilized. It would be impossible to act if we tried to adhere to them all. The role of the ego is to balance between reality and the world of our desires, and between reality and the world of rules. This is the part of the self that tells you to "Chill," that is, to slow down and think things through before you do something that may ultimately be self-destructive. Sometimes the ego is successful, and sometimes it isn't.

According to Freud, the self is the arena in which these three forces confront each other—making it hard to know what you are thinking, let alone why. To help us explain our selves, Freud developed a series of techniques designed to try to make the unconscious mind reveal itself. If we knew what desires were directing our behaviour, if we knew what rules we have stored away in our memory, then we might be able to devise a means for reconciling them with the realities of our daily lives. His famous talking cure, "psychoanalysis," which many of us visualize as someone lying on a couch telling a psychoanalyst about their childhood, is one such technique. By talking about our past experiences, Freud thought that the unconscious would come to the surface and reveal unresolved conflicts that inhibit our progress. Similarly, he found such clues to what lies beneath the surface of the self in analyzing slips of the tongue, word associations and dreams, and memories recovered using hypnosis.

Freud's view of the self has had an enormous effect on modern conceptions of identity. He complicated our understanding of the self with his introduction of the unconscious mind. He showed how the self could be divided against itself. This led to a new appreciation of the complexity of our relationship with others. If you don't know what you are doing or why, and I don't know what I'm doing or why, and the two of us are engaged in an intimate relationship, well, needless to say, we've got trouble. Freud's theories helped to explain why relationships, particularly with those whom we most love, are so difficult. And he made it evident that we need to sit back and reflect on our actions and beliefs, preferably before acting, in order to avoid doing things that will ultimately hurt us.

Freud also recognized that the mind and body are more intricately intertwined than many of his predecessors had acknowledged. The id has a biological base and its instinctual urgings direct much of our thoughts and behaviour. Yet the mind can powerfully affect the body in cases involving, for example, psychosomatic illness. Such understandings of the self have been so influential that it's hard for us really to imagine what we were like—how we thought about the self—before Freud.

However, like Descartes, Freud was left at the end of his life with more questions about the self than he had answers, questions that continue to be raised about his theory. Is the self really so mysterious? Critics have questioned Freud's claim that we are constantly at war with ourselves. Sure, there are times when we experience conflicts within, but for the most part we seem to be at peace with ourselves. This has led other commentators to speculate that we do, in fact, know what the self is and how it works, but it just isn't all that interesting compared to discussions of thanatos and eros. So, to liven up the stories of our lives, we accept Freud's notion of the unconscious mind. To relieve us from our boredom, we convince ourselves that there are such things as the id and the superego, and go on to ascribe to our actions all sorts of complicated and intriguing motivations.

Perhaps the most important criticism of Freud's theory of the self, however, concerned the very existence of the mind itself. To make this point clear, think for a minute about unicorns. Do you believe unicorns exist? Most of us don't. We believe that if you can't see it or touch it, it just isn't real. Well, have you seen your mind? Can you point to it? If I showed you a picture of your brain, would you be satisfied that you had seen your mind? Freud and Descartes asked us to believe in something as intangible as unicorns. They asked us to believe in a mind that we can't see or study or, for the most part, understand. It seems clear to many that the mind simply doesn't exist.

The search for alternative explanations of identity has led many theorists to return to that part of the self that Descartes had discarded as unreliable and unworthy of our attention, namely, the body. Most contemporary theories of the self emphasize that if we have a mind at all it must be located in a body that exists in time and space. Indeed, who I am—what I do, the way people treat me and the way I treat myself—is largely a consequence of my body, i.e., my physical makeup. Descartes and Freud were too quick to focus on the mind. They greatly underestimated the extent to which the body is the self.

Explanations of the self that centre on the body aren't new. Early attempts to explain behaviour and personality in terms of biology and physiology focused on the circulation of blood. Others looked at the shape and structure of the skull to try to explain why people behaved in particular ways. As ridiculous as these theories may sound to us now, they were used by "experts" in the past to try to explain why people acquired certain qualities and characteristics. Why did we turn to the body for information about the self? It seems pretty clear. The body is tangible. It can be observed and examined. We can study it, quantify our results, use them to predict future outcomes and, if possible, intervene. The body is knowable and predictable and therefore seems to provide a more reliable foundation on which to build a theory of identity.

Clearly the most significant development in this school of thought was the discovery of DNA (deoxyribonucleic acid). While the chemical itself was first identified in 1869, it was not until 1953 that James Watson and Francis Crick were able to unlock the structure of DNA. And in doing so, they changed the way we see the world. Just as the scientific revolution led human beings to question many of their long-held beliefs about themselves and the world around them, so too would the genetic revolution.

DNA is a genetic code found in every cell in your body. We are used to seeing it represented by a double helix—that is, by two lines or polymers that intertwine with each other. The helix is divided into 24 distinct and separate units known as chromosomes. Along these chromosomes lie genes that hold within them a blueprint for how a person is likely to grow and develop. Just as Morse code is composed of messages translated into a series of dots and dashes, the messages in our genes are encoded in the form of four basic acids known as nucleotides: adenine, guanine, cytosine and thymine. If you are wondering how this connects to the self, researchers participating in the Human Genome Project argue that their work tells us quite a lot about the self.

The Human Genome Project was initiated in 1990 with the goal of mapping out the complete human genetic code. The human genome consists of approximately 30 000–40 000 genes that send messages to the rest of our body. These genes contain information that predisposes us to develop certain physical traits, particular diseases and syndromes, and, according to some researchers, specific aspects of our personality. With researchers in over 15 countries and a yearly budget that exceeded $30 billion (U.S.), the project completed its first draft on June 26, 2000—when the dispositions associated with every human gene had been initially identified. Within the genome over 500 hereditary conditions including ALS, multiple sclerosis, Alzheimer's disease and breast cancer have been located and, relying on this knowledge, scientists have already been developing new treatment procedures and therapies. Looking at a person's DNA, doctors and researchers can not only come up with a sketch of what the person is like at this moment in time, they are also able to predict what that person's life will be like in the future. Clearly, such discoveries have been deemed miraculous. But with such findings also comes controversy.

Debates have emerged as researchers speculate on the existence of a gay gene, a serial-killer gene and an intelligence gene. Just how much of who we are is programmed by our genes? And if our behaviour and attitudes are the result of genetic encoding, how is it possible for us to be held responsible for our actions? Further questions were raised as to what should be done with the findings from this project. While the Human Genome Project is mapping the genetic code, other scientists are developing the techniques necessary to alter DNA patterning. A whole series of ethical issues arises around genetic screening and the treatment of patients for diseases and syndromes that they might acquire in future. What are we going to do with this new knowledge of the self? What, if any, limits should be placed upon its use? The questions raised by this research centre on our very understanding of what it means to be human.

The questions being raised by the genetic revolution should sound familiar. They are remarkably similar to those raised during the time Descartes was writing as the new science of his day began to challenge received beliefs about personal identity. Like our predecessors, we worry that this new view of the self—the self as a consequence of inherited nucleotides—will turn our whole world upside down by undermining belief in the mind and eliminating the concept of personal responsibility. And like our predecessors, to a great extent our worries about this science and its implications are exaggerated.

Genetic research is not a study of certainties. The science of the 21st century doesn't deal in laws of nature but rather with probabilities. Scientists acknowledge that at best genetic markers can tell us about dispositions, about the likelihood that a person will develop a particular disease or syndrome or physical feature. But dispositions are far from certainties. This leaves room for the environment to play a role in shaping the selves that we become. Indeed, it recognizes that there is much about the self that will continue to be a mystery.

Perhaps as researchers continue to study the effects of combining different gene patterns, we will gain more certainty about the self and its workings. Or maybe we will discover that the more we try to explain the self in scientific terms, the more it will escape us. Just as Descartes found himself unable to discuss the mind without making reference to the body, maybe geneticists will discover that they are unable to discuss the body without making reference to the mind.

But there still seems to be something missing from these accounts of the self. It would be a neat solution to say that the self is the mind and the body combined, if we lived alone in a box. But we don't live in a box. We live in a world in which we affect and are affected by others. Think of how someone, maybe even a stranger, can just look at you in a particular way and change the way you see yourself. Maybe that changes you for the better, or maybe it changes you for the worse, but you are changed. The accounts of the self offered by Descartes, Freud and contemporary geneticists failed to give ample consideration to the fact that we are to a great extent constructed by the society in which we live. That is, they failed to emphasize the important role that the environment plays in shaping the self that we become.

Relying on the works of Ivan Pavlov and B. F. Skinner, behaviourists argue that the self is shaped or conditioned by the responses we receive to our actions (or lack of action) in our environment. Think for a minute about the fact that on even the coldest mornings, on those mornings when we are exhausted and want nothing more than to stay in our nice, warm, cozy beds, we nonetheless get up at ridiculously early hours, brave the cold and spend hours parked on the highways, just to get to work. Have you ever thought about why we do this? I know, this might seem like a rhetorical question. Clearly, the number-one reason that we get up each and every morning and arrive at work on time is because we want—we need—money. Think for a minute about all the strange and unusual things that we are willing to do for money. Not only are we willing to get out of bed in the morning and sit on the highway for hours, we are also willing to wear uncomfortable clothes and do work that we find boring or even morally reprehensible. In other words, money reinforces our behaviour. Reinforcement involves pairing something that an individual desires with a particular action or response. Most often we use positive reinforcements; that is, we use something that the person desires to shape their behaviour. We might rely on money or material goods to get others to act in a desired manner, but we could also use more subtle stimulants such as reputation, social acceptance or friendship to shape behaviour. Why do businesses post pictures of the employee of the month? Why do they take their whole office to a baseball game? These are clearly ways that employers try to offer their employees the non-material things they desire as a consequence for good workplace performance. In conditioning, we can also rely on negative reinforcements. A negative reinforcement eliminates some existing annoyance or negative stimulant from the environment when the person acts in the desired manner. What happens, for example, when you first wake up in the morning? You hear that annoying buzz of your alarm clock. How do you get it to stop? You not only have to wake up, but you also have to reach over and turn the alarm off. This is an example of how your behaviour might be modified using negative reinforcement.

While many employers rely on reinforcement to get their workers to arrive on time and to work harder and longer hours, others rely on the second principle of conditioning—punishment—to shape the behaviour of their employees. In order to ensure that employees arrive on time, your boss might put in place a policy of deducting wages from your pay cheque or giving you a lousy schedule or delegating to you the worst work assignment to try to ensure that you arrive on time for work. When we punish someone, we try to change his or her behaviour by pairing a particular action (or non-action) with something that the person wishes to avoid.

Using these two principles of conditioning, behaviourists argue that you can explain much about the self. Think about all the subtle and not so subtle ways you are reinforced and punished for certain behaviour in the environment in which you live. In this context it is important to look at your workplace, but it is also important to consider how other forces such as your family, peers, religious organizations, government institutions, the media and even the physical environment in which we live manipulate not only how we act but also, over time, what we say and how we think.

Behaviourism has been remarkably successful. When you sit back and think about it, it really does seem that we are the consequence of the history of reinforcements and punishments to which we have been subjected. We get up in the morning and go to work. We pay taxes. We quit smoking and stop biting our nails, to a great extent because these principles work. Indeed, in institutions, these principles have been used to control large populations. Prison systems often work on a merit system. If you are a good inmate, you receive cigarettes, television time and even conjugal visits. If you break the rules, you are not only denied such things, but you may also be given the worst work detail or placed in solitary confinement.

But while behaviourism has been useful in changing people's behaviour, it has been less successful in explaining the motives for our behaviour and in changing attitudes. It has a hard time explaining, for example, why people living and working in the exact same environment can come to act and behave so differently. Co-workers who live in the same city, the same neighbourhood, and sometimes even the same household can have entirely different work habits. How is this possible? If the environment is key to shaping identity, how is it possible that workers in as diverse cultural settings as Japan, Canada and India all seem to want basically the same things for themselves and their families? Maybe it is the result of globalization: everyone everywhere wears Nike, drinks Coke and watches CNN. Or, maybe, it is because, regardless of the culture we live in, the work we do or the families that we are part of, there remain some features of human nature that stubbornly assert themselves no matter what the environmental influences.

Even more questions have been raised about the effectiveness of reinforcement and punishment. It is hard to determine what constitutes reinforcement and punishment because what we value and dislike varies from group to group and person to person. Something that I consider desirable, you might consider something to be avoided. Consider business travel in this light. My boss may think that sending me on a trip is a great opportunity, but I might not like the idea because I have Raptors tickets for that night. My boss thinks that she is reinforcing my performance at work, when, in fact, she is doing the opposite. Moreover, reinforcements only seem to work for a period of time before the person wants more in order to act in the desired manner. You might be willing to accept a fifty-cents-per-hour raise when you first start working. In time, you would want more and more money and, eventually, you may decide that the money just isn't worth getting out of bed on cold winter mornings. Similar problems arise with respect to punishment. Studies have shown that even though we have an inclination to believe that punishment is effective, in fact, it is not a particularly successful means for modifying behaviour. If you threaten to fire an employee if he or she arrives late again for work and then you don't go through with it, don't expect that tactic will work again in the future. Further, even if you do follow through with your threat, you need to recognize that a punishment extinguishes quickly. If you punish someone over and over again, eventually that person will rebel and may even go so far as to challenge you to "come and get me." What this suggests is that the self is not as malleable or as easily manipulated as behaviourists believe. It seems that we don't always want reinforcement and don't always fear punishment. Nonetheless, we keep using these techniques wishing that people were so easy to change.

It may seem that this look at some theories of the self has not really got us very far. What is the self? We still don't have a clear definition. Indeed, if anything, we might be more confused about the answer to this question than before we began. It is true that none of the thinkers discussed here arrived at a completely convincing account of the self. Many of them recognized this inadequacy themselves. Freud, for example, determined at the end of his career that he really did not understand human beings (particularly women) very well at all. Like others who have tried to explain the self, he found that his works were incomplete and full of inconsistencies. However, we should not be too quick to conclude that the works of Freud and others were written in vain.

The philosopher Friedrich Nietzsche offered a view of the self that lets us appreciate even incomplete and incoherent theories of identity. For Nietzsche the self was not something that could be discovered. We cannot locate the self in the mind or in the body. The self was not the product of the environment or of our DNA. Instead, Nietzsche argued that the self was a statement of our style.

Nietzsche challenged his readers to "give style to their character," that is, he dared them to create the self that they wanted to be. The self is not something that exists in the world waiting to be revealed; rather, it is something that we create. Each one of us, according to Nietzsche, is an artist. True, not all of us can paint or sing or write, but what we all share in common is the ability to create the person we want to become. Each day, we paint the canvas of our lives. How is this possible? How can I create who I am when, as the theorists we've discussed make clear, I am a mind attached to a particular body that has been shaped by the environment in which I live?

Friedrich Nietzsche

At first, it sounds like this is an easy project. You simply sit back and decide who it is that you want to be. But it's not so easy once you start. Indeed, you quickly discover that it is a lot harder to be an original than you think. Everywhere you look—on television, in ads, in music, in your conversation with your friends—you find people trying to create your self for you. It's hard to figure out just what exactly you want to make of your life without falling prey to someone else's image of who you should be. Moreover, while you may have always wished you could play in the NBA/WNBA, for example, you soon realize that there are some facts about your life that are unalterable. Our family and our genetic inheritance can't be just wished away.

To create the self is to write the story of our lives. It is to take those things that have happened to us and to interpret them in such a way as to give meaning to our existence. This is not an easy task. We need all the help that we can get to accomplish this goal. We look to past masters—to artists, to writers, and to philosophers, indeed to all those who have dared to think and to write about the self. We glean from them many insights—ideas, concepts and structures—that we can use to shape our lives. We need then to think hard about what they have said and decide what aspects of their creations we wish to incorporate in our work of art. Moreover, we fill our lives with experiences. We travel and dance. We laugh, and in so doing, we give ourselves the materials—the colours and shapes, the experiences and the feelings—that we need in order to create. But even this is not enough. We can sit around and dream all that we want but unless we risk living the life we have created, it is of little value. We need courage to create and also to live a life with style.

Nietzsche's theory may seem incomplete. While he told us to read and look at great works of art, we want a 12-step program to make us more interesting, more profound and, hopefully, more successful. But just as painters and writers have a hard time describing the process that they go through when they work, so too did Nietzsche find it difficult to put down into words how it is that we should create a life. If he sat down and made us long lists of dos and don'ts and we followed them to the letter, there would still be something missing. To create the self we must act on our own. We need to be brave as we risk presenting to the world our own creation. Who knows what people will think? I may think I've created a great masterpiece while others may think my work of art is a disaster. How can we judge the selves that we create?

Judging the beauty of a life is analogous to judging the beauty of a work of art. In doing so, we must look both at the form and the content of the work we have created. We need to evaluate it objectively, examining the consequences that our actions have on those around us. But we must also evaluate the self from a subjective standpoint. Are we satisfied with what we have created? Is the life we have created beautiful in our own eyes?

It's important to note that in describing the self as a work of art, Nietzsche didn't mean to lessen its importance. Indeed, quite the opposite is true. If the self is a creation, it is our creation and we must be willing to take responsibility for what we have made. If we choose to make ourselves into a sit-com character, we must be willing to accept the fact that we have chosen not to be taken seriously. Similarly, if we make ourselves into a drama queen or king, we have to recognize that it is as a result of our own decisions that people roll their eyes when we begin to tell them our latest tale of passion and woe. According to Nietzsche, there is nowhere to run and nowhere to hide. You can't shift the blame for who you are onto someone or something else. You cannot blame your id or your mother or your DNA for the person you have become. You are responsible for the self that you are today and the self that you may choose to become tomorrow.

According to Nietzsche, we create the self that we become, we give style to our character—relying upon the experiences and the ideas that we have acquired throughout our lives. This means that while it is true that the self will always remain a mystery to a great extent, the insights offered to us by Descartes, Freud, contemporary geneticists and behaviourists are of great value. What these authors offer us are the tools and the materials that we can use not to discover but rather to create a self. That is, if we are willing to take up the task, if we are willing to explore the wisdom that great minds have to offer us.

# My Brain and I Are One

## Richard Restak

I once attended the wedding of a thirty-five-year-old patient who five years earlier had come to me after seeing in broad daylight the ghost of her dead first husband.

At our first meeting she told me about the ghostly visitor, but only after I had asked a simple question: "Has anything strange . . . you know . . . out of the ordinary ever happened to you?"

"Like what?" she responded, fixing upon me a pair of now fully dilated eyes.

She then revealed that on occasion she experienced a wave of fear accompanied by "strange sensations," such as a metallic taste in her mouth or a smell in the environment like that of burning rubber. On other occasions while in her home she felt as if everything had been "somehow altered." Sometimes the alteration involved her own sense of herself as somehow split into two people: an observer who commented on her actions, and an actor who carried them out. ("Yet both of them are me," she said.)

When I asked for further details, she said: "It's as if I'm a character in a science fiction novel who inhabits one dimension of reality while the rest of the world lives in another."

The electroencephalogram, which measures the brain's electrical activity, provided me with proof of what I already suspected. Karen's disturbed sense of herself originated from an epileptic discharge deep within the left temporal lobe of her brain.

The temporal lobe is responsible for our sense of connectedness, our personal identity, the feeling of belonging we get from familiar surroundings. When it functions normally, we have no apprehensions about who we are, our situation, or the nature of things. But when the temporal lobe is diseased, strange things can occur. A seizure originating in the temporal lobe can produce disorientation, feelings of having previously experienced events happening at the moment (*déjà vu*), or equally troubling feelings that familiar objects and people are new and vaguely threatening (*jamais vu*).

"My Brain and I Are One," is from Richard Restak's *The Brain Has a Mind of Its Own: Insights from a Practising Neurologist*. New York: Random House, 1991. Reprinted with permission.

Another temporal lobe epileptic I once treated spent long hours in the middle of the night writing philosophy. He filled notebook after notebook with philosophical ramblings that in broad daylight he was able to recognize as not likely to be of much interest to anybody but himself. A serious man, he made me think of prophets and seers. At times his **ruminations** on the nature of the spiritual world became ecstatic, almost sexual. Dostoevsky, a temporal lobe epileptic, described the process in *The Idiot*:

> *There was always one instant just before the epileptic fit . . . when suddenly in the midst of sadness, spiritual darkness and oppression, his brain seemed momentarily to catch fire, and in an extraordinary rush, all his vital forces were at their highest tension. The sense of life, the consciousness of self, were multiplied almost ten times at these moments which lasted no longer than a flash of lightning. His mind and his heart were flooded with extraordinary light; all his uneasiness, all his doubts, all his anxieties were relieved at once; they were all resolved into a lofty calm, full of serene, harmonious joy and hope, full of reason and ultimate meaning. But these moments, these flashes, were only a premonition of that final second (it was never more than a second) with which the fit began. That second was, of course, unendurable. Thinking of that moment later, when he was well again, he often said to himself that all these gleams and flashes of supreme sensation and consciousness of self, and, therefore, also of the highest form of being, were nothing but disease, the violation of the normal state; and if so, it was not at all the highest form of being, but on the contrary must be reckoned the lowest. Yet he came at last to an extremely paradoxical conclusion. "What if it is disease?" he decided at last. "What does it matter that it is an abnormal intensity, if the result, if the instant of sensation, remembered and analyzed afterwards in health, turns out to be the acme of harmony and beauty, and gives a feeling, unknown and undivined till then, of completeness, of proportion, of reconciliation, and of startled prayerful merging with the highest synthesis of life?"*

An encounter with a person suffering from temporal lobe epilepsy raises a question philosophers have argued about for centuries: What is the relationship of mind to brain? How can a disturbance within a fairly circumscribed area of the brain produce such **transcendental** experiences? Most experts have taken refuge from such questions in a vague and untidy dualism that, until fairly recently, was supported by our experiences with physics and machines.

Dualism, the metaphysical conception that body is separated from mind, originated with the seventeenth-century philosopher René Descartes. Descartes proposed that the body, especially the brain, is a machine with functions that can be explained by the mathematical laws of physics. But over the past sixty years physics has changed greatly. According to the principles

**ruminations**
reflections

**Dostoevsky**
Russian novelist

**transcendental**
heightened beyond all expectations

of **quantum physics** the observer cannot be meaningfully separated from the experiment that he or she is conducting. Indeed, the viewpoint of the observer often determines what is recorded by the experiment. . . .

The observer effect holds true for brain/mind dualism. . . . When I listen to my patients tell me about a frightening vision or hallucination—something far removed from everyday experience—I'm encountering the world of mind. But if I record my patient's brain waves during a hallucination and detect an epileptic seizure within the temporal lobe, I've shifted my focus . . . from one aspect of reality to another.

Marcus Raichle, head of the brain study group at the Washington University School of Medicine in St. Louis, suggests another way of thinking about such a **paradox**: "Because the brain is a physical structure, it exists in space; but the mind operates in time alone."

The brain as I stare at it depicted on a CAT scan or set out upon an autopsy table is very much an object. It takes up space; I can see it or its representation; I can pick up the autopsy specimen. We're talking about spatial matters here.

Mind, in contrast, can be captured only in the temporal dimension. My thoughts require time before I can communicate them to you in the form of words. Without motion or some form of behavior, mind cannot be inferred. Indeed, if I don't move or speak, can you really be sure I'm thinking at all?

The closer we look, the more difficult it is to maintain any neat division between mind and brain. Suppose I shout the word *fire* in a crowded theater. That word, *fire*, is conveyed by means of sound waves that stimulate the tympanic membranes in the ears of the listeners. Within milliseconds electrochemical events occur in the auditory nerve. They then traverse the labyrinthine pathway within the brain from auditory cortex to auditory association area to limbic system. There the word *fire* is loaded with fears traceable to the first caveman who burned his fingers before a campfire. Sound waves stimulate tympanic membranes, and physical alterations take place in the brain. Milliseconds later, thanks to the limbic involvement, the hypothalamus and sympathetic nervous system are drawn into the fray: heart rate increases, blood pressure rises, breathing becomes constricted and labored. The result: hundreds of people jump up from their seats to rush toward the exit—all in response to a concept conveyed by a mere word. Shouting the word *fire* exerted a powerful influence on matter. At a minimum the physical structure of the brain has been changed, albeit momentarily.

**quantum physics**
the study of the dynamic structure and motion of atoms and molecules that constitute all physical objects in the universe

**paradox**
puzzling contradiction

Other words and phrases of a different sort (*You're a failure; I want a divorce; I love you*) exert more permanent modifications within the brain. The PET scan of a schizophrenic or a manic-depressive shows a distinct variation from what, for lack of a better term, we call a normal brain. On the whole it's likely that these distinctions represent differences in the organization and function of the brains of those unfortunates who suffer from these illnesses. Alter the brain and you alter thoughts, feelings, and personal identity. And if you change an attitude or modify your own or someone else's behavior, you've worked a miracle, performed a successful experiment in **psychokinesis**: you've used the intangible mind to transform something in the physical world.

**psychokinesis**

moving objects with the mind alone

Mind can affect brain; brain can affect mind. But can either be separated from the other? Not any more than the other side of this paper can be separated from the side that you are now reading.

My experience with temporal lobe epileptics has raised a haunting personal question: How many of my own habits and propensities are determined for me by my brain? To what extent am I anything other than my brain? Is there any way of separating the brain from the person who just asked that question? My way of coping has been to fashion a simple mantra I repeat silently from time to time: "My brain and I are one. My brain and I are one." But even as I think and speak these words—my brain changing all the while as I do so—I still find it difficult to believe that this three-pound mass of protoplasm with the consistency of an overripe avocado is the seat of who I am, of who we all are.

# Personality and Science: The Assumptions of Materialism

Peter Morea

> I have no need of that hypothesis.
>
> *Laplace, French astronomer and mathematician, referring to God*

> My fundamental premise about the brain is that its workings—what we sometimes call 'mind'—are a consequence of its anatomy and physiology and nothing more.
>
> *Carl Sagan*, The Dragons of Eden

Traditional materialism, which is the basis of the natural sciences, and particularly of classical physics, dates from the sixteenth and seventeenth centuries, and is partly responsible for the success of science. According to scientific materialism, everything which exists is matter, and matter works by cause and effect; and matter operates according to consistent, enduring and discoverable laws. Matter is irreducible, and usually thought of as characterized by its being extended in space and time. Matter is the fundamental stuff of everything, and everything can largely be explained by reducing it to its material parts—though matter itself needs no explanation.

Modern psychology extended traditional materialism to the study of human beings. Modern psychology for the most part has held that the actions of human personality can be explained by the laws of physical matter. Scientific psychology assumes, in accordance with evolutionary theory, that mind and its activities are part of the natural world and can be explained by the physical brain of traditional materialism. Cognitive psychology, like most of modern psychology, holds that mind and the brain of **orthodox** biology are the same. The attempt in philosophy to argue that mind is brain, and that mind can be accounted for in traditional materialist terms, is called identity theory.

**orthodox**
established

There are several versions of identity theory, but all assert that mind is identical with brain. Identity theory says that mind and mental states exist, but that they are physical. Having a good idea, classifying objects as

"Personality and Science: The Assumptions of Materialism" is a chapter from Peter Morea's *In Search of Personality: Christianity and Modern Psychology*. London: SCM Press, 1997. Reprinted with permission.

squares or triangles, feeling pain or softness, are physical processes of the brain, nothing more. Even complex workings of the mind, such as apparent freedom in decision-making, originality in language, and creativity in the arts and sciences, are the brain alone at work.

Modern psychology's materialist assertion, the 'mind equals brain' of identity theory, was questioned early on from within psychology by William James. In his *Principles of Psychology* (1890), James argued that there is a non-material dimension to personality. There is, says James, a 'self of all the other selves', a principle of personal identity, an active dimension in a human being which goes out to meet the content of thought. He hypothesized a '**non-phenomenal** Thinker' independent of what is thought. This raises the question of who or what the thinker is. James concludes that we have to consider this thinker in terms of soul, spirit, or some other **transcendental** principle. At this point, for James, the problem becomes **metaphysical**, beyond the scope of a scientific psychology.

Science is concerned with material data and seeks to explain physical phenomena in terms of the material world. So James proposes an alternative view, that the identity of the human thinker consists in a stream of passing thoughts. Such an account of human identity is acceptable to scientific materialist psychology. James holds that a scientific psychology has to content itself with equating the thinker with this train of passing thoughts. But he points out that this does not square with human experience; our experience is that behind the passing thoughts is a thinker. Common experience suggests that thoughts and the thinker are not the same. Common experience suggests that there exists, independent of our thoughts, a thinker usually called consciousness or 'I'.

For James, explaining the thinker, consciousness or 'I', in terms of something like spirit or soul, is as valid as any materialist psychological explanation. He holds that scientific solutions, like his own stream of passing thoughts explanation, are not necessarily more true than spiritual and transcendental explanations. In holding this position, James is rejecting scientism, the view that a complete and adequate explanation of humans can be given using the methods of natural science. Implicitly James is touching on the nature of the different perspectives provided by religion and science.

As a science, psychology is concerned with the material world, with the physical cause of things, with events which can be observed or whose effects can be observed. In practice, modern psychology makes the materialist assumption that human actions can be reduced to physical laws

**non-phenomenal**
not perceivable by the senses

**transcendental**
non-physical

**metaphysical**
beyond the physical world

which determine the behavior of all inanimate and animate matter. But the question of whether matter as conceived by traditional materialism is enough to account for human personality remains unanswered. Whether brain as conceived by orthodox biology equals mind has not yet been demonstrated.

When it comes to the existence or non-existence of God, modern psychologists, apart from Freud and Jung, have little to say. Scientific personality theorists have by and large adopted the agnostic view that we cannot know whether God exists and should regard the question as irrelevant; or they have taken Freud's atheistic stance.

Freudian psychoanalytic theory points out that feelings about parents influence the view we have of God. But Freud goes further and declares that God is no more than an **exalted** father-figure and that religion in part derives from **ambivalent** feelings about Father. He notes that young people often abandon religious beliefs as they mature and reject the authority of parents. Freud regarded God as an infantile residue from childhood; he saw reason, education for reality and science as eventually replacing such infantile illusion.

Though Freud was a **reductionist**, he did not deny the reality of mind. As a therapist he was particularly aware of the reality of people's anxieties and phobias and fantasies; he saw mind as playing a part in all these. After all, the point of Freudian psychoanalytic therapy is to reduce anxiety and phobia and depression by working on mind. Freud would like to have demonstrated that mind was brain and that there was only the physical body and brain. In an early work, 'Project for a Scientific Psychology', he tried to do this. He never published the 'Project' and subsequently described the work as balderdash. So he asserted, while holding that there was only biological body and brain, that mind and its products, such as thoughts and memories as well as fantasies and phobias, are real enough.

By the end of the nineteenth and the beginning of the twentieth century, academic psychology had abandoned words like 'spirit' and 'soul' and was exploring mind by means of **introspection**. Early in the twentieth century, behaviourist psychologists largely stopped studying 'mind', which still seemed contaminated by its historical association with non-material soul and spirit. Behaviourism no longer regarded psychology as the study of mind, but rather as the study of behaviour. Behaviorists chose to ignore, even to deny, the existence of mind and to concentrate on the study of actual behaviour which could be observed. Behaviourism was central to psychology for many decades and remains influential.

**exalted**
glorified

**ambivalent**
both positive and negative

**reductionist**
one who believes human nature can be reduced to biology

**introspection**
self-examination

Behaviourism regards human beings as blank slates with a massive capacity for learning. This learning is not related to internal processes such as mind but is the result of external rewards and punishments. According to behaviourism, the rewards and punishments of the external environment shape our behaviour; what we do is the product of such conditioning. Mind does not enter into it—or, at least, we can ignore mind in the behaviourist account. Behaviourist psychology, seeing behaviour as responses to external stimuli, regards humans as being like any other animal, just better at learning, and not really free.

Behaviourism's attempt to account for human beings in terms of observable behaviour was a justifiable and worthy attempt to create a scientific psychology. Behaviourism was able to explain much human behaviour in terms of conditioning by reward and punishment. But behaviourism had difficulty in accounting for higher human activities such as language, abstract thought, culture, science, the arts, moral behaviour. These are very real activities, central to human beings. We usually regard such activities as the product of mind, which behaviourism ignored.

It seems that mind cannot be ignored for long or just left on the periphery of explanations of humans. If humans think that they think, the first 'think' seems to clinch it. Descartes' 'I think, therefore, I am' seems a reasonable basis on which to conclude not only that I exist but that, whatever else I am, I am a thinking thing. I may doubt the existence of others but I cannot doubt that I am doubting. Thinking, doubting, reasoning, remembering seem real enough in human experience. If they are real, they suggest the existence of mind. The difficulty for psychology has been that of observing mind at work, and until recently introspection had appeared the only way. This altered with the arrival of the computer.

In the 1960s, psychology changed direction. Cognitive psychology asserted that mind was central to human activities such as thinking, understanding, learning, language, reasoning, planning, creativity, recognizing patterns, remembering. According to cognitive psychology, behaviourism was misguided in ignoring mind and suggesting that mental processes do not exist or are irrelevant. According to cognitive psychology, at present a dominant force in psychology, mind is central to human behaviour. With the computer, there was now a method for studying mind scientifically which seemed superior to the earlier approach of introspection.

A digital computer is a machine which manipulates symbols according to rules, such as those contained in its programme. A digital computer takes in data, which it transforms, stores, retrieves, transmits. Isn't this what a human mind does? The computer takes information and processes this information according to certain rules. Doesn't the human mind work by logically processing information and manipulating symbols according to rules? There have certainly been philosophers who thought so. Hobbes, for example, regarded thinking as calculations using symbols instead of numbers; Hobbes' 'reasoning is but reckoning' view has been held by some for a long time.

Cognitive psychologists start from the position that the human mind is an information-processing system, like a computer; humans use mind to sort out information. Cognitive psychologists regard the human mind as a system that accepts, transforms and stores information, and retrieves, uses and transmits that information, just like a computer. In the cognitive account, activities of the mind such as thinking and remembering and recognizing are forms of processing information according to rules. Cognitive psychologists regard humans and computers as two kinds of information-processing systems; humans and computers are different subspecies of the species, information-processing systems.

This information-processing approach avoids problems of purpose and choice raised by other accounts of mind. The actions of a computer are caused; with the computer as model, a scientific mechanistic cause-and-effect explanation of mind is guaranteed. The distinction between the obviously caused behaviour of a computer and the apparently purposeful actions of humans is illusory, according to many cognitive psychologists. A central-heating system, turning itself on and off as the temperature falls and rises, appears just as purposive as the householder who turns the heating system on 'to warm the house up' and switches it off 'because it is now hot enough'. In the cognitive-psychology account, the actions of both heating system and householder are caused.

By producing apparently intelligent behaviour which resembles what humans do, the computer seems to lay to rest one of the oldest problems about human personality, that of the body-mind relationship. For traditional materialism, the body-mind question comes down to: how can mind be explained without resorting to a ghost in the machine? Behaviourism dealt with the problem by denying, or ignoring, the existence of mind. But, as I have said, the reality of mind cannot be denied for long. Once concede its existence, and the question returns of explaining mind without resorting to spirit or soul. If we adopt as a model the programmed computer, a machine apparently intelligent like a human, and certainly with no spirit or soul, the problem seems solved.

Cognitive psychology regards the relationship of mind to brain as resembling that of wired-in programme to computer. With a human being, this wired-in programme is the specific innate features of the human brain. If the brain is like a computer, then mind resembles the programme and is a kind of innate pre-programming. In the cognitive account, a human being is not a blank slate, as behaviourism alleged. Cognitive psychology adopts an innate position, holding that there is something already written on the slate when humans are born. To behaviourism's adage, taken from Locke, that 'there is nothing in the intellect that was not first in the senses', cognitive psychology following Leibniz adds, 'Nothing—save only the intellect itself.'

Cognitive psychologists have amassed a wealth of valuable data and understanding relating to mind and its activities. But there are now queries about whether the human mind does work as an information-processing system. Experts had predicted that in a short time computers would equal and even surpass what the human mind can do. But the achievements of artificial intelligence over a period of thirty years have proved much less successful than was predicted. Compared with humans, the competence of computers is (as yet) limited. This raises queries about whether the human mind is only an information-processing system. Perhaps we do not reason, remember, understand, recognize, in the way that computers do, by logically processing information and manipulating symbols according to rules. Or if we do, perhaps this is not only what we do, and the human mind reasons and remembers and understands and recognizes patterns by other means as well. If the human mind is an information-processing system, this is possibly not the sum total of what mind is. Perhaps cognitive psychology is too restrictive in taking the information-processing model, the equivalent of **Pascal's mathematical mind**, as the complete explanation. After all, Pascal goes on to suggest that human personality also works with an intuitive mind.

The doubt about whether humans operate as information-processing systems goes further. Computers handle information and data by reducing them to bits. But it seems that the human mind does not work with information and data in this reductionist way, first breaking them down into bits of knowledge, then building them up again. **Gestalt psychology** always emphasized that 'the whole is greater than the sum of its parts', and stressed that parts can be understood only in relation

---

**Pascal's mathematical mind**

a process of reasoning based entirely on the application of rules of logic

**Gestalt psychology**

holistic study of the individual's perception and behaviour

to the whole. Is human thinking, use of language, remembering, artistic and scientific creativity, built up from discrete elements in the way that a programmed computer works? Do people recognize the faces of friends by a building-block process of assembling parts of the face? Current evidence suggests that the answer to these questions is 'No'. And if the human mind does not work in a reductionist and additive way only, then the information-processing computer as a model of the human mind is inadequate.

Programmes have been written which enable computers to learn. But such programmes have equipped computers with a very limited capacity for learning, and only over a restricted area. There are, for example, programmes for playing **draughts** which improve by storing information from previous games. But the human capacity to learn remains superior to that of the computer and extends over a wide area. Humans have a capacity for learning which is general and not specific to draughts or language vocabulary or skills in a particular sport. Of course, it remains possible that in the future more powerful computers will equal the human mind's comprehensive capacity to learn.

**draughts**
a British term for checkers

It is also becoming clear that the human mind functions in terms of an everyday knowledge of the world. We know how we are expected to behave at meal times, to dress for work, to act when we go shopping. At present it is difficult to provide computers with programmes for how to operate in such everyday situations. Humans, as a result of childhood and adult experience, have an easy grasp of contexts in which everyday life takes place. Computers have to be specifically programmed for these, and this is a vast task which as yet has not been satisfactorily done. Humans can think and apply their cognitive processes not in one area only, but generally; human beings have a sort of general all-round intelligence. Computer programmes for thinking or problem-solving as yet operate only in specific areas, such as a particular kind of algebra or chess.

Certainly one area where the computer equals the achievement of the human mind is chess. Programmed computers now play chess at a level where they would win against nearly all human players. This serves to make a point about computer accounts of how the mind works. Cognitive psychology is concerned with understanding the human mind. What is really relevant for psychology is not whether a computer plays chess well, but how it plays. Does the computer decide moves in the way that a competent human player does? It now seems unlikely. The interest of serious chess players in analysing past games, like medical specialists recalling similar cases in the past when attempting a diagnosis,

is perhaps significant. It seems clear that when faced with a problem the human mind does not always, perhaps does not usually, start from first principles. The research suggests that the human mind often starts by trying to find out what worked in the past. When the chess-playing computer wins, the rule-following information-processing computer is equalling and surpassing the achievement of the human mind, but it may not be replicating how the human minds works.

The cognitive-psychology account of humans as information-processing and rule-following systems may eventually prove inadequate. But the achievements of computers could still be taken to demonstrate that something completely physical, like a computer, thinks and understands. There is no ghost, spirit or soul in the computer machine, so if computers really think and understand, then the problem of the body-mind relationship seems solved. Whether or not computers exactly parallel the way in which the human mind works, the achievement of computers would appear to prove that a traditional materialist account of mind may eventually be possible. That a computer, something wholly material, apparently thinks, recognizes, remembers, understands, is regarded as very significant by many psychologists. Such psychologists, and some philosophers, see the computer as providing evidence for the traditional materialist position. Margaret Boden (1990) asks, 'So why shouldn't some future tin-can have feelings and sensations, too?'

But even with the advent of computers, there remain problems for the materialist position on mind. Cognitive psychology proposes that human minds resemble computers in that both operate by following rules. But the sense in which computers and humans follow rules seems different. The mechanical and electrical reactions of a clock are determined by its design; in a similar way, the actions of a computer are laid down and determined by its circuitry and programme. In this sense, clock and computer are both following rules. Is this what we mean when we say that the human mind operates by following rules?

A friend tells me how to get to his house. 'Once you have passed the railway station, go straight across the next three crossroads.' This rule, 'go straight across the next three crossroads,' means something to me. The rule has meaning, which I understand. Humans follow rules the content of which has meaning that they understand; they are guided by the meaningful content of a rule. As I pass the station, and when I approach a crossroad, I will remind myself of this 'go straight across the next three crossroads' rule. But this is different from the rules that computers and, for example, planets follow. Planets do not say to themselves: 'The rule is, just keep on swinging to the left', or, 'I must follow an ellipse whose diameter is . . .' Similarly, computers do not tell themselves what to do, since they are not guided by the meaning-content of any rule. Computers, like planets, appear to 'follow rules' in a way that is very different from the way in which humans do.

The actions of computers are caused and determined, like the actions of any machine or planet. If we describe as rule-following the caused and determined reactions of the computer to its programme, it is only as a kind of metaphor. It does not imply that rules have any meaning for computers in the way that 'Go straight across all the traffic lights until you come to a bridge' means something to a human. A computer does not react to any understanding of rules. A programme mechanically determines that the computer will follow certain procedures; what the computer does is determined. Computers and humans do not 'follow rules' in the same way.

Cognitive psychology has provided much understanding by seeing the human mind as an information-processing rule-following system like a computer. But when it comes to computers (and planets), rather than speak of their following rules, it might be more correct to describe their behaviour as law-like. The human mind is usually responding to the meaning contained in rules, but a computer is not. A thought-experiment proposed by Searle (1984) makes this clear.

In Searle's thought-experiment a man sits in a room, with a set of rules in English and a box full of statements in Chinese. The man speaks English but not Chinese; so he has no understanding of the statements in the box. When messages in Chinese are posted into the room, he has no understanding of these either. The set of rules in English, which he understands, do not explain what these messages in the Chinese language mean, but they do tell him what to do when he receives one. So when the messages in Chinese are posted in, he looks at the rules. The rules instruct him that when a particular specified set of Chinese symbols is posted in, he should take from the box and post out another particular specified set of symbols. He picks up a message in Chinese posted in, and he posts out the statement in Chinese which the rules specify. He continues to do this, but neither what is posted in, nor what he posts out, means anything to him.

The people outside the room are posting in questions in Chinese. And what the man in the room unknowingly is doing, by following the set of rules in English, is posting out correct answers. Soon the man in the room is adept at processing what to him are meaningless symbols, but what to Chinese speakers outside are meaningful questions and answers. Those outside might conclude that inside the room there is someone who understands Chinese. But this is not the case. And no matter how long the man in the room processes these symbols, he will never in this way learn to understand a word of Chinese. He knows what to do with the symbols in front of him, because of his set of rules in English. What he does not know is the meaning of the questions and answers in Chinese.

The analogy is with the computer. A programme could be written which enables a computer to do what the man in the room does. A question in Chinese is fed in; the computer matches the question against its memory or data base; the computer produces an answer in Chinese. The man in the room, by following the rules, has given the impression to those outside that he understands Chinese, but he does not understand a word. Similarly, the computer running through its programme understands not a word. All a computer has is what the man in the room has, a set of rules called a programme, for processing Chinese words which mean nothing to him.

What Searle's thought-experiment illustrates is the difference between thinking which involves understanding and 'thinking' which involves no understanding. And normally thinking, remembering, perceiving and other human cognitive processes involve understanding; such processes have meaningful content for the mind. However, for the computer, just as for the man in the room, such processes have no meaningful content.

What computers do, and they do very well, is to process symbols which mean nothing to them, in the way that the Chinese words are meaningless to the man in the room.

Searle underlines the difference by imagining the English-speaker in the room having questions in English posted in. Here the man understands the content of question and answer. The human mind may operate according to certain rules like a programme, but what human minds work on normally has meaningful content. Humans not only follow rules, but they also understand the meaning of the material which they are processing using rules. The human mind reacts to meaning (semantics) as well as to rules telling it what to do (syntax). Most activity of the human mind involves meaning and understanding in a way that the operations of a computer do not.

Even if in the future an improved computer provided answers as good as, even better than, those of someone who speaks Chinese, nothing would have changed; the computer's situation would still be no different from that of the non-Chinese speaker in the room. Should the technology of computers improve so that they achieve what human minds achieve, it would still be misleading to describe the machine as having understanding and intelligence. For intelligence and understanding, both syntax (rules) and semantics (meaning) are required. In the digital computer, or any machine, we have only the rules of syntax. The symbols in a computer programme can refer to anything—words, atoms, incidence of disease, nails; this illustrates how devoid of specific meaning they are. Searle's contention is that in no sense does a computer have understanding.

Another relevant scenario is where a computer-controlled train crashes, injuring passengers, because of some failure in the circuitry or program. Ought the public to demand that the computer be tried in a court of law? Would we now, or could we in the future, have a judicial trial of the computer for committing such a serious error? The differences between the mind of a human being and the 'mind' of a computer are real and are not dependent on the state of the art in computer technology.

Following the decline of behaviourism, with its emphasis on external behaviour, cognitive psychology emerged and, using the computer, has returned mind to psychology. Modern psychology reasserts the reality and centrality of mind. And according to cognitive psychology, human mind is characterized by innate pre-existing structures. But the scientific materialism assumed by psychological accounts of mind and personality has yet to be demonstrated. Materialist assumptions, that personality and mind consist only of the body and brain of traditional materialism, and that God does not exist or is irrelevant to personality, remain unproven.

# Am I Free or Determined?

Melanie Chaparian

Each of the theories of self discussed earlier in Unit 1 takes a stand on the philosophical debate between determinism and libertarianism. On one side of the debate, determinism is the position that all human actions are determined, or caused, by natural and/or environmental forces beyond human control. According to this theory, people do not have any free will. The field of cognitive psychology, as discussed in Morea's "Personality and Science: The Assumptions of Materialism" for example, views human beings as sophisticated computers that can only perform the operations with which they are programmed.

On the other side of the debate, libertarianism is the view that at least some human actions are free. Although many actions may be determined, there are some situations in which people can exercise their free will. Unlike computers, human beings seem to be capable of making real choices between alternative courses of action. Nietzsche's theory of the self, as discussed in "From Biography to Biology: A Brief History of the Self," for example, takes the position that people have free will.

## An Argument for Determinism

Determinism may be defended on the basis of the following rather simple argument: Every event in the world occurs because of cause and effect. Like every other event, human actions must be determined by cause and effect as well. If all of our actions are caused, we cannot possess free will because the same action cannot be both caused and free at the same time. Therefore, all human actions are determined, and no human actions are free.

Let's look at this argument in more detail. Few people today question the universality of cause and effect in the natural world. Traditional science teaches us that every natural phenomenon is the effect of a cause or set of causes. Indeed, most science assumes a deterministic model of the world. It is the very nature of science to look for the causes of the phenomena

"Am I Free or Determined?" is by Melanie Chaparian of Humber College. Used by permission.

it studies. The nature of causality is such that there is an *inevitable* connection between a cause and its effect: if the cause occurs, the effect *must* also occur. For example, if heating water to a temperature of 100°C *determines* the water to turn into steam, then every time water is heated to that temperature it *must* turn into steam. Heating water to 100°C is the *cause* and the water turning into steam is the *effect*. We never entertain the possibility that boiling water, or any other natural phenomena, occurs because of pure chance. Scientists always try to discover the causes of the phenomena they study. Indeed, when they are unable to identify the cause of a particular phenomenon, such as the memory loss suffered by people affected by Alzheimer's disease, they do not conclude that no cause exists but rather that it simply has not *yet* been discovered.

But the deterministic view is not limited to the natural sciences such as physics, chemistry, biology and medicine. Determinism is also frequently assumed by the social sciences, such as psychology and sociology, which usually attempt to study and *discover the causes of human behaviour*. A determinist would agree that, although we may believe ourselves to be unique creatures, human beings are just as subject to the world of cause and effect as boiling water and Alzheimer's disease.

The determinist argues that our distinctive nature only means that the causes that determine our actions are more complex, and therefore harder to discover, than those that cause other events. The *kinds* of causes determining human behaviour depend on the determinist's particular view of human nature. Some point to *nature*, such as hereditary or instinctual forces, as the primary cause of a person's actions. Other determinists argue that a person's behaviour is fundamentally determined by *nurture*, that is, by environmental factors. Many, if not most, determinists, however, acknowledge that a *combination* of nature and nurture determines a person's actions. A Freudian psychologist, for example, believes that an individual's behaviour is caused by the way the *ego* moderates between drives of the *id*, which are determined by instinct or heredity, and the moral demands of the *superego*, which are determined by early childhood environment. Regardless of the kinds of causes they point to, all determinists agree that all human actions are determined or caused.

No matter how long and hard we may deliberate between different courses of action, the "choice" we finally make has already been decided for us by hereditary and/or environmental causes over which we have no control. This applies to all of our actions, from the most trivial to the most significant.

According to the determinist, an analysis of the motivations of different people reveals the various causes that result in the difference in their behaviour. The determinist is quick to point out that you do not freely choose what interests you. Your interests are determined by your nature, your environment or, most likely, by a combination of both. For example, you probably wish to pursue academic success. Why is this important to you? Maybe you have been gifted with a naturally intellectual mind. This is not an attribute that you freely chose to acquire. Or perhaps your family has always encouraged good grades. Again, the determinist points out that you have no control over the values your family has conditioned into you. You may be aware that good grades are essential for the new graduate to secure a decent position in today's highly competitive job market. Once again, the determinist points out that you have no control over the increasingly high academic requirements demanded by employers. *Your* actual motivations for persevering through your homework probably include some of those discussed here as well as a number of others. But whatever they may be, the determinist argues, they reveal that you do not freely choose to study hard.

At this point, you may be convinced that *your* actions are caused by forces outside your control. But how does the determinist explain the actions of other students in your class who socialize at the expense of studying and consequently earn low marks? After all, most of them also come from families that stress academic success, and all of them want good jobs after they graduate. It *seems* that these negligent students are making a free, although foolish, choice.

Things are not always as they first appear. According to the determinist's theory, if your negligent classmates are subject to exactly the same causal forces that determine your behaviour, they would of necessity be studying as hard as you are. The very fact that they sacrifice study time to socialize indicates that their personal histories are very different from yours. Perhaps their families have not so much *encouraged* academic success as relentlessly *pressured* them to do well in school. If so, they may have been determined to rebel by going to all the college parties instead of studying. Just as you have no control over the encouragement you receive, the rebellious students have no control over the pressure they suffer. Other students who neglect their homework may simply not have the maturity required for self-discipline. Having fun may be as important to them, or even more so, as earning good marks or preparing for their future. If so, the determinist points out that a person cannot simply decide to become mature. This is a developmental process that is determined by an individual's nature and upbringing. There is a host of other causes that may determine some students to neglect their studies. Whatever these causes may be in any actual case, the determinist argues that negligent students do not freely choose to ignore their homework. Although they may feel guilty that they are not studying, they simply cannot choose to do so. Therefore, neither the diligent student nor the negligent student really makes a genuine choice between studying or not studying. The course of action each takes is determined by causes over which neither has any control.

Nor do we have the freedom to make genuine choices concerning even the most important aspects of our lives. Nature or nurture, or both, determine such things as which profession we pursue, who we fall in love with, and how many children we have. According to the theory of determinism, *all* human actions are the effect of causes over which we have no control; consequently, free will is merely an illusion.

Because we usually pride ourselves on our freedom, we may feel reluctant to accept the determinist's conclusion. But this in itself is not a good reason to reject determinism. It would be hard to deny that the deterministic model has helped to advance our knowledge of the natural world in general and the human world in particular. Discovering the cause of an event not only increases our understanding of that phenomenon but also allows us to *predict* and sometimes *control* its future occurrence. If, for example, we know that a virus causes an illness in the human body, we can predict that a person will become ill when infected by that virus, and, moreover, we can control that illness by finding ways to prevent the virus from infecting more people. Or, if we know that a moderate amount of parental pressure causes a student to succeed in school, we can predict that a student subjected to that amount of guidance will earn good grades, and we can control such successes by teaching parents how to provide the proper dose of encouragement. The deterministic model also helps us to make sense out of our personal lives. We are often remarkably successful, for instance, in predicting the actions of our close relatives and friends. If such predictions are not merely lucky guesses, the determinist argues, they must be based on our relatively extensive knowledge of the hereditary and environmental causes that determine the behaviour of those relatives and friends. The fact that we may not *like* the theory of determinism does not negate the wealth of evidence for its accuracy.

# James' Critique of Determinism

Willliam James

In his famous lecture entitled "The Dilemma of Determinism," William James, an American philosopher and psychologist who lived from 1842 to 1910, defends libertarianism, the theory that human beings have free will. Before he actually begins his argument for this theory, however, James shows that determinism—its appeal to science notwithstanding—cannot be scientifically demonstrated.

Science cannot really tell us, for example, if the negligent student's background is causing him to rebel. The fact that he does consistently neglect his assigned readings is not in itself conclusive proof that the student is determined to take this course of action. Moreover, *before the fact*—that is, before the student entered college—no one, not even the most learned determinist, could ascertain whether the student's background would lead him to socialize or to study. For instance, it would not have seemed inconceivable to suppose that the excessive family pressure would prompt the student to study harder than any other student. Nor would it have been unreasonable to surmise that this pressure would compel him to overcome his immaturity and set his priorities in a more beneficial way. *Before the fact*, this series of events seems as likely to occur as the events that actually came to pass; thus, James argues, *after the fact*, there is no way to prove that the student was determined to neglect his studies. The same argument applies to all human actions. James therefore concludes that the determinist cannot prove that all actions are the inevitable effects of prior causes. While this in itself does *not* disprove determinism, it certainly dispels the myth that determinism has the weight of science on its side, and, furthermore, suggests that libertarianism should at least be reconsidered.

# James' Argument for Free Will

Different libertarians disagree among themselves on how far human freedom extends. On one extreme, existentialists such as Nietzsche claim that all human actions are potentially free. On the other extreme, some libertarians only argue that actions performed in the face of moral demands are free. In this discussion, we will focus on the views of William James, who defends a relatively moderate version of libertarianism. According to James, we are free whenever we have a genuine choice between at least two possible and desirable courses of action. This does not mean, of course, that we are free to perform any conceivable action whatsoever. Nor does this even mean that we are free to do anything we may desire, for the action that we find most tempting may not be included within the choice before us. All that is required to render an action free is the existence of one other alternative action that it is possible for us to perform.

Essential to James' definition of free will is the existence of *possible actions*: that is, actions that a person is not inevitably determined to do but may perform nonetheless. If an action is the result of free will, then it is, before the fact, merely one of two or more genuinely *possible* alternative actions that the person can *freely choose* to perform; and, after the fact, it is correct to say that the individual *could have acted otherwise* by choosing another alternative. For instance, the negligent student may have freely chosen to spend his time socializing instead of at the library; and even though he made this choice, he could have chosen to study instead. It is the idea of possible actions that puts James in stark opposition to determinism, which states that every action is the *inevitable* effect of a cause.

We have already discussed James' argument that determinism cannot be scientifically demonstrated. He does not attempt, however, to disprove this theory nor to prove libertarianism true. This is because he believes determinism and libertarianism to be two alternative theories of reality, neither of which can be objectively proven true or false. Thus, he claims that the best we can do is to examine both theories to see which one offers us the most rational explanation of human behaviour. According to James, a "rational" theory should not only explain objective reality but must account for subjective human experience as well. James' defence of libertarianism consists in the argument that the free will position is more rational in this sense than determinism.

A significant fact of human life is the *feeling of freedom* that we often experience. James argues that any theory of human behaviour must adequately explain this feeling. Unlike determinism, libertarianism conforms to our ordinary experience: we often feel free to choose between alternative courses of action. Of course, the determinist argues that this feeling is merely an illusion because our course of action has already been decided for us by causes beyond our control. But the "illusion" persists in our inner, subjective experience nonetheless. For example, the good student probably *feels* that he or she could have chosen to go to more parties while the negligent student likely *feels* that he or she could have decided to study harder. In his or her practical affairs, even the most staunch

There is nothing more wholesome for us than to find problems that quite transcend our powers.

*Charles Pierce*

## TO STUDY OR TO PARTY

### Free Will Reconsidered

Suppose you have an examination tomorrow and a friend asks you to forgo studying and spend the evening at a party. Your friend does not urge or threaten or coerce you. You consider the alternatives, and after a moment's thought, decide to give up studying for the night and go to the party. We would ordinarily say that you are responsible for your decision. We think of such cases as actions in which you are free to decide one way or the other.

Contrast this to a situation in which a headache leads you to lie down and fall asleep on your bed instead of continuing to study. In this case it would not make sense to say that you are free to decide one way or the other about studying.

The dispute between advocates of free will and advocates of determinism is basically a dispute whether incidents like the two so cited, which feel so different, are really radically and essentially different when viewed objectively.

Whereas the advocate of free will would perceive these two sorts of acts as essentially different, the determinist would not. The determinist might argue that although you may believe that your decision to stay home to study for the exam was an expression of free choice, nevertheless closer scrutiny would reveal that your behaviour was not really free after all. What you thought was a free choice was really a choice dictated by your desires, which in turn spring from your character,

which in its turn is fashioned by the forces of heredity and environment, which are clearly beyond your control.

The central affirmation of determinism is that every event has a cause. By an analysis of the causes of any one of your actions, the determinist would cause your so-called freedom to vanish in a chain of causes that stretches back into the remote recesses of your heredity and environment. Nature and nurture, genes and society—those are the factors that made you what you are and cause you to act the way you do. The notion that you are free is really a misapprehension, an illusion.

Adapted from *An Introduction to Modern Philosophy* by Donald M. Borchert.

---

determinist probably *feels free* to choose between alternative courses of action. No matter how solidly convinced we may be that determinism offers us a rational account of all natural phenomena and perhaps most human behaviour, we still find it difficult—if not impossible—to *believe* subjectively that we are never free. Thus, determinism requires us to reject as illusory a universal human experience. Libertarianism, on the other hand, acknowledges the feeling of freedom as a natural part of the experience of exerting our free will. According to James, this is a good reason to adopt the free will thesis. While he concedes that determinism is a rational theory of reality from an objective standpoint, James argues that libertarianism is an even more rational position because it can account for our inner, subjective experience of freedom.

Another important fact of human experience that James believes a rational theory must explain are *judgements of regret*. Our dissatisfaction with the world, especially with human behaviour, leads us to regret, that is, to "wish that something might be otherwise." After receiving a poor mark in the course, for instance, the negligent student may *regret* that he chose to spend all his time socializing. And because we regret the actions of others as well as our own, you may also *regret* that he had not studied. The most significant regrets concern the moral sphere. We do not accept as inevitable the senseless murders, rapes and cases of child abuse we read about in the newspaper; instead, we judge such acts to be bad or immoral to the highest degree and regret that they are part of our world.

A regret implies that something is bad, and "calling a thing bad means that the thing ought not to be, that something else ought to be in its stead." When we label someone's action immoral, we imply that it should not have been done and that the person should have acted otherwise. For instance, when we proclaim that a murderer is guilty of the highest moral offence, we mean that he should not have committed homicide and should have instead treated his victim in a peaceful, humane manner. Regrets obviously assume the existence of free will. For this reason, libertarianism offers us a better explanation of our regrets than does determinism.

The source of our deepest regrets is the recognition that the world is fraught with immorality. According to determinism, even the most heinous crimes are as much the result of cause and effect as the routine activities we do every day. Knowing the causes of immoral actions does not eliminate our regret that they occur, but it does make our regret merely futile hope. Libertarianism, on the other hand, recognizes immoral actions as the result of free will and, as such, acknowledges that other actions could have been performed instead. Since this applies to future as well as past actions, there exists the possibility that the world—although certainly imperfect—may be made a better and more moral place through free human action. Thus, from the libertarian viewpoint, regrets may virtually be taken at face value—as expressions of our belief that immoral actions *can* be avoided and *should not* take place. This, according to James, renders libertarianism a more rational theory of human existence.

James admits from the outset that his defence consists of the argument that libertarianism is more rational than determinism because it offers a better account of our feelings of freedom and judgements of regret. This is not a claim that can be proven objectively, but one that can only be "verified" by consulting our inner, subjective sense. Although James argues that determinism is also incapable of objective demonstration, he acknowledges that determinism appeals to a different kind of rationality, perhaps what we might call a scientific rationality. Even though James finds libertarianism to be more rational than determinism, it remains for each of us to study both theories to see which of the two *we* find to be the most rational.

# UNIT 2

# Change and the Social World

We make history ourselves, but, in the first place, under very definite antecedents and conditions. Among these the economic ones are ultimately decisive. But the political ones, etc., and indeed even the traditions which haunt human minds also play a part, although not the decisive one . . .

*Frederick Engels*

Though women do not complain of the power of husbands, each complains of her own husband, or the husbands of her friends. It is the same in all other cases of servitude; at least in the commencement of the emancipatory movement. The serfs did not at first complain of the power of the lords, but only of their tyranny.

*J. S. Mill*

It is understood that in a developed society *needs* are not only quantitative: the need for consumer goods; but also qualitative: the need for a free and many-sided development of human facilities, the need for information, for communication, the need to be free not only from exploitation but from oppression and alienation in work and leisure.

*A. Gorz*

## Introduction

John Steckley

# Sociological Imagination

We have looked at the individual from various perspectives. Now we will broaden the scope and look at society, the context in which the individual lives. To shift focus from the level of the individual alone to that of the individual in society involves what sociologist C. Wright Mills terms the "sociological imagination." This "quality of mind," as Mills referred to it, involves being able to locate ourselves in terms of our social characteristics (e.g., gender, age, class, ethnicity) and the social forces of our time (e.g., economic trends, political movements), and to see how these factors influence many aspects of our personal life (e.g., our marriage, our relationships with employers, and our main worries in life).

Think of it like this: You are a twenty-year-old student who works part time in a convenience store. Your boss does not treat you with respect and has actually said, "If you don't like these working conditions, I can replace you with someone who does." You are in a significant relationship, but it is not serious enough to consider marriage. Use your sociological imagination: Why does your boss say that? It could have little to do with you personally, but everything to do with the fact that there are many people in your position, and so your boss has power because it is currently a "buyer's market" for unskilled workers. Similarly, you might not feel you can get serious about marriage at this point in your life because you need to build your career first. Join the club.

# Change

The central fact about society today is change. Things are not what they were just a few short years ago, and most of us are struggling to find some meaning in these changes. Are computers really improving the lives of most people or, instead, just increasing the distance between the "haves" and the "have nots"? Is the family dying, or improving, or just adapting? Is multiculturalism broadening our perspective, or disguising inequality among groups, or creating more division in Canadian society?

# Five Interpretations of Change

In Unit 1 we looked at different theories of the self and discovered that no one theory has all the right answers. The same holds true for theories of social change. Here, we will look at five interpretations of change: modernism, conservatism, post-modernism, evolution and fashion. For any given change, it is up to you to decide which interpretation or which combination of interpretations fits best.

## Modernism

Modernism holds that change equals progress, that the modern or new will be better than the old, that newer automatically means better. It portrays society as progressing along a straight line of improvement. From the early to the mid-twentieth century, modernism was expressed in the feeling that science and technology were going to create a material heaven on earth. Science would become a rational, hard, evidence-based religion that would take over from the traditional religions built on faith, on "unproven" and "unprovable" belief. Technology would free people from having to perform hard physical labour on the job. At home, robots would do all the housework. Freed from tedious labour on the job and at home, we would all have plenty of leisure time to do with as we pleased.

More recently, particularly in television ads, we are told that computer technology offers us increased freedom to do what would have taken many people a lot of time to do before. We can communicate with more people via the Internet. We can work at home. Look at how many people compose and record multi-instrument music in one-person, home-based operations today.

Modernist notions of politics incorporate the ideas that societies are constantly improving by becoming more democratic, that respect for human rights is on the rise, that the barriers between societies are fading—all leading to the reduction of the possibility of war. Indeed, this was the ideal behind the founding of the United Nations after World War II.

In the last few decades, however, we have discovered some of the weaknesses of modernism. Science has not significantly lessened the human need for religion. People today seek the spiritual in ways both traditional and new, even in scientific strongholds such as medicine and biology. Technology has created problems of pollution that we need to solve more by how we live than by adding more technology. Car pooling, riding bicycles, walking and using public transit will do more to reduce pollution than having more efficient mufflers on new cars. As we will discuss in Unit 4, ethical principles must come from society in general, not from scientists and technicians concerned more with "Can we . . . " than with "Should we . . . " People with jobs seem to be working harder than in decades past, putting in more hours. Leisure time is not increasing. Computers appear more to reduce the number of jobs we have available to us than to reduce the amount of work we do. There seems to be no end to all the learning we have to do to stay current and competitive, not to mention the money we have to spend to upgrade once we have become addicted to these clever machines. And even today, governments with little apparent respect for democracy, human rights or peace still maintain a visible presence.

## Conservatism

The second interpretation of change can be termed conservatism, although conservationist would be almost as accurate. This perspective sees change as being potentially more destructive than constructive, especially in emotion-charged areas such as the family, gender, sexuality and the environment.

Although it is easy to dismiss conservatism as only representing old-timers romanticizing the past, redneck reactionaries, or anti-progress, tree-hugging nature "freaks," it would be misleading to do so. Some values and customs need to be preserved. Their loss is neither inevitable, nor desirable. Take the feeling of community, for example. I live in a small town just north of Toronto. Sometimes it seems to be little more than a collection of subdivisions, but other times it feels like a community. When my stepson played on a baseball team, I was one of a gang of parents who drove our team around the Southern Ontario countryside, watching and loudly cheering for "our boys." I began to feel that all the players on the team were "my kids," a reminder of my childhood summers in Prince Edward Island, when I had many supportive "aunts" and "uncles," not all of whom were related to me.

## Postmodernism

Postmodernism is difficult to define. In postmodernist interpretation, society can be divided into two kinds of groups. One kind has a strong voice: its perceptions dominate media such as books, scientific journals, newspapers, television, radio and schools. The other kind has little opportunity to have its voice heard. Society's understanding of this kind of group (and its impact on society) typically comes from the words and perceptions of the dominant group. The first group can be termed the "Subjects," and the second group the "Objects." In a postmodernist interpretation, part of the dominance of the typical Subject groups (e.g., white, middle-class, middle-aged, English-speaking males) is that they successfully establish their worldview as "objective," "neutral," "value free" and the worldview of the Objects (typically women, Natives, people of colour) as "subjective," "biased," "value laden." Postmodernists argue that complete objectivity is impossible and that no one can be neutral in talking about society, because we are all influenced by gender, race, ethnicity, age and class. They advocate that all groups should get a chance to act as Subjects and Objects; otherwise distortion and bias too powerfully affect what is seen.

An example is the following: writers of introductory sociology textbooks in Canada are usually males and almost always white. In chapters on aging, they follow one of two patterns with respect to presenting Natives. Usually they talk about how the life expectancy of Natives is about six or seven years shorter than that of non-Natives in Canada, and how that is nonetheless an improvement over earlier years. The second pattern is to talk about a particular Inuit practice that happened in a few unusually desperate circumstances. When there was a severe shortgage of food, in some instances the old people would walk away from family and community to starve and freeze to death. Sociologists often present this as if it were a common practice, an ingrained part of Inuit culture. It is not. How would the Native "Objects" of study write about aging if they were permitted to have a voice in sociology textbooks? They would speak of how elders are valued for their knowledge, wisdom and leadership. Think of the different impressions student readers would get of Natives and aging if Natives were included in the Subjects who contribute to sociology textbooks.

How can this model be used to interpret change? Postmodernism poses similar questions to both modernists and conservatives: Improving for whom? Getting worse for whom? Think of how modernist media usually present computers and computer-related products and services as bringing about benefits to everyone. How often do you hear the opinions of those who can't afford computers or the education necessary to use them? When conservatives complain about how values have diminished in Canada, how often might they be really complaining that their ethnic group is no longer as dominant in Canada as it once was?

# Evolution

Evolution is best described as "survival of the best fit," that is, of that which fits best into a specific set of circumstances. This fit is not one step up on a modernist ladder of continual improvement, but a change reflecting a situation limited in time and place. A biological example will illustrate this concept.

Guppies swimming the rivers of Venezuela come in two basic colour patterns. High in the hills, where the rivers begin, the guppies are brightly coloured. In that way they are more likely to attract a mate and reproduce. In the lower waters, there are more predators around to eat those guppies that are easily seen. The guppies there are more dully coloured. Neither colour pattern is a general improvement in the species, just a better fit into the local environment.

Human societies typically possess good local adaptations to unique circumstances. Interpreting these different adaptations in modernist terms, with one being seen as "more modern" and therefore better than others, can lead to "ethnocentrism." Ethnocentrism is the principle that one culture sets the absolute standard by which all cultures should be judged, with difference in any form perceived as a mark of inferiority. Some North American businesses lose millions of dollars of potential business every year because they operate on the false assumption that "modern" business is run the same way across the world (i.e., North American style). Every society has its business culture, which involves adaptation to the rest of the culture. Outsiders thinking otherwise are often ethnocentric, and they make fewer deals.

The family can be seen as following an evolutionary model. In the 1950s and early 1960s, the ready availability of well-paying jobs for young people meant that Canadians married and had children earlier than they had in previous decades (or since). The time of marriage and of the birth of children was an adaptation to economic circumstances. Today, it usually takes longer for people to get their careers on track. As an adaptation to this economic situation, people tend to marry and have their first child at an older age than was the case with the previous generation.

# Fashion

Even though we love stability and predictability, we often seek out the new as much for the fact that it is new as for any other, more "logical" reasons. This need for novelty can be a source of creativity, or it can be just a money-making scheme for enticing people to buy something that is currently "in style" and "hot." We can call this change fashion. Fashion is not limited to clothes. New car features can be more fashionable than they are practical. Old coaches are fired and new coaches hired sometimes just to "shake things up." As Wendy O'Brien explains in "Fashion Statements," causes and theories go in and out of style as well.

Fashion benefits from our need to fit in with the group. Once a change has begun to emerge, others "must have it." This works well with peer pressure on children. People growing up in the 1990s went from Pogs to "virtual pets" as "must haves" in short succession. Outdoor Christmas lights seem to be one of the newest areas of fashion statement. Icicle lights became popular in the mid 1990s, only to be replaced in popularity by sculpted shapes with lights attached to them by 2000.

# The Subject Areas

We will be looking at change in four areas of life: multiculturalism, family, gender and work. Try to interpret them in more than one way before you form a definite opinion.

## Multiculturalism

A culture is a way of living. It is composed of such diverse aspects as language, religion, food, clothing, family structure and gender roles. Multiculturalism involves the existence of people of different cultures as part of one political unit (e.g., a country or nation-state). Although our federal policy of multiculturalism is relatively new, Canada has been multicultural for a long time. Europeans first coming to this country encountered diverse Native nations speaking more than 60 different languages. Our Black and our Italian history both began more than 300 years ago.

Today, multiculturalism is a controversial issue, which can be interpreted in several ways, as we will see in Greg Narbey's "Multiculturalism and Equity." Multiculturalism is seen by many as progress, a Canadian path to improvement of society. However, conservatives sometimes see multiculturalism as threatening to change long-held customs and perceptions of what Canada and Canadians are like. A postmodernist view on multiculturalism is that it hasn't really come into effect, and won't, until some of the newer Canadians have a more powerful Subject role in defining and interpreting what Canadian society is. Evolutionists look at multiculturalism as a necessary adaptation to the globalized world in which we live.

## Family

Family is hard to define, as it has taken many forms. We can say that it involves raising children, and the recognition of both biologically and more socially defined ties (e.g., godparent and clan ties).

In the Huron language there are two words for family. One means matrilineage, a family line determined only on the mother's side. You belong to the line of your mother, her mother, and so on deep into time. The other word means "clan," a social unit identified with a totem (an Ojibwe word meaning "clan") animal (e.g., bear, wolf or turtle) that traditionally comprised thousands of people. There is no term meaning only parents and children exclusively. That would be considered too small a unit to be a family.

In Vivian Smith's "Family Matters," you will see a debate between a view of family that is relatively new in Canada and one that is relatively old. The first reflects the evolutionary position that family is an adaptation to particular circumstances and can take many forms. The second takes the conservative stance that family is connected to a specific structure and that any change away from that is destructive. It is a very emotional debate, as there are always strong feelings tied to family. Look at the debate from both sides before you decide what your informed opinion is.

Obviously, a modernist would put a positive spin on family in Canada today, pointing out that couples are more likely to communicate better than they did in earlier decades. A postmodernist might note that when the media commentators negatively remark on "single-parent families," as they often do, certain minority groups get targeted for condemnation, directly or indirectly. Media commentators on family tend to come from a very limited Subject group.

## Gender Roles

Closely connected with family are gender roles, the sets of expectations linked with being a particular gender. Cultures differ in their views on what is gender-appropriate behaviour. For instance, traditional Plains Indian culture had very clear notions of what men should be like. It included high standards of personal bravery and physical toughness. Yet, at the same time, if a male was interested in things deemed female, sometimes including physical attraction to the male gender, that was accepted. Similarly, the Blackfoot, a Plains people, had the concept of the "manly hearted woman," a woman who was bold, aggressive, a successful property owner, even a warrior. These women were (and are) highly respected.

In the 1960s, when I was one of the first guys in my high school to have long hair, I was often taunted as being a "long-haired fag." When my social dancing gym class had more males than females, I had to play a "female" part in having a male partner lead while I followed. It was meant to shame me into having my hair "more like a regular guy." The destructiveness of this kind of inflexible attitude toward gender roles is discussed in Earl Reidy's "Being and Becoming."

Change in gender roles is a complex matter, well described by the old expression, "Damned if you do; damned if you don't." If a woman doesn't adhere to traditional gender roles, then, to some conservatives, she is considered to be less like a woman, more like a man. Likewise, if a woman shows what to a modernist might be too many signs of being like a traditional female, then she is somehow "behind the times." A postmodernist turn on gender roles is to look at the need to redefine gender roles in the family so that there is greater equity. A postmodernist might question the extent to which gender roles within the family have become more equal or equitable over the last few decades, conceding that women have taken on greater job equity but without their partners significantly taking on more traditional "women's work" around the home.

## Work

The changing world of work intimidates us all, as we wonder what our place will be. Much has been written in the business press about the new economy and what it means to be a "free agent" worker. Jason MacLean, in "The New Capitalism—and What It Means for You," takes a critical look at this new corporate culture and the resulting erosion in the quality of our social relations. Ultimately, MacLean's article asks whether we want to accept capitalism's newest response to global forces so passively, or whether we want to actively affirm that our relationships "extend far beyond our economic usefulness to each other, and act accordingly."

The great English poet W. H. Auden, in "Work, Labor, and Play," deals with the distinction between negatively valued "labour" and more positively valued "work." This distinction is critical when you consider that your goal in the job world involves more than just earning money but also includes a key psychological dimension.

The changing nature of our psychological, social and even political connection to the world is forcefully articulated in Ellen Ullman's "The Museum of Me." The Web has brought us the possibility of reducing if not eliminating the social aspects of commerce, "capitalism without salespeople." But the way we shop is not all that is affected; Ullman argues that the extremes of individualism encouraged by the Web both isolate us and undermine our sense of community.

# Fashion Statements

Wendy O'Brien

A recent attempt to make space in my clothes closet got me thinking about fashion and ideas. Now, I have to admit at the outset that I don't understand much about fashion. I don't know why it is that one season I'm buying sixties-style bell bottoms and the next I'm trying to fit myself into pants that are so tight that they cut off my circulation. I don't know why one year I'm wearing platform shoes and the next I'm walking around on spikes so high that I'm afraid I'm going to break my legs. I don't understand why lime green and wide collars are ever fashionable. Yet, although I am perplexed by these matters, I go out every year and I buy what's in style.

And I don't think that I'm alone in this matter. Most of us have little knowledge why some styles become trendsetting while others become errors in judgement. Can you explain why platform shoes and polyester are making a comeback? Why is it that snug-fitting pants are passé while the convict look complete with baggy jeans that display underwear is all the rage? When I watch the faces of people going through racks of clothes at the local mall or leafing through fashion magazines, it's pretty clear that many of us are at a loss when it comes to understanding fashion. But all of us walk out of stores laden with bags and packages of what is new this season. Why are we so willing to buy what we don't understand and what often doesn't fit or feel right? That's easy. All of us understand one important principle: either you're in or you're not. And whichever you are, others are sure to let you know about it.

Knowing that this is the case explained why I had decided it was time to sort through my clothes. My closet had become so full that its contents had begun to spill onto the floor. Yet while there were jeans and dress pants, long skirts and short, shirts with low necklines and those with high collars, pieces that were purple, white, beige and black, every morning I never failed to complain that I had "nothing to wear." As I began to pile these clothes on the bed, I realized that fashion is about dissatisfaction. No matter what I had in my closet, no matter how many jeans or T-shirts, how many suits or dresses, I could never find what

"Fashion Statements," is by Wendy O'Brien of Humber College. Used by permission.

was just right. Oh sure, I could find shoes that were comfortable, but they weren't trendy enough. Or I could find a pair of shoes just like the ones I saw advertised in *Elle*, but they gave me blisters. Whether I went in search for comfort or for fashion I always seemed to miss the mark.

My dissatisfaction with the contents of my closet was further compounded by the fact that I never was as happy with what I saw on myself as I was with what I saw on the models in the stores or in magazines. How many things in my closet had I bought because they looked good on Naomi Campbell or Elle MacPherson? I admired how others wore their clothes and often times bought items keeping in mind their body types not mine. Bringing home those spandex dresses, I believed that I could look as good as them. But the reality of what I saw in the mirror in my own home was something different. The clothes clung in all the wrong places, and how do you sit down in these things anyway?

As the clothes closet began to empty out, I realized that those in the fashion industry not only understood that we are difficult if impossible to please, but they also understood our desire for novelty. I always want something different, something new. I needed to have the long, flowered dresses or the halter-tops of this season, just for a change. The pinstriped suit that I thought that I looked good in and that felt so comfortable just couldn't be worn this season. If I did wear it, what would everyone think? And, well, that T-shirt from the concert that I went to last summer had to go even though it was probably the most comfortable thing that I owned. The band had begun to remake disco tunes. Yes, fashion is a fickle business.

Looking at the army boots and the tights, I could see clearly that the harder that I tried to keep pace with what was new, the more I would never be able to succeed. As fast as one style of clothing becomes the thing to wear, another one takes its place. One day we are back to the sixties and the next day it's a return to more contemporary styles. And most of us are probably caught somewhere in between wearing something that is a little out of date and something that is a little out of this world. The more we try to be fashionably dressed, the more that we just miss the mark. Trends change constantly and with each season we return to the stores and buy what is offered to us.

And whether we wanted to admit it or not, we were all buying the same things. You know, I always thought that my clothes somehow were a statement of my identity. That is, they made me an individual, they

showed the world that I was unique. Whether I chose long skirts or
micro minis, Adidas or Nike, I was telling the world who I was and what
I believed in. I was conservative or a rebel, I was "the one with the three
stripes" or I "just do it." The clothes I chose revealed *my* sense of style.
But as I sorted through the shirts and skirts, I saw how ironic this claim
was. Fashion is an industry. Items used to express my individuality were
marketed not only on the runways of Paris but also in fashion magazines sold worldwide. My fashion statements were mass produced and sold

by the millions. I was buying the image of myself that someone miles away who had never even heard of my name had created for me. What I considered novel and daring was in fact domesticated. There were hundreds if not thousands of other women walking around wearing exactly the same pair of jeans that I had spent hours painstakingly choosing.

Moreover, I never *really* wanted to be an individual. Most of the clothes I wore were not on the cutting edge but rather they were quite conventional. I wouldn't dare to wear jeans to work or wear a formal gown to dinner at my best friend's home. While I might wish I owned a dress by Versace, would I ever really wear it? And how many times have you put on clothes that you think look great only to be told through either words or looks that you really need to go and change? And, most importantly, how many times have you in fact changed? Even though we think that we are expressing our individuality through the clothes we wear, in fact, we are in search of recognition from others. We wear clothes designed by other people, deemed trendy by fashion "authorities," and regarded as conventional by those around us. Where is the individuality in all of this?

As I began to sort through my clothes, deciding which ones were to be returned to the closet and which were to be sent off to the Goodwill, I noticed that it wasn't just the clothes that I was keeping or discarding: it was also the ideals that they represented. There were the "earthmother" dresses from my days concerned with environmentalism, and the black, lots of black, clothes from my radical feminist stage. There were business suits from my "successful career woman" days and T-shirts galore representing any number of causes and events I had been committed to at one time or another. There on the bed were my clothes, but there was also more. Strewn across the comforter were my beliefs and values. And looking at them lying out in that manner, I realized that they were as much subject to the influence of fashion as were my dresses, pants and sweaters.

There amidst my clothes were the ideals I had at one time or another endorsed. Seeing my "One Canada" T-shirt, my Calvin Clan (Interesting typo don't you think? Actually, I think this may be more accurate) jeans and my lace blouse, I realized that when my ideas had lost their fashionableness, they had been abandoned at the back of my closet for the newest trend. My interest in women's issues evolved into a concern for multiculturalism, which gave way to worries about information technology, just as mini skirts had evolved into floor-length dresses, which in turn gave rise to micro minis.

What amazed me was that it was as easy to put on these new ideas, these new beliefs, as it was to put on this summer's long, floral prints. Everyone from media personalities to songwriters to advertisers to the people that I encountered in my local grocery store was sporting the same views. From them I learned not only what social causes were "in," I learned the words to say, the logos and the slogans. "Reduce, Reuse and Recycle," "Save the Whales," "Give Peace a Chance" were as easy to rhyme off as "Just Do It" and "Dare to Be Different." I thought as little of the ideals behind these slogans as I did of the bell bottoms, the spandex dresses and the blue business suits I had purchased. But I used them, boy did I use them. And when they became passé, when the issue became tired, it was abandoned as I began to learn the language of the next trend.

That was the great thing about fashion. There was always another new season just around the corner. I always knew that a new trend was just about to happen. When my ideas became the run of the mill, when everyone was wearing the same concerns, and I got tired of seeing and hearing myself on every street corner, the next season came along. And there I was buying the new striped polyester sweaters and hip-hugger jeans. That was how I acquired political correctness and Native rights. Boredom and the desire to be daring (but not too daring) had directed my attention away from even those issues that I truly believed in, those ideas that fit well and I could wear with ease and comfort. I really did believe that we needed to be concerned with the greenhouse effect, and that the image of women in the media needed to be challenged. But given that public interest in these issues had waned, what was I to do? Who was I to question public opinion?

Besides, maybe change wasn't such a bad thing. There were many fashion errors lying on my bed. Knee socks, silver shirts, Hawaiian prints. These had been replaced with silk nylons, cotton sweaters and solid colours. Sometimes the next season's clothes were more appealing. Sometimes they fit better or they were manufactured in more attractive colours. Sometimes. And sometimes they didn't feel right at all. The heels were too high, the neckline too low and the pants too tight. Sometimes homophobia gave way to gay pride or women were permitted to enter the military. But sometimes there was a rise in gay-bashing or a backlash against women. It really didn't matter. I acquired what was in style unabashedly.

Returning the items to my closet, I picked up a pair of Jordache jeans that I had bought when I was in my late teens. At the time these were trendsetters but they quickly were replaced by Kleins and then Bluenotes. Now, to tell you the truth, these were the most comfortable pair of jeans I owned. They didn't pull or pinch, they weren't too tight or too loose. But, I mean, they were stitched in silver with the name Jordache. Did I give them away or did they return to the closet? Dare I wear them on streets filled with Pepe products? It would be easy to say "Of course." It would be easy to say that I wasn't subject to fashion trends. It sounded good to say that I had my own sense of style, that I wanted to be different. But it would be a lie. It was easier to be a part of the crowd than to stand apart. It was easier to look like everyone else amidst a crowd lining up to see a movie or walking in the park on a beautiful summer day than to risk being shot that "I can't believe she's wearing that look" from strangers on the street. There was great comfort in looking into the dressing room mirror and seeing thousands of other women looking back at me. It was hard to stand out in the crowd. And hey, you could always find a store open.

Having finished the task at hand, I noticed that I actually had a little space in my closet. I could fit in at least two or three new things. Maybe the halter dress I saw on Saturday? Or what about the white shirt I saw at the Gap? It was so easy to shop around for new clothes, new ideas. Holding onto those things that weren't trendy wasn't worth it. Fashion saved me tons of time. I didn't have to think about what I should wear. The magazines and store clerks took care of that. I just needed to follow. And when people asked tough questions, well I could claim, it wasn't really my style anyway and now I was wearing . . . I never had to think too hard to be in style.

# If It's in the US, It's News. If Not, Forget It

## Martin Kettle

Seven more people were reported dead last week from the worst heat-wave in years. They brought the total of dead so far to 79. In the tinder-dry mountains, fires rage. In some areas water is running short. Farmers are being ruined as their crops fail and their animals die of thirst. In the capital city the temperature is more than 40C. But all this is happening in India, so you don't really want to know.

In the past month disasters of various kinds have taken place all over the world. There was a mudslide in Colombia that killed 41 people, many of whom were trying to help victims of an earlier slide when a second catastrophe struck. In Congo 63 people died from a terrible killer fever, similar to Ebola, that is wreaking havoc among the workforce in the country's mining belt.

Then there have been the manmade disasters. Nineteen villagers were killed in Sumatra. (Or was it 31? The reports differ.) A similar number were killed in East Timor. In Mogadishu 23 people died in gang battles. Ten Kurdish guerrillas were shot by Turkish security forces.

These examples have been assembled from two weeks' foreign pages of *The Guardian* and the *New York Times*, and from a couple of websites. With the exception of Yugoslavia, though, none has been given pages of coverage in the United States or British press. None has made it to a television news bulletin.

When will they learn, a character in Seinfeld observed as he put down his copy of the newspaper, that China is just not a page-turner? What is true of China is also true of India and, well, almost everywhere. But not quite everywhere. It would be different, if the fires, the drought and the deaths were taking place in the US. If 41 people died in a landslide in California, you would soon get to know about it—and you would soon want to know. For when catastrophe strikes the US, it is not just an American affair, and we are all page-turners.

Martin Kettle, "If It's in the US, It's News. If Not, Forget It," from *The Guardian*, Vol. 160, Number 20, week ending May 16, 1999. Reprinted with permission.

Last week's tornadoes in Oklahoma and Kansas devastated whole villages. Homes were flattened across vast areas of what is sometimes called "Tornado Alley." At the last count 46 people were killed, roughly the same number as died in the Colombian landslips last month. But the reflexes triggered by the two events are continents apart.

Why are we so much more interested in the death and devastation caused by the one than in those caused by the other? It's an important question, and there isn't a simple, straightforward answer. But it's a question that news organisations ought to be asking more often.

One reason is that the victims are white, the survivors speak English. But it's not really a kith and kin thing. It's because it's the US. I suspect that the British would not be quite as gripped if the tornadoes had killed 43 Canadians in Alberta.

And it's not as though we're all saying, "There but for fortune" about the Oklahoma twisters, either. At least, post-**Dunblane**, you could say such a thing about the **Littleton** shootings. And with a tornado in Florida you could say how lucky it didn't strike while cousin Jim was at Disney World. But who do you know who has been on holiday to Oklahoma?

Part of the response is to life imitating art (if one can apply such a word as art to the dreadful movie *Twister*, which told the story of a bunch of people who get excited chasing tornadoes). And part of it is simply to do with the accessibility of pictures. The US media set up the live coverage and did the interviews. The rest of us regurgitated it.

But all this begs the question. British journalists do not work in newsrooms with 24-hour Colombian or Indian television news channels hovering perpetually in their peripheral vision. But they do have US news channels. Look up and there's CNN. Check the news agency wires and you read American **AP**, not French **AFP**. It's a supply thing. It's not exactly a conspiracy, but it's certainly a stacked deck. American input, American output.

That's not a problem if you are American. But what about citizens of other lands? The British are given so much information about the US that at times they think they are part of the US. And so, in some ways, they are. But not in all ways. Oklahoma is simply not their backyard any more than Uttar Pradesh is.

In her recent book, *Compassion Fatigue*, the US critic Susan Moeller argues that the US media has developed a need to Americanise the news, wherever it occurs, partly to provide a sugar coating to make foreign news

**Dunblane**

a Scottish village that was the scene of a school massacre in 1996

**Littleton**

a Colorado town that was the scene of a school massacre in 1999

**AP**

Associated Press

**AFP**

Associated French Press

palatable to US audiences. Hence the Kosovo crisis is reported in terms of the three captured GIs and their families, and ultimately may be reported in terms of the "body bag" syndrome. But why do the British insist on swallowing the same pill too?

Moeller suggests that US audiences can cope with news of disasters in their own country with much greater **equanimity** than with news of disasters in the rest of the world. Catastrophe in Africa or India is too troubling and too bottomless, because it is too difficult to deal with. Catastrophe in Oklahoma is simply more finite. You can rest easy knowing that, however awful the experience they have had, the survivors will be OK in the end. We can, quite literally, switch it off.

But does this apply to the British? After all, there is no logic for saying that what happens in Kansas is more newsworthy to the British than what happens in Colombia or Catalonia.

Perhaps the truth is that the British secretly enjoy transatlantic misfortune too much. Perhaps, in an era of US global **hegemony**, they secretly need to be reassured that their masters are gun-obsessed crazies or that their lovingly constructed Oklahoma suburban homes can be smashed to smithereens within seconds by some arbitrary forces of nature. Serve them right for being top nation.

It is more than merely disquieting to think that the rest of the world appears to feel such *schadenfreude* about the death of American families as they slept in their beds. Or is it simply media laziness that is to blame? How else to explain the compulsive interest in Littleton or Oklahoma alongside the indifference to Colombia or India? How else can we explain the fact that US death has become so compulsive a fact of British life?

**equanimity**

calmness

**hegemony**

control and power

**schadenfreude**

a German term meaning enjoyment of others' misfortunes

# The Judgment of Thamus

## Neil Postman

You will find in Plato's *Phaedrus* a story about Thamus, the king of a great city of Upper Egypt. For people such as ourselves, who are inclined (in Thoreau's phrase) to be tools of our tools, few legends are more instructive than his. The story, as Socrates tells it to his friend Phaedrus, unfolds in the following way: Thamus once entertained the god Theuth, who was the inventor of many things, including number, calculation, geometry, astronomy, and writing. Theuth exhibited his inventions to King Thamus, claiming that they should be made widely known and available to Egyptians. Socrates continues:

> Thamus inquired into the use of each of them, and as Theuth went through them expressed approval or disapproval, according as he judged Theuth's claims to be well or ill founded. It would take too long to go through all that Thamus is reported to have said for and against each of Theuth's inventions. But when it came to writing, Theuth declared, "Here is an accomplishment, my lord the King, which will improve both the wisdom and the memory of the Egyptians. I have discovered a sure receipt for memory and wisdom." To this, Thamus replied, "Theuth, my paragon of inventors, the discoverer of an art is not the best judge of the good or harm which will accrue to those who practise it. So it is in this; you, who are the father of writing, have out of fondness for your off-spring attributed to it quite the opposite of its real function. Those who acquire it will cease to exercise their memory and become forgetful; they will rely on writing to bring things to their remembrance by external signs instead of by their own internal resources. What you have discovered is a receipt for recollection, not for memory. And as for wisdom, your pupils will have the reputation for it without the reality: they will receive a quantity of information without proper instruction, and in consequence be thought very knowledgeable when they are for the most part quite ignorant. And because they are filled with the conceit of wisdom instead of real wisdom they will be a burden to society.

I begin my book with this legend because in Thamus' response there are several sound principles from which we may begin to learn how to think with wise circumspection about a technological society. In fact, there is even one error in the judgment of Thamus, from which we may also learn something of importance. The error is not in his claim that writing

From Neil Postman's *Technopoly*. New York: Alfred A. Knopf, 1992. Reprinted with permission.

will damage memory and create false wisdom. It is demonstrable that writing has had such an effect. Thamus' error is in his believing that writing will be a burden to society and *nothing but a burden.* For all his wisdom, he fails to imagine what writing's benefits might be, which, as we know, have been considerable. We may learn from this that it is a mistake to suppose that any technological innovation has a one-sided effect. Every technology is both a burden and a blessing; not either-or, but this-and-that.

Nothing could be more obvious, of course, especially to those who have given more than two minutes of thought to the matter. Nonetheless, we are currently surrounded by throngs of zealous Theuths, one-eyed prophets who see only what new technologies can do and are incapable of imagining what they will *undo.* We might call such people Technophiles. They gaze on technology as a lover does on his beloved, seeing it as without blemish and entertaining no apprehension for the future. They are therefore dangerous and are to be approached cautiously. On the other hand, some one-eyed prophets, such as I (or so I am accused), are inclined to speak only of burdens (in the manner of Thamus) and are silent about the opportunities that new technologies make possible. The Technophiles must speak for themselves, and do so all over the place. My defense is that a dissenting voice is sometimes needed to moderate the din made by the enthusiastic multitudes. If one is to err, it is better to err on the side of Thamusian skepticism. But it is an error nonetheless. And I might note that, with the exception of his judgment on writing, Thamus does not repeat this error. You might notice on rereading the legend that he gives arguments *for* and *against* each of Theuth's inventions. For it is inescapable that every culture must negotiate with technology, whether it does so intelligently or not. A bargain is struck in which technology giveth and technology taketh away. The wise know this well, and are rarely impressed by dramatic technological changes, and never overjoyed. Here, for example, is Freud on the matter, from his doleful *Civilization and Its Discontents:*

> One would like to ask: is there, then, no positive gain in pleasure, no unequivocal increase in my feeling of happiness, if I can, as often as I please, hear the voice of a child of mine who is living hundreds of miles away or if I can learn in the shortest possible time after a friend has reached his destination that he has come through the long and difficult voyage unharmed? Does it mean nothing that medicine has succeeded in enormously reducing infant mortality and the danger of infection for women in child-birth, and, indeed, in considerably lengthening the average life of a civilized man?

Freud knew full well that technical and scientific advances are not to be taken lightly, which is why he begins this passage by acknowledging them. But he ends it by reminding us of what they have undone:

> If there had been no railway to conquer distances, my child would never have left his native town and I should need no telephone to hear his voice; if travelling across the ocean by ship had not been introduced, my friend would not have embarked on his sea-voyage and I should not need a cable to relieve my anxiety about him. What is the use of reducing infantile mortality when it is precisely that reduction which imposes the greatest restraint on us in the begetting of children, so that, taken all round, we nevertheless rear no more children than in the days before the reign of hygiene, while at the same time we have created difficult conditions for our sexual life in marriage … And, finally, what good to us is a long life if it is difficult and barren of joys, and if it is so full of misery that we can only welcome death as a deliverer?

In tabulating the cost of technological progress, Freud takes a rather depressing line, that of a man who agrees with Thoreau's remark that our inventions are but improved means to an unimproved end. The Technophile would surely answer Freud by saying that life has always been barren of joys and full of misery but that the telephone, ocean liners, and especially the reign of hygiene have not only lengthened life but made it a more agreeable proposition. That is certainly an argument I would make (thus proving I am no one-eyed Technophobe), but it is not necessary at this point to pursue it. I have brought Freud into the conversation only to show that a wise man—even one of such a woeful countenance—must begin his critique of technology by acknowledging its successes. Had King Thamus been as wise as reputed, he would not have forgotten to include in his judgment a prophecy about the powers that writing would enlarge. There is a calculus of technological change that requires a measure of even-handedness.

So much for Thamus' error of omission. There is another omission worthy of note, but it is no error. Thamus simply takes for granted—and therefore does not feel it necessary to say—that writing is not a neutral technology whose good or harm depends on the uses made of it. He knows that the uses made of any technology are largely determined by the structure of the technology itself—that is, that its functions follow from its form. This is why Thamus is concerned not with *what* people will write; he is concerned *that* people will write. It is absurd to imagine Thamus advising, in the manner of today's standard-brand Technophiles, that, if only writing would be used for the production of certain kinds of texts and not others (let us say, for dramatic literature but not for history or philosophy), its disruptions could be minimized. He would regard such counsel as extreme naïveté. He would allow, I imagine, that a technology may be barred entry to a culture. But we may learn from Thamus the following: once a technology is admitted, it plays out its hand; it does what it is designed to do. Our task is to understand what that design is—that is to say, when we admit a new technology to the culture, we must do so with our eyes wide open.

All of this we may infer from Thamus' silence. But we may learn even more from what he does say than from what he doesn't. He points out, for example, that writing will change what is meant by the words "memory" and "wisdom." He fears that memory will be confused with what he disdainfully calls "recollection," and worries that wisdom will become indistinguishable from mere knowledge. This judgment we must take to heart, for it is a certainty that radical technologies create new definitions of old terms, and that this process takes place without our being fully conscious of it. Thus, it is insidious and dangerous, quite different from the process whereby new technologies introduce new terms to the language. In our own time, we have consciously added to our language thousands of new words and phrases having to do with new technologies—"VCR," "binary digit," "software," "front-wheel drive," "window of opportunity," "Walkman," etc. We are not taken by surprise at this. New things require new words. But new things also modify old words, words that have deep-rooted meanings. The telegraph and the penny press changed what we once meant by "information." Television changes what we once meant by the terms "political debate," "news," and "public opinion." The computer changes "information" once again. Writing changed what we once meant by "truth" and "law"; printing changed them again, and now television and the computer change them once more. Such changes occur quickly, surely, and, in a sense, silently. **Lexicographers** hold no plebiscites on the matter. No manuals are written to explain what is happening, and the schools are oblivious to it. The old words still look the same, are still used in the same kinds of sentences. But they do not have the same meanings; in some cases, they have opposite meanings. And this is what Thamus wishes to teach us—that technology imperiously commandeers our most important terminology. It defines "freedom," "truth," "intelligence," "fact," "wisdom," "memory," "history"—all the words we live by. And it does not pause to tell us. And we do not pause to ask. . . .

**lexicographers**

writers of dictionaries

Here, there are several more principles to be mined from the judgment of Thamus that require mentioning because they presage all I will write about. For instance, Thamus warns that the pupils of Theuth will develop an undeserved reputation for wisdom. He means to say that those who cultivate competence in the use of a new technology become an elite group that are granted undeserved authority and prestige by those who have no such competence. There are different ways of expressing the interesting implications of this fact. Harold Innis, the father of modern communication studies, repeatedly spoke of the "knowledge monopolies" created by important technologies. He meant precisely what Thamus had in mind: those who have control over the workings of a particular technology accumulate power and inevitably form a kind of conspiracy against those who have no access to the specialized knowledge made available by the technology. In his book *The Bias of Communication,* Innis provides many historical examples of how a new technology "busted up" a traditional knowledge monopoly and created a new one presided over by a different group. Another way of saying this is that the benefits and deficits of a new technology are not distributed equally. There are, as it were, winners and losers. It is both puzzling and poignant that on many occasions the losers, out of ignorance, have actually cheered the winners, and some still do.

Let us take as an example the case of television. In the United States, where television has taken hold more deeply than anywhere else, many people find it a blessing, not least those who have achieved high-paying, gratifying careers in television as executives, technicians, newscasters, and entertainers. It should surprise no one that such people, forming as they do a new knowledge monopoly, should cheer themselves and defend and promote television technology. On the other hand and in the long run, television may bring a gradual end to the careers of schoolteachers, since school was an invention of the printing press and must stand or fall on the issue of how much importance the printed word has. For 400 years, schoolteachers have been part of the knowledge monopoly created by printing, and they are now witnessing the breakup of that monopoly. It appears as if they can do little to prevent that breakup, but surely there is something perverse about schoolteachers' being enthusiastic about what is happening. Such enthusiasm always calls to my mind an image of some turn-of-the-century blacksmith who not only sings the praises of the automobile but also believes that his business will be enhanced by it. We know now that his business was not enhanced by it; it was rendered obsolete by it, as perhaps the clearheaded blacksmiths knew. What could they have done? Weep, if nothing else.

We have a similar situation in the development and spread of computer technology, for here too there are winners and losers. There can be no disputing that the computer has increased the power of large-scale organizations like the armed forces, or airline companies or banks or tax-collecting agencies. And it is equally clear that the computer is now indispensable to high-level researchers in physics and other natural sciences. But to what extent has computer technology been an advantage to the masses of people? To steelworkers, vegetable-store owners, teachers, garage mechanics, musicians, bricklayers, dentists, and most of the rest into whose lives the computer now intrudes? Their private matters have been made more accessible to powerful institutions. They are more easily tracked and controlled; are subjected to more examinations; are increasingly mystified by the decisions made about them; are often reduced to mere numerical objects. They are inundated by junk mail. They are easy targets for advertising agencies and political organizations. The schools teach their children to operate computerized systems instead of teaching things that are more valuable to children. In a word, almost nothing that they need happens to the losers. Which is why they are losers.

It is to be expected that the winners will encourage the losers to be enthusiastic about computer technology. That is the way of winners, and so they sometimes tell the losers that with personal computers the average person can balance a checkbook more neatly, keep better track of recipes, and make more logical shopping lists. They also tell them that their lives will be conducted more efficiently. But discreetly they neglect to say from whose point of view the efficiency is warranted or what might be its costs. Should the losers grow skeptical, the winners dazzle them with the wondrous feats of computers, almost all of which have only marginal relevance to the quality of the losers' lives but which are nonetheless impressive. Eventually, the losers succumb, in part because they believe, as Thamus prophesied, that the specialized knowledge of the masters of a new technology is a form of wisdom. The masters come to believe this as well, as Thamus also prophesied. The result is that certain questions do not arise. For example, to whom will the technology give greater power and freedom? And whose power and freedom will be reduced by it?

I have perhaps made all of this sound like a well-planned conspiracy, as if the winners know all too well what is being won and what lost.

But this is not quite how it happens. For one thing, in cultures that have a democratic ethos, relatively weak traditions, and a high receptivity to new technologies, everyone is inclined to be enthusiastic about technological change, believing that its benefits will eventually spread evenly among the entire population. Especially in the United States, where the lust for what is new has no bounds, do we find this childlike conviction most widely held. Indeed, in America, social change of any kind is rarely seen as resulting in winners and losers, a condition that stems in part from Americans' much-documented optimism. As for change brought on by technology, this native optimism is exploited by entrepreneurs, who work hard to infuse the population with a unity of improbable hope, for they know that it is economically unwise to reveal the price to be paid for technological change. One might say, then, that, if there is a conspiracy of any kind, it is that of a culture conspiring against itself.

In addition to this, and more important, it is not always clear, at least in the early stages of a technology's intrusion into a culture, who will gain most by it and who will lose most. This is because the changes wrought by technology are subtle if not downright mysterious, one might even say wildly unpredictable. Among the most unpredictable are those that might be labeled ideological. This is the sort of change Thamus had in mind when he warned that writers will come to rely on external signs instead of their own internal resources, and that they will receive quantities of information without proper instruction. He meant that new technologies change what we mean by "knowing" and "truth"; they alter those deeply embedded habits of thought which give to a culture its sense of what the world is like—a sense of what is the natural order of things, of what is reasonable, of what is necessary, of what is inevitable, of what is real. Since such changes are expressed in changed meanings of old words, I will hold off until later discussing the massive ideological transformation now occurring in the United States. Here, I should like to give only one example of how technology creates new conceptions of what is real and, in the process, undermines older conceptions. I refer to the seemingly harmless practice of assigning marks or grades to the answers students give on examinations. This procedure seems so natural to most of us that we are hardly aware of its significance. We may even find it difficult to imagine that the number or letter is a tool or, if you will, a technology; still less that, when we use such a technology to judge someone's behavior, we have done something peculiar. In point of fact, the first instance of grading students' papers occurred at Cambridge

University in 1792 at the suggestion of a tutor named William Farish. No one knows much about William Farish; not more than a handful have ever heard of him. And yet his idea that a quantitative value should be assigned to human thought was a major step toward constructing a mathematical concept of reality. If a number can be given to the quality of a thought, then a number can be given to the qualities of mercy, love, hate, beauty, creativity, intelligence, even sanity itself. When Galileo said that the language of nature is written in mathematics, he did not mean to include human feeling or accomplishment or insight. But most of us are now inclined to make these inclusions. Our psychologists, sociologists, and educators find it quite impossible to do their work without numbers. They believe that without numbers they cannot acquire or express authentic knowledge.

I shall not argue here that this is a stupid or dangerous idea, only that it is peculiar. What is even more peculiar is that so many of us do not find the idea peculiar. To say that someone should be doing better work because he has an IQ of 134, or that someone is a 7.2 on a sensitivity scale, or that this man's essay on the rise of capitalism is an A– and that man's is a C+ would have sounded like gibberish to Galileo or Shakespeare or Thomas Jefferson. If it makes sense to us, that is because our minds have been conditioned by the technology of numbers so that we see the world differently than they did. Our understanding of what is real is different. Which is another way of saying that embedded in every tool is an ideological bias, a predisposition to construct the world as one thing rather than another, to value one thing over another, to amplify one sense or skill or attitude more loudly than another.

**aphorism**
brief statement

This is what Marshall McLuhan meant by his famous **aphorism** "The medium is the message." This is what Marx meant when he said, "Technology discloses man's mode of dealing with nature" and creates the "conditions of intercourse" by which we relate to each other. It is what Wittgenstein meant when, in referring to our most fundamental technology, he said that language is not merely a vehicle of thought but also the driver. And it is what Thamus wished the inventor Theuth to see. This is, in short, an ancient and persistent piece of wisdom, perhaps most simply expressed in the old adage that, to a man with a hammer, everything looks like a nail. Without being too literal, we may extend the truism: To a man with a pencil, everything looks like an image. To a man with a computer, everything looks like data. And to a man with a grade sheet, everything looks like a number.

But such prejudices are not always apparent at the start of a technology's journey, which is why no one can safely conspire to be a winner in technological change. Who would have imagined, for example, whose interests and what world-view would be ultimately advanced by the invention of the mechanical clock? The clock had its origin in the Benedictine monasteries of the 12th and 13th centuries. The impetus behind the invention was to provide a more or less precise regularity to the routines of the monasteries, which required, among other things, seven periods of devotion during the course of the day. The bells of the monastery were to be rung to signal the canonical hours; the mechanical clock was the technology that could provide precision to these rituals of devotion. And indeed it did. But what the monks did not foresee was that the clock is a means not merely of keeping track of the hours but also of synchronizing and controlling the actions of men. And thus, by the middle of the 14th century, the clock had moved outside the walls of the monastery, and brought a new and precise regularity to the life of the workman and the merchant. "The mechanical clock," as Lewis Mumford wrote, "made possible the idea of regular production, regular working hours and a standardized product." In short, without the clock, capitalism would have been quite impossible. The paradox, the surprise, and the wonder are that the clock was invented by men who wanted to devote themselves more rigorously to God; it ended as the technology of greatest use to men who wished to devote themselves to the accumulation of money. In the eternal struggle between God and Mammon, the clock quite unpredictably favored the latter.

Unforeseen consequences stand in the way of all those who think they see clearly the direction in which a new technology will take us. Not even those who invent a technology can be assumed to be reliable prophets, as Thamus warned. Gutenberg, for example, was by all accounts a devout Catholic who would have been horrified to hear that accursed heretic Luther describe printing as "God's highest act of grace, whereby the business of the Gospel is driven forward." Luther understood, as Gutenberg did not, that the mass-produced book, by placing the Word of God on every kitchen table, makes each Christian his own theologian—one might even say his own priest, or better, from Luther's point of view, his own pope. In the struggle between unity and diversity of religious belief, the press favored the latter, and we can assume that this possibility never occurred to Gutenberg.

Thamus understood well the limitations of inventors in grasping the social and psychological—that is, ideological—bias of their own inventions. We can imagine him addressing Gutenberg in the following way: "Gutenberg, my paragon of inventors, the discoverer of an art is not the best judge of the good or harm which will accrue to those who practise it. So it is in this; you, who are the father of printing, have out of fondness for your off-spring come to believe it will advance the cause of the Holy Roman See, whereas in fact it will sow discord among believers; it will damage the authenticity of your beloved Church and destroy its monopoly."

We can imagine that Thamus would also have pointed out to Gutenberg, as he did to Theuth, that the new invention would create a vast population of readers who "will receive a quantity of information without proper instruction…[who will be] filled with the conceit of wisdom instead of real wisdom"; that reading, in other words, will compete with older forms of learning. This is yet another principle of technological change we may infer from the judgment of Thamus: new technologies compete with old ones—for time, for attention, for money, for prestige, but mostly for dominance of their world-view. This competition is implicit once we acknowledge that a medium contains an ideological bias. And it is a fierce competition, as only ideological competitions can be. It is not merely a matter of tool against tool—the alphabet attacking ideographic writing, the printing press attacking the illuminated manuscript, the photograph attacking the art of painting, television attacking the printed word. When media make war against each other, it is a case of world-views in collision.

In the United States, we can see such collisions everywhere—in politics, in religion, in commerce—but we see them most clearly in the schools, where two great technologies confront each other in uncompromising aspect for the control of students' minds. On the one hand, there is the world of the printed word with its emphasis on logic, sequence, history, exposition, objectivity, detachment, and discipline. On the other, there is the world of television with its emphasis on imagery, narrative, presentness, simultaneity, intimacy, immediate gratification, and quick emotional response. Children come to school having been deeply conditioned by the biases of television. There, they encounter the world of the printed word. A sort of psychic battle takes place, and there are many casualties—children who can't learn to read or won't, children who cannot organize their thought into logical structure even in a simple paragraph, children who cannot attend to lectures or oral explanations for more than a few minutes at a time. They are failures, but not because they are stupid. They are failures because there is a media war going on, and they are on the wrong side—at least for the moment. Who knows what schools will be like 25 years from now? Or 50? In time, the type of student who is currently a failure may be considered a success. The type who is now successful may be regarded as a handicapped learner—slow to respond, far too detached, lacking in emotion, inadequate in creating mental pictures of reality. Consider: what Thamus called the "conceit of wisdom"—the unreal knowledge acquired through the written word—eventually became the pre-eminent form of knowledge valued by the schools. There is no reason to suppose that such a form of knowledge must always remain so highly valued.

To take another example: In introducing the personal computer to the classroom, we shall be breaking a 400-year-old truce between the gregariousness and openness fostered by orality and the introspection and isolation fostered by the printed word. Orality stresses group learning, cooperation, and a sense of social responsibility, which is the context within which Thamus believed proper instruction and real knowledge must be communicated. Print stresses individualized learning, competition, and personal autonomy. Over four centuries, teachers, while emphasizing print, have allowed orality its place in the classroom, and have therefore achieved a kind of pedagogical peace between these two forms of learning, so that what is valuable in each can be maximized. Now comes the computer, carrying anew the banner of private learning and individual problem-solving. Will the widespread use of computers in the classroom defeat once and for all the claims of communal speech? Will the computer raise egocentrism to the status of a virtue?

These are the kinds of questions that technological change brings to mind when one grasps, as Thamus did, that technological competition ignites total war, which means it is not possible to contain the effects of a new technology to a limited sphere of human activity. If this metaphor puts the matter too brutally, we may try a gentler, kinder one: Technological change is neither additive nor subtractive. It is ecological. I mean "ecological" in the same sense as the word is used by environmental scientists. One significant change generates total change. If you remove the caterpillars from a given habitat, you are not left with the same environment minus caterpillars: you have a new environment, and you have reconstituted the conditions of survival; the same is true if you add caterpillars to an environment that has had none. This is how the ecology of media works as well. A new technology does not add or subtract something. It changes everything. In the year 1500, 50 years after the printing press was invented, we did not have old Europe plus the printing press. We had a different Europe. After television, the United States was not America plus television; television gave a new coloration to every political campaign, to every home, to every school, to every church, to every industry. And that is why the competition among media is so fierce. Surrounding every technology are institutions whose organization—not to mention their reason for being—reflects the world-view promoted by the technology. Therefore, when an old technology is assaulted by a new one, institutions are threatened. When institutions are threatened, a culture finds itself in crisis. This is serious business, which is why we learn nothing when educators ask, Will students learn mathematics better by computers than by textbooks? Or when businessmen ask, Through which medium can we sell more products? Or when preachers ask, Can we reach more people through television than through radio? Or when politicians ask, How effective are messages sent through different media?

Such questions have an immediate, practical value to those who ask them, but they are diversionary. They direct our attention away from the serious social, intellectual, and institutional crises that new media foster.

Perhaps an analogy here will help to underline the point. In speaking of the meaning of a poem, T. S. Eliot remarked that the chief use of the overt content of poetry is "to satisfy one habit of the reader, to keep his mind diverted and quiet, while the poem does its work upon him: much as the imaginary burglar is always provided with a bit of nice meat for the house-dog." In other words, in asking their practical questions, educators, entrepreneurs, preachers, and politicians are like the house-dog munching peacefully on the meat while the house is looted. Perhaps some of them know this and do not especially care. After all, a nice piece of meat, offered graciously, does take care of the problem of where the next meal will come from. But for the rest of us, it cannot be acceptable to have the house invaded without protest or at least awareness.

What we need to consider about the computer has nothing to do with its efficiency as a teaching tool. We need to know in what ways it is altering our conception of learning, and how, in conjunction with television, it undermines the old idea of school. Who cares how many boxes of cereal can be sold via television? We need to know if television changes our conception of reality, the relationship of the rich to the poor, the idea of happiness itself. A preacher who confines himself to considering how a medium can increase his audience will miss the significant question: In what sense do new media alter what is meant by religion, by church, even by God? And if the politician cannot think beyond the next election, then *we* must wonder about what new media do to the idea of political organization and to the conception of citizenship.

To help us do this, we have the judgment of Thamus, who, in the way of legends, teaches us what Harold Innis, in his way, tried to. New technologies alter the structure of our interests: the things we think *about*. They alter the character of our symbols: the things we think *with*. And they alter the nature of community: the arena in which thoughts develop. As Thamus spoke to Innis across the centuries, it is essential that we listen to their conversation, join in it, revitalize it. For something has happened in America that is strange and dangerous, and there is only a dull and even stupid awareness of what it is—in part because it has no name. I call it Technopoly.

# The Museum of Me

Ellen Ullman

Years ago, before the Internet as we know it had come into existence—
I think it was around Christmas, in 1990—I was at a friend's house,
where her nine-year-old son and his friend were playing the video game
that was the state of the art at the time, Sonic the Hedgehog. They
jumped around in front of the TV and gave off the sort of rude noises
boys tend to make when they're shooting at things in a video game, and
after about half an hour they stopped and tried to talk about what they'd
just been doing. The dialogue went something like this:

"I wiped out at that part with the ladders."

"Ladders? What ladders?"

"You know, after the rooms."

"Oh, you mean the stairs?"

"No, I think they were ladders. I remember, because I died there twice."

"I never killed you around any ladders. I killed you where you jump
down off this wall."

"Wall? You mean by the gates of the city?"

"Are there gates around the city? I always called it the castle."

The boys muddled along for several more minutes, making themselves
more confused as they went. Finally they gave up trying to talk about their
time with Sonic the Hedgehog. They just looked at each other and
shrugged.

I didn't think about the two boys and Sonic again until I watched my
clients try out the World Wide Web. By then it was 1995, the Internet as
we know it was beginning to exist, but the two women who worked for
my client, whom I'd just helped get online, had never before connected
to the Internet or surfed the Web. They took to it instantly, each disap-
pearing into nearly an hour of obsessive clicking, after which they tried
to talk about it:

"It was great! I clicked that thing and went to this place. I don't remember its name."

"Yeah. It was a link. I clicked here and went there."

"Oh, I'm not sure it was a link. The thing I clicked was a picture of the
library."

Ellen Ullman, "The Museum of Me," from *Harper's*, May 2000. Reprinted with permission
from the author.

"Was it the library? I thought it was a picture of City Hall."

"Oh, no. I'm sure it was the library."

"No, City Hall. I'm sure because of the dome."

"Dome? Was there a dome?"

Right then I remembered Sonic and the two boys; my clients, like the two boys, had experienced something pleasurable and engaging, and they very much wanted to talk about it—talking being one of the primary ways human beings augment their pleasure. But what had happened to them, each in her own electronic world, resisted description. Like the boys, the two women fell into verbal confusion. How could they speak coherently about a world full of little wordless pictograms, about trails that led off in all directions, of idle visits to virtual places chosen on a whim-click?

Following hyperlinks on the Web is like the synaptic drift of dreams, a loosening of intention, the mind associating freely, an experience that can be compelling or baffling or unsettling, or all of those things at once. And like dreams, the experience of the Web is intensely private, charged with immanent meaning for the person inside the experience, but often confusing or irrelevant to someone else.

At the time, I had my reservations about the Web, but not so much about the private, dream-like state it offered. Web surfing seemed to me

not so much antisocial as asocial, an adventure like a video game or pin-ball, entertaining, sometimes interesting, sometimes a trivial waste of time; but in a social sense it seemed harmless, since only the person engaged in the activity was affected.

Something changed, however, not in me but in the Internet and the Web and in the world, and the change was written out in person-high letters on a billboard on the corner of Howard and New Montgomery Streets in San Francisco. It was the fall of 1998. I was walking toward Market Street one afternoon when I saw it, a background of brilliant sky blue, with writing on it in airy white letters, which said: *now the world really does revolve around you.* The letters were lower-case, soft-edged, spaced irregularly, as if they'd been skywritten over a hot August beach and were already drifting off into the air. The message they left behind was a child's secret wish, the ultimate baby-world **narcissism** we are all supposed to abandon when we grow up: the world really does revolve around me.

What was this billboard advertising? Perfume? A resort? There was nothing else on it but the airy, white letters, and I had to walk right up to it to see a URL written at the bottom; it was the name of a company that makes semiconductor equipment, machinery used by companies like Intel and AMD to manufacture integrated circuits. Oh, chips, I thought. Computers. Of course. What other subject produces such **hyperbole**? Who else but someone in the computer industry could make such a shameless appeal to individualism?

The billboard loomed over the corner for the next couple of weeks. Every time I passed it, its message irritated me more. It bothered me the way the "My Computer" icon bothers me on the Windows desktop, baby names like "My Yahoo" and "My Snap"; my, my, my; two-year-old talk; infantilizing and condescending.

But there was something more disturbing about this billboard, and I tried to figure out why, since it simply was doing what every other piece of advertising does: whispering in your ear that there is no one like you in the entire world, and what we are offering is for you, special you, and you alone. What came to me was this: Toyota, for example, sells the idea of a special, individual buyer ("It's not for everyone, just for you"), but chip makers, through the medium of the Internet and the World Wide Web, are creating the actual infrastructures of an individualized marketplace.

What had happened between 1995, when I could still think of the Internet as a private dream, and the appearance of that billboard in 1998

**narcissism**
self-love

**hyperbole**
exaggeration

was the near-complete commercialization of the Web. And that commercialization had proceeded in a very particular and single-minded way: by attempting to isolate the individual within a sea of economic activity. Through a process known as "disintermediation," producers have worked to remove the expert intermediaries, agents, brokers, middlemen, who until now have influenced our interactions with the commercial world. What bothered me about the billboard, then, was that its message was not merely hype but the reflection of a process that was already under way: an attempt to convince the individual that a change currently being visited upon him or her is a good thing, the purest form of self, the equivalent of freedom. The world really does revolve around you.

In Silicon Valley, in Redmond, Washington, the home of Microsoft, and in the smaller silicon alleys of San Francisco and New York, "disintermediation" is a word so common that people shrug when you try to talk to them about it. Oh, disintermediation, that old thing. Everyone already knows about that. It has become accepted wisdom, a process considerered inevitable, irrefutable, good.

I've long believed that the ideas embedded in technology have a way of percolating up and outward into the nontechnical world at large, and that technology is made by people with intentions and, as such, is not neutral. In the case of disintermediation, an explicit and purposeful change is being visited upon the structure of the global marketplace. And in a world so dominated by markets, I don't think I go too far in saying that this will affect the very structure of reality, for the Net is no longer simply a zone of personal freedoms, a pleasant diversion from what we used to call "real life"; it has become an actual marketplace that is changing the nature of real life itself.

Removal of the intermediary. All those who stand in the middle of a transaction, whether financial or intellectual: out! Brokers and agents and middlemen of every description: good-bye! Travel agents, real-estate agents, insurance agents, stockbrokers, mortgage brokers, consolidators, and jobbers, all the scrappy percentniks who troll the bywaters of capitalist exchange—who needs you? All those hard-striving immigrants climbing their way into the lower middle class through the penny-ante deals of capitalism, the transfer points too small for the big guys to worry about—find yourself some other way to make a living. Small retailers and store clerks, salespeople of every kind—a hindrance, idiots, not to be trusted. Even the professional handlers of intellectual goods, anyone who sifts through information, books, paintings, knowledge, selecting and summing up: librarians, book reviewers, curators, disc jockeys, teachers, editors, analysts—why trust anyone but yourself to make judgments about what is more or less interesting, valuable, authentic, or worthy or your attention? No one, no professional interloper, is supposed to come between you and your desires, which, according to this idea, are **nuanced**, difficult to communicate, irreducible, unique.

**nuanced**
subtle

The Web did not cause disintermediation, but it is what we call an "enabling technology": a technical breakthrough that takes a difficult task and makes it suddenly doable, easy; it opens the door to change, which then comes in an unconsidered, breathless rush.

We are living through an amazing experiment: an attempt to construct a capitalism without salespeople, to take a system founded upon the need to sell ever greater numbers of goods to ever growing numbers of people, and to do this without the aid of professional distribution channels—without buildings, sidewalks, shops, luncheonettes, street vendors, buses, trams, taxis, other women in the fitting room to tell you how you look in something and to help you make up your mind, without street people panhandling, Santas ringing bells at Christmas, shop women with their perfect makeup and elegant clothes, fashionable men and women strolling by to show you the latest look—in short, an attempt to do away with the city in all its messy stimulation, to abandon the **agora** for home and hearth, where it is safe and everything can be controlled.

**agora**
marketplace

**myriad**
many

The first task in this newly structured capitalism is to convince consumers that the services formerly performed by **myriad** intermediaries are useless or worse, that those commissioned brokers and agents are incomplete, out for themselves, dishonest. And the next task is to glorify the notion of self-service. Where companies once vied for your business by telling you about their courteous people and how well they would serve you—"Avis, We Try Harder"—their job now is to make you believe that only you can take care of yourself. The lure of personal service that was dangled before the middle classes, momentarily making us all feel almost as lucky as the rich, is being withdrawn. In the Internet age, under the pressure of globalized capitalism and its slimmed-down profit margins, only the very wealthy will be served by actual human beings. The rest of us must make do with Web pages, and feel happy about it.

One evening while I was watching television, I looked up to see a commercial that seemed to me to be the most explicit statement of the ideas implicit in the disintermediated universe. I gaped at it, because usually such ideas are kept implicit, hidden behind symbols. But this commercial was like the sky-blue billboard: a shameless and naked expression of the Web world, a glorification of the self, at home, alone.

It begins with a drone, a footstep in a puddle, then a ragged band pulling a dead car through the mud—road warriors with bandanas around their foreheads carrying **braziers**. Now we see rafts of survivors floating before the ruins of a city, the sky dark, red-tinged, as if fires were burning all around us, just over the horizon. Next we are outside the dead city's library, where stone lions, now coated in gold and come to life, rear up in despair. Inside the library, red-coated Fascist guards encircle the readers at the table. A young girl turns a page, loudly, and the guards say, "Shush!" in time to their marching step. We see the title of the book the girl is reading: *Paradise Lost*. The bank, too, is a scene of ruin. A long line snakes outside it in a dreary rain. Inside, the teller is a man with a white, spectral face, who gazes upon the black spider that is slowly crawling up his window. A young woman's face ages right before us, and in response, in ridicule, the bank guard laughs. The camera now takes us up over the roofs of this post-apocalyptic city. Lightning crashes in the dark, red-tinged sky. On a telephone pole, where the insulators should be, are skulls.

Cut to a cartoon of emerald-green grass, hills, a Victorian house with a white picket fence and no neighbors. A butterfly flaps above it. What a relief this house is after the dreary, dangerous, ruined city. The door to this charming house opens, and we go in to see a chair before a computer screen. Yes, we want to go sit in that chair, in that room with candy-orange walls. On the computer screen, running by in teasing succession, are pleasant virtual reflections of the world outside: written text, a bank check, a telephone pole, which now signifies our connection to the world. The camera pans back to show a window, a curtain swinging in the breeze, and our sense of calm is complete. We hear the Intel-Inside jingle, which sounds almost like chimes. Cut to the legend: Packard Bell. Wouldn't you rather be at home?

In sixty seconds, this commercial communicates a worldview that reflects the ultimate suburbanization of existence: a retreat from the friction of the social space to the supposed **idyll** of private ease. It is a view that depends on the idea that desire is not social, not stimulated by what others want, but generated internally, and that the satisfaction of desires is not dependent upon other persons, organizations, structures, or governments. It is a profoundly libertarian vision, and it is the message that underlies all the mythologizing about the Web: the idea that the civic

braziers
containers holding lit wood and coal

idyll
sanctuary

space is dead, useless, dangerous. The only place of pleasure and satis-faction is your home. You, home, family; and beyond that, the world. From the intensely private to the global, with little in between but an Intel processor and a search engine.

In this sense, the ideal of the Internet represents the very opposite of democracy, which is a method for resolving differences in a relatively orderly manner through the mediation of unavoidable civil associations. Yet there can be no notion of resolving differences in a world where each person is entitled to get exactly what he or she wants. Here all needs and desires are equally valid and equally powerful. I'll get mine and you'll get yours; there is no need for compromise and discussion. I don't have to tolerate you, and you don't have to tolerate me. No need for messy debate and the whole rigmarole of government with all its creaky, bothersome structures. There's no need for any of this, because now that we have the World Wide Web the problem of the pursuit of happi-ness has been solved! We'll each click for our individual joys, and our only dispute may come if something doesn't get delivered on time. Wouldn't you really rather be at home?

But who can afford to stay at home? Only the very wealthy or a cer-tain class of knowledge worker can stay home and click. On the other side of this ideal of work-anywhere freedom (if indeed it is freedom never to be away from work) is the reality that somebody had to make the thing you ordered with a click. Somebody had to put it in a box, do the pa-perwork, carry it to you. The reality is a world divided not only be-tween the haves and have-nots but between the ones who get to stay home and everyone else, the ones who deliver the goods to them.

The Net ideal represents a retreat not only from political life but also from culture—from that tumultuous conversation in which we try to talk to one another about our shared experiences. As members of a cul-ture, we see the same movie, read the same book, hear the same string quartet. Although it is difficult for us to agree on what we might have seen, read, or heard, it is out of that difficult conversation that real cul-ture arises. Whether or not we come to an agreement or understanding, even if some decide that understanding and meaning are impossible, we are still sitting around the same campfire.

But the Web as it has evolved is based on the idea that we do not even want a shared experience. The director of San Francisco's Museum of Modern Art once told an audience that we no longer need a building to house works of art; we don't need to get dressed, go downtown, walk from room to room among crowds of other people. Now that we have the Web, we can look at anything we want whenever we want, and we no longer need him or his curators. "You don't have to walk through *my* idea of what's interesting to look at," he said to a questioner in the audience named Bill. "On the Web," said the director, "you can create the museum of Bill."

And so, by implication, there can be the museums of George and Mary and Helene. What then will this group have to say to one another about art? Let's say the museum of Bill is featuring early Dutch masters, the museum of Mary is playing video art, and the museum of Helene is displaying French tapestries. In this privatized world, what sort of "cultural" conversation can there be? What can one of us possibly say to another about our experience except, "Today I visited the museum of me, and I liked it."

# Work, Labor and Play

## W.H. Auden

So far as I know, Miss Hannah Arendt was the first person to define the essential difference between work and labor. To be happy, a man must feel, firstly, free and, secondly, important. He cannot be really happy if he is compelled by society to do what he does not enjoy doing, or if what he enjoys doing is ignored by society as of no value or importance. In a society where slavery in the strict sense has been abolished, the sign that what a man does is of social value is that he is paid money to do it, but a laborer today can rightly be called a wage slave. A man is a laborer if the job society offers him is of no interest to himself but he is compelled to take it by the necessity of earning a living and supporting his family.

**antithesis**

opposite

The **antithesis** to labor is play. When we play a game, we enjoy what we are doing, otherwise we should not play it, but it is a purely private activity; society could not care less whether we play it or not.

Between labor and play stands work. A man is a worker if he is personally interested in the job which society pays him to do; what from the point of view of society is necessary labor is from his own point of view voluntary play. Whether a job is to be classified as labor or work depends, not on the job itself, but on the tastes of the individual who undertakes it. The difference does not, for example, coincide with the difference between a manual and a mental job; a gardener or a cobbler may be a worker, a bank clerk a laborer. Which a man is can be seen from his attitude toward leisure. To a worker, leisure means simply the hours he needs to relax and rest in order to work efficiently. He is therefore more likely to take too little leisure than too much; workers die of coronaries and forget their wives' birthdays. To the laborer, on the other hand, leisure means freedom from compulsion, so that it is natural for him to imagine that the fewer hours he has to spend laboring, and the more hours his is free to play, the better.

What percentage of the population in a modern technological society are, like myself, in the fortunate position of being workers? At a guess I would say sixteen per cent, and I do not think that figure is likely to get bigger in the future.

"Work, Labor and Play," excerpted from W. H. Auden's *A Certain World, A Commonplace Book*. New York: Curtis Brown: 1970. Reprinted with permission.

Technology and the division of labor have done two things: by eliminating in many fields the need for special strength or skill, they have made a very large number of paid occupations which formerly were enjoyable work into boring labor, and by increasing productivity they have reduced the number of necessary laboring hours. It is already possible to imagine a society in which the majority of the population, that is to say, its laborers, will have almost as much leisure as in earlier times was enjoyed by the aristocracy. When one recalls how aristocracies in the past actually behaved, the prospect is not cheerful. Indeed, the problem of dealing with boredom may be even more difficult for such a future mass society than it was for aristocracies. The latter, for example, ritualized their time; there was a season to shoot **grouse**, a season to spend in town, etc. The masses are more likely to replace an unchanging ritual by fashion which it will be in the economic interest of certain people to change as often as possible. Again, the masses cannot go in for hunting, for very soon there would be no animals left to hunt. For other aristocratic amusements like gambling, dueling, and warfare, it may be only too easy to find equivalents in dangerous driving, drug-taking, and senseless acts of violence. Workers seldom commit acts of violence, because they can put their aggression into their work, be it physical like the work of a **smith**, or mental like the work of a scientist or artist. The role of aggression in mental work is aptly expressed by the phrase "getting one's teeth into a problem."

grouse
wild fowl

smith
blacksmith

# The New Capitalism— and What It Means for You

Jason MacLean

> The reality now facing young workers with at least two years of college is that they will change jobs, on average, at least eleven times in the course of their working lives.
>
> —*AT&T Executive, 1997*

By all accounts, ours is an era of unprecedented material prosperity and consumer choice. Stock markets around the world seem to close each day at a record high. The reign of downsizing, the management gurus proclaim, has passed. We now worship at the altar of a bull market.[1] The high priests of Wall Street prophesy unlimited economic growth and next to full employment.[2]

What is wrong with this picture?

The answer to this question, like most others, depends in large measure on who you ask.

Proponents of the new capitalism are unshakable in their faith in our apparent economic utopia. Not only can everyone who wants to work easily find work, they say, but the *nature* of work itself has evolved for the better. The new work environment, the gurus promise, is challenging, flexible, and vastly rewarding. Modern technology has banished work that is dull and routine to the innards of the new machines, freeing ever more workers to perform complex tasks with autonomy and self-direction.

Or so the story goes.

Critics of the new capitalism, however, offer a far different answer. True, the nature of work has changed radically. But false, counter the critics, is the belief that all of us are benefitting from the transformation of capitalism. Flexibility, for instance, is to the social critics but a **euphemism** for instability and the insecurity that go along with it: short-term jobs, permanently part-time positions, "projects" and "contract work" replace stable careers; skills are continuously redefined and

**euphemism**

a mild or indirect description that at least partially conceals the reality of a harsher alternative

---

"The New Capitalism—and What It Means for You" is reprinted by permission of the author.

devalued; the middle class experiences anxieties that were in an earlier era mostly confined to members of the "working" class.

This essay chronicles the debate over the human consequences of the new capitalism. Along the way, we will address the following questions: How is the new political economy changing our relations with our families, friends, neighbours and co-workers? How do the changing patterns of our working lives spill over into our lives as democratic citizens? And, not least, what does the new economy mean for our understanding of ourselves?

Meet Mary Johnson.[3] Mary is a field technician who works for a telephone company. Mary's employer recently "re-engineered" its maintenance process in order to increase efficiency. Central to this new way of working are small teams of field technicians like Mary, each of whom is responsible for keeping a specific group of customers satisfied with their service. This involves fixing phones when necessary, performing preventive maintenance, even promoting and selling add-on services and anticipating new customer needs. Mary and her "teammates" schedule their own work and make decisions independently upon arriving at each customer site. Mary describes her new way of working like this:

> I've been at the company for twenty-three years, and I always thought we were over-managed, over-controlled and over-supervised. They [management] treated us like children. We're having a very good time under the new system. They've given us the freedom to work on our own. This is the most intelligent thing this company has done in years. It's fun.

Mary is a poster girl for the new capitalism. Her new way of working, according to the management consultants, stands in stark opposition to the classical industrial model in which workers perform specialized tasks under layer upon layer of bureaucratic management—and oversights. In order to understand the nature of the new capitalism better, a few remarks about its predecessor are in order.

At the centre of the history of economic growth is a puzzling paradox: as material growth occurs, the qualitative experience of the work itself tends to become increasingly impoverished.

The age of classic capitalism—which for the sake of convenience can be said to span the two centuries following the publication of Adam Smith's *The Wealth of Nations* in 1776—was an era that lusted for sheer quantitative expansion. It was also an era witness to mass poverty and a widening of the gap between the haves and the have-nots.

Adam Smith, one of the first philosophers to write about capitalism, argued that a complex division of labour was promoted by the adoption of *laissez-faire*[4] economics and the expansion of free markets with ever greater numbers of goods, services and workers in circulation. Society was not unlike a honeycomb, with each new cell the place for ever more specialized tasks. Consider the case of the pin maker. A pin maker working independently, doing everything himself, could make no more than a few hundred pins each day. Not a bad day's work, you might think. Smith observed, however, that if the craft of pin manufacturing was broken down into its component parts, and each worker was made responsible for only one such component part, a team of pin makers could produce more than 48,000 pins per day. The workaday experience of making pins, however, would be fundamentally altered. Pin makers suddenly found themselves condemned to a numbingly boring job, hour after hour, day after day, devoted to the repetition of the same oversimplified task.

This coupling of impressive material growth and the degradation of the quality of the work experience is known as "*Smith's Paradox*." Smith's Paradox first manifested itself in our time as "**Fordist production**," the kind of assembly-line work Henry Ford organized in his Highland Park plant in Michigan during the First World War and the kind of work that persists in factories and plants in North America and throughout the world today. Fordist production builds on the division of labour observed by Smith and makes it still more efficient by automating more and more of the tasks involved in the production process. Once the initial investment in new technology is paid for, the automation of production allows owners to produce even more goods in the same amount of time, at once reducing labour costs and increasing profit.

In step with the automation of production was a corresponding revolution in the nature of work: "*scientific management*." Although the term itself was not coined until 1911, this new approach to factory management, popularized by the engineer Frederick W. Taylor, was established near the end of the previous century. Scientific management, as Taylor imagined it, involved the following steps: 1) shift the responsibility of making decisions from workers to managers, a new, middle-level class of workers who answered to owners; 2) use scientific methods to determine the most efficient way of performing a task and then redesign the task accordingly; 3) provide a detailed description of how to do each task of each job to both managers and workers; and 4) monitor workers' performance closely.

**Fordist production**

mass production

Taylor was convinced that worker "soldiering," or deliberate laziness, was the largest obstacle standing in the way of increased productivity and profits. His solution was to determine scientifically how to increase the speed of production by conducting *time-and-motion studies* of each step of each job. A quota level would then be established for each job. If a worker exceeded the quota, the worker would be given a bonus. If, however, the worker failed to satisfy the quota, no matter how high it might be, that worker would be replaced. Still, Taylor believed his method was beneficial to owners, managers and workers alike. On the other hand, some critics, and not a few workers, believed that Taylorism, as this method came to be known, only worsened Smith's Paradox by minutely fragmenting jobs, reducing skill requirements and eliminating workers' input about how their jobs should be done.

Charlie Chaplin's classic movie *Modern Times* humorously depicts the impact of both Fordism and Taylorism on working conditions. Chaplin plays a stressed-out factory worker whose job has been analyzed and re-designed by stopwatch-wielding efficiency experts. Every few seconds, Chaplin tightens a nut as yet another identical piece of equipment zips past him on the assembly line. Chaplin's character is little more than a robot programmed by the production system. Once out on the street after work, he continues repeating the same motions on anything that fits his two wrenches.

*Modern Times* (1936)

The mass production method, as familiar as it may appear to us today, is now considered completely unsuited to the new economic environment in which consumers demand perfection at a cheap price. The classic industrial model, in the view of the new experts, is too slow, too costly and too inflexible to satisfy consumer demands. The result, the new, re-engineered capitalism, represents nothing less than the total abandonment of the Fordist and Taylorist models. This change is not restricted to Mary Johnson's company; it leaves no sector of the new economy untouched. A few examples make the point:

- At GTE Telephone operations, now GTE Network Services, a new position has been created called the "customer care advocate." This new job consolidates three previously separate and independent jobs into one. Gone are the customer-service representative who used to handle customer calls, the line checker who used to try to resolve problems by means of a computer system and the dispatcher who used to send out a field technician when necessary.

- At Owens Corning, orders are now filled by a team composed of people representing the departments of customer service, finance and transportation. Together they now share collective responsibility for each order.

- At Progressive Auto Insurance, calls from customers with accident claims go directly to a claims representative who is now responsible for ensuring that claims are settled immediately. The claims representative does as much as possible over the phone and arranges for the vehicle to be inspected by a teammate in the field.

- At the Trane Company, a manufacturer of air-conditioning equipment, newly formed production teams schedule their own work and communicate directly with suppliers to acquire the parts they need.

- At Duke Power, a division of the Duke Energy Corporation, line technicians are each given a week's worth of work instead of a day's amount and expected to schedule each task on their own. If the line technician then decides that the instructions for a job are incorrect, he or she has the authority to depart from them and restructure the duties. The line technician also has control over a wide range of issues, from selecting cable sizes to placing lights, decisions previously the exclusive preserve of highly trained electrical engineers.

- At Nabisco Canada Limited, managers and supervisors across various functional areas (e.g., marketing, finance, accounting, etc.) used to rely upon personal assistants to handle various administrative tasks. No longer. Managers and supervisors now use voice mail to accomplish these tasks. In a similar move, Nabisco managers now schedule meetings and conferences directly using the new organizational intranet.

These are but a few examples of the transformation of work. According to proponents of the new capitalism, the new jobs are comparatively more fulfilling and rewarding than the old jobs left behind. Just ask Mary Johnson.

The designers of the new economy are not unaware of their critics, however. In a popular classic about modern economic organizations, *Re-engineering the Corporation*, authors Michael Hammer and James Champy defend "re-engineering" against the charge that it is a mere cover for simply firing people: "downsizing and restructuring," they argue, "only mean doing less with less. Re-engineering, by contrast means doing *more* with less."

We should pause here to consider how the "less" in the authors' defence of re-engineering resonates with the denials of an older species of Social Darwinism: those who are not "fit," those who do not adapt, will disappear.[5] We should also note that the shelf-life of the latest management buzz-word is no more than three years. Hammer, for example, recently published a book entitled *Beyond Re-engineering*, which replaces re-engineering with "process." The basic idea, however, is essentially unchanged. The rationale for the change in terminology, consistent with both the old and the new capitalism, is simply to sell more books.

Now meet Bob Smith.[6] Bob works in a cubicle at a financial services firm in Toronto. Like the five others who work in this unit, Bob is a survivor. Bob has withstood the downsizing, the restructuring and, yes, the re-engineering. Still, Bob perseveres. His job was taken from him temporarily, altered and redefined, and returned to him, awkward and misshapen. Bob is married with two children. He is still a manager, although he now manages not people but information. Ask Bob how he is doing and he will answer, in tune with his five co-workers, that he is getting by. That he is coping.

But there came a day in the spring of 1998 when things got to Bob more than usual. He had just learned through the company grapevine that yet another instance of re-engineering was imminent. Bob arrived at work the next morning earlier than usual in order to write a note to each of his five teammates. Each note was the same, reading, *"I'm going to blow your brains out."*

Bob is now back at work with the same five colleagues, but not before he was taken away and held for a seventy-two hour psychiatric assessment. Not before he volunteered for an additional two weeks of intensive psychiatric scrutiny. And not before his threatened and understandably shaken colleagues had received a thorough psychological debriefing. All of which is the standard operating procedure for dealing with what is known as "workplace rage."

"MADDER THAN EVER" ran the banner of a career report in the 2 November 1998 edition of the *Los Angeles Times*, a section which detailed the tantrums, outbursts, and assaults (both verbal and physical) that have increasingly come to characterize workplace rage. Bob Smith is certainly not alone. Just short of 25 percent of respondents to a 1996 U.S. Gallup telephone survey on 1000 adults aged eighteen and over who were then employed either part or full time indicated that they were "generally at least somewhat angry at work."

Workplace rage is a relatively new term. The anxieties and stresses it describes, however, are nothing new at all. Karl Marx, a German historian who lived through the initial phases of the Industrial Revolution in Germany and England, was one of the first critics of capitalism. Marx used the term *alienation* to develop his critique of the nature of work under capitalism. Marx argued there was an interactive, or dialectic, relationship between human beings and nature. When we alter nature, we alter ourselves. To Marx, the same principle applied to work. When we work, we interact with nature and, in so doing, we transform it. At the same time, nature interacts with us and changes us. Through work, then, our consciousness is transformed. We are, in other words, what we do. To Marx, work was a positive activity closely connected to the very essence of what it means to be human.

Under the capitalist system, however, work changed. People no longer worked for themselves or for the intrinsic value of the work itself, but, instead, people began to work for someone else. The labour performed by workers no longer belonged to them. Ironically, as workers became separated from the end product of their labour, they began to resemble the end product itself. How? When workers labour for someone else in exchange for a wage, the end product is nothing more than a good or a service to be sold to a faceless consumer—it is stripped of the original meaning it once held for the worker. Similarly, when a worker sells his or her labour to someone else, the worker becomes just another commodity to be bought and sold by an employer. The worker who sells his or her labour for a wage not only is made an *alien* to the end product of work, over which he or she no longer has any control, but also becomes an alien, a stranger, *to his or her own self*. If you hate your work, according to Marx's logic, you will hate yourself.

The concept of alienation allows us to understand the case of the cubicle worker Bob Smith better. Alienation describes the larger context of day-to-day work. At first glance, it might have appeared that the problem was not the re-engineering of the new capitalism, but perhaps Bob himself. But on closer examination, it becomes clear that Bob's irrational behaviour was an understandable and predictable response to increased workplace alienation. And while workplace rage is clearly an extreme phenomenon, it is, like alienation, nonetheless indicative of the tensions and pressures inherent in the new capitalism. Indeed, many critics argue that the new capitalism of today is even more alienating than the capitalism of Marx's era.

If, however, this critique of the new capitalism appears less than persuasive, then consider another line of argument. The most convincing evidence of the perils of the new economy arguably comes from the reactions of corporations themselves. Workplace rage and the far more common, subtle forms of workplace dissatisfaction, like performing the bare minimum of tasks just to get by, are, after all, bad for business. Statistics Canada, for example, estimates the annual cost of work time lost due to stress at $12 billion. Not surprisingly, then, corporations are already busy trying to stem the tide of employee resentment.

Management leaders have decided to go to the heart of the problem—literally. The shelves of the business section in your local bookstore are stocked to the limit with tomes expounding the ethical and spiritual potential of corporations. Representative titles include *The New Corporate Cultures: Revitalizing the Workplace after Downsizing, Mergers and Re-engineering; The Ethical Imperative: Why Moral Leadership Is Good Business; The Way of the Leader: Applying the Principles of Sun Tzu and Confucius; Soaring with the Phoenix: Renewing the Vision, Reviving the Spirit and Re-Creating the Success of Your Company* (from the best-selling co-author of *Flight of the Buffalo* and *Teaching the Elephant to Dance*); *Healing the Downsized Organization: What Every Employee Needs to Know about Today's Workplace;* and *Going Deep: Exploring Spirituality in Life and Leadership.*[7]

The presence of spirituality in the workplace is not limited to the shelves of your local bookstore. Spirituality now reaches directly into corporations themselves. For the past six years, for example, 300 Xerox Corporation employees—including people from mailroom clerks to senior managers—have taken part in "vision quests," or camping trips, to places such as the deserts of New Mexico and the Catskill Mountains of New York to seek guidance from nature about how to produce the perfect photocopier. Companies such as Taco Bell, Pizza Hut and Wal-Mart now hire army-style chaplains to lead 24-hour "God squads" who visit sick employees in hospitals, deal with nervous breakdowns and respond to employee suicide threats. According to the Fellowship for Companies for Christ International, over 10 000 bible study and prayer groups now meet regularly in workplaces across Canada and the United States. It should come as little surprise, then, that 48 percent of recently polled Americans responded "yes" to the question: "Have you had occasion to talk about your religious faith in the workplace in the past 24 hours?" God is open for business.

Ethics and spirituality, however, are not for everyone. Many corporations are turning elsewhere to heal the wounds of chronic change. Enter humour consultants. Historically traditional and conservative organizations like IBM, the Federal Reserve Board, Charles Schwab, Fidelity Investments and the U.S. Postal Service have called upon highly paid humour consultants—who can command up to $5000 an hour—to ease workplace tensions and facilitate cooperation between managers and employees.

Lexmark International, for example, is a computer printing products company, located in Lexington, Kentucky, that recently hired a humour consultant to conduct seminars during the company's second re-engineering period. "The 'r' word brings fear to a lot of people, so we had to use humour to get people ready," reports the firm's education manager.

Neither humour or spirituality, however, is a universal cure. As one prominent humour consultant notes about his experience lecturing to a group of disenchanted brewery workers, "You can't use humour as a piece of candy to resolve your hunger. These guys were damn resentful. Some of them turned their bodies 90 degrees to avoid looking at me."

Spirituality, ethics and humour each appears to be largely unrelated to capitalism. Historically, none of these things ever crossed the minds of capitalists like Henry Ford or efficiency engineers like Frederick Taylor. Indeed, on any given day, traditional capitalists concentrated on business problems by thinking in terms of three kinds of capital: financial, physical and human. Financial capital, straightforwardly enough, refers to money and investments and taxes and the like. Physical capital, its financial value aside, refers to the actual means of production, like forklifts, staplers, and computers. Human capital measures the sum of the education, training and skills of the workforce.

Lately, the new capitalists have started paying attention to a fourth kind of capital: social capital. Sociologists use the concept of social capital, which refers to the quality of social relations between individuals and groups, to measure the strengths of various social institutions, like government, the family, the educational system, the church and local communities. Social capital is made up of several elements, but the most important ones tend to be equality, trust and cooperation.

Recently, economists and sociologists alike have begun to apply the concept of social capital to the realm of business in order to measure the strength of the relations between employers and employees, on the one hand, and among fellow employees, on the other. A consensus among both theorists and practitioners quickly emerged that social capital—equality, trust and cooperation—is as important, if not more so, to efficiency and productivity as are the traditional kinds of capital. If, for instance, the workers of company X are on an equal footing, they will be more likely to trust—rather than to compete with—each other. The more workers trust each other, the more they will cooperate with each other. Cooperation, which involves, among other things, sharing existing ideas and collaborating on new ones, should lead to creativity, which, in turn, is considered to be the key to productivity and profits in the new economy. While returns to the traditional forms of capital are limited and costly to develop, the potential of social capital appears to be virtually infinite. Viewed in this new light, spirituality, ethics and even humour are suddenly crucial ingredients to success in the new economy. Small wonder corporations are in such a hurry to increase their stock of social capital.

The real-world difficulty with such attempts at quick-fix change embraced by corporations and governments throughout the world, however, is one of time—or, more precisely, the lack thereof. Time, in fact, is central to the social and political critique of the new capitalism. Indispensable social bonds like trust, cooperation, loyalty, obligation and empathy require a long time to develop and strengthen. A meaningful sense of community simply cannot be instantly created by an act of will, no matter how pure the intention. Time, too, is crucial to the development of a solid sense of personal worth. Stable and enduring personal time, in short supply in the new economy, is necessary to establish a coherent narrative of one's life.

In the previous capitalist era, stability became a precarious dimension of time. The progress of nineteenth-century capitalism was anything but linear and smooth, swinging instead from disaster to disaster in the stock markets and in irrational capital investments. A certain kind of character type—equally familiar in the pages of Balzac[8] as in the mundane annals of finance—thrived on disorder, possessing if nothing else a quality for disloyalty. For every socially responsible industrialist like Andrew Carnegie,[9] there were hundreds of Jay Goulds,[10] adept at emerging unscathed from crises of their own design.

Max Weber's famous image of modern life confined in an "iron cage" gives short shrift to the virtues of stability. The "Protestant work ethic" of reliable, self-denying, life-long effort and thrift that Weber argued to be key to the development of capitalism is the same kind of ethic that allowed many of his own contemporaries to purchase a home, and home ownership in the nineteenth and early twentieth century was one of the few bulwarks against the storm of capitalism, not to mention a source of significant personal and family honour. That much remains true to this day.

Weber feared the rise of large national and corporate bureaucracies that exploited this service ethic, by which workers traded loyalty to their organizations in return for job security. Weber doubted that loyal servants made for objectively minded citizens. Yet petty bureaucrats derived a sense of status and public honour from their positions within large bureaucracies. T. H. Marshall, the intellectual father of the modern British welfare system, understood this well: however resistant large bureaucracies are to change from within, they nevertheless provide their members with a sort of scaffolding of mutual respect and trust that spills over into their lives as democratic citizens. The bureaucrat as model citizen is admittedly not a pretty picture, but then, Jay Gould had no interest in the subject at all.

The current rush to dismantle this institutional architecture promises to undo the civic, social and personal foundations of stable time. Take loyalty, for instance. In the emerging political economy, as people increasingly perform shifting, problem-centred jobs, loyalties to institutions diminish and promise to disappear entirely. The young people of society, the next generation of workers, citizens and parents (that means *you*) is hardest hit by these changes. They will in growing numbers enter institutions that guarantee nothing in return for their time and energy. Organizations now routinely replace permanent workers with temporary ones. More and more work is "farmed out" to "off-shore" destinations. Job-creation statistics, no matter how encouraging, reveal little about who will have access to the new jobs. Complex computer code, for example, can be written just as effectively in Bombay for a third to a seventh of its cost if written in the home offices of IBM in the United States. Nor do the statistics indicate how long the new jobs will actually last. Compounding the problem is that increasingly mobile workers are often unable to transfer their skills from job to job because their experience is overly specialized and is all too quickly rendered obsolete by technological change. People need time to accumulate experience within institutions in order to trust their co-workers and supervisors. The new economy provides few opportunities of this kind, preferring instead to be "mean and lean."

The human consequences of the new capitalism extend well beyond the workplace. Thirty-six percent of women and thirty-three percent of men in Canada presently report a high level of "work-life conflict," with work being the hands-down winner in the struggle for people's personal time. Forty-one percent of professional and managerial workers in Canada report experiencing this conflict, including forty-nine percent of men in this category. Working men and women are now more than ever caught in a "time bind" that is diminishing the quality of both their working and personal lives. As work takes up more and more time there is little left over for family, community involvement, friends and, just as important, personal reflection.

So who is right? Mary Johnson or Bob Smith? Whose story best captures the reality of work today? Michael Hammer, the outspoken proponent of the new capitalism, asserts that the question whether the new world of work is good versus bad is beside the point. Like it or not, Hammer argues, the new capitalism is inevitable. It is here to stay. Corporations and employees who fail to adapt will be replaced. Survival of the fittest. Such is the new economic environment.

Do we really have so little control over how we work and live? Reflecting upon this question philosophically, we can acknowledge that modernity is both fleeting and fragmented. To accept life in its disjointed pieces is an adult experience of both freedom and responsibility. Yet these pieces must still have some place to call home, a place that allows them to grow and endure. The problems posed by modernity in general and the new capitalism in particular demand of each generation a collective response capable of providing for our fundamental need of *Sicherheit*, the German word for a shared sense of safety, security and certainty. At present, as citizens of democratic societies, we look to the principle of perfect competition within free markets to solve our social and political problems. As Adam Smith put it, "It is not from the benevolence of the butcher, the brewer or the baker, that we expect our dinner, but from their regard to their own self-interest." This reliance on individual competition, however popular now, is still a mistake. We would do well to heed the warning of cultural historian Richard Hofstadter, whose remarks of over thirty years past resonate just as loudly today:

> *Today our greatest domestic fear lies not in our failure to produce enough goods because we do not have enough competition, but in our failure to render certain humane, healing, humanly productive and restorative social services that are not comprehended at all in the ethos of competition. At its best, business will not perform such services. At its worst, it can sustain a class of men who will prevent them from being performed.*

It is thus our responsibility to continually question existing institutional arrangements and intellectual ideas and try to imagine something better for all of us. The choice, after all, is ours to make. We are no more slaves to fashionable voices of the present than to fading echoes of the past. We can, *if we choose*, acknowledge that our obligations as citizens, neighbours and co-workers extend far beyond our economic usefulness to each other, and act accordingly.

# Notes

[1] Two adjectives are commonly used to describe the health of any economic market: bull and bear (bullish and bearish, respectively). A bull market is considered strong and friendly to prospective investors. A bear market, by contrast, is considered weak and dangerous to potential investors. A bull market tends to increase wages and decrease unemployment. The opposite is true under bearish market conditions.

[2] Economists tend to agree that 4 to 6 percent unemployment is optimal for economic productivity. Why? Having 4 to 6 percent of the labour force unemployed at any given time allows for both individual and organizational *flexibility*. Critics, however, argue that this aspect of capitalism is part of its destructive nature. Karl Marx, whose ideas will be discussed later in this essay, called the unemployed a "reserve army of labour." Maintaining a small pool of continuously unemployed workers provides capitalists with leverage over their employees. Capitalists are able to compel workers to do more for less because workers fear that if they do not comply they may be replaced with a member of the unemployed pool of labour.

[3] Mary Johnson is a pseudonym for a real person with a real job. The details are true.

[4] *Laissez-faire* is French for "allow to do," but roughly translated it means "hands-off." Applied to economics, *laissez-faire* means that the government should not attempt to play a role in the management of the economy. Adam Smith thought competition free of government interference would act like an "invisible hand" that would guide individuals and organizations to make rational and efficient decisions.

[5] Social Darwinism refers to the application of the long-term theory of biological evolution, first developed by Charles Darwin, to the short-term realm of culture and day-to-day life. In Darwin's original theory, biological evolution is the result of random mutations selected for by the environment in unpredictable ways over the course of thousands, sometimes millions, of years. Social Darwinism, by contrast, tries to justify social inequality by suggesting that those who are not successful are somehow biologically unfit. Darwin himself did not support the extension of his ideas to explain conscious human behaviour. Darwinism, more technically known as the theory of natural selection, argues that human beings are powerless to alter the course of biological evolution. This, of course, may soon change as the field of genetic engineering develops. This will in no way, however, validate the pseudo-scientific claims of Social Darwinists.

[6] Again, Bob Smith is a pseudonym for a real person with a real job. The story, however disturbing, is true.

[7] Note, however, that right next to the books listed above one can also find such titles as *Digital Darwinism: 7 Breakthrough Strategies for Surviving in the Cutthroat Web Economy*, *Strategy Safari: A Guided Tour through the Wilds of Strategic Management*, and the equally inviting *The New Machiavelli: The Art of Politics in Business*.

[8] Honoré de Balzac (1799–1850) was a French writer who produced a vast collection of novels and short stories called *La Comédie Humaine* (The Human Comedy). Balzac contributed to the invention of the classic novel and is generally considered one of the greatest fiction writers of all time.

[9] Andrew Carnegie (1835–1919) was a Scottish-born American industrialist who led the enormous expansion of the steel industry during the nineteenth century, key to the Industrial Revolution in the U.S. Carnegie was one of the most important philanthropists of his era. Carnegie also wrote frequently and eloquently about political and social matters. In his most famous article, entitled "Wealth" and written in 1889, Carnegie argued that men of great wealth have a responsibility to use their surplus wealth for "the improvement of mankind." He later wrote that "A man who dies rich dies in disgrace." Carnegie himself donated $350,000,000 to various trusts he himself established that remain in existence today (e.g., The Carnegie Endowment for International Peace).

[10] Jay Gould (1836–1892) was a railroad tycoon, financier, and speculator. At the height of his power, Gould owned Western Union Telegraph, the New York Elevated Railway, and Union Pacific Railroad. Gould is remembered as one of the most unscrupulous "robber barons" of nineteenth-century America.

# Multiculturalism and Equity

## Greg Narbey

Canadians live in a society that is formally committed to multicultural-ism in our laws and public policy. While laws and public policy may evolve and change, it is undeniable that Canada is multicultural, in the sense that it is a society made up of people who can trace their origins and their cultural background to many different parts of the world. Our commitment to multiculturalism means that not only are people of dif-ferent racial, ethnic and cultural backgrounds welcomed in Canada, but also, once here, newcomers are not forced to conform to the dominant culture, nor can they be discriminated against for continuing to value and practise their cultural and religious customs.

In recent years this policy of multiculturalism has come under attack on two fronts. Some argue that a policy of multiculturalism concentrates too much on what makes us different, on what divides us, and not enough on what we share in common as Canadians. On the other hand, others argue that multiculturalism represents only a surface support for cultural minority groups while neglecting the continued exclusion of these groups from the institutions of power in Canadian society. Multiculturalism, it is charged, is a smoke screen that encourages people of different ethnic and racial backgrounds to open up restaurants and continue certain artis-tic pursuits (dance, music, etc.) while at the same time failing to ac-knowledge that discrimination against some cultural groups results in an inequitable access to power, education, housing and jobs.

These two views can conflict, with one group thinking that multi-culturalism already goes too far in emphasizing differences, and with the other group thinking that it doesn't go far enough in promoting the fair and full sharing of power. Many people have a difficult time accommodating the changing reality of Canada, and it is not unusual for individuals to go through an adjustment period when confronted with difference in their world. Multiculturalism attempts to smooth the transition by reassuring the diverse groups that they will be treated with fairness and respect. Equity law is an attempt to insist that we progress through this adjustment with fairness.

"Multiculturalism and Equity" is by Greg Narbey of Humber College. Used by permission.

The debate over multiculturalism and equity is complicated by two fundamentally different conceptions of equality. One view is sometimes called *formal equality* because it is concerned more with ensuring everyone is treated the same (procedural fairness) regardless of personal characteristics. The second version of equality may be called *substantive equality* because it takes differences into account in order to compel change.

# Formal Equality

This basic understanding of equality is that *people should be treated the same way regardless of their culture, race, education, class or social standing.* Different people must be treated equally before the law; a person's cultural background, for example, should not affect the administration of justice.

This account of equality often conforms to the way we think the world should be. In fact, however, it is precisely because the world is not this way that legislation is often required to secure equality. It has come to be accepted that, as a human being, one has the same right as anyone else to equal treatment before the law, to access to housing and to securing employment. For example, when visible minorities apply for a job, most Canadians probably feel that their belonging to a minority group should in no way prevent them from being the successful candidate. In other words, there is no theoretical barrier just because one belongs to a minority group.

# Substantive Equality

There may be no theoretical barrier, but what if it becomes apparent that hiring practices over a period of time indicate that there is a *functional* barrier? That is, visible minorities are not represented in certain occupations in proportion to their numbers in the general population. Diversity in the population at large is not necessarily reflected in the job population. *Substantive equality* represents an attempt to remedy this imbalance, and recognizes that sometimes in order to treat people equally you must recognize and accommodate their differences. Those who favour substantive equality argue that formally recognizing a person as being equal before the law, or eligible for certain positions, is insufficient if that person lacks the wealth, education or self-esteem to take advantage of his or her equality. To paraphrase Anatole France, the law equally permits the millionaire and the beggar to sleep on park benches.

Of course, it is only the poverty-stricken that would need to sleep on park benches; thus, the law in this case appears to be equal but ignores substantial differences of wealth. Substantive equality goes beyond formal equality by attempting to right old imbalances by ensuring that if two roughly comparable candidates for a job are interviewed and one belongs to a minority group, the minority group candidate should be hired.

# The Critics of Multiculturalism

For some people, the emphasis on substantive equality and a broad toleration of different cultural norms and values represent a threat to the standards and values of the more established community. Thus, in recent years, there has been a number of criticisms directed at both the governmental policy of multiculturalism and the fact of multiculturalism. The critics of multiculturalism often can be divided into two identifiable approaches, *liberal* and *conservative*.

The *liberal* critics of multiculturalism most often object to the disregard for formal equality required by multiculturalism. Often the liberal critics of multiculturalism would like to see something like the American "melting pot." This approach favours an integration (assimilation) of new immigrants into the existing institutions and norms of the society. It is hoped that this integration would make substantive equality (the accommodation of differences) unnecessary. Furthermore, liberal critics of multiculturalism are concerned that multiculturalism distributes political rights on the basis of group identification. These liberal critics argue that political rights ought to belong to individuals equally, not to groups. Their concern is that collective rights may be oppressive to an individual and in the long run lead to stereotyping and ghettoization of minority groups.

The *conservative* critics of multiculturalism are concerned that the traditions and values that make our society attractive to others are undermined by multiculturalism, which emphasizes the equality of all cultures. As the Canadian writer George Grant stated, "A society only articulates itself as a nation through some common intention among its people." The conservative critics point out that multiculturalism makes it difficult to promote the core values and norms of our society, and they fear that promoting all cultural values and norms as equal will eventually lead to the disappearance of respect for our society's current values and norms. The conservative critics differ from the liberal critics insofar as they emphasize the community and community standards as the foundation for what brings people together. If there are no common community standards and values, they argue, society may fall apart due to a break down in social cohesion. This concern about an absence of "common intention" among the people of Canada takes on a heightened importance within the context of Quebec's desire for sovereignty. Many conservative critics of multiculturalism are concerned that if Quebec were to separate, there might not be enough in common in the rest of Canada to prevent the rapid absorption of English-speaking Canada into the United States. Thus, multiculturalism is seen as undermining the common sense of values required to keep Canada together.

# Response to the Critics of Multiculturalism

The *liberal* critics of multiculturalism underestimate just how much new immigrants and established minority groups are attracted by the promise of formal equality and toleration. In fact, the long history of Canadian immigration suggests that the promise of formal equality attracts the vast majority of immigrants to Canada; thus, a belief in formal equality becomes a cornerstone of what they value most about being Canadian. The value placed on formal equality sometimes takes time to evolve, but that is partly because the experience of new immigrants to Canada often falls short of the promise of equality. Whether it was Irish immigrants in the late nineteenth century, Chinese immigrants during the building of the national railway, Ukrainians after World War I, Italians after World War II or those from the Caribbean in the 1970s, the experience of the first generation of immigrants is that they are not treated according to the principles of formal equality and they are often discriminated against. However, as these groups of new arrivals become more settled in the country, the early experience of discrimination often fades and then they become the beneficiaries of and defenders of formal equality.

The *conservative* critics of multiculturalism, in emphasizing the importance of core values and institutions in knitting a society together, often overemphasize how much agreement there already is in Canadian society. Cultural differences aside, Canadians have vastly different standards regarding sexual morality, religious practices, publicly acceptable behaviour, and so on. One might well ask the conservative critics of multiculturalism what Canada's core values and norms are that they

## INDIVIDUAL RIGHTS AND GROUP RIGHTS

It has been commonly regarded by those who favour formal equality that laws that protect individuals from unfair interference by the state or society can only recognize and protect individuals. Adherents of formal equality support individual rights. For example, the state has a responsibility not to interfere with whom you associate with provided you do not intend to harm others. Additionally, no matter how offensive other people find your ideas or religion, the state has an obligation not to interfere with your right to practise your religion or exercise your right to free speech (again, as long as there is no harm to others). This approach to rights has emphasized the separation between individual and society.

Those who support substantive equality often support group rights. They argue that all human beings develop and thrive within communities and groups and therefore the state has an obligation to extend protection and recognition to those groups and communities when they are in danger of being overwhelmed by a larger group or a majority culture. This approach recognizes that people are discriminated against because of the groups they are associated with, e.g., discrimination against a Muslim individual occurs because they are part of a larger community of Muslims. Therefore, minority groups and cultures have a right to protection and recognition, collectively, from the state; otherwise the basic foundation for being treated equally will not exist.

would like to see new immigrants accept. My suspicion is that even among the conservative critics of multiculturalism agreement on core values and institutions could not be reached.

## Multiculturalism and Equality

Much of the debate about multiculturalism rests on the conflict between those who support formal equality and those who favour *substantive equality*. Supporters of multiculturalism usually support substantive equality and often argue that if differences are not taken into account then those differences can be used to deny equal opportunity. For example, the employer who says, "I won't hire you because you must leave work before sundown on Friday," may claim to be applying equal standards in hiring, but in fact has excluded any person (e.g., an orthodox Jew) whose religion requires observance of the Sabbath beginning Friday at sundown. The supporters of substantive equality claim that *formal equality* (treating everyone the same) may require some to abandon religious beliefs, for example, in order to be "just like everyone else." In this respect they claim that the formal approach is only really equal for those of a dominant culture.

Supporters of substantive equality often charge that formal equality can lead to *systemic racism*. Systemic racism occurs when "business as usual" leads to discrimination against individuals and groups of people;

this form of discrimination is usually the unintended result of a lack of policies and procedures meant to ensure equality. An example of systemic racism is a high school Canadian history course that discusses only the historical contributions to the development of Canada made by Canadians of European origin while neglecting the contributions of Canadians of other racial or cultural backgrounds. When a group of people is ignored or not recognized in this manner, the effect can be similar to being directly discriminated against.

The danger for supporters of substantive equality is to be clear that recognition of differences does not mean that the majority can then end formal equality for minority groups. In short, it is one thing for minority groups to request recognition and support from the state; it is entirely another to be segregated by the state regardless of the minority groups' wishes.

Caribbean groups retain their sense of identity through activities such as Toronto's Caribana Festival.

Recognizing the different conceptions of equality put forward by those debating multiculturalism does not eliminate the debate. Indeed, Quebec takes a fundamentally different position on this issue. While those who have been educated in an English-speaking school in Quebec may choose to enroll their children in an English- or French-speaking school, newcomers to Quebec must send their children to a French-speaking school. The choice open to some Québécois is not available to all (a denial of formal equality). In their defence, many Québécois view multiculturalism as an attack on the "two founding nations" theory of Canada, undermining the unique position of French Canadian culture by making it one of many, rather than an equal, partner in the construction of Canadian identity. Consequently, many Québécois argue that preservation of Quebec culture necessitates the unequal treatment of minority cultures within Quebec.

It should be kept in mind, however, that while people may be discriminated against because of racial, or cultural, identities, they are also more than the sum of those identities. Thus the recognition of differences should not result in the refusal of formal equality on the part of the majority culture.

Recognizing the different conceptions of equality being put forward does enable us to move past strongly **enculturated** responses, based often on opinion, and ask questions about the underlying claims being made by the contending parties. Trying to understand which conception of equality is being appealed to, and why, gives us the opportunity to reason about the validity of a claim.

**enculturated**
learned, culturally determined

A recent incident in Ontario gives us an opportunity to see how difficult it can be to reconcile formal and substantive equality. A Muslim taxi driver refused to accept a blind woman as a passenger in his cab because she was accompanied by her seeing eye dog. Some Muslims consider dogs to be unclean animals and for religious reasons some Muslim taxi drivers do not want the dogs in their cars. In this case, the taxi driver is appealing to a conception of formal equality: all dogs are unclean and they won't be permitted in the cab. On the other hand, the blind woman may reasonably argue that if her dog cannot be transported, her ability to shop, work and enjoy the company of friends will be hampered—her dog is not like a family pet.

This appears to be a no-win situation—the taxi driver, for religious reasons, will not allow the dog in his taxi, and the blind woman would have little reason to get into the taxi if she cannot be accompanied by her seeing eye dog. In this instance an Islamic religious leader in Ontario argued that while the Koran identifies dogs as unclean animals, it also specifies that assistance to another human being is of higher importance. Thus, in this case, the uncleanliness of the dog is less important than the assistance required by the blind woman and in the future Muslim taxi drivers should transport blind people accompanied by seeing eye dogs. This is an example of substantive equality taking difference into account. The Islamic religious leader recognized that seeing eye dogs are not simply pets and that without them many blind people would be unable to lead full, active lives.

This is a rather straightforward illustration of how this debate can be conducted at the level of fundamental claims about equality rather than at the level of name calling. These conceptions of equality are not always reconcilable. Nevertheless, as a society we consider both of them to be true at different times. Much of the underlying disagreement about multiculturalism is about which version of equality should take priority over the other. There are no easily applicable rules for deciding this question. In a democratic society these competing conceptions of equality will be open for discussion in the news media, public forums, political rallies and classrooms.

However, to discuss the underlying claims being made in the debate enables us to understand the reasons for disagreement. To give someone you disagree with a reason for your position is to recognize that person as someone worth talking to. It is a sign of respect. On the other hand, to call someone a name, or say, "This is the way we do it around here because we can, or because we like it that way," is to treat that person as less than a worthy partner in a discussion. The debate about multiculturalism, while it is sometimes difficult to recognize, is a discussion about what it means to treat people equally and what we have a right, as individuals and communities, to expect from our fellow citizens in terms of equal treatment.

# Family Matters

## Vivian Smith

Despite all the dire predictions that the family is doomed, people continue to knit themselves together like tapestries—sometimes like crazy quilts—no matter what.

Candace and Patrick recently became the absolutely over-the-moon parents of a bouncing baby boy. But Patrick doesn't live with Candace and their son, he lives with Douglas. Douglas meanwhile, is married to Candace. And Patrick is married to Diana, who lives with Candace. Are you with me?

It is an intriguing situation. Some will find the optimism in these relationships breathtaking, the determination of the child's parents inspiring, their commitment to each other enviable. Others will feel threatened, sickened and outraged that this nervy little band even calls itself a family. Their tale is thrilling, appalling, dangerously deviant, of huge public importance or none of your damn business.

It seems their story could not be told at a more critical juncture: The mainstay of Canadian social order, the family, is reputed to be in its worst crisis ever. Married couples with children now represent less than half of all Canadian families. Gruesome divorces are commonplace, custody fights break our hearts, deadbeat dads flee in droves, family violence and incest cases cram the courts, teen-agers run amok, hard-working parents lose their jobs and slink into food banks. What fresh hell awaits if we do not return to traditional family values?

But whose values, whose families and what traditions? Obviously, families are in the midst of incredible, exhausting change. That, however, is eternally the case. There is no such thing as an ideal family structure, and the one we think of as traditional—devoted mother and father, treasured kids—only exists as a nostalgic fantasy. By looking at history and other social sciences, we can roughly outline the shapes, functions and processes that Canadian families (and those of other Western nations) have really taken over time, and discover likely reasons why they change. In most ways, family life is better than it has ever been, starting with the

"Family Matters" is from *The Globe and Mail*, October 5, 1996. Reprinted with permission.

simple fact that more people are now living long and healthy enough lives to actually enjoy the pleasures of family life through several generations. Our obsession with family matters may also be a simple function of demography: The big fat baby-boom bulge is in its middle-age, a time of life when family matters seem to take up the whole day and half the night. The boomer is child, parent, sibling and spouse all at the same time.

There is one truly disturbing issue regarding the Canadian family, however. By accepting a largely American, neoconservative warning that the institution of the family is in peril, we lose our ability to react to real changes in a way that keeps families, and therefore society, strong. And let's face it: How can seven million Canadian families actually conform *en masse* to one nostalgia-based construct, even if all the politicians, religious leaders and conservative activists in the world tapped their heels together three times and said, there's no place like the nuclear family?

Which brings us back to our cutting-edge baby in Vancouver (who also happens to be cutting teeth). We are calling this baby Kim because everyone involved, while allowing themselves to be photographed and have their lives laid out in unblinking black and white, fears for their personal safety if last names are used. This request reflects the two couples' sense of vulnerability as a "different" family even in hip, seen-it-all Vancouver. "I don't want the Christian Coalition picketing outside our apartment," says Douglas. "I don't want him kidnapped," says Candace, in a voice that says she believes it could happen.

Candace, 42, and Diana, 61, are lesbians who have been together nearly seven years. Patrick, 37, and Douglas, 31, are a gay couple who have been partners for nearly nine years. The two couples are good friends and live near each other. Both pairs thought it was unjust that they couldn't qualify for the family benefits (such as dental care) that heterosexual couples receive from the company that both Patrick and Candace work for. So in 1992 they decided to get married for the purposes of enjoying those benefits: Candace to Douglas, Patrick to Diana. (Diana was married once before, and divorced years ago.)

Meanwhile, Candace, who is now estranged from her parents and siblings, has dreamed of being a mother since she was nine. "Diana and I have discussed the idea of having a child for five years," says Candace. "I'm old-fashioned. I knew I wanted my child to have two parents."

Patrick and Douglas, too, had thought the only thing missing in their lives was a child. Two years after her marriage to Patrick, Candace brought up the idea of having children. After a year of consideration, all four agreed. Health tests were conducted, legal agreements drawn up and insemination ensued. Much to everyone's delight—and not a bit of relief, since she was by now 41—Candace became pregnant. The four were in close contact during pregnancy. When Candace went into labour, Patrick was away on business and Diana witnessed the birth. Kim came into the world by Caesarian section, but he was a perfect baby boy.

Some colleagues were thrilled for the four, others wouldn't even look at them. Not a few lesbian friends were extremely critical, accusing Diana, who is an artist, of forfeiting her career to some nutty idea of parenthood, and at her age! But on the whole the reactions have been positive. Strangers coo over Diana, Candace and Kim when they travel, thinking they are Grandma, Mom and son. Residents in Patrick and Douglas' apartment building fight over babysitting rights. Members of the three extended families (remember Candace and hers do not speak) have expressed delight, and many knitted things have arrived by mail from relatives back East.

Douglas says people have already asked such questions as "Are you going to raise him to be gay?" When they think of that kind of comment reverberating throughout Kim's life, the foursome are determined to be optimistic and honest, although they acknowledge it won't be easy. "Every kid gets laughed at in the school yard over something," says Candace.

Kim is not likely to suffer from lack of attention. His four parents reason that he has twice as many people to wipe away tears, and even if one parent ends up leaving his or her partner, there will still be three parents, not a single mom or dad, left to cope. Already, Kim spends two or three days a week with Patrick and Douglas but he won't stay overnight with them until he is older. Patrick has read Hillary Rodham Clinton's book on family called *It Takes A Village,* and agrees with her take on the importance of community in child-rearing. "We are fortunate. Not only do we have the resources of four people, we have all our extended families and our neighbourhood," says Patrick. (They live in the Strathcona area, a vibrant, ethnically mixed area near downtown.)

So what are we to make of this family? We can call it aberrant, line these people up with the likes of the English writer Vita Sackville-West and her husband Harold Nicolson, two homosexuals who lived apart, took male and female lovers and wrote each other about 10 000 letters about the dreariness of everyone else. Or we can go to see Hollywood movies like *The Birdcage,* a recent remake of *La Cage Aux Folles,* in which we chuckle at the wacky antics of a gay couple trying to pass muster with a "traditional" middleclass family.

Or we can accept that historians are having a really hard time finding a single static family shape. Instead, they are discovering an endless process of changing relationships. Certainly, there isn't a clan like Kim's wheeling a stroller through every mall in town, but research by social scientists around the world shows that the diversity Kim's family embodies has been common to families around the globe and throughout history.

Roderick Phillips, who teaches history at Carleton University and edits the scholarly *Journal of Family History*, says any notion that there is a point beyond which the family cannot go without self-destructing is simply nonsense. "There was a great debate in Canada in the early 1900s over legalizing divorce here. It was felt that Canada was too 'moral' for divorce," says Prof. Phillips. "At the end of the 18th century (leading up to the French Revolution), there was a big debate on the family. It was supposed to be corrupt, on its last legs. This debate also took place in the 15th century, and again in the 16th when Protestants were convinced the Catholics were ruining the family. The family seems to be taking a very long time to die."

No doubt some form of public debate on the family began in prehistoric times, when Paleolithic (or Old Stone Age) Mom worked outside the cave gathering food while men hunted. From 3100 to 600 B.C., "historical events and social forces did bump up against one another, resulting in a kaleidoscope of shifting patterns of power relations among men and women and changing forever family dynamics and affective bonds," writes American historian and psychoanalyst Shari L. Turner in her recent book *The Myths of Motherhood*.

For medieval families, the home and the workplace were one sphere. And in their crowded dwellings, the kids might be barely noticed, for the medieval family included employees, servants, apprentices and others. Villages and communities, not families, were the dominant institutions and the arbiters of morality. Marriage was for the purpose of acquiring property and ensuring reproductive continuity. Sex for any other purpose than procreation was a sin. Most marriages lasted fewer than 15 years, and were dissolved by death. The surviving spouse remarried and a second family began.

There was no point in medieval parents being sentimental about children, as their kids either died young or were sent away as apprentices. Dr. Tamara Hareven, an author and professor of family history at the University of Delaware, says, "There is an idealization of the preindustrial family as three generations living together." But these were not

The Waltons. It was only two generations—few lived long enough to become grandparents—who dwelled together, and a host of unrelated people wedged in as well.

Medieval wives did not have equal status with men, true. But there were exceptions. While their noble husbands were off crusading, noble wives ran huge manors. On farms, wives worked alongside their husbands and children in the fields. Women were neither idolized as nurturers (as in Victorian times) nor decried as witches. Essentially, they were labourers and breeders.

In the 18th century, industrialization began the separation of work from home, husbands from wives and children, but not even the industrialization of the Western world could stop families from regrouping. In a study of Quebec families that left to take factory jobs in New England, in the mid-19th century, Dr. Hareven found that industrialization did not dismantle families as was believed. The first wave of French Canadians found work and homes for family members who later joined them. They arranged for relatives to live on the same streets. Throughout the dislocation, family groups maintained close ties, and when factories closed, the exiles would return to Quebec and renew their ties there.

"We assume that today's 'family crisis' was created by women's participation in the workforce. This masks the reality that women have always worked," says Dr. Eric Sager, a professor of history at the University of Victoria. He is heading a five-year, national study called the Canadian Families Project that is using 1901 census data to create a benchmark for comparisons of historical Canadian family structures and functions with later periods.

Dr. Sager and a dozen of his colleagues across Canada have discovered enormous diversity in households of a century ago. "The 'traditional' family is there," says Dr. Sager, "but there were also lodgers, boarders, servants and a large number of broken or fragmented families."

Divorce was extremely rare—only about 135 divorces were granted to Ontarians by act of Parliament between 1900 and 1920. Most families split apart because of death, separation or desertion. Court records show that bigamy was not uncommon, as men deserted one woman and then later married another. Women were lone heads of households in roughly one-tenth of Canadian families, about the same percentage as they are today.

While middleclass women at the turn of the century were idealized as "natural" child rearers and mostly stayed at home, their more numerous working-class sisters contributed income to the family. But before the coming of social-welfare programs, one in seven Canadian families could not survive on paid work. "Family members literally would die," Dr. Sager says, and surviving children would be sent out to steal, prostitute themselves, scrounge and beg. Parents depended on teen-agers' income to support the family. Adult children returned home not for a free meal, but out of a duty to pitch in during tough times.

Family violence was as much a reality as it is today, but was dealt with within the household.  A lodger might be aware of wife-beating and intervene, for example. Incest was handled similarly. If a new stepfather arrived and began eyeing an older daughter, she would be shipped off to someone else's home. "We assume these families were harmonious, stable, heterosexual. That's a filtered idea, not historical," says Dr. Sager.

The 20th century has been a rollercoaster for the Western family and society as a whole: two world wars, a depression, an economic boom and the more recent shocks of feminism, the Pill, fertility drugs, test-tube babies, a lessening of faith in religion, looser divorce laws, great leaps in health care, medicare, government pensions and access to education, more recession. It goes on and on. Marriages are not the economic unions they once were: People marry for love, leisure-time companions, to have a therapist around the house. Children are not labourers helping to shore up the family: They are adored, costly dependents.

Certainly families appear to be taking a battering. Men have not embraced child-rearing with quite the same enthusiasm that women have shown for careers and the workplace. So magazines are filled with stories about angst-ridden women deciding to go back home to the kids. The proliferation of tabloid tell-all talk shows would lead us to believe that families are in a state of profound crisis. But Rosemary Cozens, a Toronto family counsellor and psychotherapist, says that these shows have raised people's awareness that their own families aren't so weird. She says the shows actually make many people feel optimistic. So is the family doomed or is it indestructible?

If you are on the side of the doomsayers, you may think feckless couples today are all shacked-up or split-up, and in either case sowing seeds of social collapse. But look again at the statistics. Yes, it is true that common-law unions are increasing, but Canadians are actually marrying today at the same rate as they did 75 years ago. Yes, the number of divorces has risen dramatically since 1950, but so has the number of marriages. And it's all because more marriages are remarriages, which would indicate that when it comes to wedlock, we don't give up easily.

What is really happening here is that despite all attempts to create guilt, worries and disasters for families, they are continuing to knit themselves together like tapestries—in some cases, like crazy quilts—no matter what. And judging by the things people say they value about family life, things like commitment, forgiveness, humour, comfort, love, support, nurturing and protection of children, kindness, respect and a profound connection to others★—there is reason to believe that function, not form, is what ultimately defines a family best.

(★The above list of family values was compiled by Candace, Diana, Patrick and Douglas. It was inspired by Kim.)

## A RESPONSE TO "FAMILY MATTERS"

### Who's Vivian Smith trying to kid anyway?
### ("Family Matters"—Focus, *The Globe and Mail*, Oct. 5, 1996)

I found her paean to the brave new lesbian/homosexual conglomerate family with its picture of baby Kim held aloft—"Look Mom, Mom, Dad, Dad, no hands!"—ill conceived and unconvincing. Considering the faulty premises on which Ms. Smith has tried to base her approval of this untried model, my conclusion is hardly surprising.

Ms. Smith's bald statement, of either astonishing dishonesty or ignorance, "There is no such thing as an ideal family structure, and the one we think of as traditional—devoted mother and father, treasured kids—only exists as a nostalgic fantasy," signals another propaganda piece in *The Globe and Mail*'s ongoing campaign on behalf of the homosexual cause.

Unfortunately for the propagandists, the facts are not on their side. To give only a few examples:

Fact: Most married Canadians—e.g., 83 per cent—remain married to their original partners (Angus Reid, *The State of the Family in Canada,* June, 1994).

Fact: Compared to divorced and separated individuals, 82 per cent of married couples described their life as happy (Angus Reid, June, 1994).

Fact: The results of the authoritative University of Chicago study, *Sex in America* (1994), indicated that nearly 75 per cent of married men and 85 per cent of married women have been faithful to each other. (Compare this with the very low rates of monogamy—a proven factor in high abuse rates for kids—within the homosexual community.)

Fact: Children living with their biological parents are far less likely to be abused than those living with non-biologically-related adults ("Our Cheating Hearts," *Time*, Aug. 15, 1994).

Not only has traditional marriage/child-bearing-rearing proven to be comparatively safe environment for children and women (only two per cent of married women are abused by their husbands, Canadian Centre for Justice Statistics, 1993), across time and in all societies, this model has overwhelmingly proven to be the basis for personal and communal stability, a fact attested to in a companion article, "The Trouble With Men," also found in the Oct. 5 issue of *The Globe and Mail.*

In fact, from every reputable source these days the data confirm that as marriage has declined, the rates of child and partner abuse have increased dramatically. It is a fact—even Margaret Mead agrees—that the most reliable prescription for stable societies is the socialization of its young males. Across all cultures, the socialization of young men has been accomplished by married fatherhood, which reinforces both an alliance with the mother of their children and paternal investment in those children. Historically, children who live outside such an alliance have not generally fared well.

That the adult-centric "circle of love" so coyly photographed and so cozily described in Ms. Smith's article is at a far remove from this tried-and-true model (it may not be perfect, but it's the best we've been able to devise) puts baby Kim and other children of the counterculture in the unenviable position of being guinea pigs in an experiment of breath-taking audacity.

As a person who does treasure kids, I hope that things work out well for the children involved in these brash experiments. However, considering the horrendous fallout that the narcissism of the sexual revolution has wreaked upon our children over the past 30 years, such an outcome is far from a sure thing.

Judy Anderson,
Ontario Chapter President,
Real Women of Canada
Ottawa

# Being and Becoming

Earl G. Reidy

Who am I? What am I? These fundamental questions are commonly asked by people throughout the world many times during their lives. They are complex questions related to who and what we are as individuals and as part of groups. There are no simple answers. Each of us is unique, the result of a combination of many experiences and conditions, some learned, others influenced by our biology. In the natural and social sciences, the issue has often been over-simplified as a question of "nature" or "nurture." Frequently, today, those terms that relate to how we become who and what we are have been replaced by "essentialism" (the result of our nature or biology) and "social constructionism" (the result of social forces strongly influencing the construction of our identities), although the argument remains fundamentally the same.

Relatively early in our lives we begin to recognize, from urges within ourselves (our biology) and from external social forces (our family, peer group, the media, etc.), that our sexuality is a powerful force that helps to define our self concept, one which, as young people, we often find difficult to understand and manage. What we are usually unaware of is the degree to which social institutions play a crucial role in conditioning our biological urges and fashioning them into socially acceptable sexual behaviours that are always framed in a heterosexual context. In other words, we are taught through social influences by the family, the school, religion, the media, political, economic and other institutions to become erotically and affectionally attracted to persons of the opposite sex. There is a great deal of debate within the social scientific community about the extent to which our sexuality is the result of deliberate social engineering.

Until recently, there has been an almost unexamined assumption that human beings are naturally attracted (a result of our biology) sexually to persons of the opposite sex. Cross-cultural and cross-species studies have seriously challenged those assumptions. For example, Gilbert Herdt, an anthropologist studying a group he identifies as the Sambia in New Guinea, has documented social practices where all Sambian men are actively involved throughout their lives in what we would classify as

"Being and Becoming" is by the late Earl G. Reidy, formerly of Humber College. Used by permission.

same-sex (homosexual) behaviours that are socially acceptable and even necessary for the maintenance and survival of their society. A number of other studies illustrate similar situations in other societies and among our closest non-human, primate relatives.

Others have suggested that our sexual and affectional selves are the result of biology, that our sexuality is programmed either fully or largely by genetic factors. For example, a recent and highly controversial study by Simon Levay, an American pathologist, suggests that there may be some differences in brain size between gay and non-gay men. It is important to note, though, that Levay himself does not make any claims that this can be generalized to the total population. This, though, if proven, would indicate that we are "born with" certain potentials over which, as individuals, we have no control.

Sexual orientation, regardless of our gender, is a critical and complex part of who and what we are. To whom we are sexually and emotionally attracted is not a static one-time decision which we consciously make, although it may appear so. Most of us accept, without question, our society's assumption of heterosexuality. Some of us don't. A number of women and men throughout the world and throughout time have recognized that their sexual, affectional and erotic desires lean toward persons of the same sex either for a lifetime or for varying periods of their life.

Support groups help end a feeling of isolation.

The sexual identities available to us in Western culture include hetero-sexual (opposite sex), gay (male same-sex), lesbian (female same-sex) and bisexual (attraction to both sexes). It is important to note, though, that while a sexual/affectional identity is crucial in a person's life, it should not be the only criterion by which we evaluate ourselves or other people. We are all multidimensional.

It is unclear whether the process of self-definition is the same for all people even within a single culture. For example, a number of factors such as gender, social class, racial and ethnic group, and age, influence how we recognize, develop, accept or deny sexual and affectional feelings and desires.

Another difficulty in assessing our sexual and affectional identities is tied in with learning our gender roles. The social presentation of a male identity in Western culture, for example, often includes behaviours that deny males the opportunity to express emotional and affectional ties toward each other. Our culture tends not to do that to women as much; they are often encouraged to express their emotions. It has been suggested that this restriction is placed on males as a result of "patriarchal" (male domi-nated and controlled) social institutions that set up strict expectations of masculine behaviour as a means of defending and reinforcing male privilege and power. Such a defensive position produces very strong and negative attitudes toward males who may display any behaviours that are considered to be feminine, and thus weak. This, many feminist theorists tell us, supports the status quo, male power arrangement and keeps women sub-servient and males "in line." George Smith, a sociologist at the Ontario Institute for Studies in Education, says that one of the most important ways that North American society maintains a strict interpretation of masculinity is through what he calls the "ideology of fag." Perhaps you can recall using the term "fag" or hearing others use it. It is a powerful het-erosexist[1] and homophobic[2] weapon used to force males to conform to the dominant interpretation of acceptable masculinity. When a male be-gins to recognize that he is sexually and affectionally attracted to other males, he quickly realizes that he must hide this from others because he be-comes vulnerable to physical and verbal abuse. This form of self-protection is often referred to as being "in the closet." Women also report that they experience homophobic verbal and physical abuse that calls their femininity and sexual identities into question. The female equivalents of "fag" include "lezzie" or "dyke," derogatory and hurtful terms that are also used to reinforce male power since, according to patriarchal notions, women are supposed to seek and find their identity only in relation to males.

When does a person begin to recognize that he or she may not "fit" the expected heterosexual norm? That is a very difficult question to answer, since each person's development is so unique. However, it is important that we distinguish between same-sex feelings and a gay or lesbian identity. The Kinsey studies on male and female sexual behaviour, although flawed, are the most comprehensive and important pieces of research we have regarding the sexual behaviour of North American men and women. Kinsey and his researchers found that a number of men and women may have erotic or affectional feelings for people of the same sex for short or long periods of their lives, but never develop or assume a gay or lesbian identity.[3] Laud Humphreys, an American sociologist, discovered that many men who firmly identify as "straight" often participated in impersonal, same-sex behaviours. These findings reinforce the idea that how humans construct their sexual identities is very complex.

The *Ontario Human Rights Code* prohibits all types of discrimination against people on the basis of sexual orientation.

## KNOW YOUR RIGHTS

### Sexual Orientation and the Human Rights Code

The *Ontario Human Rights Code* prohibits discrimination on the basis of sexual orientation in services, goods and facilities; accommodation; employment; contracts; and vocational associations. This means that a person cannot be treated unequally in these areas because he or she is gay, lesbian, heterosexual or bisexual, for example.

The Code prohibits all types of unequal treatment, from the denial of a job, service or accommodation to comments, displays and jokes that may make an individual uncomfortable, because of his or her sexual orientation.

- If you were denied a service or treated unequally by a store, restaurant, theatre, club, government agency, school, hospital, dentist's or doctor's office or other provider of services, goods and facilities because of your sexual orientation...

- If you were denied employment or treated unequally in your place of work because of your sexual orientation...

- If you were denied accommodation or treated unequally by your landlord because of your sexual orientation...

Contact your local office of the Ontario Human Rights Commission. You may be able to file a complaint.

Current research indicates that recognition of a gay, lesbian or bisexual identity depends on a number of factors. My own studies of gay, male community college students regarding the development of their sexual identities confirm reports that males tend to realize earlier than females that their primary attraction is to persons of the same sex. Males report that they often knew about their difference during their elementary school years, but generally did not know what it meant nor even what to call it. Many of them said that since such feelings preceded any social knowledge of a gay identity, they believe they were "born that way." Females, on the other hand, report recognizing their lesbianism much later, sometimes after they had married and produced children.

Early recognition of a gay or lesbian state often produces, especially for young people, a great deal of confusion and pain as they begin to experience the negative, social response to gay and lesbian people that results in stigmatized status. These youths feel isolated because they don't know others like themselves and there are few visible role models to help them construct their sense of self as a lesbian or gay person. Most feel that they cannot turn to their families, friends, schools or other social groups for help. A 19-year-old male college student reported that when he told his mother he was gay, she told him, "I wish I had never given you birth."

Studies of Canadian and American gay and lesbian youths indicate that many of them consider, attempt or commit suicide as a result of extremely negative social pressures. A fortunate few, mostly those who grow up in big cities, may have access to gay and lesbian support groups, but many young people have to struggle, mostly alone, without the benefit of accurate information, to construct, deconstruct (as they get access to more information) and then reconstruct their identities, sometimes many times over. Among the many questions the youthful gay male or lesbian must grapple with, in addition to other concerns of growing up, are: am I gay or lesbian; what is a gay or lesbian; what is it like to be gay or lesbian; how does my gender identity as a male or female "fit into" being gay or lesbian; am I a bad person; what will this mean to my life, my relationships and my future; can I live with this identity? For gay males, the fear of HIV disease must also be confronted. This growth process can be made even more difficult as a result of religious, racial and ethnic group membership. Some gays and lesbians have been abused or rejected by their families, in extreme cases being declared actually dead, as a result of religious beliefs or because of attitudes that their families or other members of their racial/ethnic communities have brought with them from other cultures or social groups.

It is crucial to understand that a sexual identity is not just about sexuality; it becomes part of the person's core, inner-being and helps to structure how they see themselves and their relationships with the rest of the social world. Identities also differ for men and women. Once people work through the painful and difficult process of accepting their sexual identity, they need to integrate it with other aspects of their personality. This is the coming-out state that results from social interaction. Most major cities in the world have gay and lesbian communities that offer a variety of support services including groups for young gays and lesbians. It is within these communities that people begin to learn that they are not alone, that there are role models available to help in constructing their identity. Coming out is not a one-time event; it can be never-ending. There are parents, other family members, friends, business associates to tell or not tell. Gays and lesbians have to learn how to structure and live their partner relationships outside the social construction of marriage and how to explain their partner when they are asked to participate in social events and family gatherings. It can get very complicated.

For young men and women who identify as bisexuals, their lives become even more problematic. Drawn sexually and emotionally to people of both sexes, they are often misunderstood and shunned by the lesbian, gay and heterosexual communities.

Conditions for lesbians and gays in North America, and in some European countries, have improved significantly in recent years. This has largely been the result of political activities by lesbian and gay groups. In Canada, there is now federal and provincial legislation prohibiting discrimination; many union contracts contain anti-discrimination clauses; and almost every employment category—including the military and many religions—is now open to lesbians and gays. Popular culture, including literature, film and television, is now beginning to portray lesbians and gay men more positively, thus informing the public, helping to reduce negative and harmful stereotypes and producing more realistic role models for isolated youth. However, there still is resistance to providing accurate information to young people, especially in schools.

Unfortunately, it has also been necessary for police departments in some Canadian and American cities to develop "hate crime" units because of continuing violence, often referred to as "gay bashing," against lesbians and gay men who become scapegoats for others' insecurities. Systemic homophobia, often combined with sexism and racism, continues to be a problem for North American societies.

# Conclusion

In the development of "who we are," some men and women must come face-to-face with the recognition that they don't fit taken-for-granted expectations of a major part of their personality—their sexual identity. The process of "becoming" a sexual person, whether straight, bisexual, gay or lesbian is complex and may involve both biology and social learning acting in complicated and, as yet, largely unknown ways. For those who do recognize they do not fit the assumed heterosexual pattern, the development of their self-concept, their very identity as a person, frequently becomes, because of hostile social responses, extremely difficult and painful. More accurate and available information, support from family, friends and social institutions—especially schools—and greater social intolerance of homophobic verbal and physical abuse would make their lives far less problematic. Society must seriously question whether it can afford the incredibly high personal and social costs of prejudice and discrimination, whether directed against racial, ethnic or sexual minorities.

# Notes

[1] Heterosexism is usually defined as the assumption that everybody is heterosexual, and if they aren't, they should be.

[2] Homophobia is defined as an irrational hatred or fear of gay men and lesbians. Homophobia, as both a condition and a practice is, like sexism and racism, often well entrenched in social institutions and can be used to justify verbal and physical violence against lesbians and gay men.

[3] Results of a 1993 American study of American males, reported in *Time Magazine*, disputes the Kinsey findings. That survey, by the Batelle Human Affairs Research Centers in Seattle, Washington, noted that only 2.3 percent of the sample reported having sex with men in the past 10 years. The study has been widely criticized as being methodologically unsound. No figures were reported for females.

# UNIT 3

# The Individual and the Collective: Conflict and Cooperation

No man is an island entire of itself; every man is a piece of the continent, a part of the main. If a clod be washed away by the sea, Europe is the less, as well as if a promontory were, as well as if a manor of thy friend's or thine own were. Any man's death diminishes me, because I am involved in mankind, and therefore never send to know for whom the bell tolls; it tolls for thee.

*John Donne*

One always bakes the most delicate cakes
Two is the really superb masseur
Three sets your hair with exceptional flair
Four's brandy goes to the Emperor
Five knows each trick of advanced rhetoric
Six bred a beautiful brand-new rose
Seven can cook every dish in the book
And eight cuts you flawlessly elegant clothes
Do you think those eight would be happy
if each of them could climb so high
and no higher
before banging their heads on equality
if each could be only a small link
in a long and heavy chain
Do you still think it's possible
to unite mankind. . .

*Marquis de Sade in the play* Marat-Sade *by Peter Weiss,*
*adapted by Adrian Mitchell*

Out of timber so crooked as that from which man is made nothing entirely straight can be built.

*Immanuel Kant*

# Introduction

The central problem of any group of individuals that assembles to live together, as a collective, is balancing the conflicting claims of freedom and authority, of individual liberty and the needs of the community. How does a group organize itself so that the necessities of life are obtained and fairly distributed? How does it ensure that the weaker members of society are protected and provided for? How does a society ensure that one group or faction does not gain a disproportionate share of power? Who should govern? What are the responsibilities of citizens? The rights? These are the root questions of politics, and every government starts by recognizing the importance of these questions and proposes a system that resolves the conflict inherent in them. The answers suggested throughout history have been many and varied.

A framework proposed for the understanding of political life is a *political ideology* or philosophy. Such an ideology provides answers to the questions listed above. More importantly, it is made up of assumptions, either spelled out or taken for granted, about human nature, society and the universe as a whole. Whether drawn from Socrates or Aristotle, Hobbes or Locke, Rousseau or Marx, a political ideology provides a coherent structure of ideas about how people interact together. It paints a picture of how political communities work and, often, how an ideal society should function.

It is not the purpose of this book to study any of these ideologies in depth. Rather, it is to highlight the fact that different governments and political leaders embrace different ideologies and to remind students that the commentaries and articles that you read or hear reflect a particular ideological bias. These ideologies have consequences in the world in which you live, influencing health care, jobs, military expenditure, taxes—the list includes virtually every part of your daily life. Someone believing that human nature is essentially selfish would have very different views about government than someone who believes that human nature is essentially social and cooperative. It is important, therefore, to attempt to understand the ideas behind what people say. Individually and collectively, we are ultimately responsible for the government we get.

How, then, does an individual get behind the utterances of a politician or public figure to the core of his or her political ideology? Since every ideology addresses the fundamental issues addressed above, by asking these questions in a consistent fashion we can come to an understanding of any ideological position. While our list is certainly not complete, by looking for the answers to them in what people say and do, we can gain understanding of exactly what picture of reality they are working from.

| | |
|---|---|
| *Human Nature* | What are the fundamental characteristics of human nature? |
| *Society* | What are the fundamental characteristics of society? |
| *Change* | When is change needed and how should it be accomplished? |
| *Structure* | How are political communities organized and how should they be organized? To what purpose? |
| *Citizenship* | What should be the rights and responsibilities of citizens? |
| *Authority* | Who should govern society? Why? How should government authority be used? |
| *Justice* | How should the fruits of society be distributed? Why? |

These are the questions that any ideology attempts to answer. By asking them of those in government office, we can gain a better understanding of the ideas and beliefs that motivate them as well as predict what actions any particular individual might take if elected to office. It is through formulating our own answers to these questions that we can make informed choices about issues that matter.

In the first selection in this unit, "Politics in the Life of the Individual," you are invited to look at the political theories of several theorists whose ideas have had a significant impact on the evolution of Western political ideology. Thomas Hobbes, John Locke, Karl Marx and John Stuart Mill produced theories that provide the foundations for most Western governments. "The Great Law of Peace," furthermore, outlines the influence on the structure of the American government of the ideas of the legendary First Nations leader known as the Peacemaker. After this general introduction to these thinkers, we look at a number of related themes.

Perhaps the most urgent of these issues is the question of whether the ends ever justify the means. In other words, is it sometimes acceptable to use violence to fight injustice? This question is introduced in "Soul Force versus Physical Force" with reference to the conflicting views of Mahatma Gandhi and Martin Luther King, Jr., on one hand, and Malcolm X on the other.

A closely related issue is what is called the *politics of identity*. Our traditional concept of citizen, one who is aware of and cares about the issues facing society as a whole, is under attack. Faced with an ever growing complexity and a barrage of often conflicting and confusing information as a result of new communication technologies, individuals are retreating from involvement with the larger society. Instead, they seek comfort and understanding within smaller groups. Rather than identifying themselves as members of a particular country, individuals see themselves as primarily members of a particular racial, ethnic, linguistic or religious group. They may believe that the rights of their selected group take precedence over the more general interests of humankind: equal rights, respect for the dignity of the individual, universal satisfaction of basic needs, etc. In "A Cosmopolitan among the True Believers," Michael Ignatieff examines the reasons that lead individuals to place greater and greater emphasis on the characteristics that distinguish one group from another. As difference becomes more important, it becomes that much easier to deny the basic humanity of those not part of a given group.

This focus on difference results in intolerance, and it is the consequences of intolerance that are addressed by Mitchell Lerner in his essay, "On Inhumanity." As he discusses the horrors of genocide, the intent "to destroy, in whole or in part, a national, ethnic, racial or religious group," he forces the reader to confront our human capacity to become inhuman. A necessary precursor to genocide is the dehumanization of the "target" group. They, the Jews, the Tutsis, the Serbs . . . —we can fill in the blank—must first be made less than human. This will justify the removal of their basic rights and, ultimately, their right to life. The issues that both Ignatieff and Lerner raise are of immediate concern to the world within which we live. The overvaluing of difference leads to dehumanization, which, in turn, can all too easily lead to genocide.

Benjamin Barber, in his essay "Jihad vs. McWorld," focuses on the forces of change in the modern world. Looking at the tension between two major ideologies, capitalism and fundamentalism, he attempts to show that the victim of both forces is democracy. In what he calls the battle between the "bloody politics of identity" vs. the "bloodless economics of profit," Barber describes the assault on the modern nation, the one structure that has allowed democracy to take root and flourish. Capitalism, inherently destructive of traditional human values, seeks to maximize profit at any cost. Fundamentalism (exemplified by ethnic, tribal or religious fanatics) destroys common human values through intolerance and, once again, hatred directed at the "other."

Faced with such dismal portraits of humankind, what possible course of action can an individual take in this complex and confusing world? When we feel so isolated and powerless, what choice do we have but to seek solace in a group of like-minded individuals? It is easy to understand the reasons that societies fragment, because the attractiveness of choosing to be a part of an understandable group has an echo in all of us. The more difficult choice is to look for commonality, to struggle with the questions raised earlier and find answers to what is right and what is just. For this is the nature of living in communities—the only choice if human beings don't want to live in a fragmented, violent world. It is the nature of being human.

# Politics in the Life of the Individual

Morton Ritts

## Politics

As we saw in the previous unit, we live in a time of unprecedented change. Technology, demographics and the clash between old and new values are just some of the things that cause change. But so is something we haven't paid much attention to yet—politics. Whether we care or not, politics matters. Political decisions affect jobs, taxes, social policy, immigration and other current issues. Politics helps to define our society's notions of freedom, law and justice.

Politics isn't something that happens only at election time. Politics occurs when students protest higher tuition fees, business groups lobby for free trade, unions go on strike, women and minorities fight for employment equity, and governments act—or don't act.

In its broadest sense, politics refers to the complex relations among various members and groups in society. There is politics between you and your boss, you and your parents, you and your teachers, you and your boy- or girlfriend. Politics is about power—competing for it, sharing it, imposing it. We want power not simply because we want things our own way. We want power because it gives us the feeling that we have some control over our lives, that we are free.

Obviously certain individuals and groups in society are more powerful than others. What is the basis of this power? Does "might make right"? Does sex, race, wealth, intelligence, status or tradition? Or moral or religious authority? Or a commitment to ethical principles? In some way, these are all factors in determining how much or how little power people have.

## Government

Simply put, government is the mechanism that regulates power relations and the rights and duties of citizens and their rulers. According to the Greek philosopher Aristotle, there are basically three kinds of government:

"Politics in the Life of the Individual" is by Morton Ritts of Humber College. Used by permission.

government by one person; government by the few; and government by the many. Every government is an example of one of these three basic forms.

Whatever the case may be, some individuals and groups have more rights than others. And this in turn, as we've already suggested, depends to a large extent on a society's notions of freedom, law and justice. Later we'll examine how political thinkers like Thomas Hobbes, John Locke, John Stuart Mill and Karl Marx thought about these issues.

Whatever our political philosophy, however, we must acknowledge the role that government plays in our daily lives. Consider a government's monetary and fiscal policies, which affect everything from inflation to interest rates—in other words, everything from your ability to find a job to your ability to borrow money to start a business, or to buy a house or car.

At the same time, consider the degree to which a government is involved in economic and social matters. Those who argue for more state intervention claim that government investment in areas such as education, health care and transportation is vital for the national interest. They argue that government regulation is also necessary to ensure that businesses don't pollute the environment, treat employees unfairly or take advantage of consumers.

On the other hand, those who adopt a "laissez-faire," or hands-off approach, believe that government involvement in social and economic matters should be minimal and that it is best to allow the "market" to regulate itself.

Another important question about government is constitutional. How should power be divided among central, regional and local governments? Over the past 30 years in Canada, an extraordinary amount of energy has been devoted to the question of federal-provincial relations. Compared to other countries, Canada is already very decentralized, and many people who objected to the Meech Lake and Charlottetown agreements did so because they feared that these agreements would further weaken the federal government's power.

Of all forms of government, democracy (in theory at least) encourages the greatest redistribution of power and the greatest amount of change. In Canada and the United States, women, visible minorities, the disabled, aboriginals, environmentalists, gays and lesbians—all the groups we talked about in Unit 2—have been in the forefront of such controversial political issues as employment equity, human rights, land claims and same-sex benefits.

Of course, this kind of freedom to challenge the status quo and to fight for political change doesn't exist in every society. Freedom of speech and individual rights are values that we associate with liberal democracy. You don't have to look beyond the nearest headline or newscast to see that most of the time most governments around the world suppress human rights, crush dissent and persecute minorities.

When governments act this way, we often aren't surprised. Because many of us, consciously or otherwise, seem to accept self-interest as the norm in politics, we tend not to have a very high opinion of those who practise it. And too often their actions fail to shock us: patronage, corruption, dirty tricks, broken promises, slush funds, sex scandals—the dirty laundry list of unsavoury political practices, even in a liberal democracy, can turn us off any interest in politics at all.

## Apathy and Activism

apathy

lack of interest or concern

Many political theorists argue that such **apathy** is dangerous, however. Whether we vote or not, politics affects us in large and small ways. It determines the programs we watch on TV and the music we hear on the radio—because decisions about Canadian content are political decisions. It determines whether there is room for us at college or a job when we're finished—because education and employment policy decisions are political. So are decisions about how much money comes off our paycheques, what social programs our taxes will fund and which regions of the country will get them.

But apathy is only one response to the frustration that we may feel about how we are governed.  Another, and opposite, reaction is to become politically engaged. Such activism may even take the form of new political parties, like the Canadian Alliance or the Bloc, which capitalize on public discontent.

Of course, political activity isn't always legal or peaceful. The Los Angeles riots in the aftermath of the first Rodney King verdict were a spontaneous and violent expression of rage against the L.A. police and state authorities. In Quebec, the tense stand-off at Oka was the result of years of frustration by the Mohawks against all levels of Canadian government.

The ultimate reaction to an insensitive or unjust government is revolution. This occurs when governments lose touch with people and efforts at legal and peaceful reform have failed to produce a satisfactory redistribution of power. The consensus that has bound people together breaks down, and a new political structure is needed. The violent overthrow of the existing order is seen as the only way to make this happen.

# The Social Contract

Many of you may be familiar with the film *The Road Warrior* or the novel *Lord of the Flies*. In these and similar works, we're presented with a vision of the world in which law and order, morality and peace have broken down. In such apocalyptic, or end-of-the-world visions, life is ruled by naked power—by selfishness, fear, superstition, mistrust, brute force. Without the guiding authority of tradition, laws and institutions, without consensus, society may descend into anarchy.

For this reason, no political philosopher would argue that we should trade society for the raw state of nature—not even the great French social philosopher Jean Jacques Rousseau (1712–1778), whose writings contrast the natural goodness of people with the largely destructive impact of social institutions. But while Rousseau denounced his own artificial, class-ridden society with the famous words, "Man was born free, and everywhere he is in chains," he nevertheless understood that we are first and foremost social beings. We are united, he argued, by the arrangement that we make with each other to surrender at least some of our desires in exchange for at least some of our needs. Rousseau, Thomas Hobbes and John Locke called this arrangement "the social contract."

For them, the effectiveness of the social contract depends on our ability to obtain a satisfactory balance between what we want and what we're prepared to give up to get it. The social contract breaks down when people believe they're surrendering too much or not getting enough in return. Or when they lose the trust that binds them to others and to a government that may be incompetent, unfair or tyrannical.

In the absence of effective government, then, the social contract crumbles and no one has any security. Freedom, laws, justice and human rights are ignored, replaced by the social chaos of Bosnia and Rwanda. We need government to maintain the social contract, and we need the social contract if we want to survive.

# What Kind of Government Is Most Desirable?

The answer to this question depends on a number of things, but mainly what people believe to be the purpose of government. Is it to maintain peace and stability at any price? To promote a particular set of religious beliefs? To promote the interests of an elite, land-owning class? To preserve the rule of a king or queen? Or to guarantee freedom, rights, law and justice, which we have said are the underlying principles of liberal democracy?

Our definition of the most desirable form of government may depend on more than what we believe to be government's purpose. It may depend on some of the most fundamental questions that we ask about human nature. Are people good or bad? Are they ruled by reason or emotion? Which people are best suited to make decisions? How much freedom should ordinary people have? Are we motivated by self-interest or a desire to help others?

By the time we reach college, we have no doubt asked at least some of these questions to try to determine what kind of relationship ought to exist between ourselves and others in society, what we are willing to give up to fulfill our part of the social contract and what we expect in return.

Political philosophers since the time of Plato have tried to describe which arrangements they believe will make society function most effectively. And they often begin by trying to identify what motivates the social contract in the first place. Thomas Hobbes (1588–1679), for example, argued that it was primarily fear.

# The Fear Motive

Thomas Hobbes

Hobbes lived through a tumultuous period in English history when civil war had torn his country apart, and when law, order and security had broken down. The war reinforced Hobbes' view that people were naturally aggressive, violent and competitive, dominated by their emotions and instincts, or by what Freud would later call "the id."

Because this is human nature, Hobbes argued, people have the natural right to secure whatever they want by any means within their power. And, since we have unlimited desires and not enough resources, this leads us to inevitable conflict with others. Thus people live in a constant state of fear, and therefore their first impulse is to overpower others before being overpowered themselves. Hobbes described this state of nature before the social contract as a situation in which "every man is enemy to every man" and life is "solitary, poor, nasty, brutish and short."

Imagine that all laws in your city have been suspended for 24 hours and that the police are on strike. In effect, this would be a one-day "state of nature." Is this the time to fly off for a holiday? Or would you stay home with a shotgun and make sure that no one tried to grab your property? According to Hobbes, fear would keep you at home. What's more, he argued, you may decide to take this opportunity to relieve any defenceless neighbours of their property.

In other words, Hobbes said that we are indeed creatures of greed and passion who are driven by a desire to dominate and control. Hobbes painted a picture of human beings who are nothing more than pleasure-seeking machines. As such, they constantly seek to maximize pleasure and minimize pain.

But we're also reasonable creatures who realize that our interests are better served within a framework of law, morality, peace and security than in a state of violence and anarchy. Fear motivates us to agree to the social contract and to accept the power of government to enforce it. And the job of government, or what Hobbes called "the sovereign," is to make sure that the social contract doesn't become unstuck.

How much power should the sovereign, or governing authority, have over us? Hobbes believed that whether the sovereign is autocratic, oligarchic or democratic, it should have absolute power to do its job well. That means giving up not only some of our desires but also most of our rights—such as freedom of speech, the right to assembly and anything else that could threaten political and social stability. But, like Freud, Hobbes believed that such stability came at a price, although unlike Freud he thought the price was rarely too high.

Hobbes personally favoured autocracy as the most desirable form of government, believing that a single ruler could act far more efficiently than any government requiring the support of a fickle electorate and the unpredictable mechanics of democracy.

# The Property Motive

John Locke

Like Hobbes, John Locke (1632–1704) lived in a time of great social and political upheaval when the belief in an absolute monarch who ruled by divine right was being challenged and power was being transferred from the king to the people in the form of parliamentary democracy. Locke fully supported these radical changes.

Locke believed that all people are born free, equal, rational and moral. He also believed that we have certain God-given natural rights of life, liberty and property, which form the basis of the social contract and which it is the chief purpose of government to protect. To do so, it must be given the power to resolve conflicts and restrain violent and criminal acts. If the government fails to do its job properly, the people have the right to overthrow it—violently if necessary. To avoid this possibility, Locke advocated a system of checks and balances in which the branches of representative government are separate and distinct.

Locke's ideas on natural rights had an influence that extended well beyond the development of liberal democracy in England. They also helped to shape the thinking of the leaders of the American Revolution in their fight for independence. Indeed, Locke's theory that natural rights form the basis of the social contract is the **ideology** of liberal democracies everywhere, particularly in the United States where individual rights are paramount. The core of these rights, Locke argued, is private property.

But what exactly is private property? And why is it the defining feature of that economic system we call capitalism? Private property is more than the piece of land we own or the house we live in. It is, Locke said, whatever "we mix with our labour." It includes "the labour of [our] body and the work of [our] hands." It is also the fruits of our labour—the products we make and the goods we buy. They belong to us because we've earned them.

For Locke, private property is important because it defines the boundaries of individual freedom. Within the boundaries of their property, the individual has the right to do as he or she wishes and the state has no right to intrude. This principle may seem obvious to us, to the point where we take it for granted. But it wasn't always the case, certainly not before Locke's time, when land defined wealth and most of the land was owned by a relatively small aristocratic elite or the sovereign.

Locke believed in extending the right of private ownership beyond the privileged few. In doing so, he also endorsed the right to privacy itself, a mainstay of a free and open society. In 1968, Prime Minister Pierre Trudeau echoed Locke's view when he proclaimed, "The state has no business in the bedrooms of the nation." In the privacy of our own homes, Trudeau meant, the state has no business defining what is acceptable or unacceptable sexual behaviour between consenting adults. (Locke, of course, could never have anticipated how the rapid growth of technology in the latter part of the twentieth century made us more vulnerable than ever to invasions of privacy. The "information highway" allows governments, corporations and individuals to gain access to our bank accounts, medical records, political affiliations and other forms of highly personal information. Despite the warnings of the federally appointed Privacy Commissioner, we are becoming an increasingly closely monitored society.)

**ideology**

system of beliefs

As industrial capitalism in Western Europe and North America developed, Locke's notion of ownership and private property was expanded to include the tools, machines, factories, transportation systems, capital and human resources that made further accumulation of property possible. But clearly not everyone benefitted under such a system, and the freedom, rights, laws and justice that protected the privileged minority class did not extend to the masses.

So where Locke saw private property as the basis of freedom, socialist thinkers like Karl Marx saw it as the basis of exploitation. And where Locke argued that property was the basis of liberty, Marx replied that it was the basis of inhumanity. According to Marx, private ownership created an intolerable conflict between the "haves" and "have-nots." The only way to eliminate this conflict was to eliminate private property.

# The Class Motive

Born in Germany and living much of his life in exile, Karl Marx (1818–1883) analyzed the great divide in terms of wealth and power between the owner/capitalist class and the workers or proletariat. Rejecting Locke's view of the sanctity of individual ownership, Marx called for a revolution to redistribute social, economic and political power. According to Marx, history showed that it was not natural rights that defined the nature of our relationship to society. It was class status—rich and poor, haves and have-nots, the powerful and the powerless. To resolve the conflict between the classes and re-organize the social order in a way that guaranteed true freedom, rights and justice, it was necessary to abolish private property.

Karl Marx

Marx disagreed with those historians and political philosophers who contend that our innate human nature predisposes us to one kind of society or another. According to Marx, it is the other way round: the kind of society we live in determines our consciousness, or how we act and think. If people are selfish and greedy, the reason has little to do with human nature and much to do with social conditions.

As proof, Marx turned to capitalism. Throughout industrialized Europe, Marx saw men, women and children working long hours in unsafe mines and factories for wages that were a fraction of what their labour entitled them to. They had no pensions, health insurance or safety protection. They had no collective agreements, job security or social safety net. Capitalism, Marx argued, really offered only two possibilities: be a loser or a winner, exploit others or be exploited yourself.

Marx believed that this "survival of the fittest" mentality was the very essence of industrial capitalism. The division of labour and alienation that turned workers into products, into property belonging to someone else, destroyed the human spirit and caused untold suffering. If life is a Hobbesian war of all against all, it is not, according to Marx, human nature that causes this war but a society based on class conflict.

Marx did not look to government or the church to change this situation. In his view, government, religion, media, the education system—all the institutions of capitalist society—served the interests of the owners who controlled them and kept the workers in their place. Marx was especially critical of the role played by organized religion ("the opiate of the people"), which, he said, made people passive and accepting of their misery in this life by promising them rewards in the next.

But there is no afterlife, Marx argued, only this one. And he looked to the proletariat to lead the revolution that would destroy class conflict, eradicate scarcity and alter the course of world history: "Workers of the world unite!" he wrote in *The Communist Manifesto*, adding, "You have nothing to lose but your chains!"

Marx's view of history led him to reason that just as slavery had given way to feudalism, and feudalism to capitalism, so too capitalism would inevitably lead to socialism. Under socialism, ownership of the means of production would be collective, not private. Under socialism, the welfare of people would come before profit, and everyone would share in society's resources and wealth—"from each according to his abilities, to each according to his needs." Beyond socialism lay the "classless society" of communism, the promised land where, according to Marx, the state itself would "wither away."

Marx's influence on the twentieth century is undeniable. Until the collapse of the Soviet Union, over a third of the world's population claimed to be living under some form of communism. But whether Marx would have been happy with those who have practised what he preached is highly unlikely. Communist revolutions in Europe, Asia, Latin America and Africa have resulted in nothing like the free, classless and just societies that Marx envisioned.

Nevertheless, Marx's socialist ideals have had a profound impact on capitalism itself. Today free schooling to age 16, government loans and scholarships after that, universal health care and progressive taxation policies are characteristic of many capitalist societies. And so is the belief in a mixed economy of public and private ownership. Ironically, Marx's legacy may have been to help renew the very capitalist system that he was so certain was doomed.

# The Happiness Motive

For John Stuart Mill (1806–1879), yet another English political theorist, the purpose of life was the pursuit of happiness. And this, not natural rights or class conflict, is the guiding principle of human action. According to Mill's "utilitarian" philosophy (derived from Jeremy Bentham [1748–1832]), actions are good if they promote the greatest happiness for the greatest number of people. But this position doesn't include just any kind of happiness. Mill argued that some types of happiness are better than others; as he said, "it is better to be a human being dissatisfied than a pig satisfied." In other words, it is better to aspire to intellectual and aesthetic pleasures than to simply satisfy physical desire. Mill believed that a society that valued rights, laws and justice was the best guarantee of both individual and collective happiness.

John Stuart Mill

In what kind of society can happiness best be achieved? A society, Mill argued, liberal enough to allow individuals maximum freedom to do whatever they wanted, as long as their actions don't harm others. Because he believed that people are basically decent and by nature are rational, cooperative and sensitive to the needs of others, Mill trusted people's ability to choose what they thought best for themselves. And what is "best," of course, is whatever makes people happy.

Mill argued that the primary job of government was to preserve individual rights and freedoms. He rejected the libertarian notion that government should simply stand back and let people fend for themselves. He advocated instead the idea of government intervention—not to tell people what to do or to curtail their liberty—but rather to provide the means for them to make choices through enlightened education, progressive laws and a fair justice system.

As we have already suggested, Mill believed that once government had made the advantages of liberal democracy available to all, it should restrain an individual's actions *only* when they significantly harmed or interfered with the actions, interests or liberty of others. But some of us may have problems with the "harm principle." For example, how can we be sure when you smoke that I, a non-smoker, am not harmed? You can argue that you'll take responsibility if you get lung cancer. But your second-hand smoke can give me lung cancer too. So where does your right to smoke end and my right to clean air begin?

You might also argue that the government has no right to enforce measures of individual choice like whether you wear a seat-belt. You may say you'll take your chances in your own car, thank you very much. But if you go through the windshield, whose tax dollars will help to pay for your rehabilitation—assuming you survive?

And then, of course, there's the issue of freedom of speech. Does free speech mean that you have the right to say things that could threaten the interests, rights and even physical well-being of certain racial, religious or other groups?

Mill's "harm principle" does not deal fully with problems resulting from the impact that an individual's actions may have on others (abortion is an even more troubling example). However, Mill did anticipate objections to his utilitarian principle of "the greatest happiness for the greatest number."

You may recall that in Unit 2 we noted how the ideas, customs, laws, privileges and opportunities that bring happiness to the greatest number in society can sometimes bring misery to minorities. Mill acknowledged the potential dangers of this "tyranny of the majority." He believed, therefore, that a democratic society should not only be liberal (i.e., promote individual rights), but should also be representative and pluralistic (i.e., safeguard minority rights).

Unlike Marx, Mill did not call for the demise of capitalism. Nor did he view history as a class conflict between owners and workers, haves and have-nots. The issue for Mill was the conflict between individual freedom and government control. Mill believed strongly that in this struggle the balance of power should rest with the individual because the purpose of government was to serve the people, not the other way round.

## THOMAS HOBBES

Whatsoever therefore is consequent to a time of war, where every man is enemy to every man; the same is consequent to the time, wherein men live without other security, than what their own strength, and their own invention shall furnish them withal. In such condition, there is no place for industry; because the fruit thereof is uncertain: and consequently no culture of the earth; no navigation, nor use of the commodities that may be imported by sea; no commodious building; no instruments of moving, and removing, such things as require much force; no knowledge of the face of the earth; no account of time; no arts; no letters; no society; and which is worst of all, continual fear, and danger of violent death; and the life of man, solitary, poor, nasty, brutish, and short.

Thomas Hobbes, *Leviathan*

## JOHN LOCKE

The great and chief end, therefore, of men's uniting into commonwealths and putting themselves under government is the preservation of their property. To which in the state of nature there are many things wanting:

First, There wants an established, settled, known law, received and allowed by common consent to be the standard of right and wrong and the common measure to decide all controversies between them. . . .

Secondly, In the state of nature there wants a known and indifferent judge with authority to determine all differences according to the established law. . . .

Thirdly, In the state of nature, there often wants power to back and support the sentence when right, and to give it due execution. . . .

Men . . . enter into society . . . the better to preserve himself, his liberty and property— . . . the power of the society, or legislative constituted by them, can never be supposed to extend farther than the common good. . . . And so whoever has the legislative or supreme power of any commonwealth is bound to govern by established standing laws, promulgated and known to the people, and not by extemporary decrees. . . .

John Locke, *Second Treatise on Government*

## KARL MARX

The State, therefore, has not existed from all eternity. There have been societies which managed without it, which had no conception of the State and State power. At a certain stage of economic development, which was necessarily bound up with the cleavage of society into classes, the State became a necessity owing to this cleavage.

As the State arose out of the need to hold class antagonisms in check, but as it, at the same time, arose in the midst of the conflict of these classes, it is, as a rule, the State of the most powerful, economically dominant class, which by virtue thereof becomes also the dominant class politically, and thus acquires new means of holding down and exploiting the oppressed class. Thus the ancient State was above all the slaveowners' State for holding down the slaves, as a feudal State was the organ of the nobles for holding down the peasantry, bondmen and serfs and the modern representative State is the instrument of the exploitation of wage-labour by capital.

Karl Marx, *The German Ideology*

# JOHN STUART MILL

The object of this Essay is to assert one very simple principle, as entitled to govern absolutely the dealings of society with the individual in the way of compulsion and control, whether the means used be physical force in the form of legal penalties, or the moral coercion of public opinion. *That principle is, that the sole end for which mankind are warranted, individually or collectively, in interfering with the liberty of action of any of their number, is self-protection.*[1] That the only purpose for which power can be rightfully exercised over any member of a civilized community, against his will, is to prevent harm to others. His own good, either physical or moral, is not a sufficient warrant. He cannot rightfully be compelled to do or forbear because it will be better for him to do so, because it will make him happier, because, in the opinion of others, to do so would be wise, or even right. These are good reasons for remonstrating with him or reasoning with him, or persuading him, or entreating him, but not compelling him, or visiting him with any evil, in case he do otherwise. To justify that, the conduct from which it is desired to deter him, must be calculated to produce evil to someone else. The only part of the conduct of anyone, for which he is amenable to society, is that which concerns others. In the part which merely concerns himself, his independence is, of right, absolute. Over himself, over his own body and mind, the individual is sovereign.

✳✳✳✳✳

The worth of a State, in the long run, is the worth of the individuals composing it; and a State which postpones the interests of *their* mental expansion and elevation to a little more of administrative skill, or of that semblance of it which practice gives, in the details of business; a State which dwarfs its men, in order that they may be more docile instruments in its hands even for beneficial purposes—will find that with small men no great thing can really be accomplished; and that the perfection of machinery to which it has sacrificed everything will in the end avail it nothing, for want of the vital power which, in order that the machine might work more smoothly, it has preferred to banish.

John Stuart Mill, *On Liberty*

# Notes

[1] Italics are the editor's.

# Soul Force versus Physical Force

## Morton Ritts

Marx argued that social change could only come about as a result of revolutionary economic change. Mill, on the other hand, believed that social change was the result of enlightened political reform. Like Mill, Mahatma Gandhi (1869–1948) was also a reformer. But he believed that social change was the result of spiritual change—a transformation of the soul that would be the basis of a new and truly just social order.

This revolutionary idea was embodied in Gandhi's criticism of the Hindu caste system, which separated people into various classes from Brahmin at the upper end to the Untouchables at the lower. Rejecting his own high-caste background, Gandhi sought to eliminate the enormous social divisions created by such a hierarchy and replace them with a classless society (similar to Marx's) that affirmed the brotherhood and sisterhood of all.

Gandhi had a very benign view of human nature, believing that people are good, the world is ultimately just and that peaceful political change is eminently possible. According to Gandhi, real and lasting change was achieved not through violence but through the Hindu principle of "ahimsa," or non-violence. Gandhi believed that "ahimsa" was a universal spiritual force within all humans that could be awakened by example.

The way to awaken the conscience of one's oppressor was through non-violent acts of civil disobedience that Gandhi called "satyagraha"—"soul force" as opposed to "body force." This turning of the other cheek wasn't some masochistic invitation to be beaten by the police or army during strikes, mass demonstrations or marches. Instead, satyagraha was a way to change an enemy's hatred to love, his or her resistance to acceptance.

Despite his charismatic leadership and his great victory in gaining Indian independence from Britain in 1948, Gandhi's non-violent politics of liberation has its critics. Theorists who side with Darwin, Freud or Hobbes think Gandhi's views of human nature and political change are naive and simplistic. Moreover, they argue that while non-violence may have been successful in the struggle against British colonialism, it would have been useless against the radical evil of Nazi Germany. Gandhi's harshest critics believed him to be an impractical and even dangerous idealist.

"Soul Force versus Physical Force" is by Morton Ritts of Humber College. Used by permission.

# "We Are All Created Equal"

But Gandhi has had his supporters—social reformers inspired by his spirituality and the philosophy of satyagraha. One man who was strongly influenced by Gandhi was the American civil rights leader, Martin Luther King Jr. (1929–1968). Like Gandhi, King believed in the innate goodness of human nature, that "we are all God's children," and that the universe is a moral and just place.

One of the great public speakers in American history, King was a Baptist minister from the American South steeped in the prophetic tradition of the Bible, which he saw as a narrative of liberation and deliverance. King's Jesus was a social activist who championed the rights of the poor and downtrodden. It wasn't difficult for King to identify with Gandhi's struggle against the bondage of colonialism. After all, the United States was a country that claimed to be a beacon of freedom and equality, but a hundred years after the Civil War, black Americans had a long way to go before they could enjoy the "liberty, equality and freedom" that the Constitution promised everyone.

Like Marx, King saw the struggle between haves and have-nots as the defining feature of history. But unlike Marx, for whom religion was an oppressive institution, King saw religion as a liberating force that led to social and political change. He believed that white America was ultimately a just society but, like Gandhi, disagreed with Marx's ideology of violent revolution. Violence, he argued, led only to more violence. It could never form the basis of a viable social contract.

King believed it was possible to achieve his goal of an integrated society by changing people's hearts and minds. Reform the spirit, he preached, and you will reform the attitudes and laws that bar blacks from being part of the American Dream. Few leaders in the world today dare to talk about issues like rights and freedom in a spiritual context. King did, and succeeded in raising the debate over justice to a level of moral significance not seen in American political culture since the time of Lincoln.

In his famous "Letter" from Birmingham Jail, where he was briefly imprisoned for breaking a local ordinance against political demonstrations, King pointed out that there were two kinds of laws: just and unjust. Just laws were those that uplifted the human spirit. People have a legal and moral obligation to obey them. Unjust laws, on the other hand, were those that degraded the human spirit—laws that prohibited blacks from using "whites only" washrooms and restaurants, or denied

Martin Luther King

them the same opportunities as whites for employment, housing and education.  According to King, we have a moral responsibility to actively disobey unjust laws.

His argument has profound implications for human behaviour. For example, if more people had acted like Oscar Schindler and resisted the laws and official directives that sent millions to the Nazi death camps in World War II, they could have changed the course of history. King's moral universe of civil disobedience based on principle exists in direct contrast to the usual political motives of expedience and self-interest.

But for King, as we've said, civil disobedience had to be non-violent. Like Gandhi, he had no doubt that soul force was stronger than physical force, loving one's enemy the only way to truly humanize and change him. Throughout the late 1950s and 1960s, King helped to organize countless voter registration drives, freedom rides, sit-ins, marches and rallies involving thousands of black and white Americans who were often harassed, threatened, beaten, arrested and killed for their efforts.

In the end, the civil rights movement stirred the conscience of America and the world. Landmark civil rights legislation was introduced in 1965 and King won the Nobel Peace Prize. But he paid dearly. He was assassinated in 1968. Like Moses, he led his long-suffering people to the Promised Land, and, like Moses, he didn't live to enter.

# "By Any Means Necessary"

Martin Luther King promoted non-violence as the means to reform an unjust society because, like Gandhi, he believed in the fundamental decency of human nature and in a world where, in the end, good triumphs over evil. But just as Gandhi had his critics, so did King. And since his death some of their voices seem to speak more loudly to black Americans than his.

In the United States today, for example, the Nation of Islam has a powerful following among those African-Americans who argue that racial integration can't work, that the separation of black and white races is both desirable and necessary, and that blacks must reconnect with their African roots. If such views sound surprising in light of King's reputation, it is important to remember that even at the height of the civil rights movement's popularity, King was only one of several major African-American leaders who didn't always agree on ideology or strategy. One of King's major rivals for the loyalty of black Americans was Malcolm X (1925–1965).

Malcolm X's critical analysis of white American society and his prescription for change differed radically from King's. Malcolm X came into contact with the ideas of the Nation of Islam while in prison. Subsequently, he changed his surname from "Little" to "X" to indicate that, as the descendant of slaves, he'd been stripped of his ancestral identity.

Once out of prison, he soon became chief spokesman for the Nation of Islam and its founder, Elijah Muhammad. In brilliant speeches that were inflammatory and confrontational, Malcolm X condemned white people as "blue-eyed devils" who could never be trusted. He rejected Christianity as a racist, oppressive, "white man's religion" that didn't speak to the true black identity, which was African. King and other black Christians had "sold out," Malcolm X said.

The philosophy of the Nation of Islam stressed the need for black pride, independence, discipline and power. These could be achieved if African-Americans challenged whites on their own terms by developing their own banks and businesses, their own churches and schools, their own social and cultural support systems. Only through "black power" would African-Americans gain the freedom, justice and equality that was their right.

For the Nation of Islam, black power meant separation, not integration. Black Muslims also disagreed with King's philosophy of non-violence.

Self-preservation "by any means necessary" was justified, Malcolm X said. This meant fighting back, not turning the other cheek.

In 1964, Malcolm X went to Mecca in Saudi Arabia, the spiritual capital of Islam. There he met Muslims of all races and nations worshipping together in peace, equality and dignity. The experience moved him to reject racial hatred as a liberation strategy. He began to view the struggle against oppression in universal terms, not exclusively African-American.

After returning to the United States, he broke with Elijah Muhammad and the Nation of Islam, becoming an orthodox Sunni Muslim who believed that the social order should embrace all peoples. It was while preaching this new message of hope and solidarity that he was gunned down on February 21, 1965. He was 40 years old. Malcolm X, Martin Luther King and Mahatma Gandhi may have shared similar violent ends, but their words and actions continue to haunt and shape contemporary politics.

# By Any Means Necessary

## Malcolm X

You make my point, that as long as a white man does it, it's all right. A Black man is supposed to have no feelings. So when a Black man strikes back, he's an extremist. He's supposed to sit passively and have no feelings, be nonviolent, and love his enemy. No matter what kind of attack, be it verbal or otherwise, he's supposed to take it. But if he stands up and in any way tries to defend himself, then he's an extremist.

No, I think that the speaker who preceded me is getting exactly what he asked for. My reason for believing in extremism—intelligently directed extremism, extremism in defence of liberty, extremism in quest of justice—is because I firmly believe in my heart that the day that the Black man takes an uncompromising step and realizes that he's within his rights, when his own freedom is being jeopardized, to use any means necessary to bring about his freedom or put a halt to that injustice, I don't think he'll be by himself.

I live in America, where there are only 22 million Blacks against probably 160 million whites. One of the reasons that I'm in no way reluctant or hesitant to do whatever is necessary to see that Black people do something to protect themselves [is that] I honestly believe that the day that they do, many whites will have more respect for them. And there will be more whites on their side than are now on their side with this little wishy-washy "love-thy-enemy" approach that they've been using up to now.

And if I'm wrong, then you are racialists.

As I said earlier, in my conclusion, I'm a Muslim. I believe in the religion of Islam, I believe in Allah, I believe in Muhammad, I believe in all of the prophets. I believe in fasting, prayer, charity, and that which is incumbent upon a Muslim to fulfill in order to be a Muslim. In April I was fortunate to make the **hajj** to Mecca, and went back again in September to try and carry out my religious functions and requirements.

But at the same time that I believe in that religion, I have to point out I'm also an American Negro, and I live in a society whose social

hajj

pilgrimage to Mecca

system is based upon the castration of the Black man, whose political system is based on castration of the Black man, and whose economy is based upon the castration of the Black man. A society which, in 1964, has more subtle, deceptive, deceitful methods to make the rest of the world think that it's cleaning up its house, while at the same time the same things are happening to us in 1964 that happened in 1954, 1924, and in 1894.

They came up with what they call a civil rights bill in 1964, supposedly to solve our problem, and were murdered in cold blood. And the FBI head, [J. Edgar] Hoover, admits that they know who did it. They've known ever since it happened, and they've done nothing about it. Civil rights bill down the drain. No matter how many bills pass, Black people in that country where I'm from—still, our lives are not worth two cents. And the government has shown its inability, or its unwillingness, to do whatever is necessary to protect life and property where the Black American is concerned.

So my contention is that whenever a people come to the conclusion that the government which they have supported proves itself unwilling or proves itself unable to protect our lives and protect our property because we have the wrong colour skin, we are not human beings unless we ourselves band together and do whatever, however, whenever is necessary to see that our lives and our property is protected. And I doubt that any person in here would refuse to do the same thing, were he in the same position. Or I should say, were he in the same condition.

Just one step farther to see, am I justified in this stand? And I say, I'm speaking as a Black man from America, which is a racist society. No matter how much you hear it talk about democracy, it's as racist as South Africa or as racist as Portugal, or as racist as any other racialist society on this earth. The only difference between it and South Africa: South Africa preaches separation and practises separation; America preaches integration and practises segregation. This is the only difference. They don't practise what they preach, whereas South Africa preaches and practises the same thing. I have more respect for a man who lets me know where he stands, even if he's wrong, than one who comes up like an angel and is nothing but a devil.

The system of government that America has consists of committees. There are sixteen senatorial committees that govern the country and twenty congressional committees. Ten of the sixteen senatorial committees are in the hands of southern racialists, senators who are racialists.

Thirteen of the twenty congressional committees were in the hands of southern congressmen who are racialists. Which means out of the thirty-six committees that govern the foreign and domestic direction of that government, twenty-three are in the hands of southern racialists—men who in no way believe in the equality of man, and men who would do anything within their power to see that the Black man never gets to the same seat or to the same level that they are on.

The reason that these men from that area have that type of power is because America has a seniority system. And these who have that seniority have been there longer than anyone else because the Black people in the areas where they live can't vote. And it is only because the Black man is deprived of his vote that puts these men in positions of power, that gives them such influence in the government beyond their actual intellectual or political ability, or even beyond the number of people from the areas that they represent.

So we can see in that country that no matter what the federal government professes to be doing, the power of the federal government lies in these committees. And any time any kind of legislation is proposed to benefit the Black man or give the Black man his just due, we find it is

Malcolm X

locked up in these committees right here. And when they let something through the committee, usually it is so chopped up and fixed up that by the time it becomes law, it's a law that can't be enforced.

Another example is the Supreme Court desegregation decision that was handed down in 1954. This is a law, and they have not been able to implement this law in New York City, or in Boston, or in Cleveland, or Chicago, or the northern cities. And my contention is that any time you have a country, supposedly a democracy, supposedly the land of the free and the home of the brave, and it can't enforce laws—even in the northernmost, cosmopolitan, and progressive part of it—that will benefit a Black man, if those laws can't be enforced, how much heart do you think we will get when they pass some civil rights legislation which only involves more laws? If they can't enforce this law, they will never enforce those laws.

So my contention is that we are faced with a racialistic society, a society in which they are deceitful, deceptive, and the only way we can bring about a change is to talk the kind of language—speak the language that they understand. The racialists never understand a peaceful language. The racialist never understands the nonviolent language. The racialist we have, he's spoken his language to us for 400 years.

We have been the victim of his brutality. We are the ones who face his dogs that tear the flesh from our limbs, only because we want to enforce the Supreme Court decision. We are the ones who have our skulls crushed, not by the Ku Klux Klan but by policemen, only because we want to enforce what they call the Supreme Court decision. We are the ones upon whom water hoses are turned, with pressure so hard that it rips the clothes from our backs—not men, but the clothes from the backs of women and children. You've seen it yourselves. Only because we want to enforce what they call the law.

Well, any time you live in a society supposedly based upon law, and it doesn't enforce its own law because the colour of a man's skin happens to be wrong, then I say those people are justified to resort to any means necessary to bring about justice where the government can't give them justice.

I don't believe in any form of unjustified extremism. But I believe that when a man is exercising extremism, a human being is exercising extremism in defence of liberty for human beings, it's no vice. And when one is moderate in the pursuit of justice for human beings, I say he's a sinner.

And I might add, in my conclusion—In fact, America is one of the best examples, when you read its history, about extremism. Old Patrick Henry said, "Liberty or death!" That's extreme, very extreme.

I read once, passingly, about a man named Shakespeare. I only read about him passingly, but I remember one thing he wrote that kind of moved me. He put it in the mouth of Hamlet, I think it was, who said, "To be or not to be"—he was in doubt about something. "Whether it was nobler in the mind of man to suffer the slings and arrows of outrageous fortune"—moderation—"or take up arms against a sea of troubles and by opposing end them."

And I go for that. If you take up arms, you'll end it. But if you sit around and wait for the one who's in power to make up his mind that he should end it, you'll be waiting a long time.

And in my opinion the young generation of whites, blacks, browns, whatever else there is—you're living at a time of extremism, a time of revolution, a time when there's got to be a change. People in power have misused it, and now there has to be a change and a better world has to be built, and the only way it's going to be built is with extreme methods. And I for one will join in with anyone. I don't care what colour you are, as long as you want to change this miserable condition that exists on this earth.

# Non-Violent Resistance

Mohandas K. (Mahatma) Gandhi

## Means and Ends

*Reader:* Why should we not obtain our goal, which is good, by any means whatsoever, even by using violence? Shall I think of the means when I have to deal with a thief in the house? My duty is to drive him out anyhow. You seem to admit that we have received nothing, and that we shall receive nothing by petitioning. Why, then, may we not do so by using brute force? And, to retain what we may receive we shall keep up the fear by using the same force to the extent that it may be necessary. You will not find fault with a continuance of force to prevent a child from thrusting its foot into fire? Somehow or other we have to gain our end.

*Gandhi:* Your reasoning is plausible. It has deluded many. I have used similar arguments before now. But I think I know better now, and I shall endeavour to undeceive you. Let us first take the argument that we are justified in gaining our end by using brute force because the English gained theirs by using similar means. It is perfectly true that they use brute force and that it is possible for us to do likewise, but by using similar means we can get only the same thing that they got. You will admit that we do not want that. Your belief that there is no connection between the means and the end is a great mistake. Through that mistake even men who have been considered religious have committed grievous crimes. Your reasoning is the same as saying that we can get a rose through planting a noxious weed. If I want to cross the ocean, I can do so only by means of a vessel; if I were to use a cart for that purpose, both the cart and I would soon find the bottom. "As is the God, so is the **votary**," is a maxim worth considering. Its meaning has been distorted and men have gone astray. The means may be likened to a seed, the end to a tree; and there is just the same inviolable connection between the means and the end as there is between the seed and the tree. I am not likely to obtain the result flowing from the worship of God by laying myself prostrate before Satan. If, therefore, any one were to say: "I want to worship God; it

Gandhi

**votary**

a person bound by vows to live a life of religious worship

"Non-Violent Resistance" is reprinted by permission of Navajivan Trust and Mahatma Gandhi Estate.

does not matter that I do so by means of Satan," it would be set down as ignorant folly. We reap exactly as we sow. The English in 1833 obtained greater voting power by violence. Did they by using brute force better appreciate their duty? They wanted the right of voting, which they obtained by using physical force. But real rights are a result of performance of duty; these rights they have not obtained. We, therefore, have before us in England the force of everybody wanting and insisting on his rights, nobody thinking of his duty. And where everybody wants rights, who shall give them to whom? I do not wish to imply that they do no duties. They don't perform the duties corresponding to those rights; and as they do not perform that particular duty, namely, acquire fitness, their rights have proved a burden to them. In other words, what they have obtained is an exact result of the means they adopted. They used the means corresponding to the end. If I want to deprive you of your watch, I shall certainly have to fight for it; if I want to buy your watch, I shall have to pay for it; and if I want a gift, I shall have to plead for it; and, according to the means I employ, the watch is stolen property, my own property, or a donation. Thus we see three different results from three different means. Will you still say that means do not matter?

Now we shall take the example given by you of the thief to be driven out. I do not agree with you that the thief may be driven out by any means. If it is my father who has come to steal I shall use one kind of means. If it is an acquaintance I shall use another; and in the case of a perfect stranger I shall use a third. If it is a white man, you will perhaps say you will use means different from those you will adopt with an Indian thief. If it is a weakling, the means will be different from those to be adopted for dealing with an equal in physical strength; and if the thief is armed from top to toe, I shall simply remain quiet. Thus we have a variety of means between the father and the armed man. Again, I fancy that I should pretend to be sleeping whether the thief was my father or that strong armed man. The reason for this is that my father would also be armed and I should succumb to the strength possessed by either and allow my things to be stolen. The strength of my father would make me weep with pity; the strength of the armed man would rouse in me anger and we should become enemies. Such is the curious situation. From these examples we may not be able to agree as to the means to be adopted in each case. I myself seem clearly to see what should be done in all these cases, but the remedy may frighten you. I therefore hesitate to place it before you. For the time being I will leave you to guess it, and if you cannot, it is clear you will have to adopt different means in each case. You will also have seen that any means will not avail to drive away the thief. You will have to adopt means to fit each case. Hence it follows that your duty is not to drive away the thief by any means you like.

Let us proceed a little further. That well-armed man has stolen your property; you have harboured the thought of his act; you are filled with anger; you argue that you want to punish that rogue, not for your own sake, but for the good of your neighbours; you have collected a number of armed men, you want to take his house by assault; he is duly informed of it, he runs away: he too is incensed. He collects his brother robbers, and sends you a defiant message that he will commit robbery in broad daylight. You are strong, you do not fear him, you are prepared to receive him. Meanwhile, the robber pesters your neighbours. They complain before you. You reply that you are doing all for their sake, you do not mind that your own goods have been stolen. Your neighbours reply that the robber never pestered them before, and that he commenced his depredations only after you declared hostilities against him. You are between Scylla and Charybdis. You are full of pity for the poor men. What they say is true. What are you to do? You will be disgraced if you now leave the robber alone. You, therefore, tell the poor men: "Never mind. Come, my wealth is yours, I will give you arms, I will teach you how to use them; you should belabour the rogue; don't you leave him alone." And so the battle grows: the robbers increase in numbers; your neighbours have deliberately put themselves to inconvenience. Thus the result of wanting to take revenge upon the robber is that you have disturbed your own peace; you are in perpetual fear of being robbed and assaulted; your courage has given place to cowardice. If you will patiently examine the argument, you will see that I have not overdrawn the picture. This is one of the means. Now let us examine the other. You set this armed robber down as an ignorant brother; you intend to reason with him at a suitable opportunity; you argue that he is, after all, a fellow man; you do not know what prompted him to steal. You, therefore, decide that, when you can, you will destroy the man's motive for stealing. Whilst you are thus reasoning with yourself, the man comes again to steal. Instead of being angry with him you take pity on him. You think that this stealing habit must be a disease with him. Henceforth, you, therefore, keep your doors and windows open, you change your sleeping-place, and you keep your things in a manner most accessible to him. The robber comes again and is confused as all this is new to him; nevertheless, he takes away your things. But his mind is agitated. He inquires about you in the village, he comes to learn about your broad and loving heart, he repents, he begs your pardon, returns you your things, and leaves off the stealing habit. He becomes your servant, and you will find for him honourable employment. This is the second method. Thus, you see, different means have brought about totally different results. I do not wish to deduce from this that robbers will act in the above manner or that all will have the same pity and love like you, but I only wish to show that fair means alone can produce fair results, and that, at least in the majority of cases, if not indeed in all, the force of love and pity is infinitely greater than the force of arms. There is harm in the exercise of brute force, never in that of pity.

Now we will take the question of petitioning. It is a fact beyond dispute that a petition, without the backing of force, is useless. However, the late Justice Ranade used to say that petitions served a useful purpose because they were a means of educating people. They give the latter an idea of their condition and warn the rulers. From this point of view, they are not altogether useless. A petition backed by force is a petition from an equal and, when he transmits his demand in the form of a petition, it testifies to his nobility. Two kinds of force can back petitions. "We shall hurt you if you do not give this," is one kind of force; it is the force of arms, whose evil results we have already examined. The second kind of force can thus be stated: "If you do not concede our demand, we shall be no longer your petitioners. You can govern us only so long as we remain the governed; we shall no longer have any dealings with you." The force implied in this may be described as love-force, soul-force, or, more popularly but less accurately, passive resistance. This force is indestructible. He who uses it perfectly understands his position. We have an ancient proverb which literally means: "One negative cures thirty-six diseases." The force of arms is powerless when matched against the force of love or the soul.

Now we shall take your last illustration, that of the child thrusting its foot into fire. It will not avail you. What do you really do to the child? Supposing that it can exert so much physical force that it renders you powerless and rushes into fire, then you cannot prevent it. There are only two remedies open to you—either you must kill it in order to prevent it from perishing in the flames, or you must give your own life because you do not wish to see it perish before your eyes. You will not kill it. If your heart is not quite full of pity, it is possible that you will not surrender yourself by preceding the child and going into the fire yourself. You, therefore, helplessly allow it to go the flames. Thus, at any rate, you are not using physical force. I hope you will not consider that it is still physical force, though of a low order, when you would forcibly prevent the child from rushing toward the fire if you could. That force is of a different order and we have to understand what it is.

Remember that, in thus preventing the child, you are minding entirely its own interest, you are exercising authority for its sole benefit. Your example does not apply to the English. In using brute force against the English you consult entirely your own, that is the national, interest. There is no question here either of pity or of love. If you say that the actions of the English, being evil, represent fire, and that they proceed to their actions through ignorance, and that therefore they occupy the position of a child and that you want to protect such a child, then you will have to overtake every evil action of that kind by whomsoever committed and, as in the case of the evil child, you will have to sacrifice yourself. If you are capable of such immeasurable pity, I wish you well in its exercise.

# The Great Law of Peace

## John Steckley

As we have seen in Morton Ritts' "Politics in the Life of the Individual," there are three basic forms of government, based fundamentally on how many people actually govern the society: one, a few, or many. One of these forms, democracy, can be called "government by the many." We can subdivide democracy into two types: majoritarian and consensus. In majoritarian democracy, "majority rules." Whichever candidate receives the most votes gets elected. Whichever party has the most elected candidates gets to form the government. In a referendum, whichever alternative—either "yes" or "no"—is chosen by most people becomes the decision of the people. For example, if three friends want to go to a rock bar one night and a fourth "votes" to go to a country bar, the group will not be line dancing that night.

In consensus democracy, everyone has a say and must agree with the decision before it can be acted upon. One form of consensus democracy is when a jury must be unanimous in its verdict. As has happened in some famous cases, it can take a long time to reach a decision in this way. However, it is one way of perhaps avoiding the danger in majoritarian democracy that J. S. Mill saw: tyranny of the majority—where the majority acts like a tyrant or dictator—which, at its worst is a version of Machiavelli's "might makes right." That is, do what we do or suffer the consequences.

In this article, we will look at the Great Law of Peace, the founding story and principles of the Confederacy of the Iroquois. Iroquois society differed from the societies in which the other political philosophers and activists described in the Ritts' article lived. The private property that John Locke attached so much significance to was only of secondary importance to the Iroquois. The most valuable property was non-material—names, songs, stories, dances, spirit guardians, respect and medicinal knowledge—and most of that property was neither privately nor publicly owned. It belonged to the clan. These clans would not fit into the category of classes that Karl Marx saw in the societies he described, as they were fundamentally equal, all possessing roughly the same amount and

"The Great Law of Peace" is by John Steckley of Humber College. Used by permission.

kind of property, all providing leaders or sachems. While some lineages or family lines had the advantage of being responsible for providing the sachems, a person from any lineage could become a Pine Tree Chief.

Further, it should be noted that the Great Law of Peace should not be considered to be just a set of rules. Like the work of Gandhi and Martin Luther King, it has a strong spiritual component. Similar to Gandhi's "soul force," the spiritual purity and strength of the Peacemaker and of Hiawatha were tested throughout the story, which is an integral part of the Great Law of Peace. Without them, there would have been little respect for the political goals that it set out.

We hear and read so much about "great political philosophers" who developed their ideas far away from Canada that we are surprised to learn that an influential political thinker lived and developed his revolutionary ideas in Ontario. He is known as the Peacemaker, his set of ideas, the *Kayanerenkowa* or the Great Law of Peace. He grew up on the north shore of Lake Ontario, near the current Mohawk community of Tyendinaga. Exactly when he lived is uncertain; estimates range from 100 to 1350 A.D. He may have been a member of the Huron-Wendat nation, who were living in the area at the time.

The Great Law of Peace is both a set of ideas and the story of how the ideas developed and came to be accepted. It brought together five warring nations, known now in English as the Mohawk, Oneida, Onondaga, Cayuga and Seneca. These five linguistically and culturally related peoples lived in villages in what is now New York State. The uniting of these peoples is termed *Rotinohsoni* in Mohawk, which means "They Build or Extend a House." It is referred to in English as the Confederacy of the Iroquois. It incorporates five key elements of traditional Native governance:

1. *Consensus democracy*—the notion that to make a decision on an issue, *everyone* must be in agreement (i.e., a consensus), rather than having the majority automatically imposing its will on a minority;

2. *Leader as speaker of consensus*—the idea that the leader or "chief" does not make decisions, but merely states the consensus that the people meeting in council have reached;

3. *Council of equals*—the notion that people who meet in council do so as equals, with no one having the power to give commands to the others;

4. *Separation of leaders of war and peace*—the notion that those who lead or speak consensus in matters of peace should not be those who lead or speak consensus in matters of war;

5. *Impeachment*—the notion that there should be a quick and efficient means of deposing a leader as soon as that person loses the respect of the people.

# The Story

The political part of the story begins with the Peacemaker crossing Lake Ontario to the country of the Mohawk, the easternmost of the five nations. Once there, he convinced a man known in English as Hiawatha that the Iroquois-speaking people should not fight among themselves, but should join together in one confederacy or union of nations. Gradually the Peacemaker's ideas were heard by all five peoples, and acceptance of his wisdom grew, sometimes through tests of the Peacemaker's spiritual purity and strength.

The last and most difficult nation to win over was the Onondaga, which was geographically the middle nation, whose leader, Thadodaha, was the most powerful and feared man in the five nations. To win over Thadodaha, the Onondaga were given the title of Fire Keepers, the ones who held the council meetings in their country, and were given the greatest number of representatives in the council. Further, Thadodaha, and those who later were to bear that name, would be the leader to speak the consensus of the Confederacy, which was a great honour.

# The Sachems

The council of the Iroquois Confederacy was made up of fifty leaders, known in English as sachems. They were divided among the five nations in the following way:

| | |
|---|---|
| Onondaga | 14 |
| Cayuga | 10 |
| Mohawk | 9 |
| Oneida | 9 |
| Seneca | 8 |

Clans were very important to the Iroquois Confederacy. Each clan owned a set of names, including those of the sachems. The three clans of the Mohawk, for example, each owned three of the Mohawk sachem names. Within each clan, lineages or family lines usually supplied the adult men with sachem names. The person who designated the sachem, and who could depose him, was the Clan Matron. She was usually an older woman who was considered wise enough to perceive and speak the consensus of the entire clan.

What would lead to the sachem being deposed? He would be deposed if he acted according to his own interests rather than those of his clan and nation, or if he lost the respect of the people for other reasons. Since the Iroquois nations were matrilineal, that is, they determined kinship along the female line, women had the authority to depose a sachem. Children would belong to their mother's clan, not their father's. Why was clan membership determined this way? Some writers connect this with the fact that Iroquois women were traditionally the farmers—the main food providers. By growing corn, beans and squash, they produced most of the food. They were the (corn) breadwinners. They also decided how food was distributed.

# Historical Example

*Tekarihogen* ("Affair or Matter Split in Two") is a Mohawk sachem name, the first named in council. It belongs to the Turtle clan. A man with the English name Seth held this title during the second half of the eighteenth century. When he died, the name was passed on to his sister's son, since he belonged to the same lineage and clan. Around 1780, that man's sister, Catherine, then the Clan Matron of the Turtle clan, named his successor upon his death, which was her son, Henry. When he died in 1830, she bestowed the title on her son, John, a child from her marriage to the famous Mohawk leader Joseph Brant (after whom Brantford is named). When John died, Catherine put her daughter's son into the position. The name Tekarihogen still exists and is still respected today.

# Pine Tree Chiefs

If you did not belong to an appropriate lineage, you could not become a sachem. However, there was a basic equality of lineages because a man of exceptional ability could become a Pine Tree Chief. This term is used for someone who was not officially part of the council of sachems, but who could have tremendous influence on it, depending on the respect with which his ideas were held. John Brant (Tyendinaga) is an example of a Pine Tree Chief. He led some 2000 Iroquois to Canada after fighting against the Americans in the American Revolution during the 1770s and 1780s.

# War Chiefs

War chiefs could not be sachems. If a sachem went on a raid, he would have to do so as an "ordinary citizen." War chiefs had their own councils, which met separately from the sachems or "peace chiefs." Compare this division with the modern alternative. In the Canadian and American systems of government, the decision to go to war is made by politicians who will not actually fight, although younger people who are not politicians will. In the Iroquois system, the people who made that decision were involved with the fighting that they initiated.

# Council Meetings

In the council house of the sachems, the Senecas, Onondaga and Mohawk who would sit on one side of the fire were called "older siblings" (i.e., a term that referred to both brothers and sisters). On the other side of the fire were the "younger siblings," the Cayuga and the Oneida. The traditional manner of dealing with issues was as follows: the Onondaga leader, Thadodaha, would state the issue. He would then pass it to the Mohawk to discuss. When the Mohawk had arrived at a consensus decision, the consensus would be passed to the Seneca. They would arrive at their own consensus and return the issue to the Mohawk, who would pass both opinions "across the fire" to the Oneida. The issue would move in this way from the Oneida to the Cayuga, back to the Oneida and then "across the fire" back to the Mohawk. The Mohawk would then pass the issue, complete with all the opinions decided upon by all the nations, to the Onondaga, who would consider what had been said and then arrive at their own decision.

At this stage, the Onondaga could do one of three things. First, if all the nations had arrived at the same consensus, Thadodaha would announce or speak the decision. Second, if the Onondaga disagreed with the consensus decision, which they could do only if that decision represented a serious breach of established custom or public policy, they could send the issue through the entire process again. Third, if the nations disagreed, an

Onondaga sachem, *Hononwiyehti*, the Wampum Keeper, would suggest a compromise. This compromise would then be discussed by the five nations in the same manner as the initial issue.

# Influence of the Great Law of Peace

For most of the seventeenth and eighteenth centuries, the Iroquois were an imposing military and political force in the Great Lakes area. During the latter half of the eighteenth century, Iroquois leaders, such as the great Seneca orator Red Jacket, influenced American political thinkers such as Thomas Paine, Thomas Jefferson and Benjamin Franklin. They learned from the Iroquois Confederacy how a group of separate nations or states could be stronger if they united as one. The American Constitution reflects some of the ideas that these men learned from the Iroquois. For example, members of the United States Congress cannot go to war without resigning their seats. Likewise, military officers must at least temporarily resign their commission before running for office. Another Iroquois concept—removing discredited holders of public office—is known as the impeachment process. All elected positions, including that of the President, are subject to impeachment. Canadians are sometimes envious of that particular American/Iroquois political feature.

In Canada, we have Mohawk communities in Ontario and Quebec, an Oneida community in Ontario, and a mixed group (mostly Mohawk, Onondaga and Cayuga) at Six Nations, near Brantford. The sixth nation is the Tuscarora, who were invited into the Confederacy when the Americans drove them out of their ancestral home early in the eighteenth century.

The sachem had official authority in Canada until 1924. At that time, the federal government arbitrarily decreed that the Confederacy was neither "modern" nor "democratic" enough to continue to exist. Perhaps the Confederacy's opposition to federal policies had something to do with that. The federal government then removed the sachem from office, changed the locks on the council doors, and made the Iroquois vote in their leaders by majority vote. The result was division within the Iroquois communities that still persists.

Now, as First Nations across Canada are looking for models of self-government, they look to the ideas contained within the Great Law of Peace. Canadians of all origins could learn a great deal as well.

# Modern Applications of the Great Law of Peace

How can the ideas of the Great Law of Peace be applied today so that they can benefit contemporary society? First, let's look at a relatively new development. A 1988 report on Natives and the Canadian justice system stated that this system had failed Natives badly, and that Native-run alternatives were needed in some areas. One idea that has come from this is that of the *justice circle*. It incorporates aspects of consensus democracy, leader as speaker of consensus and the council of equals. It works something like this. Assume for the sake of illustration that a Native has committed a crime on a reserve. The question of guilt is fairly straightforward. A group of people are put together to deal with the accused. The key notion is that punishment, social harmony, rehabilitation and reintegration of the guilty party into the community must be balanced. Included in the justice circle are the accused, the victim(s), Native social workers and police, and respected elders in the community. No one is the judge. The way the guilty party is to be treated depends on the decision the circle makes. This decision must be unanimous. Everyone must agree that the treatment of the guilty party is fair, to the accused, the victim(s), and to the community in general. The incentive of those who are accused to agree with what the others say is their desire to continue to be a part of the community, not cast out of it. That is a strong incentive that is perhaps hard for urban non-Natives to understand.

What about applying the ideas of the Great Law of Peace to a town or city council? In my town council members are always fighting. It seems they don't listen very much, and they certainly don't do much in the way of compromising. If they were not allowed to vote, but had to be unanimous in their decision, would this change the council for the better? Every time there is a vote, the group gives permission for the opinion of the minority to be ignored. The need for unanimity might encourage compromise and listening. You have to understand what the opposition wants in order to see what they might be willing to give up. If the position of mayor would be kept indefinitely, perhaps that person could function as *Thadodaha* (speaker of consensus) and/or *Hononwiyehti* (one to suggest compromises).

Let's take these ideas into the politics of business. Say there is a computer software company with fifty employees. Our standard organization would have a president, vice-president and so on down the line.

What if the company had a council of five, with a sales representative, the head technician, someone from creative development, the founder and an accountant? Could that work as a council of equals, with consensus the only way in which ideas could be advanced and decisions made?

Finally, let's look at one more potential application. There have been a few dramatic instances recently in which judges have been shown to be sexist, racist or just incompetent. The process of getting rid of such judges is complex, slow and generally inefficient. Perhaps we could use one or more of the principles of the Great Law of Peace to deal with such cases. We could form a justice circle with members of the judiciary, lawyers, but also of the general public as members. This council would not vote, but would develop a consensus as to what the judge's fate might be.

# Jihad vs. McWorld

Benjamin Barber

Just beyond the horizon of current events lie two possible political futures—both bleak, neither democratic. The first is a retribalization of large swaths of humankind by war and bloodshed: a threatened **Lebanonization** of national states in which culture is pitted against culture, people against people, tribe against tribe—a Jihad in the name of a hundred narrowly conceived faiths against every kind of interdependence, every kind of artificial social cooperation and civic mutuality. The second is being borne in on us by the onrush of economic and ecological forces that demand integration and uniformity and that mesmerize the world with fast music, fast computers, and fast food—with MTV, Macintosh, and McDonald's, pressing nations into one commercially homogeneous global network: one McWorld tied together by technology, ecology, communications, and commerce. The planet is falling precipitantly apart and coming reluctantly together at the very same moment.

These two tendencies are sometimes visible in the same countries at the same instant: thus Yugoslavia, clamoring just recently to join the New Europe, is exploding into fragments; India is trying to live up to its reputation as the world's largest integral democracy while powerful new fundamentalist parties like the Hindu nationalist Bharatiya Janata Party, along with nationalist assassins, are imperiling its hard-won unity. States are breaking up or joining up: the Soviet Union has disappeared almost overnight, its parts forming new unions with one another or with likeminded nationalities in neighboring states. The old interwar national state based on territory and political sovereignty looks to be a mere transitional development.

The tendencies of what I am here calling the forces of Jihad and the forces of McWorld operate with equal strength in opposite directions, the one driven by **parochial** hatreds, the other by universalizing markets, the one re-creating ancient subnational and ethnic borders from within, the other making national borders porous from without. They have one thing in common: neither offers much hope to citizens looking for practical ways to govern themselves democratically. If the global future is to pit Jihad's **centrifugal** whirlwind against McWorld's **centripetal** black hole, the outcome is unlikely to be democratic—or so I will argue.

**Lebanonization**
a reference to the disintegration of Lebanon as a result of civil war

**parochial**
local and limited

**centrifugal**
decentralizing force

**centripetal**
a force pulling many different things toward itself and making them the same in the process

"Jihad vs. McWorld" by Benjamin Barber is from *The Atlantic Monthly*, March 1992. Reprinted with permission.

# McWorld, or the Globalization of Politics

Four **imperatives** make up the dynamic of McWorld: a market imperative, a resource imperative, an information-technology imperative, and an ecological imperative. By shrinking the world and diminishing the **salience** of national borders, these imperatives have in combination achieved a considerable victory over factiousness and particularism, and not least of all over their most virulent traditional form—nationalism. It is the realists who are now Europeans, the utopians who dream nostalgically of a resurgent England or Germany, perhaps even a resurgent Wales or Saxony. Yesterday's wishful cry for one world has yielded to the reality of McWorld.

*The market imperative.* Marxist and Leninist theories of imperialism assumed that the quest for ever-expanding markets would in time compel nation-based capitalist economies to push against national boundaries in search of an international economic **imperium**. Whatever else has happened to the scientist predictions of Marxism, in this domain they have proved farsighted. All national economies are now vulnerable to the inroads of larger, transnational markets within which trade is free, currencies are convertible, access to banking is open, and contracts are enforceable under law. In Europe, Asia, Africa, the South Pacific, and the Americas such markets are eroding national sovereignty and giving rise to entities—international banks, trade associations, transnational lobbies like OPEC and Greenpeace, world news services like CNN and the BBC, and multinational corporations that increasingly lack a meaningful national identity—that neither reflect nor respect nationhood as an organizing or regulative principle.

The market imperative has also reinforced the quest for international peace and stability, requisites of an efficient international economy. Markets are enemies of **parochialism**, isolation, fractiousness, war. Market psychology **attenuates** the psychology of ideological and religious cleavages and assumes a concord among producers and consumers—categories that ill fit narrowly conceived national or religious cultures. Shopping has little tolerance for blue laws, whether dictated by pub-closing British paternalism, Sabbath-observing Jewish Orthodox fundamentalism, or no-Sunday-liquor-sales Massachusetts puritanism. In the context of common markets, international law ceases to be a vision of justice and becomes a workaday framework for getting things done—enforcing contracts, ensuring that governments abide by deals, regulating trade and currency relations, and so forth.

**imperatives**
essentials

**salience**
significance

**imperium**
power or rule

**parochialism**
narrow perspectives

**attenuates**
undermines

Common markets demand a common language, as well as a common currency, and they produce common behaviors of the kind bred by cosmopolitan city life everywhere. Commercial pilots, computer programmers, international bankers, media specialists, oil riggers, entertainment celebrities, ecology experts, demographers, accountants, professors, athletes—these compose a new breed of men and women for whom religion, culture, and nationality can seem only marginal elements in a working identity. Although sociologists of everyday life will no doubt continue to distinguish a Japanese from an American mode, shopping has a common signature throughout the world. Cynics might even say that some of the recent revolutions in Eastern Europe have had as their true goal not liberty and the right to vote but well-paying jobs and the right to shop (although the vote is proving easier to acquire than consumer goods). The market imperative is, then, plenty powerful; but, notwithstanding some of the claims made for "democratic capitalism," it is not identical with the democratic imperative.

*The resource imperative.* Democrats once dreamed of societies whose political autonomy rested firmly on economic independence. The **Athenians** idealized what they called **autarky**, and tried for a while to create a way of life simple and austere enough to make the polis genuinely self-sufficient. To be free meant to be independent of any other community or **polis**. Not even the Athenians were able to achieve autarky, however: human nature, it turns out, is dependency. By the time of Pericles, Athenian politics was inextricably bound up with a flowering empire held together by naval power and commerce—an empire that, even as it appeared to enhance Athenian might, ate away at Athenian independence and autarky. Master and slave, it turned out, were bound together by mutual insufficiency.

The dream of autarky briefly engrossed 19th century America as well, for the underpopulated, endlessly bountiful land, the cornucopia of natural resources, and the natural barriers of a continent walled in by two great seas led many to believe that America could be a world unto itself. Given this past, it has been harder for Americans than for most to accept the inevitability of interdependence. But the rapid depletion of resources even in a country like ours, where they once seemed inexhaustible, and the maldistribution of arable soil and mineral resources on the planet, leave even the wealthiest societies ever more resource-dependent and many other nations in permanently desperate straits.

**Athenians**

residents of Athens in ancient Greece

**autarky**

self-sufficiency

**polis**

city-state of ancient Greece

Every nation, it turns out, needs something another nation has; some nations have almost nothing they need.

*The information-technology imperative.* Enlightenment science and the technologies derived from it are inherently universalizing. They entail a quest for descriptive principles of general application, a search for universal solutions to particular problems, and an unswerving embrace of objectivity and impartiality.

Scientific progress embodies and depends on open communication, a common discourse rooted in rationality, collaboration, and an easy and regular flow and exchange of information. Such ideals can be hypocritical covers for power-mongering by elites, and they may be shown to be wanting in many other ways, but they are entailed by the very idea of science and they make science and globalization practical allies.

Business, banking, and commerce all depend on information flow and are facilitated by new communication technologies. The hardware of these technologies tends to be systemic and integrated—computer, television, cable, satellite, laser, fiber-optic, and microchip technologies combining to create a vast interactive communications and information network that can potentially give every person on earth access to every other person, and make every datum, every byte, available to every set of eyes. If the automobile was, as George Ball once said (when he gave his blessing to a Fiat factory in the Soviet Union during the Cold War), "an ideology on four wheels," then electronic telecommunication and information systems are an ideology at 300 000 kilometers per second—which makes for a very small planet in a very big hurry. Individual cultures speak particular languages; commerce and science increasingly speak English; the whole world speaks logarithms and binary mathematics.

Moreover, the pursuit of science and technology asks for, even compels, open societies. Satellite footprints do not respect national borders; telephone wires penetrate the most closed societies. With photocopying and then fax machines having infiltrated Soviet universities and **samizdat** literary circles in the eighties, and computer modems having multiplied like rabbits in communism's bureaucratic warrens thereafter, **glasnost** could not be far behind. In their social requisites, secrecy and science are enemies.

The new technology's software is perhaps even more globalizing than its hardware. The information arm of international commerce's sprawling

**samizdat**

a reference to secret publications circulated by hand in the old Soviet Union

**glasnost**

openness

The guns of Jihad contrast with the toys of McWorld.

body reaches out and touches distinct nations and parochial cultures, and gives them a common face chiseled in Hollywood, on Madison Avenue, and in Silicon Valley. Throughout the 1980s one of the most-watched television programs in South Africa was *The Cosby Show*. The demise of apartheid was already in production. Exhibitors at the 1991 Cannes film festival expressed growing anxiety over the "homogenization" and "Americanization" of the global film industry where for the third year running, American films dominated the awards ceremonies. America has dominated the world's popular culture for much longer, and more decisively. In November of 1991 Switzerland's once insular culture boasted best-seller lists featuring *Terminator 2* as the No. 1 movie, *Scarlett* as the

No. 1 book, and Prince's *Diamonds and Pearls* as the No. 1 record album. No wonder the Japanese are buying Hollywood film studios even faster than Americans are buying Japanese television sets. This kind of software supremacy may in the long term be far more important than hardware superiority, because culture has become more potent than armaments. What is the power of the Pentagon compared with Disneyland's? Can the Sixth Fleet keep up with CNN? McDonald's in Moscow and Coke in China will do more to create a global culture than military colonization ever could. It is less the goods than the brand names that do the work, for they convey life-style images that alter perception and challenge behavior. They make up the seductive software of McWorld's common (at times much too common) soul.

Yet in all this high-tech commercial world there is nothing that looks particularly democratic. It lends itself to surveillance as well as liberty, to new forms of manipulation and covert control as well as new kinds of participation, to skewed, unjust market outcomes as well as greater productivity. The consumer society and the open society are not quite synonymous. Capitalism and democracy have a relationship, but it is something less than a marriage. An efficient free market after all requires that consumers be free to vote their dollars on competing goods, not that citizens be free to vote their values and beliefs on competing political candidates and programs. The free market flourished in **junta**-run Chile, in military-governed Taiwan and Korea, and, earlier, in a variety of autocratic European empires as well as their colonial possessions.

**junta**

a group of military officers who seize control of government

*The ecological imperative.* The impact of globalization on ecology is a cliché even to world leaders who ignore it. We know well enough that the German forests can be destroyed by Swiss and Italians driving gas-guzzlers fueled by leaded gas. We also know that the planet can be asphyxiated by greenhouse gases because Brazilian farmers want to be part of the 20th century and are burning down tropical rain forests to clear a little land to plow, and because Indonesians make a living out of converting their lush jungle into toothpicks for fastidious Japanese diners, upsetting the delicate oxygen balance and in effect puncturing our global lungs. Yet this ecological consciousness has meant not only greater awareness but also greater inequality, as modernized nations try to slam the door behind them, saying to developing nations, "The world cannot afford *your* modernization; ours has wrung it dry!"

Each of the four imperatives just cited is transnational, transideological, and transcultural. Each applies impartially to Catholics, Jews, Muslims,

Hindus, and Buddhists; to democrats and totalitarians; to capitalists and socialists. The Enlightenment dream of a universal rational society has to a remarkable degree been realized—but in a form that is commercialized, homogenized, depoliticized, bureaucratized, and, of course, radically incomplete, for the movement toward McWorld is in competition with forces of global breakdown, national dissolution, and centrifugal corruption. These forces, working in the opposite direction, are the essence of what I call Jihad.

# Jihad, or the Lebanonization of the World

OPEC, the World Bank, the United Nations, the International Red Cross, the multinational corporation . . . there are scores of institutions that reflect globalization. But they often appear as ineffective reactors to the world's real actors: national states and, to an ever greater degree, subnational factions in permanent rebellion against uniformity and integration—even the kind represented by universal law and justice. The headlines feature these players regularly: they are cultures, not countries; parts, not wholes; sects, not religions; rebellious factions and dissenting minorities at war not just with globalism but with the traditional nation-state. Kurds, Basques, Puerto Ricans, Ossetians, East Timoreans, Québécois, the Catholics of Northern Ireland, Abkhasians, Kurile Islander Japanese, the Zulus of Inkatha, Catalonians, Tamils, and, of course, Palestinians—people without countries, inhabiting nations not their own, seeking smaller worlds within borders that will seal them off from modernity.

A powerful irony is at work here. Nationalism was once a force of integration and unification, a movement aimed at bringing together disparate clans, tribes, and cultural fragments under new, assimilationist flags. But as Ortega y Gasset noted more than 60 years ago, having won its victories, nationalism changed its strategy. In the 1920s, and again today, it is more often a reactionary and divisive force, pulverizing the very nations it once helped cement together. The force that creates nations is "inclusive," Ortega wrote in *The Revolt of the Masses*. "In periods of consolidation, nationalism has a positive value, and is a lofty standard. But in Europe everything is more than consolidated, and nationalism is nothing but a mania. . . ."

This mania has left the post-Cold War world smoldering with hot war; the international scene is little more unified than it was at the end of the **Great War**, in Ortega's own time. There were more than 30 wars in progress last year, most of them ethnic, racial, tribal, or religious in character, and the list of unsafe regions doesn't seem to be getting any shorter. Some new world order!

Great War
World War I (1914–1918)

The aim of many of these small-scale wars is to redraw boundaries, to implode states and resecure parochial identities: to escape McWorld's dully insistent imperatives. The mood is that of Jihad: war not as an instrument of policy but as an emblem of identity, an expression of community, an end in itself. Even where there is a shooting war, there is fractiousness, secession, and a quest for ever smaller communities. Add to the list of dangerous countries those at risk: In Switzerland and Spain, Jurassian and Basque separatists still argue the virtues of ancient identities, sometimes in the language of bombs. Hyperdistintegration in the former Soviet Union may well continue unabated—not just a Ukraine independent from the Soviet Union but a Bessarab Ukraine independent from the Ukrainian republic; not just Russia severed from the defunct union but Tatarsa severed from Russia. Yugoslavia makes even the **disured**, ex-Soviet, nonsocialist republics that were once the Soviet Union look integrated, its sectarian fatherland springing up within factional motherlands like weeds within weeds within weeds. Kurdish independence would threaten the territorial integrity of four Mid-Eastern nations. Well before the current cataclysm Soviet Georgia made a claim for autonomy from the Soviet Union, only to be faced with its Ossetians (164 000 in a republic of 5.5 million) demanding their own self-determination within Georgia. The Abkhasian minority of Georgia has followed suit. Even the good will established by Canada's once promising Meech Lake protocols is in danger, with Francophone Quebec again threatening dissolution of the federation. In South Africa the emergence from apartheid was hardly achieved when friction between Inkatha's Zulus and the African National Congress's tribally identified members threatened to replace Europeans' racism with an indigenous tribal war. After 30 years of attempted integration using the colonial language (English) as a unifier, Nigeria is now playing with the idea of linguistic multiculturalism—which could mean the cultural breakup of the nation into hundreds of tribal fragments. Even Saddam Hussein has benefited from the threat of internal Jihad, having used renewed tribal and religious warfare to turn last season's mortal enemies into reluctant allies of an Iraqi nationhood that he nearly destroyed.

disured
dissolution of legal ties between states

The passing of communism has torn away the thin veneer of internationalism (workers of the world unite!) to reveal ethnic prejudices that are not only ugly and deep-seated but increasingly murderous. Europe's old scourge, anti-Semitism, is back with a vengeance, but it is only one of many antagonisms. It appears all too easy to throw the historical gears into reverse and pass from a Communist dictatorship back into a tribal state.

Among the tribes, religion is also a battlefield. ("Jihad" is a rich word whose generic meaning is "struggle"—usually the struggle of the soul to avert evil. Strictly applied to religious war, it is used only in reference to battles where the faith is under assault, or battles against a government that denies the practice of Islam. My use here is rhetorical, but does follow both journalistic practice and history.) Remember the Thirty Years War? Whatever forms of Enlightenment universalism might once have come to grace such historically related forms of monotheism as Judaism, Christianity, and Islam, in many of their modern incarnations they are parochial rather than cosmopolitan, angry rather than loving, **proselytizing** rather than **ecumenical**, zealous rather than rationalist, sectarian rather then deistic, ethnocentric rather than universalizing. As a result, like the new forms of hypernationalism, the new expressions of religious fundamentalism are fractious and pulverizing, never integrating. This is religion as the Crusaders knew it: a battle to the death for souls that if not saved will be forever lost.

The atmospherics of Jihad have resulted in a breakdown of civility in the name of identity, of **comity** in the name of community. International relations have sometimes taken on the aspects of gang war—cultural turf battles featuring tribal factions that were supposed to be sublimated as integral parts of large national, economic, postcolonial, and constitutional entities.

# The Darkening Future of Democracy

These rather melodramatic *tableaux vivants* do not tell the whole story, however. For all their defects, Jihad and McWorld have their attractions. Yet, to repeat and insist, the attractions are unrelated to democracy. Neither McWorld nor Jihad is remotely democratic in impulse. Neither needs democracy; neither promotes democracy.

McWorld does manage to look pretty seductive in a world obsessed with Jihad. It delivers peace, prosperity, and relative unity—if at the cost of independence, community, and identity (which is generally based on difference). The primary political values required by the global market are order and tranquillity, and freedom—as in the phrases "free trade," "free

---

**proselytizing**

attempting to convert to a narrow view

**ecumenical**

having worldwide value

**comity**

courtesy

**tableaux vivants**

images that tell a story

press," and "free love." Human rights are needed to a degree, but not citizenship or participation—and no more social justice and equality than are necessary to promote efficient economic production and consumption. Multinational corporations sometimes seem to prefer doing business with local **oligarchs**, inasmuch as they can take confidence from dealing with the boss on all crucial matters. Despots who slaughter their own populations are no problem, as long as they leave markets in place and refrain from making war on their neighbors (Saddam Hussein's fatal mistake). In trading partners, predictability is of more value than justice.

**oligarchs**
members of an elite that hold power in a state

The Eastern European revolutions that seemed to arise out of concern for global democratic values quickly deteriorated into a stampede in the general direction of free markets and their **ubiquitous**, television-promoted shopping malls. East Germany's Neues Forum, that courageous gathering of intellectuals, students, and workers which overturned the Stalinist regime in Berlin in 1989, lasted only six months in Germany's mini-version of McWorld. Then it gave way to money and markets and monopolies from the West. By the time of the first all-German elections, it could scarcely manage to secure three per cent of the vote. Elsewhere there is growing evidence that *glasnost* will go and *perestroika*—defined as privatization and an opening of markets to Western bidders—will stay. So understandably anxious are the new rulers of Eastern Europe and whatever entities are forged from the residues of the Soviet Union to gain access to credit and markets and technology—McWorld's flourishing new currencies—that they have shown themselves willing to trade away democratic prospects in pursuit of them: not just old totalitarian ideologies and command-economy production models but some possible indigenous experiments with a third way between capitalism and socialism, such as economic cooperatives and employee stock-ownership plans, both of which have their ardent supporters in the East.

**ubiquitous**
occurring everywhere

**perestroika**
economic restructuring

Jihad delivers a different set of virtues: a vibrant local identity, a sense of community, solidarity among kinsmen, neighbors, and countrymen, narrowly conceived. But it also guarantees parochialism and is against outsiders. And solidarity often means obedience to a hierarchy in governance, fanaticism in beliefs, and the obliteration of individual selves in the name of the group. Deference to leaders and intolerance toward outsiders (and toward "enemies within") are hallmarks of tribalism—hardly the attitudes required for the cultivation of new democratic women and men capable of governing themselves. Where new democratic experiments have been conducted in retribalizing societies, in both Europe and the Third World, the result has often been anarchy, repression, persecution, and the coming of new, noncommunist forms of very old kinds of despotism. During the past year, Havel's velvet revolution in Czechoslovakia was imperiled by partisans of "Czechland" and of Slovakia as independent entities. India seemed little less rent by Sikh, Hindu, Muslim, and Tamil infighting than it was immediately after the British pulled out, more than 40 years ago.

To the extent that either McWorld or Jihad has a *natural* politics, it has turned out to be more of an antipolitics. For McWorld, it is the antipolitics of globalism: bureaucratic, technocratic, and meritocratic, focused (as Marx predicted it would be) on the administration of things—with people, however, among the chief things to be administered. In its politico-economic imperatives McWorld has been guided by ***laissez-faire*** market principles that privilege efficiency, productivity, and beneficence at the expense of civic liberty and self-government.

For Jihad, the antipolitics of tribalization has been explicitly antidemocratic: one-party dictatorship, government by military junta, theocratic fundamentalism—often associated with a version of the *Fuhrerprinzip* that empowers an individual to rule on behalf of a people. Even the government of India, struggling for decades to model democracy for a people who will soon number a billion, longs for great leaders; and for every Mahatma Gandhi, Indira Gandhi, or Rajiv Gandhi taken from them by zealous assassins, the Indians appear to seek a replacement who will deliver them from the lengthy travail of their freedom.

## The Confederal Option

How can democracy be secured and spread in a world whose primary tendencies are at best indifferent to it (McWorld) and at worst deeply **antithetical** to it (Jihad)? My guess is that globalization will eventually vanquish retribalization. The **ethos** of material "civilization" has not yet encountered an obstacle it has been unable to thrust aside. Ortega may have grasped in the 1920s a clue to our own future in the coming millennium.

> Everyone sees the need of a new principle of life. But as always happens in similar crises—some people attempt to save the situation by an artificial intensification of the very principle which has led to decay. This is the meaning of the "nationalist" outburst of recent years…things have always gone that way. The last flare, the longest; the last sigh, the deepest. On the very eve of their disappearance there is an intensification of frontiers—military and economic.

**laissez-faire**

a policy of non-intervention by government in the economy

**antithetical**

deeply opposed

**ethos**

spirit or character

Jihad may be a last deep sigh before the eternal yawn of McWorld. On the other hand, Ortega was not exactly **prescient**; his prophecy of peace and internalism came just before blitzkrieg, world war, and the Holocaust tore the old order to bits. Yet democracy is how we remonstrate with reality, the rebuke our aspirations offer to history. And if retribalization is inhospitable to democracy, there is nonetheless a form of democratic government that can accommodate parochialism and communitarianism, one that can even save them from their defects and make them more tolerant and participatory: decentralized participatory democracy. And if McWorld is indifferent to democracy, there is nonetheless a form of democratic government that suits global markets passably well—representative government in its federal or, better still, confederal variation.

With its concern for accountability, the protection of minorities, and the universal rule of law, a confederalized representative system would serve the political needs of McWorld as well as oligarchic bureaucratism or meritocratic elitism is currently doing. As we are already beginning to see, many nations may survive in the long term only as confederations that afford local regions smaller than "nations" extensive jurisdiction. Recommended reading for democrats of the 21st century is not the U.S. Constitution or the French Declaration of Rights of Man and Citizen but the Articles of Confederation, that suddenly pertinent document that stitched together the 13 American colonies into what then seemed a too loose confederation of independent states but now appears a new form of political realism, as veterans of Yeltsin's new Russia and the new Europe created at **Maastricht** will attest.

By the same token, the participatory and direct form of democracy that engages citizens in civic activity and civic judgment and goes well beyond just voting and accountability—the system I have called "strong democracy"—suits the political needs of decentralized communities as well as theocratic and nationalist party dictatorships have done. Local neighborhoods need not be democratic, but they can be. Real democracy has flourished in diminutive settings: the spirit of liberty, Tocqueville said, is local. Participatory democracy, if not naturally apposite to tribalism, has an undeniable attractiveness under conditions of parochialism.

Democracy in any of these variations will, however, continue to be obstructed by the undemocratic and antidemocratic trends toward uniformitarian globalism and intolerant retribalization which I have portrayed here. For democracy to persist in our brave new McWorld, we will have to commit acts of conscious political will—a possibility, but hardly a

**prescient**
possessing foreknowledge

**Maastricht**
city in Belgium where the treaty was signed to create the European Union

probability, under these conditions. Political will requires much more than the quick fix of the transfer of institutions. Like technology transfer, institution transfer rests on foolish assumptions about a uniform world of the kind that once fired the imagination of colonial administrators. Spread English justice to the colonies by exporting wigs. Let an East Indian trading company act as the vanguard to Britain's free parliamentary institutions. Today's well-intentioned quick-fixers in the National Endowment for Democracy and the Kennedy School of Government, in the unions and foundations and universities zealously nurturing contacts in Eastern Europe and the Third World, are hoping to democratize by long distance. Post Bulgaria a parliament by first-class mail. FedEx the Bill of Rights to Sri Lanka. Cable Cambodia some common law.

Yet Eastern Europe has already demonstrated that importing free political parties, parliaments, and presses cannot establish a democratic civil society; imposing a free market may even have the opposite effect. Democracy grows from the bottom up and cannot be imposed from the top down. Civil society has to be built from the inside out. The institutional superstructure comes last. Poland may become democratic, but then again it may heed the Pope, and prefer to found its politics on its Catholicism, with uncertain consequences for democracy. Bulgaria may become democratic, but it may prefer tribal war. The former Soviet Union may become a democratic confederation, or it may just grow into an anarchic and weak conglomeration of markets for other nations' goods and services.

Democrats need to seek out indigenous democratic impulses. There is always a desire for self-government, always some expression of participation, accountability, consent, and representation, even in traditional hierarchical societies. These need to be identified, tapped, modified, and incorporated into new democratic practices with an indigenous flavor. The tortoises among the democratizers may ultimately outlive or outpace the hares, for they will have the time and patience to explore conditions along the way, and to adapt their gait to changing circumstances. Tragically, democracy in a hurry often looks something like France in 1794 or China in 1989.

It certainly seems possible that the most attractive democratic ideal in the face of the brutal realities of Jihad and the dull realities of McWorld will be a confederal union of semi-autonomous communities smaller than nation-states, tied together into regional economic associations and markets larger than nation-states—participatory and self-determining in local matters at the bottom, representative and accountable at the top.

The nation-state would play a diminished role, and sovereignty would lose some of its political potency. The Green movement adage "Think globally, act locally" would actually come to describe the conduct of politics.

This vision reflects only an ideal, however—one that is not terribly likely to be realized. Freedom, Jean-Jacques Rousseau once wrote, is a food easy to eat but hard to digest. Still, democracy has always played itself out against the odds. And democracy remains both a form of coherence as binding as McWorld and a secular faith potentially as inspiring as Jihad.

# A Cosmopolitan among the True Believers

## Michael Ignatieff

Anyone whose father was born in Russia, whose mother was born in England, who was educated in America, and whose working life has been spent in Canada, Great Britain, and France cannot be expected to be much of an ethnic nationalist. For many years, I believed that the tide was running in favour of cosmopolitans like me. There seemed to be so many of us, for one thing. There were at least a dozen world cities—gigantic, multi-ethnic melting pots that provided a home for expatriates, exiles, migrants, and transients of all kinds. For the urban professional populations of these major cities, a post-national state of mind was simply taken for granted. People in these places did not bother about the passports of the people they worked or lived with; they did not care about the country-of-origin label on the goods they bought. They simply assumed that in constructing their own way of life they would borrow from the customs of every nation they happened to admire.

This cosmopolitan ethic is not in itself altogether new. We have lived with a global economy since 1700, and many of the world's major cities have been global **entrepôts** for centuries. But in 1989 we entered the first era of global cosmopolitanism in which there was no framework for imperial order. For 200 years prior, the global expansion of capitalism was shaped by the territorial ambitions and policing authority of a succession of imperial powers—the British, French, German, Austro-Hungarian, and Russian empires of the 19th and early 20th centuries and the Soviet and American joint **imperium** after the Second World War.

America may still be a superpower, but it is not an imperial power: its authority is exercised in the defence of exclusively national interest, not in the maintenance of an imperial system of global order. As a result, large sections of Africa, Eastern Europe, Soviet Asia, Latin America, and the Near East no longer come within any clearly defined sphere of imperial or great-power influence. This means that huge sections of the world's population have won the "right of self-determination" on the

**entrepôt**
trading centre

**imperium**
power or rule

"A Cosmopolitan among the True Believers" is from Michael Ignatieff's *Blood and Belonging*. Toronto: Penguin Books Canada, 1993. Reprinted with permission.

cruellest possible terms: they have simply been left to fend for themselves. Small wonder, then, that, unrestrained by stronger hands, they have set upon one another for that final settling of scores so long deferred by presence of empire.

With **blithe** lightness of mind, we had assumed that the world was moving irrevocably beyond nationalism, beyond tribalism, beyond the provincial confines of the identities inscribed in our passports, toward a global market culture that was to be our new home. In retrospect, we were whistling in the dark. The key narrative of the new world order is the disintegration of nation-states into ethnic civil war; the key architects of that order are warlords. The repressed has returned, and its name is nationalism.

Everywhere I've been, nationalism is most violent where the group you are defining yourself against most closely resembles you. A rational explanation of conflict would predict the reverse to be the case. To outsiders at least, Ulstermen look and sound like Irishmen, just as Serbs look and sound like Croats—yet the very similarity is what pushed them to define themselves as polar opposites. Since Cain and Abel, we have known that hatred between brothers is more ferocious than hatred between strangers. We say tritely that this is so because hatred is a form of love turned against itself. Or that we hate most deeply what we recognize as kin.

blithe
carefree

Civil war: "Since Cain and Abel, we have known that hatred between brothers is more ferocious than hatred between strangers."

**narcissism of minor difference**

the theory that the more minor the distinction between two groups, the more important such difference becomes to those obsessed with self-identity

Or that violence is the ultimate denial of an affiliation we cannot bear. None of this will do. There are puzzles that no theory of nationalism, no theory of the **narcissism of minor difference**, can resolve. After you have been to the wastelands of the new world order, particularly to those fields of graves marked with numberless wooden crosses, you feel stunned into silence by a deficit of moral explanation.

In his 1959 essay "What Does Coming to Terms with the Past Mean?" Theodor Adorno says, in passing, "Nationalism no longer quite believes in itself." Everywhere I went, there was a bewildering insincerity and inauthenticity to nationalist rhetoric, as if the people who mouthed nationalist slogans were aware, somewhere inside, of the implausibility of their own words. Serbs who, in one breath, would tell you that all Croats were Ustashe beasts would, in the next, recall the happy days when they lived with them in peace. In this divided consciousness, the plane of abstract fantasy and the plane of direct experience were never allowed to intersect.

Nationalism is a form of speech that shouts, not merely so that it will be heard but so that it will believe itself. It is almost as if the quotient of crude historical fiction, violent moral exaggeration, ludicrous caricature of the enemy is in direct proportion to the degree to which the speaker is himself aware that it is all really a pack of lies. But this insincerity may be a functional requirement of a language that is burdened with the task of insisting upon such a high volume of untruths. The nationalist vision of an ethnically pure state, for example, has the task of convincing ordinary people to disregard stubbornly adverse sociological realities, like the fact that most societies are not and have never been ethnically pure. That such fantasies do take hold of large numbers of people is a testament to the deep longing people have to escape the stubborn realities of life.

Nationalism, in this interpretation, is a language of fantasy and escape. In many cases—Serbia is a flagrant example—nationalist politics is a full-scale, collective escape from the realities of social backwardness. Instead of facing up to the reality of being a poor, primitive, third-rate economy on the periphery of Europe, it is infinitely more attractive to listen to speeches about the heroic and tragic destiny of Serbia and to fantasize about the final defeat of her historic enemies. Nationalist rhetoric rewrites and re-creates the real world, turning it into a delusional realism of noble causes, tragic sacrifice, and cruel necessity.

Yet there is a further element to add to the picture. As all of us can see on our television screens, most nationalist violence is perpetrated by a small minority of males between the ages of 18 and 25. Some are psychopaths, but most are perfectly sane. Until I had spent some time at the checkpoints of the new world order, until I had encountered my quotient of young males intoxicated by the power of the guns on their hips, I had not understood how deeply pleasurable it is, for some, to have the power of life and death in their hands. It is a characteristic liberal error to suppose that everyone hates and fears violence. I met lots of young men who loved the ruins, loved the destruction, loved the power that came from the barrels of their guns.

Perhaps liberals have not understood the force of male resentment that has accumulated through centuries of gradual European pacification. Liberals have not reckoned with the male loathing of peace and domesticity or with the anger of young males at the modern state's confiscation of their weapons. One of the hidden explanations behind nationalist revolts is that they tap into this deep substratum of male resentment at the civility and order of the modern state. It seems obvious that, for many, the state's order is the order of the father and nationalism is the rebellion of the sons. How else are we to account for the staggering **gratuitousness** and bestiality of nationalist violence, its constant overstepping of the bounds of either military logic or legitimate self-defence, unless we leave some room in our account for the possibility that nationalism exists to warrant and legitimize the sons' "vengeance against the father."

gratuitousness
unjustified nature

My journeys have also made me rethink the nature of belonging. Any expatriate is bound to have moments of wishing for a more complete national belonging. But I have been to places where belonging is so strong, so intense, that I now recoil from it in fear. The rational core of such fear is that there is a deep connection between violence and belonging. The more strongly you feel the bonds of belonging to your own group, the more hostile, the more violent will your feelings be toward outsiders. When nationalists claim that national belonging is the overridingly important form of all belonging, they mean that there is no other form of belonging—to your family, work, or friends—that is secure if you do not have a nation to protect you. Without a nation's protection, everything that an individual values can be rendered worthless. Belonging, in this view, is first and foremost protection from violence. Where you belong is where you are safe; where you are safe is where you belong. You can't have this intensity of belonging without violence, because belonging of this intensity moulds the individual conscience: if a nation gives people a reason to sacrifice themselves, it also gives them a reason to kill.

Throughout my travels, I kept remembering the scene in *Romeo and Juliet* in which Juliet whispers to herself on the balcony in her night-gown, unaware that Romeo is in the shadows listening. She is strug-gling to understand what it means for her, a Capulet, to fall in love with a Montague. Suddenly she exclaims,

> 'Tis but thy name that is my enemy;
> Thou art thyself though, not a Montague.
> What's Montague? It is nor hand, nor foot,
> Nor arm, nor face, nor any other part
> Belonging to a man. O, be some other name!
> What's in a name?

On the front lines in Bosnia, in the housing projects of Loyalist and Republican Belfast, in all the places where the tribal gangsters—the Montagues and Capulets of our day—are enforcing the laws of ethnic loy-alty, there are Juliets and Romeos who still cry out, "Oh, let me not be a Croatian, Serbian, Bosnian, Catholic, or Protestant. Let me be only myself."

But such people are an embattled minority. The world is run not by skeptics and ironists but by gunmen and true believers, and the new world they are bequeathing to the next century already seems a more vi-olent and desperate place than I could ever have imagined. If I had sup-posed, as the Cold War came to an end, that the new world might be ruled by philosophers and poets, it was because I believed, foolishly, that the precarious civility and order of the states in which I live must be what all people rationally desire. Now I am not so sure. I began my jour-ney as a liberal, and I end as one, but I cannot help thinking that liberal civilization—the rule of laws, not men, of argument in place of force, of compromise in place of violence—runs deeply against the human grain, and is achieved and sustained only by the most unremitting struggle against human nature. The liberal virtues—tolerance, compromise, rea-son—remain as valuable as ever, but they cannot be preached to those who are mad with fear or mad with vengeance. In any case, preaching al-ways rings hollow. We must be prepared to defend these virtues by force, and the failure of the sated, cosmopolitan nations to do so has left the hungry nations sick with contempt for us.

**sated**
satisfied

Between the hungry and the **sated** nations, there is an impassable bar-rier of incomprehension. I've lived all my life in sated nation-states, in places that have no outstanding border disputes, are no longer ruled by foreigners or oppressors, where citizens are masters in their own house. Sated people can afford to be cosmopolitan; sated people can afford the luxury of condescending to the passions of the hungry. But among the Crimean Tatars, the Kurds, and the Cree, I met the hungry ones, peoples whose very survival will remain at risk until they achieve self-determination, whether in their own nation-state or in someone else's.

What's wrong with the world is not nationalism itself. Every people must have a home, every such hunger must be assuaged. What's wrong is the kind of nation, the kind of home that nationalists want to create and the means they use to seek their ends. Wherever I went, I found a struggle going on between those who still believe that a nation should be a home to all—and that race, colour, religion, and creed should be no bar to belonging—and those who want their nation to be home only to their own. It's the battle between the civic and the ethnic nation. I know which side I'm on. I also know which side, right now, is winning.

# On Inhumanity

## Mitchell Lerner

> There is a universal tendency to avoid seeing, as well as remembering, the human capacity for evil. Adolf Hitler understood that well when, on August 22, 1939, he said to his military commanders regarding his plans for Poland: "Who, after all, speaks today of the annihilation of the Armenians?"
>
> *Donald E. Miller and Lorna Touryan Miller,* Survivors

## The Problem

"Thinking is the . . . work of a species that bears responsibility for its own survival . . . to carry on thinking [is] the authority by which we survive in human form."

*Hannah Arendt*
Life of the Mind

Ever since Cain raised his hand against his brother Abel, the Earth has witnessed inhumanity, brutality and indifference. Even as I write this essay, newspaper stories and photos convey painful images of the latest atrocity—the Rwandan civil war. In this fight between the Hutu and the Tutsi, the blood of hundreds of thousands of men, women and children has been spilled. More than a million refugees have fled to neighbouring areas, where many are dying of disease.

A million refugees here . . . ethnic cleansing there . . . the imagery of human tragedy marks both the present and the past. How do we as individuals make sense of distant suffering and death on a massive scale? How do we comprehend what is happening in Rwanda today, Bosnia yesterday, and other places 50 and 80 years ago? How do we think about the magnitude of human evil? Can thinking about what it means to be human ensure our survival?

In this essay, we address the very difficult concepts of genocide, dehumanization and the banality of evil.

## Genocide

The term "genocide" comes from the Greek word *genos*, meaning people, and the Latin word, *cide*, referring to killing. Raphael Lemkin coined the term in 1944 to describe the attempt to destroy a nation or an ethnic group either by killing them or by depriving them of the ability to live and procreate. In 1948, the United Nations resolved that genocide means an intent to destroy, in whole or in part, a national, ethnic, racial or religious group:

"On Inhumanity" is reprinted by permission of Mitchell Lerner.

a)  by killing members of the group;
b)  by causing serious bodily or mental harm to members of the group;
c)  by deliberately inflicting on the group conditions of life calculated to bring about its physical destruction, in whole or in part;
d)  by imposing measures intended to prevent births within the group;
e)  by forcibly transferring children of the group to another group.

Over the years, genocide has come to mean a form of one-sided mass killing in which a state or another authority intends to destroy a group, as that group and membership in it are defined by the perpetrator.[1]

This definition is important in several ways. First, it acknowledges that there is no reciprocity in genocide: it is not a war, although it may and often does occur in the midst of war, hiding in the **machinations** of war.

**machinations**
hostile manoeuvres

Second, genocide means that all group members are targets, regardless of individual characteristics. Einstein and Freud were Jews and, as such, didn't have the right to exist in the Nazi universe. Not long ago, the Soviets and the Americans pointed weapons of mass destruction at each other, putting humanity at great risk. The enormous power of nuclear weapons makes possible the indiscriminate destruction of entire national groups and allows us to conceive of the enemy as an entire people.

Third, those who attempt genocide regard specific populations as dispensable. The notion that entire groups of people are disposable demeans the value of human life and negates all the spiritual, religious, and cultural aspirations of the species.

The indiscriminate destruction of an entire people is genocidal, and the genocidal illusion is that we can become more pure by eradicating those who are different from ourselves. Genocide is the worst outcome of labelling and stereotyping. Blinded by prejudice, we cannot see or hear the other as they are. This, then, is the genocidal mentality—irrational, merciless, making no exceptions.

This century's first instance of genocide occurred in 1915, when the ruling government of the Ottoman empire, the Young Turks, attempted to create a new order for their state. Their ideology of Pan-Turanianism required that all of Turkey be of one religion: Muslim. The government of Enver and Talaat perceived the several million Armenians who lived in the eastern Ottoman Empire as a threat, and secretly declared them as undesirable and expendable. The Turkish Armenians were a cultured, civilized, creative, educated people who had expected to receive some form of sovereignty within the Ottoman empire.

Instead, hiding behind the smokescreen of World War I, the Turkish government implemented a bureaucratic system to destroy the Armenians.

After allying with Germany, the Turkish military invaded Armenian population centres, conducted deportations, and brutally slaughtered approximately 1.5 million Armenians. To this day, the Turkish government denies the extent of the killings, and keeps many of its documents sealed to investigators. Armenians around the world and others continue to urge political leaders to acknowledge the genocide that prefigured and predated the Nazi Holocaust by some 20 years. They contend that the present Turkish government, by not acknowledging the destruction of a people, is attempting to dispense with historical fact the way its predecessors dispensed with Armenian souls.

❖

Since 1945, at least 22 documented examples fit within the definition of genocide. The estimated number of deaths, between three and nine million people, does not include the 1.5 million Armenians or the six million Jews who died in the Nazi Holocaust.

"The most painful question of genocide," write authors Chalk and Jonassohn, "is, How is it possible for people to kill other people on such a massive scale? The answer seems to be that it is not possible. At least not as long as the potential victims are perceived as people. We have no evidence

Inmates at a Nazi concentration camp.

that genocide was ever performed on a group of equals. The victims must not only *not* be equals, but also be clearly defined as something less than fully human."[2]

When European pioneers haphazardly slaughtered North American aboriginals, when the Khmer Rouge campaigned to slaughter the urban population of Cambodia, when white slave traders ripped apart black families on the Ivory Coast, when the Hutu macheted the Tutsi, what must these individuals have been thinking? What understanding of another human being must go on in the head of a person who is shredding, burning, stabbing or enslaving human beings?

Chalk and Jonassohn raise an important and essential point. It is *not* possible for genocide to occur unless the perpetrator regards all members of the target group as less than human. The victims must be dehumanized. Since dehumanization is a process that happens over time, it contains enough warnings that it can be stopped.

# Dehumanization

Hitler's "Final Solution," the Nazi's clinical term for mass murder, involved the systematic slaughter of six million Jews. It was designed to eliminate an entire people by using the efficient mechanisms of an industrial culture. The Holocaust took place in the midst of a culture that was rich in art, music, philosophy and science. The term *Holocaust* is reserved for this particular tragedy of the 20th century, which was the ultimate ideological genocide. It refers to the period from January 1933, when Hitler seized power on a platform of racial purity and superiority, to May 1945, when the Nazi regime dissolved.

German statistics indicate that 5.8 million Jews were murdered. The recognized figure of non-Jewish civilians murdered is six million, including Gypsies, Serbs, Polish intelligentsia, resistance fighters, German opponents of Nazism, homosexuals, Jehovah's Witnesses, habitual criminals and the disabled.

European Jewish culture was destroyed, along with a host of other "less-than-humans." German technical specialists engineered mass-murder camps, known as concentration camps, and built special killing apparatus. In these devices, which included gas chambers, crematoria and burial pits, the destruction of a people transpired. Hundreds of thousands of Nazis actively participated in the ghettoizing, deportation and mass killings of the Jews, which went on for six years. Fathers, mothers, grandparents and 1.5 million children were sent up in flames.

Like all genocides, dehumanization was a necessary precondition of the Holocaust. Dehumanization involves fear of the other. Like the body's immune system, which attacks foreign elements, the mind seems to attack foreign ideas and ways before it can understand them. The process of dehumanization, of deconstructing another, is a way of asserting one's own identity. But being unlike the other does not empower you to deny those others their existence. The essence of civilization—the essence of a social contract—is the acknowledgement of shared basic rights. And none is more fundamental than that of existence. Dehumanization, then, is the process by which we devalue the other and soon remove their right to exist.

**promulgating**
promoting

**narcissistic**
self-obsessed

Possessed of a long militaristic, patriotic, nationalistic history, the Germans felt humiliated by their loss in World War I and by the excessive demands of the post-war Treaty of Versailles. By **promulgating** theories that the Germans belonged to a "master race," the Nazis redefined dehumanization and made it into a high art. The fiercely proud and **narcissistic** tendencies in German culture were exploited to the hilt by the Nazi propaganda machine. The Germans scapegoated and stereotyped their targeted group, the Jews, as inferiors and a national threat, and instituted laws to curtail their rights. The long history of anti-Semitism in Europe simplified the process.

The Nazi illusion of grandeur and perfection threatens our understanding of civilization, as formulated from ancient times. Civilization does not mean that some are superior and some inferior, or that some are masters and others are slaves. Civilization demands that we accept others as part of a broader human community; that others are different, not less than; that others are strange, not threatening. Civilization, like marriage, requires compromise. But for Hitler, his thugs and the passive European population, there was no compromise.

# The Banality of Evil

**banality**
trite predictability

We told them not to be afraid, we wouldn't do anything to them, they should just stand in front of the wall. But it was taken for granted among us that they should be killed. So when somebody said, 'Shoot,' I swung around and pulled the trigger, three times, on automatic fire. I remember the little girl with the red dress hiding behind her granny.

One sunny morning in June 1992, Borislav Herak and two other Serb nationalist soldiers gunned down a Muslim family found hiding in a basement. Later, from a jail cell, he described many crimes he had committed to a reporter from the *New York Times*. "[H]is account was offered in a matter-of-fact manner, and always with a keen attention to detail. As he shifted between one killing and another, and between rapes, the young Serb gave the names of many of his victims. He described where they were killed, what they were wearing, and what they said immediately before they died."

What does a soldier think of as he carries out the genocidal policies of his government? The soldier quoted above, like many others, seemed to be obeying orders and following the crowd, with the rules around him laid down by the circumstances of war. Where was his conscience? Why do so few people involved in genocide recognize their own ability to take a moral stand and oppose evil? The soldiers doing the hacking in Rwanda, the rape in Bosnia, the slaughter of "non-desirables" anywhere, go against conscience by participating in thoughtlessness as much as they participate in genocide.

The philosopher Hannah Arendt, whose studies of totalitarianism remain central for all scholarship on this topic, has made a simple but startling observation: there is no great demon who acts as a mastermind behind evil. Evil comes out of the hearts of ordinary people who prefer to obey rather than think. This, then, is the banality of evil. Destruction arises not from some demonic vision but from ordinary thoughtlessness, indifference and silence. Some argue that historical precedents, economic conditions or cultural conflict cause people to be seduced by what appear to be passionate but simplistic solutions. And while it may be easier to get swept away by the crowd, we need courage to stand up against it.

## Some Conclusions

Many follow the crowd, while a few say "No." Even in a world of horror there are some who act according to their conscience, such as the righteous people of Le Chambon-sur-Lignes, France, who saved 5000 Jewish lives during World War II.

For you and me, genocidal events may seem to defy ordinary language and cause us to disbelieve the truth. They may seem so irrational and incredible that we may prefer to ignore, doubt or deny the documented facts. The numbing effect of the incomprehensible may inhibit the very thoughtfulness that we need in order to resist. As hard as it is to do, we should not let the experience of the unthinkable overwhelm our ability to fasten to the truth.

All the testimonies of survivors; all the elaborate words, ideas and structures of scholars attempting to frame the subject; all the memoirs written to recall the slain and condemn the injustice—all these are words in a vocabulary of responsibility to the human family. We owe it to the victims of genocide, to each other, and to our children to respond with thoughtfulness, conscience and spirit.

# Notes

1 *Genocide Watch*. Helen Fein, Ed. Yale, 1992.

2 *The History and Sociology of Genocide*. Frank Chalk and Kurt Jonassohn. Yale, 1990.

# In Rwanda, the Smell of Death Permeates the Air

Nigel Ryan

Rwanda is a green, hilly idyll, plumb in the heart of Africa, rather like Scotland with banana trees. Bird calls replace the sounds of the electronic world: There is one that makes you look round for a telephone ringing. At night, insects click like light switches. Rwanda has Africa's densest population; its leafy roadsides hum with life. Houses apparently on fire indicate family lunch on the go; cracks in the roof serve as kitchen chimneys. Toyota minibus-taxis rattle by crammed with passengers. Pedestrians wave as you pass with smiles like grand pianos opening—the smaller they are, the louder they yell. Butter wouldn't melt in their mouths.

It is incredible to think that five years ago this graceful and charming race was overtaken by mass madness and, in a 10-week binge, a million Rwandans were hacked to death or shot—one in seven of the population. At the root of the trouble—as of human folly from Ulster to Kosovo—lay an uncontained fear. Despite its 10-to-one ratio, the Hutu majority tribe has always felt threatened by the Tutsi minority, traditionally their rulers. And with good reason: While they were conducting a once-and-for-all massacre to purge Rwanda of Tutsi influence, a Tutsi-led army invaded and seized control.

Today, 120,000 Rwandans are in custody, charged with genocide. Prisoners wear a pale-pink uniform. You see them mending the roads and working in the fields. At night, they can be heard in the overcrowded jails chanting songs learned in the Scout movement (they were all good Catholics once). There is no rush to justice. Most Rwandan lawyers refuse to represent the accused for fear of reprisals. That job falls to *Avocats Sans Frontières* (ASF), a Belgian aid organization partly funded by the European Union.

I spent a week with a group of lawyers on loan from France, Belgium and French-speaking Africa who between them are trying to establish some semblance of a judicial procedure. On my first day, I spent several hours in court (a disused school-house) with three men accused of

From *The Spectator*, June 16, 1999. Reprinted with permission.

running a local squad who were waiting with their French lawyer, Maître Hélène Celier-Geoffroy, for a judge who never turned up (most judges have other, better-paid jobs to go to).

We filled the afternoon with a visit to Murambi technical college, converted into a makeshift museum of genocide. The college was a last rallying point for 27,000 Tutsis trying to flee their persecutors. A young guide opened a door to us to what had been a dormitory of four students. On each bed were neat rows of skulls. He opened a second door, then a third . . . By the sixth we had seen enough.

I returned that night dumb with incomprehension to the sanctuary of the ASF compound, with its barbed wire and guards. I washed my hair and changed my clothes, but I could not get rid of the stale, sweet smell of death. It permeated everything, even the view. The compound veranda looks on to a magnificent panorama. In one corner is a cathedral-sized Catholic church in which 100 Rwandans were massacred. How can one start to understand what it takes to make human beings turn to mass murder? Was a whole nation insane? Did an evil cloud descend?

It was one of the African lawyers, Maître Nouga from the Cameroons, who gave me my first glimmer of insight into the psychology of ethnic cleansing: "In order to understand you first have to accept that every human being is the same. You have to say to yourself, 'Under the same

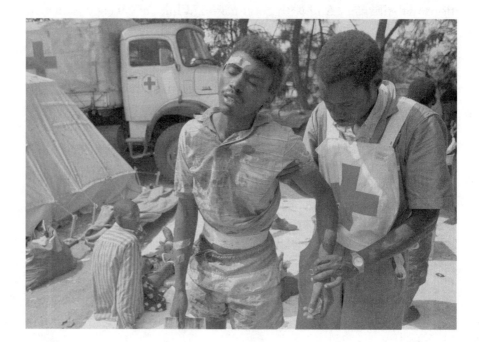

special circumstances I could have done that.' If you cannot make that leap in your mind, you have lost the battle to understand."

The special circumstances in Rwanda were exposure to a sustained, officially sanctioned campaign of hate—a variant of Nazi Germany, Ulster, Kosovo. Just as the Nazis blamed the Jews, so the extremist Hutus blamed the Tutsis for every wrong and every ill in their lives, real or imagined. Taking a leaf out of **Goebbels'** book, the extremist Radio Mille Collines (1,000 Hills) broadcast round-the-clock propaganda culminating in an open call to kill: and not just Tutsis, but moderate Hutu opposition supporters thought to be too soft on them.

Maître Nouga had studied the effect of the campaign on his clients (one of whom was called de Gaulle), using it as grounds for arguing diminished responsibility: "The first stage of the campaign is identifying the enemy and establishing them in your mind as a threat to you and your family. Feeling threatened brings out the killer in all of us." I thought of road rage when for a blind, homicidal split-second you wish the other driver dead. "Next comes the dehumanization process: These are not humans, they are vermin and they threaten your survival. It is your patriotic duty to exterminate them together with their progeny. When you believe that, you are ready to kill. And once you start it gets easier."

Cases I was to witness bore out this logic of poison. A 40-year-old soldier under sentence of death appeared on television to say he had been possessed and had taken part in rape and murder on the order of his superiors. Now he had seen God and wanted to repent. Others talked as if they had been hypnotized. A farmer had given himself up, unable to live with the thought that he had killed a Tutsi girl he found hiding in his vegetable patch; but, he said, he had acted in a trance, obeying orders from Radio Mille Collines.

Fear fuelled by propaganda and whipped into madness, the ingredients of a cocktail of evil—how else to explain husbands and wives of opposing races killing each other, doctors aborting Tutsi babies, neighbours of decades slaughtering one another?

Since trials began two years ago, 1,200 Rwandans have been sentenced: about half to death (a handful have been executed) and half to prison. At this rate, it will take 200 years to get through them all, assuming ASF stays beyond its present mandate, which ends in 18 months. What will the government do about that? Will they just have to release the convicted? There has been talk of speeding up court proceedings by means of "popular justice"—one shudders to think what that would

**Goebbels**
the Nazi Director of Propaganda in WWII

entail. For the moment the Rwandan answer is *"On verra."* That's in the future. The present has more pressing problems: life in an inherently unstable situation, a nation propped up by world aid agencies, and a minority government concerned with staying in power.

The university of Butare, Rwanda's second largest town, looks today exactly like any American place of learning. It is hard to believe in this leafy campus teachers set about butchering their own students, but they did. In the entrance hall is a memorial book with introductory words from the new rector: "Do not waste time on tears and reproaches for evil done; turn your attention instead to trying to understand it, so as to eradicate the cause. It is necessary to ensure that this cannot happen again." Pious words, but a better treatment for madness than bombing it.

At the weekend I swam in a lake with some of the ASF lawyers, after being assured that there were no crocodiles and that the hippos "usually" kept to the far bank. An otter joined us, head popping up to observe, like a submarine periscope. Overhead a corps de ballet of dragonflies with black square markings on their elegant, transparent wings performed an aerial Swan Lake. Afterwards we learned that the lake had been used to dispose of the bodies of dead Tutsis "to help them on their way to the river and back home to Ethiopia where they came from." In Rwanda, you can eat bananas, mangoes or avocados off the tree and drink fresh ginger cordial, but you can't get away from the smell of death.

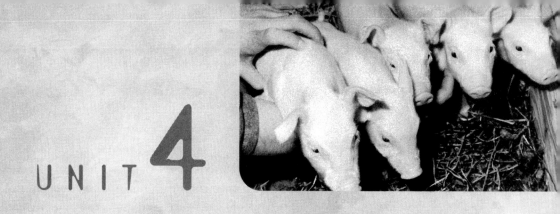

# UNIT 4

# Science and the Natural World

It seems to me that those sciences are vain and full of error which do not spring from experiment, the source of all certainty.

*Leonardo da Vinci*

I cannot believe that God plays dice with the cosmos.

*Albert Einstein*

The opposite of a correct statement is an incorrect statement, but the opposite of a profound truth is another profound truth.

*Neils Bohr*

Science cannot solve the ultimate mystery of nature. And it is because in the last analysis we ourselves are part of the mystery we are trying to solve.

*Max Planck*

# Introduction

Human beings are curious by nature, and it is this very curiosity that has led to much that is admirable in what humankind has produced. Reduced to its core, curiosity is simply asking questions. Why do people behave the way they do? What if we used this material in our building? Questions like these can lead to new theories in psychology, or find expression in a new form of architecture. The investigation of the natural world around us, normally seen as the realm of science, is really just asking a series of questions in a structured way. It also allows those questions to be answered in a consistent fashion and in a way that allows for the answers to be right or wrong. "Why are things the way they are?" may lead to "If this is the way that things are supposed to be, then shouldn't…?" The goal of this kind of questioning is the ability to predict what will happen if certain conditions are met. Ultimately, we end up with a theory that makes sense of a part of the natural world, and a framework that connects that particular part to our understanding of the whole world.

As suggested above, science is, in part, the methodical observing of a body of data; determining the relationships and regularities; figuring out the organizing and underlying patterns. This is the pedestrian side of science—a rigorous method and routine testing. The basic idea is straightforward. Starting with some knowledge, we infer that if X, then Y. Then, given some figures, we predict the likely result as exactly as possible. The prediction is put to the test of experience and is either upheld or refuted. If refuted, we either discard the **hypothesis** or try an amended version. It must be kept in mind, however, that hypotheses and theories are *not* certainties. They are conjectural in nature—educated guesses. There is conjecture involved in every use of evidence. Underlying patterns and structures are not written on every event or experience—they don't yell out, "Here I am!" The act of discovery is the act of informed speculation, the proposing of answers to questions beginning, "What if…"

This method of questioning also allows for present observation to be connected with past experience. Since any hypothesis must be verified, any evidence or findings resulting from an experiment are subject to the verdict of experience. Past experience may lead to the development of an hypothesis and consequent predictions about what will occur if something else happens. The merit of the hypothesis is confirmed or

**hypothesis**

proposition that serves as the basis for argument or experimentation disproved when that which is predicted either occurs or doesn't. The results of the experience, in turn, become part of the experience from which hypotheses may be generated. In this way, we are able to learn from mistaken ideas or failed experiments, and build a history of information that allows us to start a new investigation from a different vantage point. We are *not* condemned to repeat our mistakes and we *can* draw from the experience of others.

Both scientific method and informed speculation can be seen in the work of Edmund Halley (1656–1742). Newton's vision of gravity—a force that exerts an influence on all objects in the universe—allowed him to demonstrate mathematically the elliptical orbits described by Kepler. Newton's ideas presented a whole new way of seeing things: a whole new way of both asking and answering old questions. It also raised a new group of questions—many of them uncomfortable questions for the time. Halley, a British astronomer, began around 1695 to apply Newton's theories to the motion of comets. Comets were interesting objects to investigate. They were somewhat mysterious, partly because they exhibited no regularity whatsoever. According to Newton's theories, though, they should show an underlying regularity completely in tune with the rest of nature. Halley's "What if . . ." question was, "What if comets have very large elliptical orbits?" Halley decided to investigate a comet that he himself had seen in 1682. The observations made of this comet gave a fairly precise location to the comet's path while it was within sight. This was only a small portion of the total orbit, however, and did not allow for calculation of the overall size of the orbit or allow for the prediction of the comet's return.

Halley started doing a bit of historical research (past experience), and found a number of previous comet sightings that were detailed enough to make some comparisons. Some provocative data were provided by these comparisons. There were two earlier sightings that had recorded orbits very similar to the orbit of the comet that he had observed in 1682. Since it was highly improbable that three different comets would have the same orbit, Halley concluded that these were three different appearances of the same comet. Since the previous sightings had been in 1530–1531 and 1606–1607, Halley decided that the comet had an elliptical orbit that took about 76 years to circle the sun. Using the hypothesis of elliptical orbits within a Newtonian system, Halley further predicted the return of the comet some time in December of 1758. Both the hypothesis and the prediction stemming from it were cause for much discussion at the time. The proposed experiment, however long it might take to verify, was simple. Either the comet would appear as predicted or it would not. Although Halley died in 1742, the comet that returned on Christmas day in 1758 bears his name. The scientific community of the day conceded that Halley's hypothesis and prediction provided good justification for Newton's theories.

In light of our previous discussion of scientific method, Halley made an hypothesis that was testable. He wanted to prove that comets in general (and this comet in particular) operated within the confines of the Newtonian theory of Celestial Mechanics. More specifically, he wanted to demonstrate that a small mass was in an elliptical orbit around a large mass—the result of gravitational influence. By making a prediction, he allowed for his hypothesis to be tested. Using data on velocity and location that were available from the previous sightings, Halley was able to calculate the shape and size of the orbit and to predict its return in 76 years. His statement (that the comet would be in a certain place at a certain time) was either true or false. Its appearance at the proper time confirmed his hypothesis.

This process of question and answer, drawing from observed experience, is fundamental to the scientific process of discovery. In its more rigorous form and more structured application, it is known as the scientific method. The articles in this unit provide a range of perspectives on both the process and consequences of the application of this method.

In the essay written by Tom Olien, the author discusses the observation and structuring of information, the more pedestrian side of science. He also discusses, however, the creative leap that some scientists are able to make in order to find a grand, unifying theme. He compares this to an artist stepping "beyond the structured data and rules." Olien also draws an interesting distinction between the usefulness of science as a tool to aid us in learning the rules for understanding observable phenomena and its inappropriateness as a means of answering ultimate questions about the meaning of life. Douglas Futuyma explores the distinction between science and non-science in his article "Scientific Knowledge," which discusses debates around and within the theory of evolution. Central to his argument is the self-correcting nature of scientific endeavour, in large part enforced by the process of peer review by which science corrects itself. "Science is not the acquisition of truth; it is the quest for truth," he writes.

If science is a method of asking questions and learning and building from the answers, it is a method that we all use, to a greater or lesser degree, as we navigate throughout our lives. The degree of rigour used determines how well we learn from our experience and how clearly we see the forces at work both in the world around us and upon ourselves. As Carl Sagan writes, "Those creatures who find everyday experience a muddled jumble of events with no predictability, no regularity, are in grave peril. The universe belongs to those who, at least to some degree, have figured it out." Our role as informed individuals, actively participating in life, is to seek understanding.

As we achieve more and more understanding, our own picture becomes clearer. As we gather more experience, our own sense of "rightness" becomes more refined and we develop our own view of how the world works and how we fit in. Much as the scientist gathers and organizes data, looking for a unifying theme, individuals collect and examine various theories, find an order or unifying element and create a picture of what looks right to them.

All of the above is very theoretical. We are perhaps more accustomed to thinking about science in its many applied manifestations, the technological wonders that surround us in our daily lives. One of the more agreeable consequences of understanding how things work is the power that this understanding gives us over the world around us. We want to apply our knowledge in order to make our lives more comfortable and routine actions less strenuous. The more we learn, the more control over nature we are able to exert. However, in our enthusiastic pursuit of the fruits of science, we have often overlooked the consequences of the application of this knowledge. A number of articles in this section consider the questions related to the application of science. Freeman Dyson, in "Can Science Be Ethical?" raises the question of our responsibility to consider the ethical implications of any scientific application. Is it good (providing necessities for the disadvantaged), or is it evil (aggravating existing inequalities)? While he concludes that caution is justified and social constraints on new technologies are necessary, he also votes in favour of continued experimentation and discovery. Similarly, Brian Doyle argues that "members of a society must decide how they will use their resources to satisfy the needs of that society." His discussion of the guiding principles recommended by the Royal Commission on the New Reproductive Technologies is a good example of an ethical and responsible approach to the application of a new technology. Alan Bernstein, in "Secrets of the Human Genome," outlines some of the medical benefits arising from new scientific breakthroughs, but concludes with a cautionary note on the ethical challenges that face us in living with this new knowledge.

# The Path of Scientific Development

Tom Olien

In this course we have been exploring who we are as individuals (Unit 1), how we interact as groups (Unit 2), and how we structure power in our society (Unit 3). Later in the course (Unit 5), we will explore how we express ourselves through arts and culture. In this unit we will explore the role of scientific inquiry in understanding our natural universe, the impact of technological development as we harness the energy and resources of our planet to our own ends, and how these activities shape human self-awareness.

The scientific endeavour is a mammoth undertaking. To bring some order into this overwhelming human activity this chapter will outline a broad path of actions that lead to the development of a mature scientific discipline.

The cycle of scientific development starts with an idea, a problem to be solved, a paradox to be resolved or a speculation generated out of curiosity. In response, three primary activities are set in motion: (1) observing; (2) structuring the information; and (3) discovering or creating an underlying mechanism.

Inherent in each of these activities is a relentless process of reflection, checking equipment, correcting observations, updating techniques, confirming speculations and questioning theory. The result is the process shown in the chart on the next page. This process, exemplified by the development of major scientific disciplines such as physics, geology, biochemistry or genetics, parallels the steps of the scientific method, the discipline of curiosity used by individual scientists.

## Observing

Scientific activity starts with observation. Initially, observations were limited to the five human senses. But we now live in a world with powerful extensions to our primary senses. A simple set of binoculars drastically amplifies our ability to identify a bird in the woods or to see the stars and planets with a clarity that the most astute astronomer of 400 years ago could not imagine.

"The Path of Scientific Development" is by Tom Olien of Humber College. Used by permisson

## THE PATH OF SCIENTIFIC DEVELOPMENT

An idea, a problem, a paradox or a speculation starts the process

### The Process

**Observing**

- instrumentation that extends our senses
- skill and discipline
- objectivity

**Structuring and Using the Information**

- patterns and laws
- applied mathematical tools of analysis
- empirical rules for design and extension

**Discovering/Creating an Underlying Mechanism**

- a creative leap beyond reasoning
- a simple, elegant unifying principle
- creating new possibilities and testing new observations

Many instruments measure features of the universe that go beyond our senses. A voltmeter measures electrical potential, a feature of an electric circuit hidden from human senses except in the high values that produce a dangerous shock. A compass can detect the direction of the earth's "invisible" magnetic field while other instruments measure its strength. The Herculean forces between the rock faces of sliding continental plates can be measured as well as the temperatures of outer space or the heat in the core of a nuclear reactor.

Scientific observation requires both skill and discipline: the persistence of a keen nature observer waiting for hours to see the mating habits of an obscure species, the diligence in washing and sterilizing every piece of equipment over again to maintain the germ-free environment necessary for medical research, or the technical skill of the operator of a multi-million-dollar electron microscope.

Every area of scientific observation requires objectivity. Scientific objectivity should allow one to "see" what is really there and not what one hopes to "see." The ability to achieve this ultimate abstract objectivity is at best tainted by human frailty and at worst perverted by the massive personal, social, economic or ideological consequences of the impact of a given observation. In spite of these complications, the process of scientific observation usually converges to the point where all competent observers agree that they "see" the same thing in the same set of circumstances.

## Structuring and Using the Information

Once a body of data has been accumulated from reliable observation, the next task is to attempt to make some sense and order out of the data. Science assumes that every action follows some pattern, usually some cause-and-effect connection. Sometimes the connections are fairly simple and obvious. When a swinging golf club strikes a stationary ball on the tee, the ball takes off. The connection between force and motion is fairly direct and obvious in this case. Other times the connections are complex and obscure. The connection between cigarette smoking, lung cancer and heart disease is not so obvious. Statistically there is some relation, because large samples of smokers consistently show higher incidence of these problems than non-smokers. But we are unable to link directly one person's smoking of one pack a day to the onset of lung cancer a number of years later. There are too many factors involved to be able to make specific, direct cause-and-effect connections between these items.

Still, the search for patterns or laws, whether simple or complex, is a long term goal of science. The methods include cataloguing samples, making diagrams, enumerating lists and creating graphs. Statistical analysis and other powerful mathematical tools are all used. The details of a discovery may be tucked away in seemingly random data or "noise." Finding patterns in such circumstances is not unlike the capacity of the human ear to pick out a faint cry for help in the midst of the roar of a hurricane.

Laws and empirical rules for design and extension can be developed from these patterns and used by science and society. Using the periodic table of the elements, a chemist can predict that an element in the same column but next row can be expected to have similar properties to the one in the previous row. This may be enough guide or warning to allow one to make a useful compound or avoid a potentially explosive one.

At this stage in the path of scientific development we may have some very useful rules for how things work, but we do not know why they work as they do. There appears no obvious fundamental mechanism, only rules, often very complex and arbitrary ones connecting certain facts and events. To simplify and make sense of these rules there is an urge to discover an underlying principle.

## Discovering or Creating an Underlying Mechanism

The discovery of grand themes and fundamental theories is the crowning achievement of the creative human mind working in the arena of science. The laws of universal gravitation, relativity, evolution, continental drift and genetics are examples of underlying mechanisms.

These themes did not emerge from reason alone. Like artists, scientists must step beyond the structured data and rules. Typically a person or a group makes an educated guess or an intuitive leap that opens a new possibility and a new way of thinking. The genius of the process of science is that it doesn't stop with a good guess, but sets to testing it thoroughly. The creative guesses that were wrong have long since disappeared, leaving us only the heroic tales and legacies of the ones that worked.

A fundamental theory is often simple. Usually, it is grounded on an elegant and aesthetically pleasing unifying principle. Looking back, most people would say it is obvious, it looks so right and natural. For example, the simple, elegant and powerful $E = mc^2$ is a symbol that is recognized by almost anyone in our century.

The discovery of an underlying mechanism creates new possibilities. It begs to be used and tested in new areas. Great advances in scientific development and technological application take place following the breakthrough of a major scientific theory. Each extension is also a test of the new theory. Applications that work confirm the theory. When the extensions of the theory begin to break down and special rules and adjustments are needed to get consistent results, paradoxes emerge, and a new understanding of a fundamental mechanism is begging to be brought forward. We are thrown back to the beginning of the process. And thus science moves on, never complete, no matter how convincing, powerful and elegant a particular theory may be at one time.

We will examine how these three stages develop from examples in celestial mechanics and genetics.

# The Path to an Underlying Mechanism in Celestial Mechanics

Global navigation in the fifteenth century revived interest in the stars and planets. Little change had been made to the model of the universe developed by Ptolemy in second-century Roman times. In this theory, the earth was at the centre of the universe and at rest with no rotation or motion. The sun, moon and planets revolved around this fixed earth, their motions explained by a system of over 80 circles within circles. The system was adequate for the needs of the time (it worked as a system of navigation), but it was very complex.

Copernicus revived an old idea that had fallen by the wayside. He suggested that the system would be simpler if we treated the sun as the centre of the system of planets and rotated the earth daily to allow for the rising and setting of the sun and moon and stars. It seems obvious to us now, but not so in the context of his time. Religious dogma and our own ego demanded that we see ourselves and our earth as the pinnacle of creation and thus, axiomatically, the centre of it all. But the simplicity and elegance of the Copernican suggestion was convincing and encouraged a new wave of thinking at a time when society was opening up to new ideas and technology was evolving to allow new observations. And so the process was set in motion.

The observational step is exemplified by the Danish astronomer Tycho Brahe. He made meticulous observations of the heavens that were 100 times more accurate than previous observations, pushing the very limits of accuracy of the unaided eye. Meanwhile, making use of the newly developed optical lenses to make a telescope, Galileo extended the process of observation into new domains. He saw the rotation of the sun, the phases of Venus, and moons revolving around Jupiter. These and other observations did much to challenge the dogmas that had kept a geocentric view of the universe dominant for so many centuries. (Galileo was also instrumental in developing the experimental method and proposing theories of terrestrial mechanics that would be vital to future steps.)

To make sense of these observations, Johann Kepler, a German mathematician and astronomer, applied his analytical skills to Tycho Brahe's data. His structuring of the information led to three laws of planetary motion. These laws correctly described and predicted the motion of the earth, moon and planets about the sun. They are used to this day for calculating the orbits of satellites around the earth. But Kepler's laws lacked any viable explanation of why these laws worked.

The explanation came from the leap made by Isaac Newton. Galileo had described the action of gravity for earth-bound objects such as stones and cannon balls. The leap that Newton made was to ask if gravity actually extended to the moon. Again, it may seem obvious to us, but it represented radical new thinking at the time, and only a few

## THE PATH OF SCIENTIFIC DEVELOPMENT

### Celestial Mechanics

**IDEA**—Copernicus (1473–1543) proposed that the earth is not the centre of the universe.

#### Observing

- **Tycho Brahe** (1546–1601) gathered new, precise information about planets.
- **Galileo** (1564–1642) used the telescope to observe rotation of sun and the revolution of the moons of Jupiter.

#### Structuring and Using the Information

- **Kepler** (1571–1630) developed three laws of planetary motion: (1) the orbits of the planets around the sun are elliptical, with the sun at one focus; (2) the line drawn from the sun to a planet sweeps out equal areas in equal times; (3) the square of the period of the planet is proportional to the cube of the radius.

#### Discovering/Creating an Underlying Mechanism

- **Newton** (1642–1727) formulated the law of universal gravitation: All objects in the universe attract each other. The force increases with the product of their masses and decreases with their distance apart.

$$F = \frac{Gm_1m_2}{r^2}$$

decades earlier this idea would have been ruled out as heresy by both church and science. Newton did some calculations and found it worked for the moon. In fact it worked for all the planets, with the sun as the gravitational centre of the solar system. Kepler's laws could then be deduced as a consequence of universal gravitation rather than as a separate set of rules for our planetary system.

The mechanism of universal gravitation could be applied to objects on the surface of the earth and beyond. It explained the pattern of the tides and allowed for accurate predictions, such as the date of return of Halley's comet and the existence of the planet Neptune, finally observed in 1846.

The power of Newton's mechanical laws is seen in the word "mechanism" itself, as well as in the history of the industrial revolution. The principles of mechanics, thermodynamics and electromagnetism have led to the proliferation of machinery unimaginable before and, even more significantly, have become the model for the way of thinking in many other domains of human endeavour as well. For example, we often view and treat the human body as a complex mechano-electro-chemical machine. We talk about the machinery of government and the chemistry of relations. So great is the power of these theories in directing human activity that for a while we lost sight of them as theories, as models of reality. As theories take on the aura of reality itself they lead us to believe that science can fully explain the universe and deliver ultimate truth for us. But, "Science is not about truth, it is about the most reliable information at the time," says Paul Davies. So, we are forced to travel the path of scientific development over and over again in cyclical fashion, to let in new and grander theories that reject previous notions or treat earlier theories as a subset of a larger picture.

Only a century ago, for instance, it was suggested that the physics of the day could explain all physical phenomena. But, within 20 years, the observation of details within the atom and activities taking place at close to the speed of light showed that classical mechanics and electromagnetism did not apply at the atomic level or at very high speeds. It took Albert Einstein's Special Theory of Relativity and the development of quantum mechanics to supersede Newtonian mechanics, not making it wrong, but limiting it to objects of ordinary sizes and speeds. We were forced to encounter "realities" that were far outside our day-to-day experience. How can we talk about "now" in a universe with a finite speed of light, so that it takes seconds to communicate with the moon, minutes with the sun, hours with the planets, years to thousands of years with the stars and millions to billions of years with the galaxies. The expansion of the universe observed by Edwin Hubble in the 1920s can be seen as a metaphor for an expanding reality. Surely, no one theory can capture the full expression of such a reality.

# The Path to an Underlying Mechanism in Genetics

Although genetics is barely 100 years old, it is constantly in the news: genetic-linked diseases, genes for behaviour traits, cloning, the Human Genome Project. The field of genetics provides an excellent example of the path of scientific development and also highlights the increased speed of the whole process.

Mendel is credited as the father of genetics based on his systematic observations of cross-breeding of characteristics in pea plants. He also enunciated some basic rules to explain the patterns of genetic inheritance. About the same time, the physical location of the "inheritance material" was found in the chromosomes. These appear under a microscope as small sausage-like objects within the nucleus of the cells of an organism.

## THE PATH OF SCIENTIFIC DEVELOPMENT

### Genetics

**IDEA**—Organisms inherit characteristics of the parent.

**Observing**

- **Mendel** (1822–1884) observed the inheritance pattern in peas.

**Structuring and Using the Information**

- **Mendel** also introduced the basic form of the laws of genetics.
- Many people use the laws of genetics to improve grains and livestock and to understand and control some genetic diseases.

**Discovering/Creating an Underlying Mechanism**

- **Watson and Crick** discovered the DNA molecule that reveals the code that governs all genetics.

But there are a small number a chromosomes and a very large number of genetic features for even the simplest organism. The gene was the name given for the package of information coded for a particular characteristic. But the physical form and activity this gene took on was unknown.

For over half a century critical observations and increasingly complex rules of genetics were developed and applied to improve grains and livestock and to add to our understanding of hereditary diseases. But the gene itself remained a mystery. The fundamental mechanism driving genetics was a mystery, a **black box** with some patterns of input and output understood and many more not understood. The structure and the activity within the black box remained unknown.

It was the study of nucleic acids by Watson and Crick that opened up the black box in 1953. They illuminated the structure of the DNA molecule and its capacity to code information and replicate. The revolution in genetics had begun. Just as mechanical engineers, armed with the foundations of mechanics generated the industrial revolution in a previous era, now genetic engineers equipped with an understanding of the fundamental genetic structure are developing tools and techniques that can systematically control the features of plants, animals and human beings. The implications are exciting and frightening but with the basic mechanism understood there is no turning back the exploration.

And the story isn't over. The machine-like simplicity of the DNA molecule and its basic mode of operation is not unlike Newtonian mechanics in its ability to allow us to think we have the "whole truth" about the genetic process. At first look the DNA molecule elegantly explained evolution based on genetic mutations due to damage and replication errors in the DNA. But new data is arriving and chinks in this simple model are occurring. New scientific concepts are just over the horizon to begin to deal with this new data: autopoiesis (self-organizing systems) and complexity theory to name only two.

One hundred years ago, the terms "relativity," "**quantum mechanics**," "wave-particle duality" and "expanding universe" were not part of our vocabulary and particles such as neutrons and neutrinos were unknown. These are more than just terms understood by a handful of highly trained scientists. They are now images that deeply affect our understanding of who we are in the universe. And so, we are part of a current drama as the path of scientific development continues to cycle back on itself creating new images and new understandings of the human project.

---

**black box**

a term scientists use to describe a situation in which we know essentially what something does, but we don't yet comprehend how it operates (like machinery covered up by a black box)

**quantum mechanics**

the mathematical representation of the dynamic structure and behaviour of atoms and molecules

# The Illusion of Fundamental Mechanisms

We have seen how powerful the breakthrough to a fundamental mechanism is to scientific development. But fundamental mechanisms still beg the question of why they are there in the first place. Newton's law of universal gravitation does not really explain what gravity is but just how it acts. Einstein's Theory of General Relativity suggests that gravity may be seen as the distortion of space-time planes by the effects of mass objects, thereby reducing gravity to an issue of geometry, not an item or a force at all. There seems to be a never-ending sequence of new possibilities—an awesome and exciting possibility in itself.

An even more subtle illusion is hidden in the almost religious belief that science is about truth and the hope that the methods of science will answer all of life's questions and eventually solve the issues of a stable and satisfying life for our species on the planet. Instead we must turn to science as one of several wisdoms needed to resolve the issues of the meaning and purpose of life. Many of the noted physicists of the twentieth century were essentially mystics. They allowed the possibility of a dimension to human experience that was not accessible by the methods of their science. That doesn't mean they invoked God or some outside mystical force to explain the problems of their science. But neither did they expect science to explain the full richness of their unique life experience. Science seeks to illuminate the mechanisms of repeatable phenomena in all domains of our universe. As for the ultimate questions about the meaning of life, science may provide powerful clues, but on its own has no final answers.

# Scientific Knowledge

Douglas J. Futuyma

> It is time for students of the evolutionary process, especially those who have
> been misquoted and used by the creationists, to state clearly that evolution is
> fact, not theory . . . . Birds arose from nonbirds and humans from nonhumans.
> No person who pretends to any understanding of the natural world can deny
> these facts anymore than she or he can deny that the earth is round, rotates on
> its axis, and revolves around the sun.
>
> *Richard C. Lewontin, 1981*[1]

Before the mid-1930s, science in Russia could proudly hold its own
with any in the world. Within genetics and evolution alone, the names
Vavilov, Dubinin, Timofeef-Ressovsky, Severtzov, Schmalhausen, and
many others ranked with the best researchers in England, Germany, or the
United States. Then came Trofim D. Lysenko, a man unschooled in science but well attuned to political currents. Presenting not scientific evidence but Marxist rhetoric, he won the support of Stalin for his genetic
theories. Within a decade the best scientists in the Soviet Union had
been imprisoned, executed, or silenced. Why?

**Mendelism**

the theory of heredity advanced by
the Austrian monk and botanist
Gregor Mendel (1822–1881)

According to Lysenko, **Mendelism** was "the tool of bourgeois society,"
particularly in holding that the gene could not be altered except by mutation, and that the direction of mutation was random—meaning that mu-
tational change could not be governed by man or the environment.
This, Lysenko believed, had to be wrong; because nature, as Marxist doc-
trine showed, had to be both improvable and perfectable. Adopting a
kind of **Lamarckism**, Lysenko set out not only to destroy his Mendelian
rivals but to transform Soviet agriculture. Improved varieties of crops
could be created, he said, by allowing the environment to alter their
hereditary properties. Within a single generation, he could transform
winter wheat into spring wheat merely by changing the temperature
in which it grew. He went further, saying that species could be transformed into other species at will—wheat into rye, for instance—by
planting them in the right environment. The Darwinian idea that members of a species compete for the necessities of life was an invention of

**Lamarckism**

the theory advanced by the French
naturalist Lamarck (1744–1829)
that acquired characteristics can be
passed down to offspring

From Douglas J. Futuyma's *Science on Trial: The Case for Evolution*. New York: Sinauer
Associates, 1995. Reprinted with permission.

bourgeois science used to justify class struggle in a capitalist society. There could be no inherent competition, only altruism in nature. Seeds should be sown in clusters so that all except one would "sacrifice themselves for the good of the species."

Rapidly achieving command of Soviet biology and agriculture, Lysenko destroyed it all. From the 1930s on, biological research in the Soviet Union was perverted to Lysenko's ends, and agricultural production fell deeper and deeper into disaster. Lysenko had never given evidence for his claims; but his political power left him unassailable. Only in 1965 was he finally deposed, and Soviet biology . . . . [struggled ever after] to catch up with the West.

A grim story indeed, but what do we learn from it? That reality stubbornly refuses to be bent to our desires or ideologies. Genes cannot be altered to suit our ends, as devoutly as we may wish them to be. Truth cannot be established by the Communist Party, nor by the vote of a democratic society or a board of education. Reality does not yield to wishful thinking. There are certainly many people who believe in unicorns, or in the predictions of astrology, or in the transmigration of souls, because these beliefs satisfy their emotional needs. Such needs, however powerful, do not make unicorns or astrological influences or **metempsychosis** any more real. Nor do our wishes make unpleasant realities go away; death and disease remain grimly real.

In this light, how should we interpret such creationists' objections to teaching evolution as that it is harmful to the child because it "contradicts his innate consciousness of reality and thus tends to create mental and emotional conflicts within him"; it "tends to remove all moral and ethical restraints"; "it may tend to rob life of meaning and purpose"; it "leads to a conviction that might makes right"? In other words, don't tell people about evolution because it's unpleasant, like death. Deny the reality of evolution and you can save the child from emotional conflicts and immorality.

Even if these accusations were true, they would be irrelevant to the question of whether or not evolution is a fact. Science is science only if it limits itself to determining the nature of reality. The hallmark of science is not the question "Do I wish to believe this?" but the question "What is the evidence?" It is this demand for evidence, this habit of cultivated skepticism, that is most characteristic of the scientific way of thought. It is not limited to science, but it isn't universal, either. Many people still cling to traditional beliefs in the face of contrary evidence, out of wishful thinking, the desire for security and simplicity. But rationalism, as the

Charles Darwin

metempsychosis
reincarnation

philosopher of science Karl Popper has said, "has . . . always claimed the right of reason and of empirical science to criticize, and to reject, any tradition, any authority, as being based on sheer unreason, or prejudice, or accident."

At its best, science challenges not only nonscientific views but established scientific views as well. This, in fact, is the wellspring of progress in science. Our knowledge can progress only if we can find errors and learn from them. Thus, much of the history of science consists of a rejection or modification of views that were once widely held. Geologists once believed in the fixity of continents, but now believe in continental drift. The **Newtonian theory of physics** is now seen as a special case of a larger theory that includes relativity. Scientists realize, if they have any sense at all, that all their currently accepted beliefs are provisional. They are, at present, the best available explanations, but subsequent research may show them to be false or incomplete. I cannot stress this point too strongly. Unlike fundamentalists who will not consider the possibility that they could be wrong, good scientists *never* say they have found absolute "truth." Read any scientific paper and you will find the conclusions couched in words like "apparently" or "it appears that."

Scientists accept uncertainty as a fact of life. Some people are uncomfortable unless they have positive, eternal answers; scientists come to terms with uncertainty and mutability as a fundamental condition of human knowledge. Science is not the acquisition of truth; it is the quest for truth.

The picture I have just painted is, of course, a somewhat idealistic one. In fact, scientists are just as human as anyone else. They believe that one or another hypothesis is most likely to be true, and they engage in sometimes bitter battles to defend their ideas. Scientists' beliefs are also shaped by their political, social, and religious environment. It is undoubtedly true that **Darwin** and **Wallace** were led to the idea of natural selection because the English economic system of their day put an emphasis on competition, free enterprise, and economic progress. The history of IQ testing shows that scientists can often be misled by their social beliefs. Psychologists in the early part of this century "knew" that there were fixed hereditary differences between races in intelligence, and interpreted all the data they collected in this light. One of the pioneers in IQ testing, H.H. Goddard, "discovered" by testing immigrants that 79 percent of the Italians, 83 percent of the Jews, and 87 percent of the Russians were "feeble minded." The IQ test was in English, of course.

---

**Newtonian theory of physics**

traditional theory of physics, including the laws of gravity and of motion, established by the English physicist and mathematician Newton (1642–1727)

**Charles Darwin**

British naturalist (1809–1883) credited with being the father of the theory of evolution by natural selection

**Alfred Wallace**

A contemporary of Darwin who also worked on the theory of evolution (1823–1913)

Thus the common image of scientists as abstracted, unbiased, detached intellectuals has no foundation in reality. Scientists are often highly opinionated, even in the face of contrary evidence; and they are often not particularly intelligent, either. The spectrum of scientists, as of any other group of people, runs from the brilliant to the fairly stupid. Almost every scientist has made more than one asinine statement in the course of his or her career, and some make them habitually.

If scientists can be just as biased, subjective, and foolish as anyone else, why should we have any belief in what they say about physics, evolution, or the causes of cancer? Because scientists are motivated not only by a quest for knowledge but a quest for reputation. And there is no better way for a scientist to achieve reputation than to demolish existing ideas by finding contrary evidence, or to propose a theory that explains the evidence better. This means that although individual scientists often make errors, the body of scientists in a field eventually uncovers these errors and attempts to correct them. Every scientist's research depends on the research of others in the field; so out of pure self-interest, every scientist scrutinizes the work of others carefully, to be sure it is reliable. Science is a self-correcting process.

How are errors found? First, most scientific journals send articles to other scientists for review before accepting them for publication. Such an article is expected to present not only experimental data but a detailed description of the methods by which the data were obtained, so that others can repeat the experiment. Reviewers scrutinize these papers and often reject them for any of several reasons: insufficient data, erroneous methods, improper use of statistics, unwarranted deductions from the data. About half the papers submitted to *Evolution*, the journal that I edit, are rejected for these kinds of failings.

Certainly not all errors are caught at this stage, but many of those that slip by are pointed out by other researchers in papers they subsequently publish. Any supposed fact or theory that is at all important is soon tested by other scientists, who see if they can confirm the results. Recently, for example, some investigators claimed that immune resistance acquired during an individual's lifetime could be passed on genetically. This claim of Lamarckian inheritance runs counter to genetics and evolutionary theory; if it were true, it would be extremely important. But other immunologists immediately tried to repeat the observations and were unable to verify them. Such a claim will be held in abeyance, or rejected outright by the scientific community.

Very rarely, there are even cases of dishonesty. A recently publicized case is that of the late Cyril Burt, whose data on the IQs of separated pairs of twins provided the main evidence for a genetic basis for IQ variation. Burt's critics have now found inconsistencies in his data, and even his supporters have ultimately agreed that he must have made up data. But such cases are extraordinarily rare, because every scientist worthy of the name knows that his or her data must withstand scrutiny.

The result of this process of exploration and correction is that at any time, scientists have a body of knowledge and understanding that is reliable, within the limits of what can be known at that time. It is for this reason that I, as a biologist, can have confidence in, say, radiometric dating, or in the atomic theory of chemical reactions, even though I have no personal knowledge of these fields. Radiometric dating is so critical to physics and geology that it would not be widely used unless its validity had been repeatedly tested. A scientist therefore does not appeal to the authority of any one scientist to justify his or her beliefs, but rather to the entire body of scientific practice.

So far, I have been talking about science without defining it. Many people assume that science is the collection and cataloging of facts, but science is much more than this. Darwin saw this clearly: "About thirty years ago there was much talk that geologists ought only to observe and not to theorize; and I well remember someone saying that at this rate a man might as well go into a gravel-pit and count the pebbles and describe the colours. How odd it is, that anyone should not see that all observation must be for or against some view, if it is to be of any service!" That is, science consists of a search for explanations. The *Oxford English Dictionary* defines science as "a branch of study which is concerned with a body of demonstrated truths, or with observed facts, systematically classified and more or less **colligated** by being brought under general laws, and which includes trustworthy methods for the discovery of new truths within its own domain."

**colligated**

linked together by a shared general description or hypothesis

I have already described some of these "trustworthy methods." What makes them trustworthy is repeatability. An observation is accepted as a scientific "fact" only if it can be repeated by other individuals who follow the same methods. Thus extrasensory perception is not considered factual by most scientists, because so far it has not been possible for skeptical observers to verify the claims of people who say they have ESP.

But what are the "truths" that science is supposed to discover? "Truth," according to the same dictionary, is "conformity with fact; agreement with reality." "Fact," in turn, is "something that has really occurred or is actually the case; something certainly known to be of this character; hence a particular truth known by actual observation or authentic testimony." But whose knowledge or observation serves to establish something as fact? Certainly not the populace at large. It is very possible that most people in the world do not know the fact that the earth revolves around the sun. Then what kind of observation establishes a fact? Not direct observation, necessarily. We observe the sun moving across the sky, but not the fact of the earth's rotation. We accept the fact that material is made of atoms, but we have no personal experience of them. In the scientific sense, then, "facts" must be propositions agreed upon by individuals who have repeatedly applied rigorous, controlled methods of direct or indirect observation. All but the most trivial facts ("There is a blue chair in my office") begin life as hypotheses, and graduate to "facthood" as knowledgeable individuals come to agree upon them. The rotation of the earth was once a hypothesis; it is now a fact. Facts are merely hypotheses that are well supported by the available evidence.

The word "hypothesis" means, to many people, an ungrounded speculation. But this is not the way the word is used in science. As Sir Peter Medawar says,

> Most words of the philosopher's vocabulary, including "philosopher" itself, have changed their usages over the past few hundred years. "Hypothesis" is no exception. In a modern professional vocabulary a hypothesis is an imaginative preconception of *what might be true* in the form of a declaration with verifiable deductive consequences. It no longer tows "**gratuitous**," "mere," or "wild" behind it, and the **pejorative** usage ("evolution is a mere hypothesis," "it is only a hypothesis that smoking causes lung cancer") is one of the outward signs of little learning.

**gratuitous**
undeserved

**pejorative**
negative

The difference between a fact and a hypothesis, then, is a matter of degree, a matter of how much evidence there is. Yet people who have a vested interest in opposing scientific conclusions often claim that whatever they oppose is merely a hypothesis or a theory, not a set of facts. For several decades there has been overwhelming evidence that smoking causes lung cancer; but the tobacco industry says that this hasn't been "proven," that the relationship is a "hypothesis" instead of a "fact." In exactly the same way, **creationists** say that evolution is a theory, not a fact, and hence unproven. However, nothing in science is ever proven in this sense. There are no **immutable** facts. Every scientific claim is a hypothesis, however well supported it may be. It has never been proven

**creationists**
those who maintain that the universe was created by God as recounted in the Bible

**immutable**
unchanging

that hemoglobin carries oxygen; there is merely so much evidence for this claim that it is hardly imaginable that it could be false. Nonetheless, it is still conceivable that some revolution in chemistry could completely change the theory of chemical bonds, and that we would have to revise our notion of what hemoglobin does.

It is important to recognize that not all "facts" are susceptible to scientific investigation, simply because some observations and experiences are entirely personal. I cannot prove that someone loves his or her child. The emotions that any individual claims to have are not susceptible to scientific documentation, because they cannot be independently verified by other observers. In other words, science seeks to explain only objective knowledge, knowledge that can be acquired independently by different investigators if they follow a prescribed course of observation or experiment. Many human experiences and concerns are not objective, and so do not fall within the realm of science. As a result, science has nothing to say about **aesthetics** or morality. It cannot provide an objective basis on which to judge whether or not Beethoven wrote great music, or whether or not an act is ethical. The functioning of human society, then, clearly requires principles that stem from some source other than science. While science can provide objective knowledge, we must look elsewhere for guidance on how to use that knowledge.

**aesthetics**

theories of beauty

Scientific facts are, as Darwin suggested, usually not very interesting unless they bear on theories that explain them. "Theory" in science has a very special meaning. It does not mean mere speculation or conjecture. Rather, as the *Oxford English Dictionary* puts it, a theory is "a scheme or system of ideas and statements held as an explanation or account of a group of facts or phenomena; a hypothesis that has been confirmed or established by observation or experiment, and is propounded or accepted as accounting for the known facts; a statement of what are known to be the general laws, principles, or causes of something known or observed." Thus, relativity theory and Newtonian theory are bodies of interconnected statements that in combination explain physical events. Atomic theory is a body of statements about the structure of atoms that explains chemical reactions. Plate tectonic theory is a body of statements about forces operating within the earth that, among other things, are responsible for the movement of continents. Each of these theories relates a vast number of formerly disconnected phenomena. Plate tectonic theory, for example, brings together observations in seismology, geomagnetism, geochemistry, and various branches of terrestrial and marine geology.

When, in this way, a theory makes sense out of many otherwise myste-rious phenomena, it is likely to be accepted even before there is actually adequate evidence. Nevertheless, every such theory makes predictions, which then test the theory's validity. The Copernican theory of the solar system, although thoroughly accepted by the seventeenth century, was not definitively tested until the 1830s, when the predictions it made about stel-lar parallax (the direction of a star from different places on the earth's orbit) were verified.

One criterion of a good scientific theory is that it makes predictions which, if subsequently confirmed, serve to support the theory. It must be kept in mind, however, that even if they support it, they do not prove it true. It is always possible that another theory, yet to be conceived, would make the same predictions. Thus there is another important criterion of a sci-entific theory which most scientists accept. This is Karl Popper's dictum that a theory be in principle "falsifiable." That is, a good theory doesn't merely explain everything; it specifically predicts that certain observations, if made, would prove the theory wrong. If you propose that diseases are caused by evil spirits, there is no way in which I could possibly prove your the-ory wrong. Such "spirits" would not be detectable; and if they act at whim, I can make no predictions about who will or will not fall sick. The germ theory of disease, on the other hand, makes specific predictions about in-fectivity, physical conditions that favor the contraction of disease, and so on. It predicts that a disease could not be caused by germs if people suffer it who have never contacted infected material.

The most powerful form of science, then, consists of formulating hy-potheses, sometimes by observation and sometimes by intuition, anal-ogy, or other sources of insight that we do not fully understand; and deducing conclusions from these hypotheses that can be tested directly or indirectly by observation or experiment. The testing of hypotheses is the "body of trustworthy methods" to which the *Oxford English Dictionary* refers.

If a scientific theory is one that can be **corroborated** by observa-tions that accord with its predictions, that can be falsified by observations or experiments which are incompatible with the theory, and that relies on objective observations that can be repeated by trained, unbiased ob-servers, a nonscientific theory must be the converse. The nonscientific the-orist lives within an impregnable fortress, safe from criticism, because the hallmark of nonscientific theories is that they cannot be falsified. They are formulated vaguely, or invoke agents whose actions cannot be

**corroborated**
verified

predicted, so that they "explain" every possible outcome of a situation. Whatever your personality or history may be, a good astrologer will find some conjunction of the planets that explains why you are this way, even though as a Sagittarius you're "expected" to be the opposite.

Similarly, any "theory" that explains phenomena by recourse to the actions of an **omnipotent, omniscient** supreme being, or any other supernatural omnipotent entity, is a nonscientific theory. I could postulate that all human actions are slavish responses to the suggestions of guardian angels and **diabolical incubi,** and no one could possibly prove me wrong; for whether a person's actions look rational or irrational, good or evil, I can involve the power of supernatural suggestion. I could similarly postulate that God personally has governed the development and life of every creature that has ever been born, and if you protest that the laws of physics, chemistry, and biology explain biological phenomena, I could answer that God in his wisdom sees fit to act in an orderly way that gives the appearance of material laws of causation.

Because such a theory cannot be challenged by any observation, it is not scientific. It isn't necessarily wrong. It is just not amenable to scientific investigation. Science cannot deny the existence of supernatural beings. It cannot prove that God didn't create the universe. It can't prove that God isn't shunting electrons down the **cytochrome** molecules in your **mitochondria**. Science can neither affirm nor deny supernatural powers. Science is the exercise of reason, and so is limited to questions that can be approached by the use of reason, questions that can be answered by the discovery of objective knowledge and the elucidation of natural laws of causation. In dealing with questions about the natural world, scientists must act as if they can be answered without recourse to supernatural powers. There can be no scientific study of God.

How do these generalizations about science apply to the problem of evolution? We are dealing with two distinct questions. The first is the historical question of whether or not evolution has actually occurred: Have living forms actually descended by common ancestry from earlier forms? The second question is: If evolution has actually happened, what mechanisms have been responsible for it?

Both these questions have traditionally been subsumed under the term "the theory of evolution." But I wish to distinguish them carefully, for I consider the first question to have been resolved into fact, and the second question to fall into the category of theory. The body of statements about mutation, natural selection, **genetic drift**, and so forth

**omnipotent**

all-powerful

**omniscient**

all-knowing

**diabolical incubi**

evil spirits said to descend upon people when they are asleep

**cytochrome**

a series of compound molecules that participate in cell respiration through a transfer of electrons

**mitochondria**

very small structures found in the cytoplasm (the substance between the cell membrane and the nucleus) of most cells that are the centre of intracellular enzyme activity

**genetic drift**

evolution of a species (or part thereof) due to chance genetic changes is the theory of evolution: that is, the explanation of the historical fact that evolution has actually occurred. The mass of evidence from the geological record, embryology, comparative morphology, biochemistry, and the rest of biology indirectly proves the common ancestry of living organisms to the satisfaction of biologists generally. This may seem an elitist basis on which to judge a proposition factual, but it is no more so than the elitism we accept in astronomers or, for that matter, in physicians who attribute disease to germs rather than to spirits.

Why do biologists consider evolution to be a fact? Partly because the hypothesis of evolution is corroborated by enormous masses of consistent evidence, just as untold numbers of astronomical observations corroborate the Copernican rather than the Ptolemaic view of the solar system. Every anatomical or biochemical resemblance between species, every vestigial structure, every pattern of geographical distribution, every fossil is consistent with the idea of evolution. Again and again, new discoveries, such as the close resemblance of the DNA of humans and apes, accord with the idea of common ancestry. But there is more to a good scientific hypothesis than corroboration; it must be falsifiable. And the hypothesis that evolution has occurred could indeed by falsified. A single undisputed fossil of a flowering plant or of a human or any other mammal in Precambrian rocks would do it. Millions of conceivable **paleontological** discoveries could disprove evolution, but none ever has come to light.

paleontological
fossil-related

Unlike the historical fact of evolution, which is universally accepted by qualified biologists, evolutionary theory, that is, the theory of mutation, recombination, natural selection, genetic drift, and isolation, is subject to argument, just as there is argument about how genes are regulated during development, or how earthquakes are caused. Two major kinds of argument about evolutionary theory occur within scientific circles. There are philosophical arguments about whether or not evolutionary theory qualifies as scientific theory, and substantive arguments about the details of the theory and their adequacy to explain observed phenomena.

It is possible to ask whether or not a theory based on historical events can be tested, since such events are not susceptible to experimental manipulation or direct observation. However, if we cannot accept the idea that theories of history can be tested, most of the problems studied by scientists immediately cease to be amenable to scientific inquiry; because with the exception of some principles of physics and chemistry, most phenomena must be explained in part by recourse to history. Much of geology and astronomy, for example, deals with historical phenomena. Virtually all of biology is historical. If we ask why the forests of Long Island are dominated by pine instead of maple, the immediate answer is that the dry sandy soil of Long Island is more favorable to pines than maples; but to be fully satisfied, we must go on to ask why Long Island has sandy soils. The answer is, of course, historical: Long Island is a pile of loose rubble deposited by the most recent glacier, and does not have a mineral soil formed from underlying bedrock.

In fact, historical phenomena can be scientifically analyzed because they form patterns, showing that repeated historical events are generally associated with one or more conditions that imply causation. It is difficult, and often impossible, to rigorously test a hypothesis about any single historical event, such as why the human species is the only "naked ape," and most speculations about such unitary historical events must remain speculations rather than rigorous scientific statements. But when a particular kind of historical event is repeated, we see whether it is usually associated with specific conditions that might qualify as causes. For example, from fossil material and comparative anatomy, it is possible to test the hypothesis that new features of organisms generally evolve by modification of preexisting features.

A secondary issue then arises: Is the hypothesis of natural selection falsifiable, or is it a **tautology**? If there were no more to the theory of evolution than that "natural selection is the survival of the fittest," and we then defined the fittest as those best capable of survival, natural selection would indeed be an empty, untestable concept. The claim that natural selection is a tautology is periodically made in the scientific literature itself, and in fact had been made by Karl Popper, the chief advocate of testability in scientific theory. However, Popper . . . [later] stated that he . . . [had come to] believe natural selection to be testable: "The theory of natural selection may be so formulated that it is far from tautological. In this case it is not only testable, but it turns out to be not strictly universally true." In fact, the notion of natural selection has been tested many times. Thus, knowing that birds generalize color patterns from one insect to another, one can predict and then experimentally demonstrate that if an edible insect resembles an inedible species it will enjoy some protection from predation, and that the degree of protection increases with the degree of similarity to the unpalatable species.

The neo-Darwinian theory of evolution is also clearly falsifiable because we can postulate alternative theories which, if true, would render neo-Darwinian theory superfluous. The most obvious alternative theory is

tautology

a true statement that says little; e.g., "bald men have no hair" the Lamarckian one. If it were true that modifications acquired during the life of an organism could become hereditary, many features of organisms would evolve by the direct influence of the environment, and natural selection would not play a major guiding role in adaptation.

These are the larger philosophical questions that can be asked about the validity of evolutionary theory, and most biologists are satified with the answers. Biologists do not universally agree, however, that the neo-Darwinian theory is *sufficient* to explain all of evolutionary change, and there is a lot of debate about which of the mechanisms of evolution are most important. For example, some of the most eminent evolutionists argue that not all evolution can be attributed to natural selection. Much of evolution may proceed by genetic drift, so that not all the differences among species are necessarily unique adaptive solutions to unique adaptive problems. Moreover, they argue, mutations are not random, in that certain kinds of mutations are more likely than others. However, almost everyone agrees that the chance of occurrence of a mutation is not influenced by whether or not the current environment would favor it.

Another major area of debate is whether or not mutations of small effect are the sole stuff of evolution. Although much of evolution certainly has proceeded by gradual changes, it is possible to imagine beneficial mutations that could produce large changes. Thus some morphologists and paleontologists feel that some major changes in evolution may have entailed "macromutations" with large effects. But neo-Darwinian theory does not invoke any natural law that mutations must be small in effect. The reason for supposing that most evolutionary change has been gradual is not theoretical but empirical—the observation that most variation within and among closely related populations is due to many genes, each with a small effect.

Finally, paleontologists such as Stephen Jay Gould have written that neo-Darwinian theory is insufficient to explain the broad panorama of historical evolution. By "neo-Darwinian theory" he means the "hard-core" genetic theory that many evolutionists adhered to after the "modern synthesis" of the 1940s and 1950s: the belief that all of evolution consisted of the action of natural selection on slight genetic variations. If this is the definition of neo-Darwinian theory, then as Gould says, "the modern synthesis is incomplete, not incorrect." For such a theory would not account for nonadaptive characteristics; nor, in itself, would it account for why certain long-term series of evolutionary events occurred. In particular, Gould and certain other paleontologists have postulated that long-term evolutionary trends may be caused not just by slow, steady change in one direction within a particular species, but by a higher-level process that the neo-Darwinists didn't emphasize in the modern synthesis: rates of extinction and speciation.

For example, if the lineage from the eohippus to the modern horse increased in overall size for 60 million years, it is possible to imagine that this was the result of the steady, excruciatingly slow change of a single species. But the evolution of horses . . . included a lot of speciation: species continually proliferated new species, some larger and some smaller. Paleontologists such as Niles Eldredge, Stephen Jay Gould, and Steven Stanley favor this interpretation: new species, with various body sizes, arise quite quickly. The changes in body size occur by the processes of genetic variation and natural selection. But larger species may tend to survive longer than small species before becoming extinct. As a result, they have more of a chance to give rise to more large species than small species will to small species. Therefore, various species at any time may be evolving in both directions, but an overall trend toward larger size emerges, just because of differences in extinction rates. Such rates are not normally taken into account in the neo-Darwinian theory of natural selection within species. If the Eldredge-Gould-Stanley viewpoint is correct, we need a theory of why some species are more prone to extinction than others, to complement the genetic theory of natural selection.

The reason I am dwelling on this subject is that creationists have gleefully pounced on the writings of these paleontologists, claiming that the whole structure of evolutionary theory is going down the drain. According to Gish, "Evolutionists are saying . . . that natural selection has made no significant contribution at all to the overall course of evolution." But this is not at all what the paleontologists are saying. They are merely arguing that "macroevolution," the long-term history of life, includes important events, such as extinction, that cannot be studied in the context of "microevolution," the genetic changes of single species. Thus Gould argues that "macroevolution has some claim to theoretical independence": that understanding the history of life requires more information than genetic studies can provide, a whole level of theory that incorporates the genetic theory and adds to it.

Debates and controversies of this kind go on continually in evolutionary science and in every scientific discipline. They indicate not that the field is tottering on the brink of chaos and despair, but that scientific inquiry is flourishing: that people have found unexplored questions to answer, and new, improved theories with which to expand the scope of human understanding. New ideas come up continually and either pass the gauntlet of scientific testing or pass into oblivion. How different science is from creationism! Creationists, by their own admission, cannot test their theory. According to Gish, animals and plants "were brought into existence by acts of a supernatural Creator using special processes which are not operative today." How, then, could they be examined by any methods of science? Gish goes on: "We do not know how the Creator created, what processes He used, *for He used processes which are not now operating anywhere in the natural universe* . . . . We cannot discover by scientific investigations anything about the creative processes used by the Creator" [emphasis in the original]. Exactly because it is impossible scientifically to investigate supernatural processes, creationists can offer no more evidence for creation now than they could in 1859. They simply repeat the same arguments they have used for centuries—no new ideas, no new information. Where science frees and exercises human intellect, creationism claims the intellect is powerless. Where science offers the optimism that comes with understanding, creationism denies it. Where science grows, creationism stays stagnant. Where science offers the method of hypothesis-testing to justify its claims, creationism offers blind faith in the authority of a single book and its most rigid interpreters.

# Note

[1] Richard C. Lewontin, who holds the Alexander Agassiz professorship at Harvard University, is a leader on the genetic basis of evolution.

# The Tale of the Ancient Molecule

## Paul Davies

Inside each and every one of us lies a message. It is inscribed in an ancient code, its beginnings lost in the mists of time. Decrypted, the message contains instructions on how to make a human being. Nobody wrote the message; nobody invented the code. They came into existence spontaneously. Their designer was Mother Nature herself, working only within the scope of her immutable laws and capitalizing on the vagaries of chance. The message isn't written in ink or type, but in atoms, strung together in an elaborately arranged sequence to form DNA, short for deoxyribonucleic acid. It is the most extraordinary molecule on Earth.

Human DNA contains many billions of atoms, linked in the distinctive form of two coils entwined in mutual embrace. This famous double helix is in turn bundled up in a very **convoluted** shape. Stretch out the DNA in just one cell of your body and it would make a thread two meters long. These are big molecules indeed.

convoluted

intricately winding

Although DNA is a material structure, it is pregnant with meaning. The arrangement of the atoms along the helical strands of your DNA determines how you look and even, to a certain extent, how you feel and behave. DNA is nothing less than a blueprint—or, more accurately, an algorithm or instruction manual—for building a living, breathing, thinking human being.

We share this magic molecule with almost all other life forms on Earth. From fungi to flies, from bacteria to bears, organisms are sculpted according to their respective DNA instructions. Each individual's DNA differs from others in the same species (with the exception of identical twins), and differs even more from that of other species. But the essential structure—the chemical makeup, the double-helix architecture—is universal.

DNA is incredibly, unimaginably ancient. It almost certainly existed three and a half billion years ago. It makes nonsense of the phrase "as old as the hills": DNA was here long before any surviving hills on Earth. Nobody knows how or where the first DNA molecule formed. Some scientists even speculate that it is an alien invader, a molecule from Mars

From Paul Davies' *The Fifth Miracle: The Search for the Origin and Meaning of Life*. New York: Simon & Schuster, 1999. Reprinted with permission.

perhaps, or from a wandering comet. But however the first strand of DNA came to exist, our own DNA is very probably a direct descendent of it. For the crucial quality of DNA, the property that sets it apart from other big organic molecules, is its ability to replicate itself. Put simply, DNA is in the business of making more DNA, generation after generation, instruction manual after instruction manual, cascading down through the ages from microbes to man in an unbroken chain of copying.

Of course, copying as such produces only more of the same. Perfect replication of DNA would lead to a planet knee-deep in identical single-celled organisms. However, no copying process is totally reliable. A photocopier may create stray spots, a noisy telephone line will garble a fax transmission, and a computer glitch can spoil data transferred from hard disk to a floppy. When errors occur in DNA replication, they can manifest themselves as mutations in the organisms that inherit them. Mostly a mutation is damaging, just as a random word change in a Shakespeare sonnet would likely mar its beauty. But occasionally, quite by chance, an error might produce a positive benefit, conferring an advantage on the mutant. If the advantage is life-preserving, enabling the organism to reproduce itself more efficiently, then the miscopied DNA will out-replicate its competitors and come to predominate. Conversely, if the copying error results in a less well-adapted organism, the mutant strain will probably die out after a few generations, eliminating this particular DNA variant.

This simple process of replication, variation, and elimination is the basis of Darwinian evolution. Natural selection—the continual sifting of mutants according to their fitness—acts like a ratchet, locking in the advantageous errors and discarding the bad. Starting with the DNA of some primitive ancestor microbe, bit by bit, error by error, the increasingly lengthy instructions for building more complex organisms came to be constructed.

Some people find the idea of an instruction manual that writes itself simply by accumulating chance errors hard to swallow, so let me go over the argument once more, using a slightly different metaphor. Think of the information in human DNA as the score for a symphony. This is a grand symphony indeed, a mighty orchestral piece with hundreds of musicians playing thousands of notes. By comparison, the DNA of the ancient ancestor microbe is but a simple melody. How does a melody turn into a symphony?

Suppose a scribe is asked to copy the original tune as a musical score. Normally the copying process is faithful, but once in a while a **quaver** becomes a **crotchet**, a C becomes a D. A slip of the pen introduces a

quaver

an eighth note

crotchet

a quarter note

slight change of tempo or pitch. Occasionally a more serious error leads to a major flaw in the piece, an entire bar omitted or repeated perhaps. Mostly these mistakes will spoil the balance or harmony, so that the score is of no further use: nobody would wish to listen to its musical rendition. But very occasionally the scribe's slip of the pen will add an imaginative new sound, a pleasing feature, a successful addition or alteration, quite by chance. The tune will actually improve, and be approved for the future. Now imagine this process of improvement and elaboration continuing though trillions of copying procedures. Slowly but surely, the tune will acquire new features, develop a richer structure, evolve into a sonata, even a symphony.

The crucial point about this metaphor, and it cannot be stressed too strongly, is that the symphony comes into being without the scribe's ever having the slightest knowledge of, or interest in, music. The scribe might have been deaf from birth and know nothing whatever of melodies. It doesn't matter, because the scribe's job is not to compose the music but to copy it. Where the metaphor fails is in the selection process. There is no cosmic musician scrutinizing the score of life and exercising quality control. There is only nature, red in tooth and claw, applying a simple and brutal rule: if it works, keep it; if it doesn't, kill it. And "works" here is defined by one criterion and one criterion only, which is replication efficiency. If the mistake results in more copies made, then, by definition, without any further considerations, it works. If A out-replicates B, even by the slightest margin, then, generations on, there will be many more A's than B's. If A and B have to compete for space or resources, it's a fair bet that A will soon eliminate B entirely. A survives, B dies.

Darwinism is the central principle around which our understanding of biology is constructed. It offers an economical explanation of how a relatively simple genetic message elaborates itself over the eons to create molecules of DNA complex enough to produce a human being. Once the basic manual, the precursor DNA, existed in the first place, random errors and selection might gradually be able to evolve it. Good genes are kept, bad genes are discarded . . . . Obviously Darwinian evolution can operate only if life of some sort already exists (strictly, it requires not life in its full glory, only replication, variation, and selection). Darwinism can offer absolutely no help in explaining that all-important first step: the origin of life. But if the central principle of life fails to explain the origin of life, we are left with a problem. What other principle or principles might explain how it all began?

To solve this problem, we must seek clues. Where can we look for clues about the origin of life? A good place to begin is to ask where life itself began. If we discover the place where life started, we may be able to guess the physical conditions that accompanied its genesis. Then we can set about studying the chemical processes that occur in such conditions, and build up an understanding of the prebiotic phase bit by bit.

# Can Science Be Ethical?

Freeman Dyson

One of my favorite monuments is a statue of Samuel Gompers not far from the Alamo in San Antonio, Texas. Under the statue is a quote from one of Gompers' speeches:

> What does labor want?
> We want more schoolhouses and less jails,
> More books and less guns,
> More learning and less vice,
> More leisure and less greed,
> More justice and less revenge,
> We want more opportunities to cultivate our better nature.

Samuel Gompers was the founder and first president of the American Federation of Labor. He established in America the tradition of practical bargaining between labour and management which led to an era of growth and prosperity for labour unions. Now, 70 years after Gompers' death, the unions have dwindled, while his dreams, more books and fewer guns, more leisure and less greed, more schoolhouses and fewer jails, have been **tacitly** abandoned. In a society without social justice and with a free-market ideology, guns, greed, and jails are bound to win.

When I was a student of mathematics in England 50 years ago, one of my teachers was the great mathematician G.H. Hardy, who wrote a little book, *A Mathematician's Apology*, explaining to the general public what mathematicians do. Hardy proudly proclaimed that his life had been devoted to the creation of totally useless works of abstract art, without any possible practical application. He had strong views about technology, which he summarized in the statement "A science is said to be useful if its development tends to accentuate the existing inequalities in the distribution of wealth, or more directly promotes the destruction of human life." He wrote these words while war was raging around him.

tacitly
quietly

From Freeman Dyson's *Imagined Worlds*. Cambridge, Mass.: Harvard University Press, 1997. Reprinted with permission.

Still, the Hardy view of technology has some merit even in peace-time. Many of the technologies that are now racing ahead most rapidly, replacing human workers in factories and offices with machines, making stockholders richer and workers poorer, are indeed tending to accentuate the existing inequalities in the distribution of wealth. And the technologies of lethal force continue to be as profitable today as they were in Hardy's time. The marketplace judges technologies by their practical effectiveness, by whether they succeed or fail to do the job they are designed to do. But always, even for the most brilliantly successful technology, an ethical question lurks in the background: the question whether the job the technology is designed to do is actually worth doing.

The technologies that raise the fewest ethical problems are those that work on a human scale, brightening the lives of individual people. Lucky individuals in each generation find technology appropriate to their needs. For my father 90 years ago, technology was a motorcycle. He was an impoverished young musician growing up in England in the years before World War I, and the motorcycle came to him as a liberation. He was a working-class boy in a country dominated by the snobberies of class and accent. He learned to speak like a gentleman, but he did not belong in the world of gentlemen. The motorcycle was a great equalizer. On his motorcycle, he was the equal of a gentleman. He could make the grand tour of Europe without having inherited an upper-class income. He and three of his friends bought motorcycles and rode them all over Europe.

My father fell in love with his motorcycle and with the technical skills that it demanded. He understood, 60 years before Robert Pirsig wrote *Zen and the Art of Motorcycle Maintenance*, the spiritual quality of the motorcycle. In my father's day, roads were bad and repair shops few and far between. If you intended to travel any long distance, you needed to carry your own tool kit and spare parts and be prepared to take the machine apart and put it back together again. A breakdown of the machine in a remote place often required major surgery. It was as essential for a rider to understand the anatomy and physiology of the motorcycle as it was for a surgeon to understand the anatomy and physiology of a patient. It sometimes happened that my father and his friends would arrive at a village where no motorcycle had ever been seen before. When this happened, they would give rides to the village children and hope to be rewarded with a free supper at the village inn. Technology in the shape of a motorcycle was comradeship and freedom.

Fifty years after my father, I discovered joyful technology in the shape of a nuclear fission reactor. That was in 1956, in the first intoxicating days of peaceful nuclear energy, when the technology of reactors suddenly emerged from wartime secrecy and the public was invited to come and play with it. This was an invitation that I could not refuse. It looked then as if nuclear energy would be the great equalizer, providing cheap and abundant energy to rich and poor alike, just as 50 years earlier the motorcycle gave mobility to rich and poor alike in class-ridden England.

I joined the General Atomic Company in San Diego, where my friends were playing with the new technology. We invented and built a little reactor which we called the TRIGA, designed to be inherently safe. Inherent safety meant that it would not misbehave even if the people operating it were grossly incompetent. The company has been manufacturing and selling TRIGA reactors for 40 years and is still selling them today, mostly to hospitals and medical centres, where they produce short-lived isotopes for diagnostic purposes. They have never misbehaved or caused any danger to the people who used them. They have only run into trouble in a few places where the neighbours objected to their presence on ideological grounds, no matter how safe they might be. We were successful with the TRIGA because it was designed to do a useful job at a price that a big hospital could afford. The price in 1956 was a quarter of a million dollars. Our work with the TRIGA was joyful because we finished it quickly, before the technology became entangled with politics and bureaucracy, before it became clear that nuclear energy was not and never could be the great equalizer.

Forty years after the invention of the TRIGA, my son George found another joyful and useful technology, the technology of CAD-CAM, computer-aided design and computer-aided manufacturing. CAD-CAM is the technology of the postnuclear generation, the technology that succeeded after nuclear energy failed. George is a boat-builder. He designs seagoing kayaks. He uses modern materials to reconstruct the ancient craft of the Aleuts, who perfected their boats by trial and error over thousands of years and used them to travel prodigious distances across the northern Pacific. His boats are fast and rugged and seaworthy. When he began his boat-building 25 years ago, he was a nomad, travelling up and down the north Pacific coast, trying to live like an Aleut, and built his boats like an Aleut, shaping every part of each boat and stitching them together with his own hands. In those days he was a nature-child, in love with the wilderness, rejecting the urban society in which he had grown up. He built boats for his own use and for his friends, not as a commercial business.

As the years went by George made a graceful transition from the role of rebellious teenager to the role of solid citizen. He married, raised a daughter, bought a house in the city of Bellingham, and converted an abandoned tavern by the waterfront into a well-equipped workshop for his boats. His boats are now a business. And he discovered the joys of CAD-CAM.

His workshop now contains more computers and software than sewing needles and hand tools. It is a long time since he made the parts of a boat by hand. He now translates his designs directly into CAD-CAM software and transmits them electronically to a manufacturer who produces the parts. George collects the parts and sells them by mail order to his regular customers with instructions for assembling them into boats. Only on rare occasions, when a wealthy customer pays for a custom-built job, does George deliver a boat assembled in the workshop. The boat business occupies only a part of his time. He also runs a historical society concerned with the history and ethnography of the north Pacific. The technology of CAD-CAM has given George resources and leisure, so that he can visit the Aleuts in their native islands and reintroduce to the young islanders the forgotten skills of their ancestors.

Forty years into the future, which joyful new technology will be enriching the lives of our grandchildren? Perhaps they will be designing their

own dogs and cats. Just as the technology of CAD-CAM began in the production lines of large manufacturing companies and later became accessible to individual citizens like George, the technology of genetic engineering may soon spread out from the biotechnology companies and agricultural industries and become accessible to our grandchildren. Designing dogs and cats in the privacy of a home may become as easy as designing boats in a waterfront workshop.

Instead of CAD-CAM we may have CAS-CAR, computer-aided selection and computer-aided reproduction. With the CAS-CAR software, you first program your pet's colour scheme and behaviour, and then transmit the program electronically to the artificial fertilization laboratory for implementation. Twelve weeks later, your pet is born, satisfaction guaranteed by the software company. When I recently described these possibilities in a public lecture at a children's museum in Vermont, I was verbally assaulted by a young woman in the audience. She accused me of violating the rights of animals. She said I was a typical scientist, one of those cruel people who spend their lives torturing animals for fun. I tried in vain to placate her by saying that I was only speaking of possibilities, that I was not actually myself engaged in designing dogs and cats. I had to admit that she had a legitimate complaint. Designing dogs and cats is an ethically dubious business. It is not as innocent as designing boats.

When the time comes, when the CAS-CAR software is available, when anybody with access to the software can order a dog with pink and purple spots that can crow like a rooster, some tough decisions will have to be made. Shall we allow private citizens to create dogs who will be objects of contempt and ridicule, unable to take their rightful place in dog society? And if not, where shall we draw the line between legitimate animal breeding and illegitimate creation of monsters? These are difficult questions that our children and grandchildren will have to answer. Perhaps I should have spoken to the audience in Vermont about designing roses and orchids. Vegetables, it seems, do not have rights. Dogs and cats are too close to being human. They have feelings like ours. If our grandchildren are allowed to design their own dogs and cats, the next step will be using the CAS-CAR software to design their own babies. Before that next step is reached, they ought to think carefully about the consequences.

What can we do today, in the world as we find it at the end of the 20th century, to turn the evil consequences of technology into good? The ways in which science may work for good or evil in human society are many and various. As a general rule, to which there are many exceptions, science works for evil when its effect is to provide toys for the rich, and works for good when its effect is to provide necessities for the poor. Cheapness is an essential virtue. The motorcycle worked for good because it was cheap enough for a poor schoolteacher to own. Nuclear energy worked mostly for evil because it remained a toy for rich governments and rich companies to play with. "Toys for the rich" means not only toys in the literal sense but technological conveniences that are available to a minority of people and make it harder for those excluded to take part in the economic and cultural life of the community. "Necessities for the poor" include not only food and shelter but adequate public health services, adequate public transportation, and access to decent education and jobs.

The scientific advances of the 19th century and the first half of the 20th were generally beneficial to society as a whole, spreading wealth to rich and poor alike with some degree of equity. The electric light, the telephone, the refrigerator, radio, television, synthetic fabrics, antibiotics, vitamins, and vaccines were social equalizers, making life easier and more comfortable for almost everybody, tending to narrow the gap between rich and poor rather than to widen it. Only in the second half of our century has the balance of advantage shifted. During the last 40 years, the strongest efforts in pure science have been concentrated in highly esoteric fields remote from contact with everyday problems. Particle physics, low-temperature physics, and extragalactic astronomy are examples of pure sciences moving further and further away from their origins. The intensive pursuit of these sciences does not do much harm, or much good, either to the rich or the poor. The main social benefit provided by pure science in esoteric fields is to serve as a welfare program for scientists and engineers.

At the same time, the strongest efforts in applied science have been concentrated upon products that can be profitably sold. Since the rich can be expected to pay more than the poor for new products, market-driven applied science will usually result in the invention of toys for the rich. The laptop computer and the cellular telephone are the latest of the new toys. Now that a large fraction of high-paying jobs are advertised on the Internet, people excluded from the Internet are also excluded from access to jobs. The failure of science to produce benefits for the poor in recent decades is due to two factors working in combination: the pure scientists have become more detached from the mundane needs of humanity, and the applied scientists have become more attached to immediate profitability.

Although pure and applied science may appear to be moving in opposite directions, there is a single underlying cause that has affected them both. The cause is the power of committees in the administration and funding of science. In the case of pure science, the committees are composed of scientific experts performing the rituals of peer review. If a committee of scientific experts selects research projects by majority vote, projects in fashionable fields are supported while those in unfashionable fields are not. In recent decades, the fashionable fields have been moving further and further into specialized areas remote from contact with things that we can see and touch. In the case of applied science, the committees are composed of business executives and managers. Such people usually give support to products that affluent customers like themselves can buy.

Only a cantankerous man like Henry Ford, with dictatorial power over his business, would dare to create a mass market for automobiles by arbitrarily setting his prices low enough and his wages high enough that his workers could afford to buy his product. Both in pure science and in applied science, rule by committee discourages unfashionable and bold ventures. To bring about a real shift of priorities, scientists and entrepreneurs must assert their freedom to promote new technologies that are more friendly than the old to poor people and poor countries. The ethical standards of scientists must change as the scope of the good and evil caused by science has changed. In the long run, as Haldane and Einstein said, ethical progress is the only cure for the damage done by scientific progress.

The nuclear arms race is over, but the ethical problems raised by non-military technology remain. The ethical problems arise from three "new ages" flooding over human society like **tsunamis**. First is the Information Age, already arrived and here to stay, driven by computers and digital memory. Second is the Biotechnology Age, due to arrive in full force early in the 21st century, driven by DNA sequencing and genetic engineering. Third is the Neurotechnology Age, likely to arrive later in this century, driven by neural sensors and exposing the inner workings of human emotion and personality to manipulation. These three new technologies are profoundly disruptive. They offer liberation from ancient drudgery in factory, farm, and office. They offer healing of ancient diseases of body and mind. They offer wealth and power to the people who possess the skills to understand and control them. They destroy industries based on older technologies and make people trained in older

**tsunamis**

large tidal waves caused by underwater earthquakes

skills useless. They are likely to bypass the poor and reward the rich. They will tend, as Hardy said over 80 years ago, to accentuate the inequalities in the existing distribution of wealth, even if they do not, like nuclear technology, more directly promote the destruction of human life.

The poorer half of humanity needs cheap housing, cheap health care, and cheap education, accessible to everybody, with high quality and high aesthetic standards. The fundamental problem for human society in this century is the mismatch between the three new waves of technology and the three basic needs of poor people. The gap between technology and needs is wide and growing wider. If technology continues along its present course, ignoring the needs of the poor and showering benefits upon the rich, the poor will sooner or later rebel against the tyranny of technology and turn to irrational and violent remedies. In the future, as in the past, the revolt of the poor is likely to impoverish rich and poor together.

The widening gap between technology and human needs can only be filled by ethics. We have seen in the last 30 years many examples of the power of ethics. The worldwide environmental movement, basing its power on ethical persuasion, has scored many victories over industrial wealth and technological arrogance. The most spectacular victory of the environmentalists was the downfall of nuclear industry in the United States and many other countries, first in the domain of nuclear power and more recently in the domain of weapons. It was the environmental movement that closed down factories for making nuclear weapons in the United States, from plutonium-producing Hanford to warhead-producing Rocky Flats. Ethics can be a force more powerful than politics and economics.

Unfortunately, the environmental movement has so far concentrated its attention upon the evils that technology has done rather than upon the good that technology has failed to do. It is my hope that the attention of the Greens will shift in this century from the negative to the positive. Ethical victories putting an end to technological follies are not enough. We need ethical victories of a different kind, engaging the power of technology positively in the pursuit of social justice.

If we can agree with Thomas Jefferson that these truths are self-evident, that all men are created equal, that they are endowed with certain in-alienable rights, that among these are life, liberty, and the pursuit of happiness, then it should also be self-evident that the abandonment of millions of people in modern societies to unemployment and destitution is a worse defilement of the earth than nuclear power stations. If the ethical force of the environmental movement can defeat the manufacturers of nuclear power stations, the same force should also be able to foster the growth of technology that supplies the needs of impoverished humans at a price they can afford. This is the great task for technology in this century.

The free market will not by itself produce technology friendly to the poor. Only a technology positively guided by ethics can do it. The power of ethics must be exerted by the environmental movement and by concerned scientists, educators, and entrepreneurs working together. If we are wise, we shall also enlist in the common cause of social justice the enduring power of religion. Religion has in the past contributed mightily to many good causes, from the building of cathedrals and the education of children to the abolition of slavery. Religion will remain in the future a force equal in strength to science and equally committed to the long-range improvement of the human condition.

In the world of religion, over the centuries, there have been prophets of doom and prophets of hope, with hope in the end predominating. Science also gives warnings of doom and promises of hope, but the yearnings and promises of sciences cannot be separated. Every honest scientific prophet must mix the good news with the bad. Haldane was an honest prophet, showing us the evil done by science not as inescapable fate but as a challenge to be overcome. He wrote in his book *Daedalus* in 1923, "We are at present almost completely ignorant of biology, a fact which often escapes the notice of biologists, and renders them too presumptuous in their estimates of the present condition of their science, too modest in their claims for its future." Biology has made amazing progress since 1923, but Haldane's statement is still true.

We still know little about the biological processes that affect human beings most intimately—the development of speech and social skills in infants, the interplay between moods and emotions and learning and understanding in children and adults, the onset of aging and mental deterioration at the end of life. None of these processes will be understood within the next decade, but all of them might be understood within the . . . century. Understanding will then lead to new technologies that offer hope of preventing tragedies and **ameliorating** the human condition. Few people believe any longer in the romantic dream that human beings are perfectible. But most of us still believe that human beings are capable of improvement.

ameliorating

making better

In public discussions of biotechnology today, the idea of improving the human race by artificial means is widely condemned. The idea is repugnant because it conjures up visions of Nazi doctors sterilizing Jews and killing defective children. There are many good reasons for condemning enforced sterilization and euthanasia. But the artificial improvement of human beings will come, one way or another, whether we like it or not, as soon as the progress of biological understanding makes it possible. When people are offered technical means to improve themselves and their children, no matter what they conceive improvement to mean, the offer will be accepted. Improvement may mean better health, longer life, a more cheerful disposition, a stronger heart, a smarter brain, the ability to earn more money as a rock star or baseball player or business executive. The technology of improvement may be hindered or delayed by regulation, but it cannot be permanently suppressed. Human improvement, like abortion today, will be officially disapproved, legally discouraged, or forbidden, but widely practised. It will be seen by millions of citizens as a liberation from past constraints and injustices. Their freedom to choose cannot be permanently denied.

Two hundred years ago, William Blake engraved *The Gates of Paradise,* a little book of drawings and verses. One of the drawings, with the title "Aged Ignorance," shows an old man wearing professorial eyeglasses and holding a large pair of scissors. In front of him, a winged child is running naked in the light from a rising sun. The old man sits with his back to the sun. With a self-satisfied smile he opens his scissors and clips the child's wings. With the picture goes a little poem:

In Time's Ocean falling drown'd,
In Aged Ignorance profound,
Holy and cold, I clip'd the Wings
Of all Sublunary Things.

This picture is an image of the human condition in the era that is now beginning. The rising sun is biological science, throwing light of ever-increasing intensity onto the processes by which we live and feel and think. The winged child is human life, becoming for the first time aware of itself and its potentialities in the light of science. The old man is our existing human society, shaped by ages of past ignorance. Our laws, our loyalties, our fears and hatreds, our economic and social injustices, all grew slowly and are deeply rooted in the past. Inevitably the advance of biological knowledge will bring clashes between old institutions and new desires for human self-improvement. Old institutions will clip the wings of new desires. Up to a point, caution is justified and social constraints are necessary. The new technologies will be dangerous as well as liberating. But in the long run, social constraints must bend to new realities. Humanity cannot live forever with clipped wings. The vision of self-improvement, which William Blake and Samuel Gompers in their different ways proclaimed, will not vanish from the earth.

# On Human Reproduction and the Limitations of Science

Brian Doyle

The headline reads "Women trade eggs in try for baby." The article describes how a private clinic in Toronto had arranged for women who were unable to afford in vitro fertilization to give their eggs to couples who needed them. In exchange, the couple who received the eggs would pay for the woman's in vitro treatment. Some people were horrified at the thought of selling human eggs while others argued that it was simple economics: that is the way a free market works. There is a buyer for every seller.

The controversy surrounding the new reproductive technologies (NRTs) illustrates the difficulties we face at the frontiers of science. What principles should be used to regulate the new reproductive technologies? Should society play a role in what is usually a personal decision made by an individual or couple?

NRTs are of enormous benefit to infertile couples (couples who have tried unsuccessfully to conceive over a period of two years). Government estimates (1996) indicate that half a million Canadians suffer from infertility. The reasons are many, but may include damage to the woman's reproductive organs or an extremely low sperm count for the man. Thousands of women around the world have been able to have children because of the NRTs. Before we can deal with the controversies surrounding this issue, it is probably a good idea to review some of the recent developments in NRTs.

# What Are the NRTs?
## In Vitro Fertilization

Normally when a woman's egg is released from her ovary, it travels down the Fallopian tube to her uterus. If the egg is fertilized along the way, it will become attached to the wall of the uterus and start to develop. If the tube between the ovary and uterus is damaged, the egg may not be able to make it to the uterus. In this situation the couple may consider in vitro fertilization. This medical procedure involves a number of steps.

"On Human Reproduction and the Limitations of Science" is by Brian Doyle of Humber College. Used by permission.

First, several eggs are taken from the woman's ovaries. These eggs are placed in a petri dish and given nutrients to keep them healthy. Then the man's sperm is placed on the petri dish and the eggs are fertilized. The fertilized eggs are carefully monitored for two to three days and then several are placed inside the woman's uterus. This is called embryo transfer. The federal government estimates that in 1995 between 500 and 700 babies were born in Canada using this technology. For women not covered by insurance the cost at the publicly funded clinic I visited was $3200 for one treatment cycle. The cost to have an embryo frozen for future attempts was $700 per embryo and there was a $100 annual maintenance fee.

## Surrogacy

If a woman cannot have the embryo transferred into her own uterus or does not want to be pregnant, she might make an agreement with a surrogate to bear her child. The embryo is transferred into the surrogate mother's uterus, where it will develop until it is born. The child is then "returned" to the genetic mother.

## Egg Donation

Sometimes a woman is unable to produce a viable egg that has the potential to be fertilized and develop. This inability may be because of damage to her reproductive system. In this situation she may receive an egg from a donor—sometimes a sister or another woman willing to donate an egg.

## Prenatal Diagnosis

Tay-Sachs disease

a genetically linked enzyme deficiency resulting in nervous system damage and early death

To some extent it is now possible to determine the "genetic health" of the fetus before it is born. This often involves screening the genes of the potential parents to determine if either parent is a carrier of a disease-linked gene that may be passed on to a child.  A couple undergoing genetic screening, for example, may find that they are both carriers for **Tay-Sachs disease**; then tests can determine whether a fetus has the disease. This information may lead the couple to decide to abort the fetus; alternatively, this information may help the couple prepare for the birth (and ultimate death) of an unhealthy baby.  Although there are thousands of genetically linked diseases, only some are detectable.

## Artificial or Therapeutic Insemination

Artificial insemination is used for couples when the man's sperm cannot fertilize the egg and for women who want to have a child without a

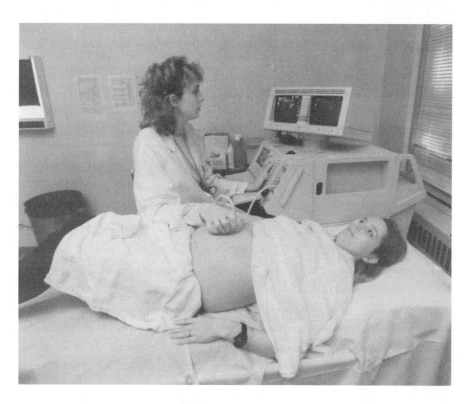

High tech comes to the aid of parents-to-be.

man. This process involves placing the man's sperm into the woman's upper vagina using a tube or syringe.

The couple may choose to use donated sperm, if the man's sperm is not viable or if he carries a genetic defect. The donated sperm may come from a sperm bank or from a specific individual. Several thousand Canadian children are born each year using this technique.

## Pre-Implantation Diagnosis

This new technique allows the physician to check embryos for genetic defects prior to implanting them in a woman's uterus. Genetically defective embryos can then be screened out.

# Guiding Principles

In order to sort out the ethical implications of this new technology, the federal government formed the Royal Commission on the New Reproductive Technologies in 1989. The Commission investigated NRTs and consulted Canadians about their concerns. In their final report the Commission took a practical approach to the ethical issues surrounding the NRTs, identifying seven guiding principles.

## 1. Individual Autonomy

People should be free to choose how they want to live their own lives, as long as they do not harm others. This principle implies that people should have control over their own bodies. For example, a person who is receiving treatment must give consent for that treatment, be informed of the different treatments available to her, and be aware of the risks involved in undergoing treatment. The prescription of fertility drugs is the most common method used to treat infertility. These drugs are used to control the number of eggs that mature and the rate of maturation. Some are used to trigger superovulation—the maturation of several eggs at once. Fertility drugs have a powerful effect on the human body and may have adverse short- and long-term effects on the body. Women undergoing treatment should be informed of the risks involved in taking these drugs. However, when the Commission surveyed women who were receiving these drugs without any additional treatment at fertility clinics across the country, less than half indicated that they had received counselling about their treatment. Women should also be aware that despite all the pain and expense, the success rate for in vitro treatment is less than 20 per cent. Only one out of every five women who undergoes in vitro fertilization treatment will give birth.

The principle of individual autonomy also limits society's ability to interfere with the individual. The reproductive technologies have led to conflict between individual rights and contemporary social values. For example, should we allow individuals to use the prenatal diagnostic techniques to determine the sex of the fetus? Some couples may use this information to select the sex of their children, aborting the fetus if it is not the sex that they desire. Some people have argued that a woman has the right to know all available information about the fetus and has the right to abort that fetus if she chooses. In contrast to this view, some prenatal clinics have stopped giving out the sex status of the fetus to expectant mothers because of concern over sex selection and abortion.

Is the practice of sex selection wide spread in Canada? Apparently not. The Commission found that just over 70 per cent of those people considering having children did not express a preference for a girl or boy.

## 2. Appropriate Use of Resources

The members of a society must decide how they will use their resources to satisfy the needs of that society. The costs of a new technical procedure must be weighed against the benefits it will provide for society. Technologies that have little benefit to society should not be funded while we need to fund those technologies that do provide benefits. For example, the NRTs were developed to help infertile couples have children. Many people have argued that too much time and money have been spent on developing the technology to deal with the problem of infertility and not enough time and money have been spent on determining the causes and working on the prevention of infertility. Sexually transmitted diseases, smoking, workplace and environmental pollution, drug and alcohol abuse, and poor nutrition are all factors that have been linked to reduced fertility or infertility. Perhaps more money should be spent on programs that address these practical problems and less on the expensive but glamorous process of developing and providing reproductive technologies. Some groups within our society—the homeless, geographically isolated communities, new immigrants to Canada—have difficulty receiving the most basic of health care services. Shouldn't providing better health care for these groups have priority over providing NRT services?

## 3. Non-Commercialization of Reproduction Technologies

For many people human life has value that cannot be measured in dollars. For them the buying or selling of human embryos or fetuses or fetal tissue is not acceptable. But for others, a woman should have the right to do what she wants with her body and that may include the selling of her eggs. Similarly, a man has the right to sell his sperm.

Why shouldn't an individual be allowed to sell her eggs? If the government attempts to stop her, wouldn't it be restricting her freedom? Dr. Anne Boetzkes, a professor of ethics at McMaster University, suggests that we need to carefully examine how any possible commercialization would affect other women in society. She argues that the sale of eggs turns the reproductive aspect of life into a commodity, reducing it to the status of any other thing you can buy, and reinforcing the view of women as reproductive vessels. Other critics of the commercialization of NRTs point to the case of Mary Beth Whitehead. In New Jersey in 1984, Mary Beth Whitehead agreed to be the surrogate mother for Elizabeth and William Stern's child. Ms. Whitehead was impregnated by artificial insemination with Mr. Stern's sperm. After "Baby M" was born Ms. Whitehead decided to keep the child and the Sterns took her to court to gain custody of the child. Many people were disturbed by the terms of the contract signed by Ms. Whitehead and the Sterns. The contract indicated that Ms. Whitehead would receive $10 000 if the pregnancy resulted in a healthy infant. She would receive only $1000 if the child was stillborn and the Sterns had the right, according to the contract, to demand that Ms. Whitehead have an abortion if the prenatal testing indicated that there was something wrong with the fetus.

Critics of the "business" of reproduction suggest that what has happened in the United States could happen in Canada if the use of these technologies isn't carefully monitored and controlled. From just 30 clinics in 1981 to over 300 in 1996, the U.S. fertility business is booming, with Americans spending over $2 billion a year at these clinics. Because the fertility services are so expensive—a single IVF treatment costs between $5000 and $15 000—few couples can afford to pay the fees. But the desire to have children can be overwhelming, and couples are willing to pay almost any amount in the hope of having a child. In this competitive and lucrative market, clinics use traditional marketing strategies to attract customers. For example, the California Pacific Fertility Clinics have a marketing professional on staff, offer "discount packages" ($13 000 gets you up to three IVF treatments), publish newsletters, hold seminars and run radio advertisements. Only recently, clinics have begun to follow U.S. legislation that requires them to track success rates and undergo an accreditation process.

## 4. The Principle of Equality

This principle indicates that each of us deserves an equal amount of respect and concern as a human being. Any activity associated with the NRTs must be measured against this principle. For example, does the buying and selling of human eggs violate this principle of equality? Dr. Boetzkes suggests that it might:

> Is a transaction like that going to set back the interests of the disadvantaged? Is it going to lead to the exploitation of the disadvantaged? So if somebody is so poor that they're looking for ways to make money and one way they're offered is to sell reproductive services. What's wrong with that? Well, what it means is that someone who is already disadvantaged because they're poor is then going to have to compromise over their human dignity in order to get ahead . . . in order to improve their situation. And a member of the group who is already well-advantaged is going to take advantage of that situation . . .

This principle of equality also implies that access to the new reproductive technologies should not be restricted by age. However, at the clinic I visited, women accepted into the clinic must be 38 years old or younger. The age restriction was in place because of health risks and because of the reduced chances of success for older women.

Our ideas of what constitutes a family are changing and the NRTs will influence this process. The principle of equality requires that access not be restricted due to marital status or sexual orientation. Single women may choose to have and raise a child without a male partner. For lesbian couples, the NRTs present an opportunity to have children of their own if they use artificial insemination. Gay male couples who wish to enter into an agreement with a surrogate mother may also have an opportunity to raise children that are biologically their own sons or daughters.

Some individuals view the use of NRTs as an attack on the traditional family. They argue that many single mothers already live in poverty and that allowing single women access to artificial insemination procedures will simply increase the number of poor mothers. Moreover, these critics claim that the lack of a male role model may lead these children to have difficulties growing up. Some writers in the United States have argued that the widespread availability of artificial insemination procedures to single women seems to be redefining what many have considered in the past to be a social problem—fatherless households—into something that is socially acceptable. They argue that the reproductive technologies may make marriage and family obsolete and that it devalues fatherhood. Others argue that a gay couple could not provide a balance of role models.

## 5. Respect for Human Life

This principle indicates that human life deserves respect at all stages of development. Some groups argue that the fact that the fetus is created by humans and is living tissue does not necessarily make it a human being. Others disagree, arguing that we become human beings at the moment of conception and therefore no one, including our mother, has the right to end our lives. For many people these two extremes are not acceptable. At what stage of development does a fetus become a human being and possess rights and protections? In March of 1991, the Supreme Court of Canada ruled that a fetus is not a person until it has completely left its mother's body. Groups such as Real Women and Canadian Physicians for Life point out that the ruling means that premature babies born at 24 weeks after conception have all the rights of Canadian law, but that a full-term fetus (40 weeks) about to be delivered does not.

Although we as a society have not reached a consensus on when human life begins, most individuals would agree with the Royal Commission report when it states, "While the law does not treat embryos and fetuses as full members of the community, they are closely connected to the community in virtue of both their genesis and their future," and therefore must be treated with respect and dignity.

What actions are disrespectful to human life? Fetal tissue is used in a variety of medical and research procedures, including the study of diseases, the development of new drugs and the education of health professionals. This use worries some individuals. They are concerned that fetal tissue may be viewed as a commodity. For example, there are studies which suggest that patients with Parkinson's and Alzheimer's disease can be helped by transplantation of fetal brain tissue. Some people have worried that women may become pregnant so that aging parents suffering from diseases such as Parkinson's could use the fetal tissue. Others fear that women may be subjected to unnecessary abortions to supply fetal tissue for research. Supporters of fetal tissue research argue that these situations could be avoided with careful monitoring and that fetal tissue research has provided remarkable benefits to society. For example, many vaccines, among them the polio vaccine, were developed using fetal tissue.

## Quantity and Quality Control

For many people the use of contraceptives to prevent pregnancy is no longer a controversial issue, although many religious leaders continue to disagree with their use. What may become a dilemma for parents is their ability to control not only the quantity of children they have, but also the quality of the children they have. This situation may develop as prenatal and pre-implantation diagnostic techniques improve. By identifying severe disabilities at or before the fetal stage and terminating the pregnancy, are we reducing human suffering, both for the individual who would have had the disability and the parents who would have cared for that individual? Joseph Fletcher believes we are. In his book *The Ethics of Genetic Control,* he describes the creation of children without the use of quality control as "sexual roulette." He writes that "we ought to protect our families from the emotional and material burden of such diseased individuals and from the misery of their simply 'existing' [not living] in a nearby 'warehouse' or public institution." Fletcher provides an example of a man with haemophilia. People who suffer from this disease have difficulty forming scabs when they are cut. In severe cases the person may bleed to death if he is cut and cannot get to a hospital. The disease is caused by a gene and is sex-linked; a father who is a carrier will pass it on to his daughters but not his sons. His daughters will not get the disease but will pass it on to their children. Fletcher argues that it is the "moral responsibility" of this man to ensure that he has only male children, aborting any female embryos that would carry the gene. "Choosing high-quality fetuses and rejecting low-quality ones is not tragedy; sad, but not agonizing."

Many groups, particularly disabled persons, strongly disagree with Fletcher's point of view. They point to the tremendous contributions made by people who happen to have genetic disabilities. By what criteria should the "quality" of the fetus be judged?

Other concerns have been raised over access to this genetic background information. Insurance company executives have indicated that it should be included in any medical history forms that are submitted by individuals applying for health insurance. In Ontario where health care is paid for by citizens' taxes it is unlikely that any health services will be denied to a person. But in the future, will parents feel pressure to abort abnormal fetuses that, if born, will be costly for taxpayers to care for and to educate?

Perhaps even more disturbing is the possibility that this technology may lead people to select embryos that contain specific, desirable traits, such as a certain eye colour or a certain level of intelligence. This possibility is similar to the idea of eugenics—the attempt through selective breeding to improve the human race. In the past, the attempt to eliminate "bad" genes resulted in compulsory sterilization laws for the mentally disabled in some provinces and U.S. states. These laws have now been repealed; however, some critics have suggested that the practice of allowing individuals to use the NRTs to "weed out" certain genes and select for other genes may lead to a revival of eugenics.

## 6. Protection of the Vulnerable

This principle indicates that individuals who are unable to look out for their own welfare should receive special consideration. Should these special considerations be extended to include children who may be born through the use of NRTs? Some groups have argued that society has an interest in protecting NRT offspring from unsuitable parents. Reports of older women giving birth—for example, a 59-year-old woman in 1993 and, more recently, a 63-year-old woman, have triggered a debate over when a woman is too old to bear a child. Dr. Arthur Kaplan of the University of Minnesota has argued that every child has the right to a mother who will not need to be in a nursing home when the child enters high school. He feels that mothers' desire for a child should not take priority over the welfare of the child. Other writers have indicated that this represents a double standard; after all, men in their 70s, without the permission of their doctor, can father children. For example, Charlie Chaplin fathered a child at 73. Up until now this has been biologically impossible for women. Supporters of older women using IVF to have babies point out that older mothers are often more financially secure, have more time to devote to a child than younger women and that even young mothers die suddenly and that all responsible parents should make arrangements for the care of their children in the case of such an event.

Should infertile couples themselves be considered "vulnerable"? Despite the high costs, fertility treatments will be unsuccessful for most of the couples who come to the clinics for help. And because they are desperate to have a child they are vulnerable and may be willing to purchase several treatments before giving up. As one clinic director in the United States suggested, "The problem with this field is that patients don't realize it's a business."

## 7. Accountability

Finally, we as members of society are responsible for the control and regulation of the new reproductive technologies. Many professions and organizations are self-regulated, but because the impact on society of the NRTs will be so profound, all members of society must have a voice in the regulation of the technologies. Regulation cannot be left to one group or individual, but ultimately is the responsibility of all members of a democratic society.

# Conclusion

The common values held by at least the majority of members of an open and free society are reflected in the laws that govern that society. In 1993, Canadians, through their participation in the Royal Commission, expressed their values and concerns and these have shaped the seven guiding principles. The federal government is now attempting to pass legislation that puts into effect the guiding principles of the Royal Commission. This legislation will create a ban on

- commercial surrogacy;
- the buying and selling of human eggs and sperm;
- egg donation in return for IVF services;
- developing artificial wombs;

- cloning;

- animal–human hybrids; and

- retrieving eggs or sperm from fetuses or cadavers for reproductive services.

Will our values as a society change over time? Certainly. So the debate over this issue, an example of our attempt to use technology wisely for our own benefit, will continue. When technology answers an important human need, there is an undeniable pressure to take advantage of the technological solution. In what way does the reproduction of human life differ from any other aspect of nature that we control through our use of technology? We must all participate in the search for the answer to this fundamental question.

# Secrets of the Human Genome

Alan Bernstein

We are in the midst of a profound revolution in health research—a revolution driven by our emerging understanding of the molecular basis of human biology and disease. Within our genome exist many of the secrets of our shared humanity, as well as the differences that make each of us distinct human beings.

Understanding the human genome will have a transformative effect on health and on our health-care system. This revolution will fundamentally alter the way we prevent, diagnose, and treat diseases even as it poses ethical problems about privacy and confidentiality that we are only just beginning to grasp.

At the moment, our health-care system is primarily reactive—we treat people when they become ill. With the new knowledge that we are gaining of the human genome, we will be able to predict who is susceptible to disease and help to prevent the disease or catch it at an earlier, treatable stage.

For example: We can now identify people who carry an altered gene that predisposes them to colon cancer. Armed with this knowledge, we can look for and remove the pre-malignant growths before they become cancerous, preventing deaths from this disease.

Diagnosis of disease will also change radically. Instead of symptom-based diagnosis—we know the car won't start, but we don't know why—we will be able to make a diagnosis based on the molecular pathways that are altered. We will know whether the car won't start because the battery is dead, or the gas tank is empty. Just as battery or gas-tank problems require different solutions, the genetic variations of a disease require different approaches. Patients will be stratified according to the genetic pathway their disease has taken, and treated appropriately.

We can already see the potential benefits of such individualized medicine. STI-571 is a drug being tested as a treatment for chronic myelogenous leukemia. It is designed to interact with the ABL protein, the protein coded for by the ABL gene that is responsible for the abnormal growth of leukemic cells. Early results are highly promising; the drug is

The following article originally appeared as "The Human Genome. Balancing Act: Science and Society" in *The Globe and Mail* on February 14, 2001.

very effective and has few side effects. In short, we are rapidly moving from reactive to proactive approaches to health and to diagnoses based on what our genes are doing, not our symptoms.

The genomic revolution, and its implications for health research, is also fuelling the growth of Canada's New Economy. For Canada, the economic potential is enormous. We have one of the world's most vibrant biotechnology sectors—companies that are leaders in developing new therapies for HIV/AIDS, cancer, infectious diseases, blindness, heart disease, etc. These companies have grown out of the innovative research carried out at our universities and research hospitals. They now employ hundreds of young Canadians, and are supported by more than $500-million annually.

But . . .

We are still far from having all the answers. If the human genome map is the Book of Life, then we still don't completely understand the language in which it is written. Deciphering that language—figuring out what our genes actually do—is going to be an exciting challenge involving more than just geneticists.

**Proteomics** will be an important piece of the puzzle, since genes are simply blueprints for proteins. **Bioinformatics** will be another part of the puzzle. Integrative physiologists and clinicians will bring their understanding of the whole person to the table, while organ specialists will help us understand how genes affect the development and functioning of our heart, lungs, liver, brain and other organs. Social scientists are essential if we are to understand the complex interplay between genetics and external factors, such as socio-economic status, lifestyle, and the environment. Some diseases such as Tay-Sachs and cystic fibrosis arise only as a result of mutations in a single gene. Others, such as diabetes and various mental illnesses, appear to reflect the complex interplay between our genetic hard-wiring and what we eat, who we know, how we live.

And more than ever, we're going to need ethicists. The genetics revolution is raising countless new ethical issues. The ability to predict disease, decades in advance, has profound implications for how we view our lives and make life decisions. How will new genetic information affect our decisions about whether to have children? What should we tell them? What should they tell us?

Issues of privacy and confidentiality are critical, as is the need to deal with the issue of discrimination in the workplace or by insurers. Will employers have the right to genetic information about potential workers? Who has the right to this information? Our bosses? Our future spouses? Our insurance agents?

proteomics

the study of the structure and function of proteins and their genetic source

bioinformatics

an emerging discipline integrating mathematical, statistical and computer techniques to analyze and manage biological information

The development of new therapies raises issues of health disparities. New drugs are expensive, and the pace of development is rapid. Access to these drugs is going to vary, not only between the developed and developing worlds, but within regions of Canada and between Canada and the United States.

Our governments need scientific, objective evidence in order to make informed policy decisions about the avalanche of new treatments. Will this ultimately mean that the health-care system becomes more cost effective? Or will costs rise as the public's expectations continue to increase?

In last month's Speech from the Throne, Ottawa recognized the driving force that health research will play in ensuring the health of Canadians and of the health-care system. It implicitly recognized that today's challenges—a vibrant and efficient health-care system, the health of our aboriginal population, healthy children, a strong and diversified economy and the branding of Canada as a country characterized by excellence, creativity, free enquiry and opportunity—require a strong culture of research. I have no doubt that Canada can lead the world in this new science and develop a uniquely Canadian approach that balances the exciting scientific opportunities with the ethical and social challenges for the benefit of all.

*Dr. Alan Bernstein is the president of the Canadian Institutes of Health Research. He is an internationally known researcher in cancer and gene therapy and the former director of the Samuel Lunenfeld Research Institute at Mount Sinai Hospital in Toronto.*

# UNIT 5

# Arts and Culture

The purpose of art is the lifelong construction of a state of wonder.

*Glenn Gould*

As an artist, one is not a citizen of society. An artist is bound to explore every aspect of human experience, the darkest corners—not necessarily—but if that is where one is led, that's where one must go. You cannot worry about what the structure of your own particular segment of society considers bad behaviour, good behaviour; good exploration, bad exploration. So, at the time you're being an artist, you're not a citizen. You don't have the social responsibility of a citizen. You have, in fact, no social responsibility whatsoever.

*David Cronenberg*

The sole substitute for an experience which we have not ourselves lived through is art and literature.

*Alexander Solzhenitsyn*

Fantasies are more than substitutes for unpleasant realities, they are also dress rehearsals. All acts performed in the world begin in the imagination.

*Barbara Grizzuti Harrison*

Confronted with a story, any story, we immediately seek to fathom it out, to know it, even though we realize that if we succeed it will no longer be interesting, it will die. Oddly, then, the greatest pleasure we can get from a story only comes when the smaller satisfaction of having explained it away is thwarted. The mind discards, as it were, the chaff of the explicable to find real repose, or real excitement, in a kernel of enigma.

*Tim Parks*

# Introduction

Throughout the course of this text, reason has helped us to examine some thorny and fundamental problems. You may recall the question of the possibility of freedom in Unit 1, the collision of necessary change and the persistence of old attitudes in Unit 2, the possibility that human nature itself imposes limits on our hopes for political solutions in Unit 3, the concern that the technological offspring of science may cause us to lose our way in the search for a better world in Unit 4. For answers to these and other questions, we have relied on reason and the methods of various disciplines such as psychology, sociology, philosophy, politics and science. In Unit 5, we shift emphasis, not in the sense of turning away from reason and method, but in the sense of adding a certain openness to imagination and a receptivity to pleasure. For the arts are about the significance of a parallel and imagined universe in the mind, a place where the real world may be reflected and criticized perhaps, but where the chief motive to explore is pleasure.

Morton Ritts, in his article "Portrait of the Arts," points out that it is sometimes easier to say what art isn't than to come to an easy definition of what it is. Perhaps that can be explained by the breadth of what can be called art. Think of the difficulty of generalizing about something that could be as concrete as a building and as delicate as a poem, as irresistible as rock 'n' roll and as difficult as much modern sculpture. Ritts ventures to point out an intriguing paradox: "Characters in novels and films who are invented, who are fictions, often reveal more about human nature than real people." Perhaps that is because we are so good at disguising what we think and feel in real life that the openness we experience in fiction seems so honest and intimate. It is the quality of revelation, the "showing" rather than the "telling" that separates art from science. Good fiction doesn't talk about or theorize the human situation; it moves in on one particular aspect of life, refines and focuses our attention to the point where we can share the experience of the fictional characters, and then moves on. In many ways, the arts leave room for a private distilling process, where we sift through the art experience and decide to take from that experience what is most valuable to us.

Ritts affirms the value of the connection between individual creativity and social need, a connection that has a vulnerability in the Canadian context, as John Steckley's article, "A Canadian Lament" forcefully explores. Canadians are avid consumers of other peoples' culture and, proportionately, it is rare for Canadians to read, see or hear their own story in novels, film or music. On the one hand, this phenomenon is understandable; we have a small population, we live next to the most vibrant producer of popular culture in the world and it is quite normal to be fascinated by American culture as are the citizens of every other country in the world. On the other hand, if we don't develop our own voice and our own story as a counterbalance to American culture, we forego a vital tool for self-understanding and will be compelled to see the problems of growing up, finding a mate, facing danger and growing old through Californian eyes.

Scott Greer and Michael Horwood also explore the connection between the individual and society in their article, "Music as History." They begin with a wonderful quote from Friedrich Nietzsche that we can all agree with: "Life without music would be a mistake." The article goes on to show how music not only is an expression of individual talent but also is a reflection of its culture and time, and how the increasingly important role of the soloist matches and parallels the emergence of individual power.

Clive Cockerton in "Serious Pleasure" explores and answers the concerns that some people have about the seductive power of art to lead us to think and do things we shouldn't. It begins with a summary of Plato's arguments for banning art from an ideal society and attempts to counter these arguments by essentially making three points:

1. pleasure and beauty are intrinsically valuable in themselves—art can revive and inspire us;

2. art provides us with insights into particular fictional lives that can have a significant impact on the way we understand our own lives; and

3. by taking us out of ourselves and into others' lives, art creates a sense of community through the realization that others experience life as we do.

In "Objectivity and Subjectivity," Cockerton picks up the theme of knowledge and asks whether we can learn anything reliable from art, or even if we can say anything reliable about something so obviously coloured with emotion as our experience of art. If we agree with the

philosopher Nietzsche that there are no facts independent from interpretation, does that mean that all interpretations are of equivalent value
or that some interpretations are more helpful and illuminating than others? If we see art through the lens of our personal history, our gender, our
social and economic class, and our racial and ethnic background, do we
each see something different according to the mix of our influences? If
the answer is yes, then there really doesn't seem much to talk about in art,
other than to exchange highly personal, cultural and gendered interpretations. Thomas Lux's "The Voice You Hear When You Read Silently"
explores the weight of personal experience—the way the voice in your
head "never says anything neutrally." And yet it is undeniable that art
works produced in different times, by different genders and different
cultures and classes, still speak to us. What is it in the art that allows us to
experience its power despite all the differences between the creators and
us? It is tempting to think that there is something in the art that can
break through the differences that divide us.

There is a great deal of difficulty in talking about art as an abstract
thing without talking about specific works of art. For this reason, two
short stories and another poem are included as lively examples of art
works that illustrate some of the more general points made in the essays.
"The Grown-up," "The Disclaimer" and "I Go Back to May 1937"
reflect on the theme of time in their own remarkable manner. Both the
stories and the poem invite us into their worlds, compelling us to stretch
to understand the cares of others and, in the process, making our own
view richer.

# Portrait of the Arts

Morton Ritts

In this unit we examine the role of the arts. Sometimes it's harder to say what art is than what it isn't. Art, for example, isn't science. As we saw in the previous unit, science is factual and **propositional**. It tries to provide knowledge that is objective and clear, with verifiable observations based on a rigorous method of enquiry.

Art, on the other hand, tends to be ambiguous and problematic. It is both factual and fictional. Indeed, on one level, narrative arts such as literature and film proclaim themselves to be not "true" at all, to be "made up." How can something that's made up be true? And yet, we know from our own experience that when we read certain novels or see certain films we're struck by just how "true to life" they are.

There is a profound paradox here. Characters in novels and films who are invented, who are fictions, often reveal more about human nature than real people. Fiction, in other words, has the capacity to provide us with greater insight into truth than truth. But fiction is just another kind of truth. All art is.

Of course, psychology and biology also provide us with truth. But their focus is always general, while art portrays the particular. As a psychological theory, Freud's **oedipal complex** is universal and abstract. But in the novel *Sons and Lovers*, D.H. Lawrence gives this theory specific, concrete form by creating a rich and complex character whose intense, troubled relationship with his mother dominates his life.

For another example compare the description of anxiety and fear in a psychology textbook with how these same emotions are depicted in a novel or film. The textbook account is analytical, factual. This is fine, but such an account doesn't convey to us what anxiety and fear "feel" like. A well-written novel or well-made film does, however, by locating these emotions in actions that compel our interest. This difference between fact and fiction is the difference between science and the arts. Science, including the social sciences, "tell," whereas the arts "show."

We've said that the arts show by giving us knowledge of the particular. As the *Sons and Lovers* example suggests, we come to know an important universal relationship (mothers and sons) in the depiction of a specific relationship.

**propositional**
proved or disproved using formal logical or mathematical procedure

**oedipal complex**
an attraction in a male for his mother accompanied by hostility towards his father

"Portrait of the Arts" is by Morton Ritts of Humber College. Used by permission.

The arts show by way of creativity, discipline, expressiveness. They give form to our experience. Sometimes the result is indirect, as in expressionist painting. Sometimes it's brutally direct, as in *The Killing Fields*, a powerful film about the genocide that occurred in Cambodia in the 1970s. Different as they are, both examples represent some important aspect of truth.

# Art and Society

One thing we can say for certain is that artists work in a social context. On the walls of the vast cathedral-like caves at Lascaux in southwestern France, our palaeolithic ancestors painted picture-stories of their communal hunts. These extraordinary images bind us to our own prehistoric beginnings some 20 000 years ago. At the same time, they're a good example of one of the underlying impulses behind art—the impulse to leave our mark, to say we were here.

Some argue that we work (not labour) for much the same reason, especially if we view our work as "play," in the sense used by Auden in Unit 2. But is there a difference between work and art? Yes and no. No doubt, what a good painter or a writer produces is always the result of hard work. But if all art is work, the opposite—that all work is art—is not true. This is because most of us work to please someone else while most artists work primarily to please themselves. In this sense, the more a job allows you to please yourself the closer you are to being an artist.

Most of us don't have this luxury. If we work in a factory, an office, a retail store or a school, our individual needs count for less than those of the company or our clients. Certainly we can find fulfillment in our work, but never at the expense of the group. While enlightened employers try to create the conditions for a balance between our individual interests and those of the company, this isn't often possible.

So in this way art is different from work. Unlike work, art, in Western culture at least, stresses the primacy of the individual. In this tradition, even performing artists, like musicians, actors and dancers, have a healthy regard for their own uniqueness. They may be part of a team, but some will always insist on shining more brightly than others—on being "stars."

Throughout history, societies have often objected to the idea of artists as individuals, arguing that their first loyalty is not to themselves but to the state. This was the case in the former Soviet Union, and is still the case in China. Even in democracies like Canada and the United States, books,

magazines, paintings, photographs and films are censored because they are deemed in some way a threat to society for reasons of obscenity, libel or blasphemy.

The Greek philosopher Plato would have heartily endorsed such censorship. For him, art was at best a distraction, at worst a danger. He believed it was difficult enough to know reality. Art only made it harder—instead of showing things as they were, it offered distorted representations of those things. Drama, poetry, painting gave us a kind of secret secondhand version of life, he argued. They served no constructive purpose.

According to Plato, only the study of science, philosophy or history enlightened us because these disciplines appealed to the mind, to our rational selves. Drama, poetry, music and the visual arts appealed to our senses, our irrational and emotional selves. In doing so, they not only distorted reality, they also threatened the security and well-being of the state because they tended to mislead, confuse and excite people.

## The Need to Imagine

Just as art differs from philosophy, science and history, writers, actors, dancers and other artists differ from philosophers, scientists and historians. Like them, artists attempt to impose their own sense of order on the random flow of life around them. But as we've already seen, their method is different—artists work with their senses, with feeling and intuition, with metaphor and imagination.

In his play, *A Midsummer Night's Dream*, William Shakespeare compared artists (poets) to lovers and lunatics. What connects them, he suggests, is precisely this power of the imagination:

> And, as imagination bodies forth,
> The form of things unknown, the poet's pen
> Turns them to shapes, and gives to airy nothing
> A local habitation and a name.

The artist, then, is someone whose imagination makes the unknown known, the invisible visible and the unconscious conscious—which is very close to the therapeutic process of Freudian psychoanalysis. Art itself is a way of exploring the mysteries of the human condition, not in the linear fashion of scientific enquiry but in the associative, circular manner of therapy. "We shed our sicknesses in books," D.H. Lawrence wrote. Art, he meant, heals.

That's perhaps one reason why people feel the need to write, paint, play an instrument or sing. Another reason, we've suggested, is the desire to leave some sign, some evidence of our existence. As children we seek even the most trivial kind of immortality, nothing more sometimes than carving our initials into the trunk of a tree or printing our name in the fresh concrete of a sidewalk.

The humanistic psychologist Abraham Maslow offers still another way of looking at the desire to create. In his hierarchy of needs, Maslow speculates that physical survival is basic. Someone who lacks the requirements for physiological well-being, including food and shelter, isn't much interested in writing novels or painting landscapes.

But once these basic needs are satisfied, we often ask ourselves, "What more is there to life?" What's more, Maslow says, are the higher level needs for love, esteem and, above all, self-actualization. More than most people, artists are obsessed by the need to self-actualize, to be the best they can at whatever they are. A tale about two modern painters, Amadeo Modigliani and Chaim Soutine, illustrates this point.

Modigliani and Soutine were friends who shared a studio in a small garret in Paris at the turn of the last century. They were almost stereotypes of the starving artist, deprived of material comforts but endowed with rich and productive imaginations.

One day, the story goes, they bought a chicken at the local butcher shop, as the subject for a "still life." They hung it from the rafters in their studio and set up their easels. In the midst of their preparation, however, it occurred to them that they hadn't had a decent meal in weeks. They'd spent their last francs on a chicken, but incredibly—foolishly, it seemed at that moment—they were intending to paint it, not eat it.

Maslow might explain their dilemma this way: If the two friends cooked the chicken, they'd satisfy their basic survival needs but not their need for art. On the other hand, if they painted the chicken, they'd satisfy their need for self-actualization, but might starve to death in the process. What to do? In fact, they arrived at one of those inspired compromises that are the mark of true genius—they painted very quickly (while the chicken was still fresh).

The story is a good example of the struggle between the demands of life and those of art. Someone once asked the great artist Picasso whether, if his house caught fire, he'd rescue his cat first or his paintings. He answered his cat. Picasso's point was that artists draw their inspiration from life. Without life there can be no art.

# Art Redraws the Boundaries of our Lives

As much as artists deal with the world of imagination and subjective perception, their messages of pain or celebration correspond in some way to life outside them, to the common experiences of humanity. When we see a film or hear a song that absorbs us, we feel this connection too. The artist redraws and enlarges the boundaries of our emotional and intellectual landscape.

At their best, the books and films and music that mean most to us tell us stories in provocative new ways. Since the beginning, the human species has always felt compelled to tell stories. There are the hunting pictures in the caves at Lascaux. There was remarkable poetry, music and painting in the Nazi concentration camps. Plato was right to suggest that art is dangerous, but perhaps that's exactly what art should be—something that pricks the bubble of illusion, that exposes pain and injustice, that challenges us to think about old things in new ways.

Art is often most dangerous when it creates an experience for us that defies what is considered politically and morally "correct." That's why one of the first acts of dictatorial regimes is to imprison a country's writers. Or why police shut down exhibitions of "offensive" paintings and photographs. Or why some governments issue death threats against artists who have allegedly committed crimes against the state.

Yet those who want to create art, and not propaganda, will always affirm their right to see with their own eyes, to speak in their own voice. Their messages may indeed be subversive. But we soon forget books or paintings or music or films or plays that merely entertain us. We remember instead those that have astonished or disturbed, moved or changed us. They're part of who we are.

# Serious Pleasure: The Role of the Arts

## Clive Cockerton

In many people's eyes, the arts are the toy department of life—occasionally amusing perhaps but in the long run a waste of time for men and women of action and purpose. The Greek philosopher Plato (427–347 B.C.) argued that art was a distraction we would be better off without. According to Plato, art was a distraction for the following reasons:

1.  Art deals with images not truth; it doesn't advance knowledge, it doesn't discover anything, it only seems to understand.

2.  Art imitates reality; to learn about reality it is much better to study reality itself rather than a pale imitation.

3.  Art is sensual and distracts us from the more important quests (such as moral or spiritual quests). In its arousal of basic instincts, in its stimulation/simulation of violence and lust, it is anarchic, a force for disorder in the community.

In short—empty, imitative and corrupting.

Since Plato, many moralists have branched off from these arguments and urged us to consider that bright colour and decoration were immoral because they call attention to the self instead of singing the praises of God, or that "realistic" novels were too shocking for the delicate sensibilities of young women, or that rock 'n' roll would corrupt and deprave youth with its primitive rhythms. At a much less passionate level, many business people are skeptical of the arts, except where they can be trained to serve the purpose of promoting consumption of goods and services in advertising. Politicians frequently see the arts as "frills," and in a time of recession the artistic community is the first to feel the cuts of government support. All of these views, whether held by philosophers, moralists, business people or politicians, have in common the conviction that art is not serious.

This doesn't mean that the effects of art can't be serious. Plato was concerned that literature and art were disruptive and corrupting. Stories need sinners to be interesting. Tales of people who always do the right thing are predictable, preachy and boring. Yet stories that embrace all that is human, the sinners as well as the saints, compel us to accept the humanity of those who lie, cheat, betray, of those who are greedy, lustful and cruel. Not just accept the humanity of others, but also recognize those very qualities in ourselves. Moralists worry that this recognition and acceptance are subversive and undermine moral authority. Whenever we encounter an argument that says that a certain film or type of music will inflame or deprave, or that violence on TV will lead to violent children, we are dealing with an offshoot of Plato's original concern.

Aristotle, a student of Plato's, developed a counter-argument that suggested that the symbolic experience of violence in the arts was actually helpful and worked like a safety valve for our violent sides. Through the emotion raised in watching a story unfold, we achieve catharsis, a cleansing and purging of destructive emotion in a safe and contained way. For Aristotle, nothing was to be gained from denying our destructive urges. Indeed, the opportunity to face our sometimes violent and immoral nature in a story lessened the threat of our urges becoming reality. In other words, in watching a violent and terrifying story, we rehearse the emotion along with the actors and are released from having to act it out. However, recent psychological tests on children who were exposed to violent television suggest that some harmful results do occur. There's no simple, mechanical process whereby children watch violent acts and then always re-enact them. It's a more subtle process of shifting the atmosphere, of weakening the inhibition to violence that over time can result in changed behaviour. However, Aristotle couldn't predict Saturday morning TV and its impact on children. His insights were an attempt to describe adult responses to serious drama and remain useful as reflections on how the adult mind responds. Even adults have terrors and nightmares, and the arts enable us to both face what horrifies us and move beyond it as well.

But can art have a harmful impact on sane, responsible adults? Recently, the Canadian legal system seemed to be saying that citizens needed to be protected from their own reactions when it seized paintings by Eli Langer of children in potentially sexual positions. This action was curiously directed at the paintings themselves rather than at the painter. The clear suggestion is that some subject matter cannot be explored, a suggestion that most artists would resist. Society clearly has interests at stake, and probably should find ways to protect itself from exploitation of sensational subject matter, but there is a great deal of difference between the sleazy exploitation of the pornographer and the serious exploration of the artist. The courts, however, have not found a reliable way of measuring that difference. Should the failure of the courts and the anxieties of moralists shut us off from discussing certain controversial subject matter? Is the danger from the arts real? As Plato writes:

> Much is at stake, more than most people suppose; it is a choice between becoming a good man or a bad; poetry, no more than wealth or power or honours, poetry can tempt us to be careless of justice and virtue. (*The Republic*)

Although Plato refers to poetry here, this fear of temptation would apply equally to other arts, because the seductive power of all arts threatens the rule of reason. Elsewhere, Plato argued that drama

> waters the growth of passions which should be allowed to wither away and sets them up in control although the goodness and happiness of our lives depend on their being held in subjection.

This idea may seem exaggerated and extreme to a modern audience, but for Plato our happiness depended on leading a good life, and a good life depended on control of the emotions by reason.

Plato's second objection, that art imitates reality, reflects his concern that we could be deceived by the distortions and exaggerations of the storytelling process. Put crudely, a film such as *Disclosure*, which presents the story of a man who is sexually harassed by his female employer, however worthwhile the story may be in artistic terms, could lead the viewer to gross misperceptions about the nature of sexual harassment and power in the workplace. Clearly, the social reality has been that men have been the dominant gender in terms of business power and are far more likely to harass employees than women. Yet the fictional story may be compelling because it touches our emotions or thrills us, and we may be tempted to think of the film as a realistic and likely representation of what really goes on in business. The reality becomes apparent when we think about it, but for Plato we are always in danger when we succumb to the pleasurable pull of a story that could lead us down a rhetorical path to error. Of course, we are all aware and a little bit wary of the common lies of film—the couple overcoming all obstacles to their love and riding off into the sunset and the hero triumphing against seemingly impossible odds. However, the creators of these stories could defend their stories by saying that they don't have to be likely, just plausible, and that the preference for heroic triumph over dismal failure is an understandable and universal audience choice.

My favourite distortion is the glaring omission that very few characters in film worry about who pays, and no screen time is consumed with the practical issues of getting and saving money that takes up so much time in the actual world. Writers and filmmakers could respond that all stories must necessarily involve compression, and that compression involves eliminating superfluous detail, leaving the essential story to stand out boldly, without being submerged in the minute and tedious chores of everyday life. I'm just not sure that our relationship to money is always so inessential.

Perhaps Plato's intellectually most interesting objection is the first one—that art involves an inevitable illusion. What we see in film is not reality; when we read fiction we enter a world that is entirely made up. For Plato, the fact that we see images and enter into fantasy worlds means that we are turning away from truth. After reading a novel, can we say we know anything about the real world? We may think we know something of the human situation focused on in the plot of the novel, but have we acquired any verifiable concepts that we might have if we had read a psychology textbook instead?

Well, perhaps not verifiable in the same controlled, scientific, experimental way, and maybe not full-blown concepts, but I would argue that, yes, novels provide us with genuine insights into human behaviour and situations. And these insights are verifiable, at least in a comparative way. When we finish a novel, we compare the truth of what we have read with our experience of the truth. In this way, every reading is some kind of experiment, some kind of verification. The fact that Hamlet or Falstaff are made-up characters in Shakespeare's plays does not prevent us from learning a great deal about ourselves and other people from them. They may be literally non-existent but it makes no sense to refer to them in this way as their creation enriches our understanding of the real. So too does the imaginative testing of possibilities involved in any serious novel. And since every testing of fictional possibilities is verified or rejected by every reader, novels that are read and endorsed by many readers probably have a lot to say to us. Perhaps novels are the most insightful artistic medium, but surely the same comparative experience operates with certain kinds of realistic film. In *American Beauty*, for instance, the film clearly tries to capture something of the mood of suburban North America. The audience naturally compares their own attitudes to the attitudes toward money, work, family and sexuality depicted in the film and almost immediately looks for answers to some interesting questions.

Is the film credible? Does it fit with my own experience or is it at least plausible given the fictional characters and situation? When we see a film that affects us, we reflect on what we have seen, we search for verification in our own lives.

We experience stories as we experience the world—from a perspective, a point of view that is both emotional and rational. Plato was wary of our emotional natures; he believed that they were not to be denied perhaps, but kept in strict control. In our day, despite the enormous success of science, we generally don't experience life as detached observers. Indeed, detachment seems too clinical, and the perspective of the scientist lacks the engagement with experience that a fulfilled life seems to require. Instead we grope about through our lives, using bits of knowledge and lots of emotion in a constantly shifting understanding—as we do in novels. We discover that emotion can be as reliable a guide to right conduct and behaviour as ideas and concepts. Some actions just don't feel right. Others, despite what we might have been taught to believe, feel liberating and joyful. Literature helps us to feel more acutely and generously as it guides us through an ever-expanding repertoire of human situations contained in its pages. It involves a passionate way of knowing, different from, but not inferior to, the relentless rationality of the philosopher or the precise observation of the scientist.

Still, literature is the most intellectual art form. Ideas are undeniably present in great works, even if they are never talked at you, or talked about, they hover in the background. The consequences of ideas are revealed, are shown to be valuable or not, but not directly in argument form. Ideas are produced by scientists, philosophers, academics, by all of us. It is in literature that ideas are given flesh, tested not in debate, but in a re-creation of life. The cold, abstract and theoretical position is abandoned and replaced with a vantage point that is passionately considered and grounded in particular lives. As the philosopher Lorraine Code writes:

> The claim that literature is a source of knowledge rests upon a belief in the value of understanding the particular. It implies that a minute and inward understanding of particulars has the capacity to go beyond itself, to show something more general … (*Epistemic Responsibility*)

Why do some particular characters' lives seem to speak to all of us, when clearly not all of our lives resemble the particular character? The writer creates an image of human complexity that draws us into the

fictional world, convinces us of its reality and at the same time throws light onto the real world. Theoretical understanding may be an essential element to knowledge, but without being grounded in the particular, theoretical understanding seems bloodless. *The Insider* examines a number of complicated issues such as the ethics of whistle-blowing, corporate control of the media and the compromises people face in the workplace. The narrative of *The Insider* takes us inside these complicated legal and ethical issues by presenting it as personal experience, thereby making it intimate. And it is precisely this intimate knowledge that might elude a purely historical perspective.

The great American poet Wallace Stevens wrote a poem whose title, "Not Ideas about the Thing, but the Thing Itself," contains the ambition most writers have to deliver directly an intimate understanding of the world. For this intimacy to be achieved, characters can't just be mouthpieces of ideas or virtues, but instead must convince us of their full individuality and their real humanity. Our lives are shaped by diverse combinations of ideas and experience, whether we are conscious of them or not. Fiction provides a means of becoming more conscious, of constantly examining and testing these ideas and experience. Through this fictional process, we learn which ideas are useful, not just as ideas but as guiding principles.

When we read a novel, we may come to know a situation or a character very well; indeed, we may know all the significant details about a person's life (thoughts as well as actions). It's possible to know fictional characters better than our close friends. By providing us with all the information we need and by coming to a conclusion, novels present a complete vision. This completeness necessarily lacks some of life's random quality. Novels conclude, life goes on. By concluding, novels ask us to stop and think. By focusing on some of the most fundamental issues (growth, independence, love, pain, death) that we encounter in the real world, novels ask us to reflect on our own lives. But they don't just ask, they seduce us with pleasure, with worlds spun from word-magic. They extend the promise of intimacy, they leave us with insight.

Whenever it occurs, the combination of pleasure, beauty and insight is life-affirming. While pleasure and beauty are frequently found on the shimmering surface of art, in the form of delight in a turn of phrase or in intensity of vision, the insight cuts to the heart of issues, toward a deeper understanding of people and human experience. The answer to Plato's desire to rid his world of art lies in the value of pleasure and insight to the individual reader and viewer. Rather than being opposed to the quest for a rational life, perhaps the arts are complementary, providing a testing board for the different ideas that call out to us. At any rate, art's value doesn't stop with beneficial experiences for the individual, but extends to a community. Indeed, the shared experience of art helps to create a sense of community. Many cold winds blow through an individual's life, but the arts tell you that you're not alone, that others have cried as hard, laughed as loud and loved as deeply. There's pleasure in that—in the community with others that the arts magically bring to us. Serious pleasure.

# A Canadian Lament

John Steckley

## Can You Hear Me?

You live in Toronto, the largest city in Canada. Yet if I asked you to come up with a song that mentioned the name of your city, could you do it? Hard, isn't it? How about I make it easier and ask you to come up with a song that mentions any place in Canada. It's still a difficult task. If you know a lot about music and have a good memory—and it helps to have lived a long time—you might be able to come up with old songs by Gordon Lightfoot, Neil Young and, of course, anything by Stompin' Tom Connors of "Bud the Spud" and "Sudbury Saturday Night" fame. If you're younger, you might bring to mind something by Blue Rodeo, the Tragically Hip, I Mother Earth or maybe a song about the Black experience in Toronto, by one of our rap deejays.

Want something easier? Try thinking of a song that mentions a place in the United States. New York, Los Angeles, San Francisco and Chicago, and if you like country, Nashville, Memphis, the states of California, Carolina (North or South), Arkansas or Kentucky, and just about every place in Texas spring to mind pretty fast.

Canadians such as Shania Twain, Alanis Morissette, Céline Dion and Bryan Adams are among the biggest musical stars in North America. But do they ever sing about where they are from? Will Shania ever mention her hometown of Timmins, as she has Arkansas in her song "Home's Not Where His Heart Is Anymore"? Will Alanis sing about how ironic it is to be raised in Ottawa? Will the lyrics of a Céline Dion song ever mention Quebec when she sings in English? When he is singing with big stars Pavarotti, Streisand or Tina Turner, will Bryan Adams ever suggest that they sing about Vancouver? Don't hold your breath.

While we are on the subject of music, think of the big-name musicals that make so much money and play so long in Toronto. They all have a setting that is outside of this country: *Ragtime* (United States), *Sunset Boulevard* (Hollywood), *Evita* (Argentina), *Phantom of the Opera* (Paris), *Les Misérables* (Paris), *Cats* (London), *Joseph and the Amazing Technicolour Dreamcoat* (Egypt), *Jane Eyre* (England), *Showboat* (United States) and

"A Canadian Lament" is by John Steckley of Humber College. Used by permission.

*Beauty and the Beast* (France). As I write, *Damn Yankees* (about the New York baseball team) is just starting to play here. Don't ever expect to see and hear a production of *How About Those Jays?*

# Can You See Me?

Move now to the television screen. A substantial number of television shows are filmed in Vancouver and Toronto, but those cities don't exist in those shows. Licence plates are always obscured in some way. You don't see distinctive features such as the CN Tower or the Lion's Gate Bridge. "Due South" was shot in Toronto, but took place in Chicago (with introductory stock footage of recognizable Chicago features). "The X-Files" used to be shot in Vancouver, but the main characters are FBI agents who travel around the United States looking for signs of aliens (not ones wearing toques, hockey sweaters and eating doughnuts—my spell check doesn't like the word "toques"). Think of American place names in television shows, past and present: "Boston Common," "L.A. Law," "LAPD," "Chicago Hope," "Streets of San Francisco," "Dallas," "Beverly Hills 90210," "Hawaii Five-0," "Miami Vice," "The Fresh Prince of Bel Air," "New York Undercover"....

American domination of movies tends to block out Canadian voices.

What about the big screen, movies? American domination is almost complete here; Canada is barely a player. Our films are like our milk: 2 per cent of the movies shown in our theatres is Canadian. Compare that with 45 per cent domestically produced films in France (a figure that they worry about as showing American domination), and 11 per cent in Australia. How many movies have you watched in the last year, 2 years, 11 years, that took place *officially* (complete with licence plates, names and recognizable landmarks) in any place in Canada? Can you think of the names of any Canadian movies? *Hard Core Logo, Dance Me Outside, Jesus of Montreal, The Sweet Hereafter*, and *The Decline of the American Empire* probably don't sound familiar to you. Count up all the different times you've seen someone play the part of the president of the United States in a movie. Now try to remember whether you've ever seen anyone play the prime minister of Canada. No wonder so many children believe that the leader of our country is a president.

Canadian stories don't get told. Bring to mind all the baseball movies that have been made. *It Happens Every Spring, Ty Cobb, Angels in the Outfield, Bull Durham, A League of Their Own, Major League, Field of Dreams, The Babe* are but a few. Now think of the teams involved: New York Yankees, California Angels, Cleveland Indians, Chicago Cubs and minor league teams in the United States. What do you feel are the chances that you'll ever see a movie that features the Toronto Blue Jays (twice World Series champs) or the Montreal Expos? There have been many movies made concerning other sports: boxing, basketball and football especially. But what about hockey? There's *Slapshot*, with Canadian actors, a very Canadian story (about a one-industry town and its hockey team) but with an American star and an American site. The *Mighty Ducks* movies serve as not-so-subtle Disney movie advertisements for a Disney-owned team. There is a flood of Canadian books out now about hockey, particularly focused in on the two greatest Canadian sports franchises of all times: the Montreal Canadiens and the Toronto Maple Leafs. There are a good number of movie-inspiring stories in those books, but they will most likely remain just on the printed page. My childhood heroes— Eddie Shack, Bobby Baun, Tim Horton, Frank Mahovlich and, even, grudgingly as a Leaf fan, "Rocket" Richard, "Boom Boom" Geoffrion and Jean Béliveau—will probably never be seen in the movies.

Didn't it seem strange in *Wayne's World* to see people playing road hockey—the youthful experience of most Canadian males and a growing number of Canadian females? I didn't realize how Canadian an experience that is until I lived a year in Scotland. One day I heard the sound of wood scraping on pavement, and ran out of my house to see whether it was the sound of someone playing road hockey. Mike Myers (Wayne) of course is Canadian. But in the movies he played road hockey in a suburb of Chicago, and even that quintessentially Canadian landmark, the doughnut shop, was named after a player for an American team, Chicago's Stan Mikita. Mike Myers grew up in Scarborough and recreated that place in Chicago, and later in San Francisco, with the Scottish family in *So I Married an Axe Murderer*. His story felt so familiar, I felt I had met his dad when I grew up in Don Mills, right beside Scarborough, but the location was wrong. I doubt if it was a San Francisco story; the expatriate Scottish presence is so much stronger in Canada than in the United States.

There is a recent exception to my "Canadian stories don't get told" declaration. In 1996 the movie *Fly Away Home* came out with some success, and as I write it is the movie with the most copies in my video rental store. It is based on Bill Lishman's autobiography *Father Goose*, which is the story of how a man who earns his living making metal sculptures such as the famous "Autohenge" (a Stonehenge made out of car wrecks) pursued a lifelong dream to fly with the birds. The story is deeply rooted in southern Ontario. He grew up near Oshawa; his first commissioned sculpture was for the opening of Yorkdale shopping mall; he made front page news with the sculpture of a metal horse that he left, as a publicity stunt, outside of Toronto City Hall; he was one of the most conspicuous figures in the opposition to the building of the airport in Pickering during the 1970s; his art adorns Canada's Wonderland and Marineland. In the early 1990s he fought Ottawa (actually a federal bureaucrat with a strong need to control) to fly in an ultralight plane largely of his design with a group of Canada geese to the southern coastal states, first Virginia, then North Carolina. The geese had "imprinted" on him, taking him and his planes for their parents. It was not only an experiment to benefit the geese, who may have to change their migration paths due to the destruction of habitat and overhunting, but it was also an experiment that may lead some day to his working with endangered species such as the whooping crane and the trumpeter swan.

Now I liked the movie. It touched the emotions without manipulating them too much. There were good shots of the southern Ontario farmers' fields and woodlots that are dear to my heart. And if I could live with the southern Californian accent of Kevin Costner when he played the role of the Englishman Robin Hood, I suppose I can deal with the southern accent of Jeff Daniels in the part of Canadian Bill

Lishman and the New Zealand accent of Anna Pacquin as the heroine Amy who had been brought up by her mother in New Zealand. I didn't very much mind them changing the story so that a young girl was the one who the geese imprinted onto. And I found it humorous that to make sure people knew that the film was taking place in Canada, pictures of the Queen were featured prominently. But somehow something was lost for me. Maybe it was the sense of place that you get about American locations in recent movies such as *Fargo* and *Leaving Las Vegas*, and pretty much any movie based in L.A. or New York. Maybe so few movies present Canadian stories, that I was hungry in this exception for more representation of where I was raised.

# Can You Read About Me?

There is constant political and economic pressure coming from the United States to further dominate our media by overturning the cultural protection statements in the North American Free Trade Agreement of 1994. Should American magazines such as *Sports Illustrated* and *Reader's Digest* be treated as "Canadian" because they have some Canadian content? The World Trade Organization, based in Geneva, tentatively answered this question with a "yes," and it has the political power to enforce that answer. "Treated as Canadian" means they would have no import taxes put on them and that Canadian companies could claim certain tax concessions when advertising in these publications. "Treated as Canadian" means that these "split-run" magazines (they have a "run" or slightly different publication in more than one place over the same publication period) can charge less for advertising. In 1993, when *Sports Illustrated* tried this, it would charge $6250 for a full-page ad, while *Maclean's*, a Canadian magazine, charged $25 400 for the same full-page ad. Most of a magazine's revenue, some 70 per cent, comes from those advertisements. These Canadian-American split-runs get to be cheaper because they ride on the money spent on the American publication. They don't have to pay any significant amount for their writers, editors or illustrators as, for the most part, that is paid for in the American run. The extra money the Canadian magazines charge for advertising comes from paying for Canadian writers, editors, illustrators and such. When people argue that there should be a "level playing field," with no government "interference," they speak not knowing that, as we have seen, there is no level playing field to begin with. The American side of the field is much higher because of their size and economic power. Government restriction would make the field more level, not less.

The American magazines were successful in obtaining the rights from the World Trade Organization to make split-runs. Canadian Heritage Minister Sheila Copps countered in December 1999 with the Canadian Magazine Fund, $150 million to be made available to Canadian-owned magazines having 80 per cent Canadian content. If this move does not prove effective, Canadian magazines will be muscled off the stands by more powerful American magazines. Fewer Canadian stories will be told, and of those that are, fewer will be written by Canadians. It could lead to other "cultural industries" being put in the same situation. The aggressive attitude that at least some highly placed Americans have can be seen in former U.S. Trade Representative Charlene Barshefsky's comments:

> We cannot allow Canadian entities to use "culture" as an excuse to provide commercial advantages to Canadian products or to evict U.S. firms from the Canadian market.[1]

I agree with Peter C. Newman's opinion that the issue is not just about magazines; it is about how two different societies view their national cultures—one aggressively international, the other geared more toward national survival and understanding:

> To Americans, culture is their most successful export; they thrive on influencing the minds, fashions, manners and outlooks of a world tuned into their movies, television, clothes, books and heroes.
>
> Canadian culture is a far more subtle and fragile commodity, involving scattered truths about our past history, current hopes and future aspirations—about why we hold our ground in this cold land with empty horizons. . . . [I]ts many expressions—including Canadian magazines—must continue to find a market in order to give it voice and shape.[2]

# Can Anything Be Done About It?
## Canadian Content Rules and Government Involvement

One way of fighting this American arts domination is through government regulations that require Canadian content make up a fixed percentage of what is heard and seen on radio and television—30 per cent for the former and 50 per cent for the latter. Should we try this with movies as well, in order to increase the impact of Canadian content laws? There are complications involved. How do you define something as Canadian? How many Canadians involved make something Canadian rather than American or British? If a band had two Canadians and two

Americans, does it qualify? Many remember how a few years ago a Bryan Adams album was determined not to be Canadian because of the number of non-Canadians involved in the production. But then, Bryan might not have become the big star he is today if he hadn't had Canadian content rules to give his early material air play.

Sometimes artistically silly situations develop. A Toronto radio station was previewing a new U2 album. They could not play the whole CD in one hour because that would violate 30 per cent Canadian content rules. So, strangely, Canadian songs were intermixed among those of the U2 CD. The radio station had been burned the year before when it had done a top 1000 greatest hits and had to do the last 15 a day after the weekend was over, so as not to violate "the rules." On the other side of the coin, we see cynical stations that play Canadian tunes during the wee small hours and the weekends when the listenership is down, a practice referred to as the "beaver bin." "And, now, insomniacs, we have the all-Rita-McNeil hour."

There is a similar practice with television stations. The Canadian Radio-television and Telecommunications Commission (CRTC) set the rule that during the "prime time" hours of six to midnight, there must be 50 per cent Canadian content. Both the two big private networks use what is called the "bookends" approach. They show news, which qualifies as Canadian content, from six to seven and eleven to midnight. Thus they don't have to show much entertainment that is Canadian. In a recent study (valid for early 1997), during the crucial seven to eleven slot during weekdays, CTV showed only two hours of Canadian production of a possible twenty, and Global showed five (three of which was hockey). The CBC had all but half an hour filled with Canadian content. No wonder that the Minister of Heritage, Sheila Copps, suggested that Ottawa exclude television news and sports from the 50 per cent. The private networks responded to her suggestion by saying that they don't have the money to produce more Canadian content. In the words of Guy Maavera, CTV's programming vice-president:

> There isn't going to be more Canadian drama created as a result of that kind of change, because there isn't going to be any more money in the system for it. All we will be doing is giving up advertising revenue from American programs."[3]

One suggested way to increase the money spent on shows having Canadian content was for a cap to be put on amounts that private Canadian broadcasters could bid for non-Canadian shows. The thinking was that it would free up money for those broadcasters to spend on the Canadian prime-time shows. That suggestion was not implemented.

There is a definite amount of economic and political pressure brought to bear to reduce or eliminate Canadian content rules. We can see something of that when the cable networks took an American country music station off the general package and substituted a Canadian one, which presented a higher percentage of Canadian country performers. The main sponsor for the American station, General Electric, was very upset, and made some pretty significant economic threats about what it might do if the American station were not returned to its former status. Finally, a compromise was achieved. Both networks, Canadian and American, became part of the general cable package.

One further comment on Canadian content rules is needed. They do not guarantee that our stories are told, our voice is heard. Much that qualifies as Canadian content is what is termed "industrial Canadian." It qualifies as Canadian because of the number of Canadians hired, but the story it tells has really nothing to do with this country. Would you say that "X-Files," when it was filmed in British Columbia, made a Canadian statement? The same negative response would come concerning "F/X" and "Nikita," both of which were mostly American-clone, fashion-statement style with good-looking Australian stars, no Canadian substance.

Government is involved beyond making Canadian content rules. The federal government, through Telefilm Canada and the Cable Fund, invests something in the neighbourhood of $250 million a year to create independently produced Canadian TV movies and dramatic series. Then there is the CBC. In addition, the federal government and some provincial governments, including Ontario, provide production-investor tax relief and tax benefits for those who advertise on Canadian stations. Canadian-produced films and television shows have benefitted from such efforts. Export sales of Canadian-produced films and television programming in 1995 amounted to about $1.4 billion, a significant increase from earlier years. This could be threatened in the future by American political and economic pressure, and by moves made by the World Trade Organization to restrict "unfair trading practices."

## The Problems of Attitude

Another part of the problem relates to our attitude. Many seem to feel that if a work is Canadian, then there is something wrong with it, that to be successful we have to copy what someone else does. One exception that we are proud of is the Group of Seven, artists who are "very Canadian" in what they portray. But they too had to confront and overcome this attitude. A.Y. Jackson, one of the Group of Seven, when faced with severe criticism from Canadian critics, came up with some good advice in 1922:

> A little less skepticism regarding the work of our own artists and a little more towards a lot of foreign work which floods our market would seem a more intelligent attitude to take. The only things to be ashamed about in Canadian art are the scarcity of people who appreciate it, and the limited and obvious views that prevail as to what a work of art should be.[4]

The CEO of Alliance, a major Canadian film and TV producer (close your eyes and see the triangle that appears as their logo), spoke the words of the self-imposed Canadian anthem of defeat when he said:

> We don't make popcorn movies. . .We have to stay out of the mainstream. Attempting to compete can only lead to failure because of what we are up against.[5]

It is wrong simply to U.S.-bash and cry in the one thing that remains Canadian—our beer. When something is given away it can hardly be thought of as stolen. Americans have a strong sense of their own culture that has much to be admired. We should exhibit a similar passion. We can't blame them for wanting to shout out who they are, nor for their desire to "start spreading the word" (as it says in the song "New York, New York"). We could take a page from their book, or maybe their magazine, which may be the only kind of magazine we read soon.

Canadians involved with the arts often seem to think that Canada won't sell, either to Canadians or Americans. But think back to the 1980s, when Bob and Doug McKenzie, the hosers (my spell check now includes that word as well as toques) from the Great White North, with their toques, their back bacon and their beer, were so popular. (Now you remember another Canadian movie, *Strangebrew*.) Part of their success in Canada was not just the jokes, but that it was just so rare and it felt so good to see something even remotely like ourselves on television. Their popularity in the United States should show us that Canadians showing Canada can sell.

We do have well-established traditions concerning singing about ourselves. One common feature among Canada's Native peoples was for people to own songs. You might receive a song in a vision, or have one presented to you as a precious gift that only you could sing. Angela Sydney, the last speaker of Tagish, gave her son returning from World War II the clan-owned song of a man who was lost for years at sea after being stranded on the ice while hunting seal. It was a song of returning back to the people after coming close to death. There were also death songs that would give you strength when you knew or suspected that you were going to die soon. Our whole landscape was filled with song when this was Native land only. Many, many rivers, rapids, lakes, hills, valleys and sacred spots had songs that referred to them. It helped to connect people with the land. Travel across that land now and there are few songs.

The Atlantic provinces provide other examples. Living in Newfoundland, I discovered a rich heritage of songs about the people, their history and culture. I was raised on the down-home music of Don Messer and his Islanders on CBC, my mother being from Prince Edward Island. The first Canadian/international star in country music, Hank Snow, would often sing of his "Nova Scotia Home."

Then there is Quebec. There is no shortage of passionate songs about Québécois life, nor plays, nor movies, nor television shows. And we have had singing Canadian "cowboys" too, not afraid to sing about where they were from. Wilf Carter and Ian Tyson spring immediately to my mind. Let's hope that cowboy-hatted "New Country" stars Terri Clarke and Paul Brandt follow suit.

Perhaps other Canadian star actors can follow Dan Ackroyd's lead. In January 1997, he played in a two-part mini-series about the Avro Arrow, an important Canadian story about the collapse of an ambitious fighter plane project during the late 1950s. He helped give the production star credibility when investors were looked for and did so for a third his usual salary. It seems to me that he has set a standard by which other Canadian stars should be judged.

This does not mean that Canadians should tell only Canadian stories. Michael Ondaatje's enormously successful book *The English Patient* has British heroes and takes place in North Africa and Italy. It is important that Canadian writers have the freedom to tell such stories. Still, it felt good when I went to see the movie and heard key supporting characters say that they were from Montreal and when someone asked, "Is there any-body from Picton?" It was rather like seeing the face of someone you know on the TV screen.

What I am talking about is more than just hearing names of places and teams that are Canadian. It is about the Canadian voice. What is this? I've never heard a definition of "voice" that I like, but I know it is about a people's capacity to tell about who they are through TV, movies, books, magazines, music and art. When your voice is taken away from you, you cannot be heard, no one gets to hear your story. It is as if you don't exist.

# Notes

[1] As cited in Marci McDonald's "Menacing Magazines," *Maclean's,* March 24, 1977, p. 54.

[2] Peter C. Newman, "The Canadian Dream Loses a Big Round," *Maclean's,* January 27, 1997, p. 56.

[3] As quoted in Sid Adilman's "TV Bosses Slam CanCon Ideas," *Toronto Star*, March 1, 1997, p. L5.

[4] Charles C. Hill, *The Group of Seven: Art for a Nation* (Ottawa: National Gallery of Canada in association with McLelland & Stewart) 1995, p. 134.

[5] As cited in Brian Johnson's "The Canadian Patient," *Maclean's*, March 24, 1997.

# Music as History: The Representation of the Individual in Western Music

Scott Greer and Michael Horwood

Life without music would be a mistake.

*Friedrich Nietzsche*

Think for a moment about what life would be like *without* music: no CDs, no music on the radio, no concerts, no dancing, not even a tune to hum to yourself. All sound would be purely functional. Talking and the mechanical humming and rattling of our technology would be all that we would hear. Sounds pretty awful, doesn't it! Fortunately we do have music, which, as an art, involves the creation or appreciation of sound *for its own sake*; it is not a by-product of something else or simply a means to an end.

Great music, like all great art, has both timeless and culturally specific qualities. This essay examines some of the great musicians and music of Western society and looks at some examples of how this music not only embodies and embraces the human spirit, but also reflects the cultural context of its historical era. And, although you may not particularly *like* so-called "classical music," hopefully the examples and ideas presented in this article will help you hear and understand the music you do enjoy in a different way.

Music *as* history? In fact, music *is* history. It is a piece of historical evidence that can tell us a great deal about other people: how they lived, celebrated, worshipped, even fell in love; it can also tell us about their philosophy, government and social structure. In a sense, music takes us through space and time to another "world." Whether we are listening to a Beethoven symphony, an Indian raga or the rhythmic drumming of an African dance, we are learning about and experiencing a part of that culture. With that in mind, it is important at least to recognize that music is more than just a mirror that reflects the culture or

Music cannot be fully appreciated unless heard. For this reason, we have included a listening guide of musical works that will help you in appreciating the music discussed in this article.

"Music as History: The Representation of the Individual in Western Music" is by Scott Greer of Concordia University and Michael Horwood of Humber College. Used by permission.

the changing face of a society. Musical forms and styles evolve in their own right, while composers react to and build upon the works of their predecessors.

It is important to remember that while music history is divided into several neat categories, these are human creations and do not always unfold in such an organized fashion. You will also find that historical labels for musical styles, such as "Renaissance" or "Baroque," have expressions in other art forms. Baroque visual art, for instance, may reflect the same concerns and stylistic response as Baroque music.

# Periods and Styles in Western Music

## The Gothic Era

Broadly speaking, the Western musical tradition began and became distinguished from folk music when monks in the early Christian church began to write down music used in their services (which basically consisted of chants). Music during the Gothic period (1100–1400) was largely based on what has come to be known as "Gregorian chant." Gregorian chant actually predates the Gothic period by several hundred years, and its name refers to Pope Gregory I, who around 600 A.D. compiled and categorized chants used by the Church. He assigned particular chants to particular religious services, resulting in the Church's "liturgy" of sacred works, thereby making music a regular feature of Church ceremonies. The most common of these is the well-known "Mass," which can be either spoken or sung.

Gregorian chant can be described as "a free melodic chanting of sacred texts, intense yet devotional and serene, drawing on the natural stress of language for its rhythm ..."[1] There are generally no specific composers associated with these works, but Gregorian chants have recently become very popular and recordings of them are now quite accessible. They also heavily influenced one of the main musical forms in the Gothic era, the "motet."

The Gothic motet is essentially an elaboration of the Gregorian chant, but its form is much more complex. Unlike chant, the motet is "polyphonic," which refers to music that combines two or more musical lines (or melodies) at a time. This music began to have a "layered" sound and often involved intricate patterns and compositional techniques.

## HIDDEN MEANINGS

Composers would even "hide" a chant or conceal symbolic musical phrases within the complexities of the music. This fascination with hidden meanings and decoding messages could well have been a result of the Crusades. In the war against the Muslims, the writings of Aristotle and other philosophers of antiquity (whose work had been lost for centuries) had been "recovered," and these new texts had to be translated, interpreted and eventually reconciled with the Bible. This project often created considerable controversy as to what was the correct translation and interpretation of a text. Many scholars viewed works such as the Bible as having hidden or coded meanings, resulting in multiple interpretations. Consequently, the Christian monks became very adept at the art of interpretation, and this practice might very well have influenced how they approached and practised the art of composition.

The Gothic period also had its "lighter" side: this was the time of the "troubadours," who were roving poets and composers, singing about the ideal of "courtly love."[2] This period was also a part of the "age of chivalry," where women became romanticized and even idealized objects of musical affections. Ironically (by today's standards), this represents a rise in the status of women in that love duets emerged, and a woman might even join with a man in a song of love. The sometimes bawdy and irreverent nature of this music contrasted sharply with the serious, devout religious music of the time. This development reflects the growing interest in secular (non-religious or worldly) activities and knowledge, which would later blossom during the Renaissance.

## The Renaissance Era

The Renaissance style of music ("renaissance" refers to the "re-awakening" after the "Dark" or "Middle Ages") began after 1400 and continued until roughly 1600. Music in the Renaissance style is homogeneous, restrained, intimate, even gentle. With its emphasis on pure melody, Renaissance music is primarily polyphonic. However, harmony emerged during this period in some musical forms, and is most apparent at the end of a piece where a sequence of harmonies closes a work. In keeping with this, by the end of the era there was a more marked avoidance of musical "clashes" or dissonances. This quality in Renaissance music was at least partly a result of the end of the Crusades. People craved a sense of stability, and the Renaissance motet responded with a form that articulated a feeling of quiet reverence.

One particularly popular musical form during the Renaissance was the "madrigal." The madrigal is a secular work, and its lyrics usually told of romantic love (probably a continuation of the troubadours' style). Popular in Italy and England, madrigals were frequently played at social occasions such as banquets, festivals and even meetings of scholarly or artistic societies. They were sometimes performed with the accompaniment of a lute or other stringed instrument, which was also undergoing a period of considerable development. In fact, by the end of the Renaissance purely "instrumental music" had emerged, which was music composed solely for a solo instrument or group of instruments.

## The Baroque Era

The Baroque era in music is a fairly long period that extends from about 1600 to roughly 1750, coinciding with the beginning of the Enlightenment. The Enlightenment is the period in history when Western civilization arose from its "reawakening" and began to make great advances in knowledge—particularly in the sciences. Galileo, Kepler, Newton, Descartes, Leibniz, Hobbes and Locke are only a few of the important philosophers and scientists whose ideas have shaped our knowledge of the world today. At a time of great social and intellectual change, the relationship between music and society became increasingly complex.

Perhaps the most obvious and immediate connection between the advances of the Enlightenment and the Baroque era was to be found in the role of human *reason*. Our ability to think logically and rationally was what enabled us to create the infinitesimal calculus, discover coordinate geometry, formulate the laws of motion, etc. Reason and all of the virtues of the sciences—the ability of the human mind to discover and understand the laws of the natural world—are celebrated in Baroque music. As a result, Baroque music has a balanced, proportional sound. Everything is logical and well prepared; the music never grows too loud or threatens to over-excite the passions. Although many people do have emotional reactions to Baroque music, the responses usually are cerebral in nature.

While there were several significant scientific advances, the Christian Church was still very much a part of the music of this period. Reason had not yet replaced faith, and the **Reformation** and **Counter Reformation** had if anything intensified religious fervour. Furthermore, it was initially believed (or perhaps hoped) that science would *confirm* rather than contradict the truths of the Scriptures, and that the scientific method was allowing us to glimpse the marvel and majesty of God's creation.

**Reformation and Counter Reformation**

periods of religious reform in sixteenth-century Europe

This hope may partly explain why much of Baroque music displays a love of the grandiose, which can be seen in the emergence of large-scale vocal works such as the opera, oratorio and cantata. These larger musical forms led to the emergence of orchestras, which usually were kept by and played for a royal court. There were, however, very few public performances; most of this music was either performed in a church or at a palace of the nobility.

This emphasis on reason and order can be heard clearly in J.S. Bach's Brandenburg Concertos. Bach's music is felt by many to represent the pinnacle of the Baroque era, and some even regard him as the greatest composer in the history of Western music. Clearly, the Brandenburg Concertos represent a few of the most popular and brilliant pieces of music ever composed.

Typically, a *concerto* is a form of music in which a soloist is accompanied by an orchestra. However, in Bach's day, this definition of a concerto had yet to evolve. The early concertos involved contrasting the orchestra with *either* a solo instrument (e.g., Vivaldi's The Four Seasons) or a group of solo instruments (e.g., Bach's Brandenburg Concertos). For example, in the second Brandenburg Concerto, a recorder, an oboe, a violin and a trumpet are highlighted against the strings. Similarly, in the fourth Brandenburg Concerto, Bach sets a violin and a pair of recorders against the rest of the orchestra, which usually consisted of about 20 players. When listening to this music, one can hear that the soloists play basically the same music as the orchestra, and there is no attempt to have this smaller group of musicians "show off" or stand out or indulge in the kind of solo virtuosity we find in later concertos.

This musical structure reflected the role of the individual within the larger social context of the time. This was a time before the "individual" emerged as the focus of society: a time before radio and television, before video games and computers, before stereos, or even before the ability for "average people" to listen to music in their own homes. The entire capitalist system of providing for the consumer who has surplus income had yet to arrive. The only "consumers" were the aristocracy and the Church, and the artists were basically considered "servants." The idea of the artist as an impassioned, creative and autonomous individual was not to arrive for almost another 100 years. Similarly, the idea of the "self" (or one's sense of personal identity) was still inextricably tied to a particular geographical region, social class, family background and (if the person was male) a trade.

## The Classical Era

By 1750, the year J.S. Bach died, the popularity of the Baroque style had begun to fade; in fact, his own sons thought their father was already a bit outdated. The next 100 years would see more changes in musical form and performance than had occurred in the entire history of music. The world was quickly changing, and music was moving from a state of passive reverence of the Divine to more "earthly," practical concerns. The feelings of awe and wonder found in the complexity of Baroque music were replaced by a more streamlined approach that valued efficiency over grandiosity. The Classical period, therefore, is known for its emphasis on musical clarity and a trimming of Baroque excess.[3]

Reason, honoured during the Baroque period as allowing us to understand God's handiwork, now became venerated for its own sake: reason was humanity's guide in the exploration and understanding of the world. After all, it had recently brought us an understanding of physics, the creation of the steam engine and the discovery of wonders such as a vaccine for smallpox. In a sense, people began to see the world less in terms of "God's creation" and more in terms of human accomplishments.

The Classical period marked the first time in the history of music where instrumental music, particularly the symphony and the solo concerto, began to supersede vocal music. There is no better example of the Classical style in concertos and symphonies than Wolfgang Mozart (his middle name was actually Amadé not "Amadeus," and he rarely used it). Perhaps more than any other Western composer, Mozart's music represents for many the ultimate in pure beauty and musical perfection. As a result, his music is very easy to follow and appreciate. Mozart, therefore, makes for the "perfect" example of the Classical concerto and symphony.

By the mid-to-late eighteenth century, the "solo concerto" had become the dominant form of concerto. By comparing the Classical period solo type of concerto with the Baroque concertos, one finds that the soloist was much more of a focus during the Classical period. The music the soloist played was often much more demanding and difficult, and thus the music the soloist played began to differ from the music played by the orchestra. In Mozart's Violin Concerto No. 3, for example, the orchestral introduction is repeated by the soloist, which gives the impression that the soloist is still included in the overall musical framework. It is only after the restatement of the main theme that the soloist is allowed to develop and elaborate on different musical ideas.

## ROCOCO STYLE

One of the first changes away from the Baroque style can be found in the "rococo" period in eighteenth-century France. Music during the Baroque and Classical periods was composed under the "patronage system," which meant that music was composed at the request of the ruling aristocracy (such as Louis XIV in France or the Esterházys in Austria). The fancy of the aristocracy was not for "great art," but for music that was entertaining and would prove to be a diverting distraction from the imminent political crises that many of these governments faced. As a result, the music of the rococo era was simple, light and frivolous. More to the point, the rococo style represented a break with the heavy polyphonic Baroque textures and paved the way for the beginning of the Classical era.

The emergence of the soloist was the result of a variety of factors, one of which was that improvements in technology yielded instruments of greater musical range and power (such as the development of the piano from the harpsichord). On a more historical level, the evolution of the concerto as a musical form represented the changing social roles and relationships within society. During this period, two extraordinarily important historical events occurred: the American revolution in 1776 and the French revolution in 1789. Both of these events were extremely significant in determining the political and social climate of the time. To get a sense of the meaning of these events, we can look at some of the themes they shared. For instance, both revolutions were against monarchies, and both were supplanting the monarchical form of government with a more democratic system. Democracy was a radical concept in the eighteenth century, but it represented political freedom and equality for the people. These revolutions signalled the beginning of a new age: an age that saw the decline of the old aristocracies and a rise in democratic forms of government. Along with these changes came a new concern for the interests and rights of the people and a new form of social power—the power of the individual to make self-determining choices. These choices were initially about laws and government, but with the coinciding emergence of capitalism these choices eventually expanded to include everything from electing officials to buying a particular brand of shaving cream. The Classical period, therefore, represents the dawn of the modern "individual self" as a source of social and political power.

## The Romantic Era

With the Romantic era, individual expression, long kept within the confines of aristocratic rule and social structure, broke free into a world where the needs and desires of the individual became paramount. With the ascendancy of the modern individual and the notion of "individuality," music began to become more dramatic. Musical themes began to present contrasts that were full of tension and conflict. Even if you do not play an instrument or read music, you can easily hear the "musical drama" that is set up by the way themes contrast with each other and then find resolution in the end. This process is not unlike that of a narrative, where characters are presented in situations that almost always involve some type of conflict. The story unfolds as the characters attempt to resolve the conflict, and usually ends "happily" with a resolution that ties together the diverse aspects of their lives and personalities. So it is with music as well. Perhaps the reason why Romantic music has remained so popular is because the struggle it represents also symbolizes, on a larger level, the predicament we all face as human beings. It may be equally true that when a resolution is found, especially after a long arduous struggle, it often brings with it "individualistic" feelings such as power, pleasure and accomplishment.

It is important to note that the term "Romantic," as it is used here, means something much more broad than "romantic love." In this context, "Romantic" has a very general meaning, usually involving feelings of heroism, fantasy, wonder or mystery and of distant or strange people and places.

The Romantic era (which is generally considered to be most if not all of the nineteenth century) brought with it many sweeping changes: the after-effects of the American and French revolutions, the subsequent Napoleonic Wars, the demise of the nobility as the ruling class, the rise

## MUSICAL THEMES

Musical themes can be developed in one of two ways, both of which can be found throughout the history of music: either through a "theme and variation" approach, which we find in the Baroque complexity of Bach or in contemporary jazz; or through a process of contrasting themes (A followed by B), which we find in the "sonata" form of Classical and Romantic symphonies.

of an affluent middle class, the industrial revolution and, musically speaking, the transition from viewing the musician as a servant to the royal court, to that of the "artist" as a uniquely gifted creator and even celebrity. The composer in the nineteenth century established an independent status for the first time in history. The old world was crumbling, and by 1800 composers could not solely rely on employment with princes or princesses. Composers therefore began to sell their music to publishers and sell tickets for concerts where they would often perform the music themselves. As the "bourgeois" in Europe grew during the mid-1800s, there was an increasing demand for music and concerts. Thus, music was being performed less often in royal palaces and more often in public concert halls. "Art," since the late nineteenth century, has come to denote the creation of an "art culture," which is defined by the relationship between the "creator" and the "consumer."

Although nineteenth-century artists had to appeal to the public for income, they did not view their works as simply articles for commercial success. The Romantic artist came to symbolize a new vision about what it meant to be human: one who is free, bold and yet deeply in touch with the emotions and passions. "Reason," worshipped during the Baroque era and glorified during the Classical, was seen as too narrow and as missing the "deeper" truth of what one *felt*.[4] "Nature" was a force beyond rational-logical comprehension. Emotion and emotional expression therefore replaced reason as the central motif during the Romantic period. As a result, "creativity" began to be valued socially during the Romantic period, and art became recognized as a form of expression that embodied these important social and philosophical ideals.

Within the history of music there has never been a single figure who had the impact of Ludwig van Beethoven. He single-handedly changed the way the world heard, thought about and felt music. He even changed the way music as an occupation and business was handled. In the space allowed, we could not really do justice to Bach and Mozart from earlier

## MUSICAL GENIUS

Beethoven's fame largely lies in the way he revolutionized musical form. If we look at history, we see that nearly all great artists fall into one of two categories: those like Beethoven who changed the existing forms and styles of artistic expression, and those like Mozart who represent the culmination and even "perfection" of a particular style or tradition.

periods, and we most certainly cannot do so with Beethoven; suffice it to say that his presence in music can hardly be overstated or overestimated.

If you have been listening to the music of other periods leading up to this era, you will hear that the sound of Beethoven is unmistakably different. The emotion, energy and raw power of his music had never before been experienced. It shocked and even revolted many of the people who first heard it—one reviewer of the Fifth Symphony thought the music must have been written by a "lunatic."

Beethoven's music reflects his personality: emotional, bold, non-conformist, powerful, uncompromising. Much of Beethoven's music conveys a sense of conflict and a struggle to find resolution, such as in the Third and Fifth Symphonies. It is a commonly held belief that at least some of this comes from the fact that Beethoven went through a torturous period of losing his hearing, eventually leading to complete deafness. As if the masterpieces Beethoven created were not stunning enough, the fact is that most of his major works were written when he was either partially or completely hearing-impaired! Without fear of exaggeration, this must surely represent one of the most super-human achievements in the history of Western culture.

In a way, what Beethoven left us was a record of his fight to express his talent and musical gifts to the world. Joining in this titanic battle, we often come away from Beethoven feeling heroic or exalted (or even intimidated), as if he has touched some part of us that understands and also shares this conflict, as if his conflict is in some way our own. Although Beethoven is usually associated with this kind of fist-pounding, soul-wrenching intensity, he also wrote music that is quite the opposite, music of astonishing beauty and tenderness. Beethoven would often use both extremes in a single work. His famous "Moonlight Sonata" is an example of this: the cool placidity of a pond in the first movement is contrasted with the fierce rage of a tempest in the last. This is part of what makes Beethoven's music so compelling.

Beethoven also instituted significant changes in the concerto. We have traced the development of the concerto from the Baroque to the Classical period, where the soloist stepped into the limelight for the first time. In the Romantic era, this focus on the individual, both musically and socially, is further intensified and magnified. Remember that in the nineteenth century a new capitalist class was emerging, and as a result the individual had many more choices and opportunities in terms of social and economic mobility. In Beethoven's piano concertos the soloist becomes even more prominent, in that the piano is set *against* the orchestra—note that "against" is the operative word here. Unlike the concertos of Mozart, where the soloist is distinct but not separate from the music played by the orchestra, the soloist for Beethoven has much more autonomy and freedom of expression. One clear example of this is Beethoven's Piano Concerto No. 5 (also called the "Emperor Concerto" for its military/march-like theme). In the opening bars there are immediate differences: the piano does not wait for the orchestra to announce the main theme, but begins with an impressive and even triumphant musical "announcement." The parallel here between the role of the soloist and the social context is unmistakable, especially since we know that Beethoven's political views were decidedly in favour of democracy and the rights of the individual.

Later in the nineteenth century, several characteristics found in Beethoven were expanded and elaborated. The breadth and grandeur found in the "Emperor Concerto" became central features of music in the Romantic era. Taking Beethoven as the model, Romantic composers created music that displayed a free and spontaneous, even improvised, sound. Musical forms and rules were remoulded or broken, signalling that the musician (and the individual) should not be hemmed in by tradition. There were more frequent and sudden changes of mood, and, overall, the sound of the music itself changed dramatically. The music became louder, and the orchestra had a larger, fuller and more powerful sound.

Accordingly, composers needed improved instruments that would meet these new demands. Such instruments were provided through developments from the industrial revolution, resulting in improved quality and standardization of instrument manufacturing. For the first time, solo performers (i.e., instrumental soloists and opera singers) became renowned virtuosos and public superstars (e.g., Liszt, Paganini), appearing to be so super-human as to cause an audience to wonder if the performer was in league with Satan! In some of the later Romantic composers, such as Wagner, Bruckner and Mahler, this resulted in music of incredible emotional energy and intensity. Musical proportions expanded as well, yielding music that was louder and longer, and requiring more and more musicians (sometimes more than 100). Perhaps the evolution of the symphony orchestra is in a way symbolic of the growing cities of Europe at the time: a collection of sounds of all kinds brought together, demanding a focus.

# The Modern Era

As we approach the twentieth century, developments in music and modes of expressing music increase at an exponential rate. Beginning in late-nineteenth-century Europe, the tonality of music underwent a series of radical shifts: there was an increase in the dissonance of the music, which began to stretch the traditional concept of "musical keys"; musical structure is broken up in favour of more fragmentary sound textures. Perhaps the most radical development is the appearance of "atonal" music: music with no key, scale or tonal centre.

In the early twentieth century, American music began to be heard, and its essential feature was diversity, which was brought about to a large extent by the impact of technology (e.g., radio and recordings). This diversity can be clearly seen in the newly formed American musical styles: "jazz," along with George Gershwin, became tremendously popular; the "blues," which were born out of southern Black spirituals; and "rock 'n' roll," which represented a mixture of Black blues and White country music in a "popular" format, as can be seen with Elvis Presley.

Since the mid–1800s, music had also become increasingly nationalistic, and pressure was exerted on composers to conform to patriotic causes. In Stalinist Russia for example, Shostakovich had a number of run-ins with the Communist party. He was repeatedly accused of not being patriotic enough and for being too "Western." As a result, Shostakovich had to produce music not as art, but as political rhetoric, censored and moulded to fit governmental policy—and with the paranoid Stalin one could never be too careful!

As mentioned above, technology has also played a huge role in the creating, playing and appreciation of music. Most significantly, the radio and the phonograph (which turns out to be an early form of CD) drastically altered how music was played and heard. Musicians could now edit separate recordings of music together, which in effect created a performance that had never actually been given. Moreover, the average person's living room could now be instantly turned into a concert hall, featuring all of the great artists of the day. After World War II, advances in technology created a music industry unparalleled in the history of music. Musical recordings were mass produced, and improvements in communication brought us live concerts from Europe and around the world. This tidal wave of technology has even resulted in musical careers that are born and flourish without ever having stepped onto a concert stage (e.g., the Alan

Parsons Project). One unfortunate result of this immense influx of technology was that the general public stopped actively learning to read and play music, but instead became just passive listeners and consumers.

Technology has also changed and diversified the type of music we like. In a vein similar to Darwin's "struggle for survival," competition for the public's musical dollar has resulted in specialization and spawned an enormous variety of musical styles: country and western, rhythm and blues, reggae, heavy metal, even easy listening (yes, *Muzak* is a type of music!), and the list goes on. One effect of this was the birth of "pop culture" in the late twentieth century, where art "for art's sake" has been replaced by art that is primarily a function of the music industry. Music is now rated, not according to musical creativity, acumen or prowess, but according to commercial success (ask any artist and he or she will tell you that "success" is not necessarily an indication of quality).

Yet, this is nothing really new. Music has always had its "popular" side; even Brahms wrote a set of "Hungarian Dances." The major difference in our society is that "pop" music and the music industry machine that drives it are so large and powerful that they threaten to eclipse the *art* of music. Consequently, as "pop culture" separates from an "artistic culture," music has become a commodity for mass consumption. This has led many artists to seriously question the future of music (as we understand it) as an art form.

John Cage, for example, was a twentieth-century American composer who promoted the idea that our traditional understanding of music may simply be a "historical accident." We normally like to think that when we look at history we find advancement and progress in the development of ideas and practices. Not so, according to Cage. The Western musical tradition may be at an end, and a fundamental new understanding of sound may be on the horizon. To illustrate his point, Cage devised a "concert" that he gave at Harvard Square. He placed a piano on an island in the middle of a busy intersection and sat down as if to give a recital. A crowd gathered and waited. And waited. Cage sat silently with his hands folded across the closed lid of the piano. After a certain period time, which was specified by the Chinese text *I Ching*, he opened the piano cover and stood. The baffled audience applauded, but where was the music? Cage's point here is that the "music" was actually the background noise of the traffic, pedestrians walking, people talking, etc. Anything can qualify as music, according to Cage; it is simply a matter of context that we see it as such.

# Conclusion

Throughout this essay we have seen examples of how music reflects the social context. From the emergence of the individual, through the rise of democracy, to the age of technology, we have been able to witness the changes in musical styles. Music embodies and expresses the human spirit, and society, in all of its whims, crises and victories. To truly appreciate music as both history and as art, we must understand it *as an end in itself.* Many of us listen to music only as a *means:* we use it to distract us, to relax us, or to simply fill empty space. The point made by Nietzsche at the beginning of this essay was that music is a life-giving and life-sustaining force. However, only when we regard music on its own terms—as an end in itself—do we experience its life-enhancing properties. When we treat music (and each other) solely as means to an end, we reduce it to the level of a mechanical contrivance or "sonic wallpaper," thereby robbing it of those defining qualities that set it apart from technology and petty consumerism. To conclude, perhaps we can gain some insight from the great conductor Bruno Walter, who saw music as a "moral force." As such, it is even more important that music not simply become an entertainment device, but is recognized as representing a vital part of our humanity.

# Notes

[1] Yehudi Menuhin and Curtis Davis, *The Music of Man* (Sydney: Methuen, 1979), p. 47.

[2] We can still see the troubadours' style today in street musicians and in the origins of musical forms such as rap.

[3] Although the term "Classical" is widely used to refer to any type of music from Gregorian chants to Stravinsky, the Classical era is actually relatively brief: from about 1750 to just after 1800.

[4] For example, Mary Shelley's *Frankenstein* represents the distrust some Romantic writers felt about reason and science.

## "SOUND ADVICE"

### Renaissance:

Any keyboard works by Byrd, Tomkins or Gibbons.
Lute music or songs by Dowland.
Palestrina: various Masses or Motets.
Josquin des Prez: various Masses or Motets.

### Baroque:

J.S. Bach: Brandenburg Concertos; Concerto for two violins.
Handel: Music for the Royal Fireworks; Water Music; Messiah.
Vivaldi: The Four Seasons.

### Classical:

Mozart: Symphony No. 35; Violin Concerto No. 3; Piano Concerto Nos. 20 and 21;
        Requiem.
Haydn: Symphony No. 104; Piano Sonatas 50–56.

### Romantic:

Beethoven: Symphonies Nos. 3 and 5; Piano Concerto No. 5 ("Emperor Concerto"); Piano
           Sonata No. 14 ("Moonlight Sonata").
Wagner: Tristan und Isolde.
Liszt: Piano Concertos Nos. 1 and 2.
Brahms: Piano Concerto Nos. 1 and 2; Violin Concerto.
Paganini: Violin Concerto Nos. 1 and 2.
Saint-Saëns: Piano Concerto No. 2.
Tchaikovsky: Piano Concerto No. 1.

### Modern:

Stravinsky: The Rite of Spring.
Schoenberg: Five Pieces; A Survivor from Warsaw.
Shostakovich: Symphony No. 13, "Babi-Yar."
Cage: Concerto for Piano and Orchestra.

# Stories: An Introduction

## Clive Cockerton

> Thanks to art, instead of seeing a single world, our own, we see it multiply until we have before us as many worlds as there are original artists.
>
> *Marcel Proust*

As we live out our lives, we are frequently involved too deeply in the day-to-day to be able to interpret the significance of what is swirling around us. Although we like to think that we are in charge of our lives, that we are authors of our destiny, we too easily lose direction and become uncertain of where we are headed. We can try to get our bearings by asking friends for advice or we can turn to a fictional world to look for clues in the stories of others. Of course, the difference between life and literature is that life has no plot, or at least no plot that we are sure of. So, while there may be many similarities between life and literature, as many of the same passions and tears and laughter occur in both places, literature lends a satisfying structure to experience. It also expands our experience, as Proust suggests, by letting us see other worlds and perspectives. It feeds our imagination, whether we are children looking for tales that make sense of a sometimes frightening world or we are adults looking for sense in a sometimes confusing world.

But stories are more than earnest searches for meaning; they are about pleasure. They can be scary, funny, sexy, and they can fill us with curiosity, suspense and wonder. They can allow us to travel to other worlds, but getting there is half the fun as we are seduced by the magic of the writer's craft to believe in the reality of what we are reading. We step into a story and the best stories compel us to leave our skepticism behind and to experience the fictional world as directly as we do our own. The best stories are full of another's consciousness; they are drunk with life and invite us to share their vitality.

Stories touch upon grand themes: love, death, marriage and betrayal. Many stories deal with our sense of time, that moment-by-moment sequence that slips through our fingers and that our parents tell us to make much of. The two stories that follow, "The Grown-up" and "The

Disclaimer," both deal with time and the quality of life that various times afford us. "The Grown-up" starts in the present tense of childhood and contrasts the child's world of pleasure and play with the adult world of tasks and talk. Because Peter Fortune has a strong imagination, he understands that he, too, will one day join the adult world and leave behind the physical energy and joyful vitality of childhood. In an imaginative leap forward in time, Peter wonders what could possibly compensate for this loss. His answer has all the grown-up adventure and excitement that he could wish for. The young boy's answer is not for him alone, as it is part of a compulsion in the universe, a compulsion to move forward, "for nothing could keep still, not people, not water, not time."

"The Disclaimer" has a very different angle, for it looks back with nostalgia from the vantage point of adulthood to the joy and innocence of young love. Nostalgia is about the failure of the present and our inability to make sufficient change in the time we have. Disappointed with what has become of us, we look back to a better time, we want to live again within the golden glow; the poignancy at the source of nostalgia lies in the fact that we don't have time to make amends, that we don't have the energy to recapture those wonderful moments except in fiction and fantasy. But "The Disclaimer" is not just sentimental and mournful; it rises above the pain with wit and style and takes the reader on a short but intense roller-coaster ride that asks the young to be wary and the old to remember.

# The Grown-up

Ian McEwan

Every August the Fortune family rented a small fisherman's cottage on the Cornish coast. Anyone who saw the place would have to agree it was a kind of paradise. You stepped out of the front door into an orchard. Beyond it was a tiny stream—hardly more than a ditch, but useful for damming up. Further on, behind a thicket, ran a disused railway track that had once brought out the ore from a local tin mine. Half a mile along was a boarded-up tunnel that the children were forbidden to enter. Round the back of the cottage were a few square yards of scrubby back garden which gave directly on to a broad horseshoe of a bay fringed with fine yellow sand. At one end of the bay were caves just deep and dark enough to be scary. At low tide there were rock pools. In the car park behind the bay there was an ice-cream van from late morning to dusk. There were half a dozen cottages grouped along the bay and the Fortunes knew and liked the other families who came in August. More than a dozen children aged between two and fourteen made up a ragged group who played together and were known, at least to themselves, as The Beach Gang.

By far the best times were the evenings, when the sun sank into the Atlantic and the families gathered in one of the back gardens for a barbecue. After they had eaten, the grown-ups would be far too content with their drinks and endless stories to set about putting the children to bed, and this was when The Beach Gang would drift away into the smooth calm of dusk, back to all their favourite daytime places. Except now there was the mystery of darkness and strange shadows, and the cooling sand beneath their feet, and the delicious feeling as they ran about in their games that they were playing on borrowed time. It was way past bedtime, and the children knew that sooner or later the grown-ups would stir themselves out of conversations and the names would ring out in the night air—Charlie! Harriet! Toby! Kate! Peter!

Sometimes, when the shouts of the grown-ups could not reach the children at the far end of the beach, they sent Gwendoline. She was the

From Ian McEwan's *The Daydreamer*. New York: Alfred A. Knopf, 1994. Reprinted with permission.

big sister of three of the children in The Beach Gang. Because there was not enough room at her family's cottage, Gwendoline was staying with the Fortunes. She had the bedroom next to Peter's. She seemed so sad, so wrapped up in her thoughts. She was a grown-up—some said she was as old as nineteen—and she sat with the grown-ups all the time, but she didn't join in their chat. She was a medical student and she was getting ready for an important exam. Peter thought about her a lot, though he wasn't sure why. She had green eyes, and hair that was so ginger you could almost say it was orange. She sometimes stared at Peter long and hard, but she rarely spoke to him.

When she came to collect the children she came ambling slowly across the beach, barefoot and in ragged shorts, and she only looked up when she reached them. She spoke in a quiet, sad, musical voice. "C'mon you lot. Bed!" and then without waiting to hear their protests, or repeat herself, she would turn and walk away, scuffing the sand as she went. Was she sad because she was a grown-up and wasn't really enjoying it? It was hard to tell.

It was in the Cornish summer of his twelfth year that Peter began to notice just how different the worlds of children and grown-ups were. You could not exactly say that the parents never had fun. They went for swims—but never for longer than twenty minutes. They liked a game of volley-ball, but only for half an hour or so. Occasionally they could be talked into hide-and-seek or lurky turkey or building a giant sand-castle, but those were special occasions. The fact was that all grown-ups, given half the chance, chose to sink into one of three activities on the beach: sitting around talking, reading newspapers and books, or snoozing. Their only exercise (if you could call it that) was long boring walks, and these were nothing more than excuses for more talking. On the beach, they often glanced at their watches, and, long before anyone was hungry, began telling each other it was time to start thinking about lunch or supper.

They invented errands for themselves—to the odd-job man who lived half a mile away, or to the garage in the village, or to the nearby town on shopping expeditions. They came back complaining about the holiday traffic, but of course, they were the holiday traffic. These restless grown-ups made constant visits to the telephone box at the end of the lane to call their relatives, or their work, or their grown-up children. Peter noticed that most grown-ups could not begin their day happily until they had driven off to find a newspaper, the right newspaper. Others could not get through the day without cigarettes. Others had to have beer. Others could not get by without coffee. Some could not read a newspaper without smoking a cigarette and drinking a coffee. Adults were always snapping their fingers and groaning because someone had returned from town and had forgotten something; there was always one more thing needed, and promises were made to get it tomorrow—another folding chair, shampoo, garlic, sun-glasses, clothes pegs—as if the holiday could not be enjoyed, could not even begin, until all these useless items had been gathered up. Gwendoline, on the other hand, was different. She simply sat in a chair all day, reading a book.

Meanwhile Peter and his friends never knew the day of the week or the hour of the day. They surged up and down the beach, chasing, hiding, battling, invading, in games of pirates or aliens from space. In the sand they built dams, canals, fortresses and a water zoo which they stocked with crabs and shrimps. Peter and the other older children made up stories they said were true to terrify the little ones. Sea monsters with tentacles that crawled out of the surf and seized children by the ankles and dragged them into the deep. Or the madman with seaweed hair who lived in the cave and turned children into lobsters. Peter worked so hard on these stories that he found himself unwilling to go into the cave alone, and when he was swimming he shuddered when a strand of seaweed brushed against his foot.

Sometimes The Beach Gang wandered inland, to the orchard where they were building a camp. Or they ran along the old track to the forbidden tunnel. There was a gap in the boards and they dared each other to squeeze through into total darkness. Water dripped with a hollow, creepy, plopping echo. There were scurrying sounds which they thought might be rats, and there was always a dank sooty breeze which one of the big girls said was the breath of a witch. No one believed her, but no one dared walk more than a few paces in.

These summer days started early and ended late. Sometimes, as he was getting into bed, Peter would try to remember how the day had begun. The events of the morning seemed to have happened weeks before. There were times when he was still struggling to remember the beginning of the day when he fell asleep.

One evening after supper Peter got into an argument with one of the other boys whose name was Henry. The trouble started over a chocolate bar, but the row soon developed into a bout of name calling. For some reason all the other children, except of course Kate, sided with Henry. Peter threw the bar of chocolate down into the sand and walked off by himself. Kate went indoors to get a plaster for a cut on her foot. The rest of the group wandered off along the shore. Peter turned and watched them go. He heard laughter. Perhaps they were talking about him. As the group moved further away in the dusk, its individual members were lost to view and all that could be seen was a blob that moved and stretched this way and that. More likely they had forgotten all about him and were playing a new game.

Peter continued to stand with his back to the sea. A sudden cool wind made him shiver. He looked towards the cottages. He could just make out the low murmur of adult conversation, the sound of a wine-cork being pulled, the musical sound of a woman's laughter, perhaps his mother's. Standing there that August evening between the two groups, the sea lapping round his bare feet, Peter suddenly grasped something very obvious and terrible: one day he would leave the group that ran wild up and down the beach, and he would join the group that sat and talked. It was hard to believe, but he knew it was true. He would care about different things, about work, money and tax, cheque-books, keys and coffee, and talking and sitting, endless sitting.

These thoughts were on his mind as he got into bed that night. And they were not exactly happy thoughts. How could he be happy at the prospect of a life spent sitting down and talking? Or doing errands and going to work. And never playing, never really having fun. One day he would be an entirely different person. It would happen so slowly he would not even notice, and when it had, his brilliant, playful eleven-year-old self would be as far away, as peculiar and as difficult to understand, as all grown-ups seemed to him now. And with these sad thoughts he drifted into sleep.

The following morning Peter Fortune woke from troubled dreams to find himself transformed into a giant person, an adult. He tried to move his arms and legs, but they were heavy and the effort was too much for him so early in the day. So he lay still and listened to the birds outside his window and looked about him. His room was much the same, though it did seem a great deal smaller. His mouth was dry, he had a headache and he was feeling a little dizzy. It hurt when he blinked. He had drunk too much wine the night before, he realized. And perhaps he had eaten too much as well, because his stomach felt tight. And he had been talking too much, because his throat was sore.

He groaned and rolled over on to his back. He made a huge effort and managed to raise his arm and get his hand to his face so that he could rub his eyes. The skin along the line of the jaw rasped under his touch like sandpaper. He would have to get up and shave before he could do anything else. And he would have to make a move because there were things that needed doing, errands to run, jobs to do. But before he could stir, he was startled by the sight of his hand. It was covered in thick black curly hairs! He stared at this great fat thing with its sausage-sized fingers and began to laugh. Even the knuckles sprouted hairs. The more he looked at it, especially when he clenched it, the more it resembled a toilet brush.

He got himself upright and sat on the edge of the bed. He was naked. His body was hard, bony and hairy all over, with new muscles in his arms and legs. When at last he stood up he almost cracked his head on one of the low beams of his attic room. "This is ridic . . ." he started to say, but his own voice astonished him. It sounded like a cross between a lawn-mower and a fog horn. I need to brush my teeth and gargle, he thought. As he crossed the room to the hand-basin, he had to cling to it while he examined his face in the mirror. With its mask of black stubble, it looked like an ape was staring back at him.

He found he knew just what to do when it came to shaving. He had watched his father often enough. When he had finished, the face looked a little more like his own. In fact rather better, less puffy than his eleven-year-old face, with a proud jaw and a bold stare. Rather handsome, he thought.

He dressed in the clothes that were lying on a chair and went downstairs. Everyone's going to get a shock, he thought, when they see I've grown ten years older and a foot longer in the night. But of the three adults slouched round the breakfast table, only Gwendoline glanced up at him with a flash of brilliant green eyes, and quickly looked away. His parents simply muttered G'morning, and went on reading their papers. Peter felt strange in his stomach. He poured his coffee and took up the paper that was folded by his plate and scanned the front page. A strike, a scandal about guns, and a meeting of the leaders of several important countries. He found he knew the leaders of several important countries. He found he knew the names of all the presidents and ministers and he knew their stories and what they were after. His stomach still felt odd. He sipped the coffee. It tasted foul, as if burnt cardboard had been mashed up and boiled in bathwater. He went on sipping anyway because he didn't want anyone to think that he was really eleven years old.

Peter finished his toast and stood up. Through the window he could see The Beach Gang running along the shoreline towards the cave. What a waste of energy so early in the day!

"I'm going to phone my work," Peter announced importantly to the room, "and I'm going to go for a stroll." Was there ever anything duller and more grown-up than a stroll? His father grunted. His mother said, "Fine," and Gwendoline stared at her plate.

In the hallway, he dialled his assistant at the laboratory in London. All inventors have at least one assistant.

"How's the anti-gravity machine coming along?" Peter asked. "Did you get my latest drawings?"

"Your drawings made everything clear," the assistant said. "We made the changes you suggested, then we switched the machine on for five seconds. Everything in the room started floating about, just as you said. Before we try again we're going to have to screw the tables and chairs to the floor."

"I don't want you to try again until I'm back from holiday," Peter said. "I want to see it for myself. I'll drive back at the weekend."

When he had finished on the phone, he stepped out into the orchard and stood by the stream. It was a beautiful day. The water flowing under the wooden footbridge made a lovely sound and he was excited about his new invention. But for some reason he did not feel like moving away from the house. He heard a sound behind him and turned. Gwendoline was standing in the doorway, watching him. Peter felt the tightness in his stomach again. It was a cold, falling sensation. He felt a little weak about the knees. Gwendoline rested her arm on the rim of the ancient water butt which stood by the front door. Morning sunlight, broken by the leaves of the apple trees, bobbed about her shoulder and in her hair. In all his twenty-one years, Peter had never seen anything so, well, perfect, delicious, brilliant, beautiful . . . there was no word good enough for what he saw. Her green eyes were fixed on his.

"So you're going for a walk," she said lightly.

Peter could hardly trust himself to speak. He cleared his throat. "Yes. Want to come?"

They went down through the orchard to the raised cinder path where the railway track had once been. They talked about nothing in particular—about the holiday, the weather, newspaper stories—anything to avoid talking about themselves. She put her smooth cool hand in his as they walked along. Peter seriously thought he might float off to the tops of the trees. He had heard about boys and girls, men and women, falling in love and feeling crazy, but he had always thought that people made too much of it. After all, how much can you really like someone? And in movies, those bits which they always had to have, when the hero and heroine took time off to get soppy and gaze into each other's eyes and kiss had always seemed to him ridiculous time-wasting junk that did nothing more than hold up the story for minutes on end. Now here he was melting away at the mere touch of Gwendoline's hand, and he wanted to shout, to roar for joy.

They came to the tunnel, and without stopping to talk about it, they stepped through the gap in the boards, into the cold smoky blackness. They clung to each other as they went further in, and giggled when they trod in puddles. The tunnel was not very long. Already they could see the far end, glowing like a pink star. Half-way along they stopped. They stood close. Their arms and faces were still warm from the sun's heat. They stood close together and, to the sound of scurrying animals and water plop-plopping into puddles, they kissed. Peter knew that in all the years of a happy childhood, and even in its very best moments, like playing out with The Beach Gang on a summer's evening, he had never done anything better, anything so thrilling and strange as kiss Gwendoline in the railway tunnel.

As they walked on towards the light she told him how one day she would be a doctor and a scientist and she would work on new cures for deadly diseases. They stepped blinking into the sunshine and found a place under the trees where blue flowers grew on slender bendy stems. They lay on their backs, eyes closed, side by side in the long grass, surrounded by murmuring insects. He told her about his invention, the anti-gravity machine. They could set off together soon, climb into his green open-topped two-seater sports car and drive through the narrow lanes of Cornwall and Devon to London. They would stop at a restaurant along the way and order up chocolate mousse and ice-cream, and lemonade by the bucket. They would arrive at midnight outside the building. They would ride up in the lift. He would unlock the laboratory and show her the machine with its dials and warmly glowing lights. He would throw the switch, and together they would bump and tumble gently in the air with the tables and chairs . . .

He must have fallen asleep in the grass as he was telling her this. Sports car, he thought dozily, chocolate mousse, midnight, stay up as late as I want, and Gwendoline. . . . It was at this point that he realized he was staring not at the sky, but at his bedroom ceiling. He got out of bed and went to his window which overlooked the beach. He could see the Gang, way in the distance. The tide was out, the rock pools were waiting. He slipped on his shorts and a T-shirt and hurried downstairs. It was late, everyone had finished breakfast long ago. He gulped down a glass of orange juice, took a bread roll and ran outside, across the tiny back garden and on to the beach. The sand was already hot under his feet, and his parents and their friends were already set up with their books and beach-chairs and parasols.

His mother waved at him. "That was a good sleep. You needed that."

Excited, he began to run towards them, and he must have been half-way when he stopped and turned to look at the grown-ups one more time. In the shade of the parasol they leaned in towards each other as they talked. He felt differently about them now. There were things they knew and liked which for him were only just appearing, like shapes in a mist. There were adventures ahead of him after all.

As usual, Gwendoline was sitting apart with her books and papers, studying for her exam. She saw him and raised her hand. Was she simply adjusting her sun-glasses, or was it a wave? He would never know.

He turned and faced the ocean. It was sparkling, right to the wide horizon. It stretched before him, vast and unknown. One after the other the endless waves came tumbling and tinkling against the shore, and they seemed to Peter like all the ideas and fantasies he would have in his life.

He heard his name called again. His sister, Kate, was dancing and hopping on the wet sand. "We've found treasure, Peter!" Behind her, Harriet was standing on one leg, hands on hips, drawing a circle in the sand with her big toe. Toby and Charlie and the little ones were jostling to take turns leaping off a rock into a saltwater puddle. And behind all this human movement the ocean bobbed and folded and slid, for nothing could keep still, not people, not water, not time.

"Treasure!" Kate called again.

"I'm coming," Peter shouted, "I'm coming!" and he began to sprint towards the water's edge. He felt nimble and weightless as he skimmed across the sand. I'm about to take off, he thought. Was he daydreaming, or was he flying?

# The Disclaimer

## Ron Carlson

This is a work of fiction, and any resemblance to actual events, locales, or persons, living or dead, is merely coincidental, except for the restaurant I call the Wild Chicken, which was a real place actually called the Blue Bird, a drive-in fast-food joint I always drove past on my way to Debbie Delucca's house. I loved the Blue Bird, all the lights on late at night, because I knew that I was going to get a cheeseburger or the vanilla shake, so many of which I enjoyed with Debbie Delucca herself, or alone if I was driving back late from her house wrecked from all the couch time with her. The couch time I put in the book was real too, as well as the couch, a kind of overstuffed nappy sofa with Debbie's mother's big red and blue afghan on the back, a blanket that wanted to get caught in the gears and dragged into the evening's activities quietly and inextricably, a beautiful bold coverlet with a repeated pattern of red geese against a blue sky. Of course the Blue Bird, which I have called the Wild Chicken, and where I stood so many midnights under the fluorescent lights picking red and blue threads out of my hair waiting for a cheeseburger and a vanilla shake, is now a Custom Tile Outlet, a place you can go if you want your fireplace to look like the one in any Hilton.

I also should add here that Debbie Delucca's house is based on her real house, a green-sided bungalow on the corner of Concord Street and Eighth South that had a long shallow porch where I stood so many nights whispering with Debbie, giving Mrs. Eisenhour across the street a little show, I suppose, as Debbie and I would stand some nights for an hour and some nights two, saying good-bye and I love you and I can't believe I've met someone like you and that was dreamy in there on the couch I love you so much, and other direct dialogue that I've used in the text absolutely verbatim, probably the easiest thing of all the things in this book to write because everything we said is alive within my head after all these years, things actually uttered on the chilly fall nights there on Concord Street and Eighth South, as we twisted closer, so lost some nights that time itself dissolved or collapsed, disappeared anyway, a phenomenon I describe better than that in the book, and a phenomenon that has not come round for me since those intoxicating nights under the huge munificent blessing of the ancient poplar tree in her front yard, a real tree that held up the sky for half a mile in every direction, a giant that dumped its leaves in unending ten-ton squadrons that fell like some kind of perfect setting for us, a backdrop, a movie—if it could give up its ten million golden secrets, a blizzard of leaves, then we could be in love. That tree is long gone, as the house in which Debbie Delucca lived exists no longer, both bladed under for the Interstate years ago so that motorists now can exit there at Eighth South for easier access to the airport. I put that tree in the book; it was too big not to, but it is a tree we'll never any of us see again.

Nothing—no resemblance to actual events, coincidental or otherwise—is going to bring that tree back, or Debbie Delucca, who was my close associate all those years, the young person with whom I invented modern love, love as we know it. Love which so many people dabble in today, but do not study or understand or allow to course through their veins like some necessary thing the way that we did. We were the last people to use love right. Debbie Delucca is now Debbie Delucca Peterson somewhere in St. Clare, where she does who knows what. I can't imagine, though I've tried.

And what am I going to do, go into the ShopMart down there and run into her at the little lunch counter they've got over by the children's department as she sits quietly sipping some chicken noodle soup and reading this very book and nodding at how accurate every word is—the things she said, the things I said in return? And I'd sit down beside her and order a vanilla shake, not even wanting their fake version of one of the world's great treasures, which doesn't even have real ice cream or real vanilla, but wanting to say the words the way I did so many nights under the bright lights of the Blue Bird Cafe, *vanilla shake,* to see if she might turn to see who's talking like this, looking up from a book that I'm sorry now I even wrote, really sorry, because I see for the first time that you can't get anything back. No coincidence at some lunch counter and twenty minutes of conversation with a girl you once knew, some woman sitting there and you know the exact location of every mole on her body, is going to make one thing in this real world different. If you want the coincidence where some character based on me gets the amazing girl back and has his heart start again under the most beautiful tree on the continent after so many years, you're going to have to look in a book.

# I Go Back to May 1937

Sharon Olds

I see them standing at the formal gates of
    their colleges,
I see my father strolling out
under the ochre sandstone arch, the
red tiles glinting like bent
plates of blood behind his head, I
see my mother with a few light books at
    her hip
standing at the pillar made of tiny bricks
    with the
wrought-iron gate still open behind her, its
sword-tips black in the May air,
they are about to graduate, they are about
    to get married,
they are kids, they are dumb, all they know is
    they are
innocent, they would never hurt anybody.
I want to go up to them and say Stop,
don't do it—she's the wrong woman,
he's the wrong man, you are going to do things
you cannot imagine you would ever do,
you are going to do bad things to children,
you are going to suffer in ways you never
    heard of,
you are going to want to die. I want to go
up to them there in the late May sunlight
    and say it,
her hungry pretty blank face turning to me,
her pitiful beautiful untouched body,
his arrogant handsome blind face turning to me,
his pitiful beautiful untouched body,

but I don't do it. I want to live. I
take them up like the male and female
paper dolls and bang them together
at the hips like chips of flint as if to
strike sparks from them, I say
Do what you are going to do, and I will
        tell about it.

# Objectivity and Subjectivity

## Clive Cockerton

When we attempt to choose a movie for Saturday night, we might begin by poring over the newspaper, scanning the listings, reading the reviews. This film is an "absolute delight," that film is "irresistible," this one "touching and sensitive." Choices, choices. How does one sort the good from the bad in such a list? Add to the questions of the intrinsic worth of the film the problem of the individual's mood. Sometimes "touching and sensitive" just doesn't stand a chance against "frivolous and fun."

In fact, most of the decisions regarding choosing a film are subjective. After all, how can one effectively compare a musical to a thriller except on the basis of how one feels at the moment? In choosing a film we make decisions based on content that is suitable to our mood and a faith that the form of the film will measure up to its content. Once we have seen the film, however, we usually wish to weigh the success of our choice. Our conclusions usually fall into two categories:

1. "I really like the film because . . ."
2. "That is a good film because . . ."

These statements are really very different from each other, with the first statement recording a subjective preference while the second attempts an objective evaluation. Preference tends to be more content-oriented as in "I really liked the ending," or "It was a great love story," while attempts to prove the worth of the film tend to be more form-oriented as in, "The photography was beautiful" or "The pace was exciting."

For most of us, whether or not we like a film is much more important than whether the film is any good.  As well, it is clearly possible to like a film we know we cannot defend as a good film. Our preference may be formed because of the presence of a favourite actor, a locale such as Africa or New York that fascinates us, or moments such as steamy love scenes or violent car chases that we find irresistible. The presence of these elements in no way forms a criterion for excellence, and the absence of these elements does not indicate a bad film. Indeed, our preference for these elements declares a lot about ourselves and our own feelings but says

"Objectivity and Subjectivity" is by Clive Cockerton of Humber College. Used by permission.

virtually nothing about the film. As well, it is quite possible to dislike a film that we know to fulfill all the requirements of a good film, again for strictly personal reasons such as the fact that the film reminds us of unpleasant or painful moments in our own lives.

Although there is clearly no possibility of argument or contradiction about personal feelings on an art object (they just simply are what they are), it is also clear that we can change our minds about works of art. A painting can look shapeless and disorganized to us until someone more expert reveals a previously overlooked organizing principle. A novel can sometimes seem obscure and difficult until we become familiar with its language and worldview. We might condemn a film as confusing and subsequently read an interview with the director in which he states that he wants his audience to feel confused. If the film achieves its aim, how can we condemn it? These examples happen frequently and point to the fact that proper artistic evaluation is more than just a subjective statement about our perspective at the moment. It is not simply a case of thinking one thing on Monday and another on Friday. We replace the first view with the second because we think that the second view more accurately and objectively describes the art. It is as if at first glance we perceive a frog, but after consultation with experts we begin to discern the prince hiding within. Of course, there are many more frogs than princes, and we are more frequently deceived by art works that initially seem good but over time don't stand up to close examination.

Experts attempt to engage our minds in the task of analyzing the aesthetic emotion. They teach us to analyze the art work, to look separately at its elements, and to establish standards or criteria to evaluate the elements. The use of this largely mental process can help us to understand more about the art work independent from our own subjective bias. Aristotle identified three criteria based on his study of Greek poetry and drama: unity, clarity and integrity. Unity (of mood, of time and place among others) as a criterion didn't have the longevity of the other two: Aristotle couldn't anticipate the successful mixing of comic and tragic mood that would take place in Shakespeare's plays and other later works. However, clarity of expression seems as useful a standard by which to judge as any. Integrity, in the relationship of the parts of the play/poem to the whole and in the relationship of the whole to reality, forms the basis of much critical judgement. If we substitute simplicity of design, or perhaps more appropriately, focus, for the concept of unity, we have a starting point in our discussions of criteria.

However, in our search for objective criteria by which to judge art objects, it must be admitted that no criteria work universally for all art objects. We praise the playful fantasy in the paintings of Henri Rousseau yet we do not condemn the paintings of Edvard Munch for lacking that quality; indeed we praise Munch for his graphic rendering of inner torment. We appreciate one novel's realistic depiction of character and delight in another's cartoon-like parodies. We appreciate the grim honesty of films like *Trainspotting* and at the same time are charmed by the simple beauty of films like *The Black Stallion*. Yet on occasion films displaying "simple beauty" or "grim honesty" lack other qualities and we find them unsatisfactory. The fact that no one criterion or element guarantees a work's value makes the job of appraisal that much more difficult. One thing is clear: On different occasions we judge by different criteria. Moreover, the skilled and open-minded consumer of art lets the individual work of art dictate by which criteria it is to be judged.

Some contemporary critics suggest that in a modern consumer society we are so overwhelmed with artistic experiences and images that the task of sorting them into piles of good and bad is a hopeless one. These critics see a rough equality of banality in all objects, and find that wit and beauty come from the perspective of the audience, and are not necessarily contained in the art. It is how you see a TV program, for instance, not the TV program itself that makes the experience lively and intelligent or dull and stupid. Some of these critics would go so far as to say that a book has no meaning by itself, that an unread book is a vacuum, and that the reader is the one who provides the meaning. Since every reader's experience is shaped by their gender, their class and cultural background, there can be no universal objective meaning, only a collection of diverse and subjective impressions. As one critic, Frank Lentricchia, writes of his relationship to literature:

> I come to the text with specific hangups, obsessions, worries, and I remake the text, in a sense, for me, for my times . . . . The moment you start talking about it, you have injected interpretation. The text is not speaking; you are speaking for the text. You activate the text.

Still other critics focus on the possibility of consensus (among informed observers) operating as a kind of objectivity. This agreement by experts operates as a kind of "rough guide" to truth. However, these "agreements by experts" do not always have the shelf life that one would expect. It is clear that some art work does not seem to travel well from one historical period to the next. The novels of Sir Walter Scott (*Ivanhoe, The Heart of Midlothian*) were extremely popular in the nineteenth century and are hardly read today. In the last hundred years, the literary reputation of Ernest Hemingway was extraordinarily high in the '20s and '30s but today Hemingway is more often seen as an interesting but minor writer.

One historical period may form an aesthetic preference for certain artistic qualities, preferring, for instance, clean and simple elegance to the previous generation's taste for exuberant and stylized decoration. When watching old films on television, we can be initially struck by what now seems bizarre fashion and style. Our experience of these films can be even more seriously undermined by outmoded attitudes, particularly sexist and racist ones. Everything that has happened to form our present consciousness stands as an obstacle to the appreciation of these films.

Even within an historical period critics sometimes disagree about the value of an individual work. Recently, films such as *Eyes Wide Shut, Gladiator* and *Erin Brockovich* have received very diverse reviews. All the critics may agree, for instance, that pace in editing and structure is a very important element in a film's success. They may all agree that pace is a problem in any particular film. But some critics will find that the other

elements of the film compensate for the weakness in pace and will give the film an overall high evaluation. Some of the disagreement can be explained by the fact that, despite agreement in theory on the importance of pace, in practice many critics habitually weigh some criteria more than others. Therefore, those critics who regard editing as the most essential creative act in film will habitually favour films that possess skillful editing in spite of other problems that may exist in the film. Other critics may habitually value elements of script, acting or cinematography more highly than editing and refuse to accept that the obvious virtues in editing make up for the perceived weakness in acting. When a preference is habitual, we can be pretty sure that its origin is rooted deeply in our own personality and experience.

In spite of the effort of art critics to focus on the art rather than themselves, to analyze and evaluate the elements of art rather than narrate and describe their own experiences, it remains obvious that elements of personality can't always be overcome or transcended. Perhaps the relationship between art and our experience of art is circular. The more we possess the inner experience, the more we grow curious about that external art object. The more we learn about art, the more we learn about what makes us who we are. That moment on Saturday night when the theatre goes dark, we watch the slowly brightening screen and wonder what this film world will be like. At the end of the film, if we have been moved by the film, the natural instinct is to be quiet, to digest our own experience before surfacing to the workaday world. But watching movies is a social activity, and it's irresistible to turn to our friends and ask, "What do you think? Wasn't it good? I really liked the part where . . ." We share our delight, and we compare experiences. Our view becomes larger.

❖

Ultimately, the question is much larger than whether our statements about art are objective or not. The question applies not only to art. It's about the world. It's just that art is a convenient place to begin the argument. If we cannot agree on the meaning of a single art object, with its known borders, its beginnings, middle and end, with its human author, how can we make statements about a limitless universe—a universe not divided into neat stages of development, ending in closure, but a universe (caused/uncaused) constantly evolving, stretching out to infinity and a universe whose author is either unknown or not available to interview.

Is the external world totally independent of us or as the Greek philosopher Protagoras held, is it us, and our perceptions that are the measure of all things? Even if we grant the existence of the external world, it doesn't seem possible to get beyond our perceptions of it. Scientists have their protocol, the scientific method, that is meant to banish subjective interpretation. In the search for the underlying principles of things as they are (remember Tom Olien's article), science took over from religion the chief role of establishing truth. And what a magnificent job science has done. In revealing the structure of sub-atomic particles, in predicting the location and timing of an earthquake or volcano, in isolating a deadly virus and developing vaccines, and in improving the quality of life for millions, science can lay claim to being humanity's most successful enterprise.

Think of the surgeon holding a human heart in his or her hands, repairing a faulty valve and placing it back into the person's chest, giving 20 years more of life. All of the knowledge, the complex theory and practical skill that go into a successful operation rest on a physician's informed judgement that an operation is called for. That judgement is fallible, as are all human judgements. For the history of science is full of examples of misreadings, of scientists finding only what they were looking for, and not finding what they weren't, of finding solutions to problems that fit not only the hypothesis but also the prevailing ideology. Ultimately, scientists too must depend on their very fallible senses (or their high-tech extensions) to draw conclusions. As well the role of the scientist confers no immunity to normal human pressures, the ego needs, the economic necessity to succeed, the political compulsion to research in certain directions. Scientists may be the most objective amongst us, but even in this highly trained class of people, subjective considerations colour many perceptions.

The truth about the world, the final objective Truth, is getting harder to find, yet meaning, subjective meaning is everywhere. A single rational explanation for the universe and all it contains may no longer be possible. Our knowledge (scientific and otherwise) has grown and grown until it has reached a point beyond which any one individual can comprehend the whole. To see the whole domain of our knowledge we need to climb a very high mountain; we haven't found the mountain yet (although on several occasions we thought we had) and are beginning to doubt if it exists.

Instead of the overview from the mountain, what we have is the micro-view of the specialist. What we have are fragments of the whole, knowledge and insight from the physicist, the philosopher, the biologist, the historian, the psychologist, the literary critic, the political economist. The fragments don't cohere into one magnificent interpretation of the universe. They exist as beams of light that illuminate the darkness for a certain time, as probes that reveal something about the world, and as a point of view.

We both rely on and are suspicious of experts. We rely on them, for their fragmentary understanding of the world is the best insight that we've got. But in a deeper sense we know them to be fallible. No political thinker predicted the collapse of communism in Eastern Europe, yet we continue to tune into the TV to hear what those experts have to say. Young parents read everything they can get their hands on about child rearing, yet are highly selective in what ideas they apply to their own children. We may listen with interest to the reasoned arguments of the nuclear power experts, but when they tell us that we have nothing to fear the shadow of Chernobyl falls over the discussion.

Every discipline of study is currently racked with conflict, with dissenting voices. If even the experts can't agree, are the rest of us just gambling on what and whom we choose to believe? It becomes so difficult to judge the worth of arguments that quickly threaten to go beyond our expertise. The difficulty causes many of us to give up the task of sifting through the ideas, adopting instead a weary and cynical assumption that all views are equal. Many of us come from school systems that value self-expression as the highest good. It doesn't so much matter what gets expressed (all views are roughly equal anyway); just so long as a view gets expressed, the system will applaud. This emphasis involves a radical turning away from the searching after truth that has so long inspired our education. If there's no truth to search for, why struggle so hard?

If there's no truth, then what we have left are competing views, subjective perceptions. My view becomes as valuable as yours because there's no way to weigh and measure them against each other. On the surface, there's an increase in tolerance as we all recognize that what may be true for me may not be true for you. But beneath the surface lurks the urge for dominance, the recognition that the prevailing view belongs to the loudest, most powerful voice.

And so we have the competition of interests and perspectives: Quebec, the West, free trade, feminists, unionists, Native peoples, blacks, environmentalists. The competition is healthy, the diversity of views enriching.

But without truth as a goal, the contest of ideas has no referee; it's too easy for reason to become a weapon to beat your opponent, not a tool to dig for understanding. Still, we're in the middle of a huge process in our relationship to the world and each other. If fragmentation into competing perspectives and specialized bits of knowledge is the current mode, perhaps all we need to do is wait for the emergence of new and better ideas that might reconcile some of the conflicts and satisfy our yearning for something to believe in. The competition of ideas has been evident throughout this text: Are we free or determined? in Unit 1; What changes and what remains the same? in Unit 2; Do we have the sense to cooperate with each other or are we doomed to conflict? in Unit 3; Can science provide the solutions to the problems it creates? in Unit 4. Do we have to make a choice? Do we have to run to the comfort of certainty? Or do we have to learn to love the paradox—to see in contradiction the breathing in, the breathing out of ideas?

The arts, particularly narrative arts such as film and the novel, may have a role to play in helping us to reconcile apparent contradiction. By successfully creating a fictional world that re-creates the real world, the artist sets artificial boundaries to what is included in the story, how many characters, subplots and themes. Fictionalizing the world tells us everything we need to know; the artist creates a vision of life that is remarkable in its completeness. The sharing of this vision creates a sense of community between artist and audience and holds out the possibility of consensus. We are not alone; others see the same world, sometimes with great clarity and undeniable insight. It's as if the film or novel creates a fictional mountain, from which we can finally see the human truth stretched out below, in all its complexity and contradiction. It is just a glimpse, but reassuring. In the midst of the darkest night-time thunderstorm, the lightning can suddenly illuminate our world in a flash of brilliant light, letting us know that the world is still there, under the cover of darkness.

# The Voice You Hear When You Read Silently

## Thomas Lux

is not silent, it is a speaking-
out-loud voice in your head; it is *spoken*,
a voice is *saying* it
as you read. It's the writer's words,
of course, in a literary sense
his or her "voice" but the sound
of that voice is the sound of *your* voice.
Not the sounds your friends know
or the sound of a tape played back
but your voice
caught in the dark cathedral
of your skull, your voice heard
by an internal ear informed by internal abstracts
and what you know by feeling,
having felt. It is your voice
saying, for example, the word "barn"
that the writer wrote
but the "barn" you say
is a barn you know or knew. The voice
in your head, speaking as you read,
never says anything neutrally—some people
hated the barn they knew,
some people love the barn they know
so you hear the word loaded
and a sensory constellation
is lit: horse-gnawed stalls,
hayloft, black heat tape wrapping
a water pipe, a slippery
spilled *chirrr* of oats from a split sack,
the bony, filthy haunches of cows ...
And "barn" is only a noun—no verb
or subject has entered into the sentence yet!
The voice you hear when you read to yourself
is the clearest voice: you speak it
speaking to you.

# The Search for Form

## Clive Cockerton

It is clear that the Canadian government, through its body of experts, believes that objective evaluations can be made about works of art and about what they can contribute to a culture. The experts reward the good art with government money and discourage the bad by withholding funding. Each of the experts from the different artistic areas brings criteria drawn from years of experience to judging art. As well as the criteria for good art, those experts also bring some sense of what might contribute to the broader Canadian culture, what might serve as Canadian cultural self-expression. The problem occurs when certain themes or styles become identified as officially Canadian, that is, promoting a standardized Canadian vision. It has been frequently said that one of our best Canadian film directors, David Cronenberg, seems somehow un-Canadian. His stories of sophisticated people in urban settings confronted with physical horrors don't address the "official" themes of Canadian culture. His films may be about victims, but they are not victims of the cold or of loneliness. They do not endure long and hard trials; rather, they explode in intense and horrific ways. How un-Canadian. Yet he is a director who has lived all his life in Toronto and who has made most of his films in Canada. If he is not Canadian, it is because we have an overly rigid expectation of what constitutes a Canadian vision. Organizations such as the Canada Council naturally tend to promote works that express a coherent view of ourselves, but this coherence can sometimes become conformity—conformity to an official version of ourselves.

More fundamentally, many people have difficulty accepting the notion that a body of experts can come to valid conclusions about works of art. We can probably all recall moments when a teacher seemed to drone on about the monumental significance of a short story that made us ache with boredom, or the deeper levels of meaning in a poem whose message totally eluded us. It is always right to be skeptical about the experts, but our challenges to authority should also be matched by a willingness to apply the rules of evidence to any work of art. Just as we must always question the officially proclaimed ideas, we must also discover that some work is simply better than others.

"The Search for Form" is by Clive Cockerton of Humber College. Used by permission.

Take the following two sentences, containing roughly the same content, and try to rank them according to merit.

Version 1: Generally speaking there are a lot more unhappy moments in life than there are happy ones.

Version 2: Happiness was but an occasional episode in a general drama of pain.

As subjectively attached as I am to Version 1 (I wrote it), it must be admitted that while it has a conversational matter-of-fact quality about its grim message, it lacks the complexity and power of Version 2. When we look at Version 2, we notice the precision of the language and the tightness of the structure. Notice how key words are twinned to heighten the contrast: occasional and general, episode and drama, and, most importantly, happiness and pain beginning and ending the sentence. You might also notice that the sounds of the first half of the sentence are softly melancholic, while the second half has a leaden heaviness and finality. No doubt about it, once you examine closely, it is easy to see that in Version 2 the content has found its clearest and most forceful expression.

Let's look at two versions of another grim sentiment.

Version A: Days go by one after the other in a monotonous way. This trivial parade of time ends in death. It is like a bad actor. Life doesn't mean anything; it is just full of noise and anger, ultimately meaningless.

Version B: Tomorrow and tomorrow and tomorrow / Creeps in this petty pace from day to day, / To the last syllable of / recorded time, / And all our yesterdays have / lighted fools / The way to dusty death. Out, out / brief candle. / Life's but a walking shadow, / a poor player / That struts and frets his hour / upon the stage, / And then is heard no more. / It is a tale told by an idiot, full of sound and fury, / signifying nothing.

Version B is probably the most famous statement of thoroughgoing pessimism in the English language. It is full of wonderful images, days lighting the passage to ultimate darkness, the ranting idiot's tale, while Version A will never be read anywhere beyond these pages, and even then quickly forgotten.

In literary terms, having the right (write) stuff has its base in the author's ability to create magical effects with language. These effects can be achieved through precise use of words, through an ability to manipulate the sound and rhythm of language, and through an ability to create haunting images.

Michael Herr, in his book *Dispatches*, a chronicle of the Vietnam war, attempts to capture the emotional texture of combat in this paragraph.

> Fear and motion, fear and standstill, no preferred cut there, no way even to be clear about which was really worse, the wait or the delivery. Combat spared far more men than it wasted, but everyone suffered the time between contact, especially when they were going out every day looking for it; bad going on foot, terrible in trucks and APC's, awful in helicopters, the worst, travelling so fast toward something so frightening. I can remember times when I went half dead with my fear of the motion, the speed and direction already fixed and pointed one way. It was painful enough just flying "safe" hops between fire-bases and lz's; if you were ever on a helicopter that had been hit by ground fire your deep, perpetual chopper anxiety was guaranteed. At least actual contact when it was happening would draw long ragged strands of energy out of you, it was juicy, fast and refining, and travelling toward it was hollow, dry, cold and steady, it never let you alone. All you could do was look around at the other people on board and see if they were as scared and numbed out as you were. If it looked like they weren't you thought they were insane, if it looked like they were it made you feel a lot worse.

This is a writer writing at the top of his game, taking the reader on a roller-coaster ride, using his craft to capture the subtle ways terror can grip.

❖

There is a deep satisfaction that comes from an appreciation of form. An arrangement of words, images, colours or notes can illuminate a moment, create powerful emotion, and so change our perceptions that we never look at life or art in quite the same way again. Art can be more than form, and to be sure it can be full of ideas, archetypes and moral discriminations. But while it can be more than form, without form it is nothing; it loses its magical hold on us.

Outside the realm of art, that perfect arrangement is harder to find in human relationships. Many of us find a sense of energy and harmony in nature, and discover a solace in contemplation of the beauties of nature. Perhaps this respect for nature explains our sense of the violation we experience when confronted with massive pollution, and explains why acid rain, the lead in the air, the depletion of ozone, the poisoning of our water, seem obscene. We have become so sensitive to this tampering with natural form that intentional pollution with toxic substances is now considered a criminal and not merely a civil offence. Companies such as Exxon become associated in the public mind with ecological disaster and do so at their peril. The public's tolerance of irresponsible and negligent behaviour on the part of private companies is slowly becoming a thing of the past, and the so-called "green movement" is emerging as a powerful political force.

In Unit 4 Tom Olien talked of the search for an underlying principle as the great creative urge of scientists. As Benjamin Barber writes in Unit 3:

> It certainly seems possible that the most attractive democratic ideal in the face of the brutal realities of Jihad and the dual realities of McWorld will be a confederal union of semi-autonomous communities smaller than nation-states, tied together into regional economic associations and markets larger than nation-states—participatory and self-determining in local matters at the bottom, representative and accountable at the top.

At any rate, we are more interconnected now than at any time in history. We listen with keen interest to reports from Russia hoping for a better life for the average Russian and a more secure future for us all. If we accept the good things of interdependence, however, it is also true that we feel more keenly the tragedies, whether they occur in Rwanda, Bosnia or China. Events that take place far away—the tearing down of the Berlin Wall or the Chinese takeover of Hong Kong—touch us because we share the same urge for freedom.

Whenever new ideas clash with an existing form, there is some dislocation, something lost as well as gained. Unit 2 of this text looked at what happens when the old values are challenged by new technologies and new ideas. People cannot see what is happening to them and vainly try to deny the impact of the change. Some societies can be aware of the process of change in varying degrees, but the task of integrating new forms with old always challenges our best efforts.

Finally, it is in our own lives that form has the greatest significance, as we attempt to find shape and meaning in the daily flow of our existence. The facts, the contents of our lives, are distressingly similar, as a comparative glance at any number of résumés shows. We are born, go to school, make friends, take part-time jobs, go to college and then on to a career. Along the way, we may form romantic attachments, get married, have children, grow older, watch children leave us, retire from our jobs and grow older still. But this sameness doesn't tell the whole story. As the old jazz lyric goes: "It ain't what you do, but how you do it." Some people's lives are tragic, while others with the same observable facts seem heroic. After we bury some people, all we can hear, after our own tears subside, is the sound of their laughter. What makes this life full and generous and that life pathetic? Clearly, it has something to do with perception, the perception of the individual who lives it as he or she contemplates the moment and discovers the pattern in the flow of daily experience. These moments of perception are often struggled for, but sustain the idea of a conscious life. To be conscious, to understand what is happening to you, and to others, here and now, is a large part of the urgency and energy of human life.

# A Chat Session:
# Why No One Looks
# Where a Statue Points

# A Chat Session: Why No One Looks Where a Statue Points

## George Byrnes

A "chat" program allows people to communicate instantaneously with each other over the Internet. Chat sessions are an even faster means of communication than e-mail since they give participants the ability to hold a "conversation" by sending short, typed messages back and forth in real-time. All chat "messages" are collected in a "transcript" on each participant's computer so they can be reviewed during the session and printed or saved for later use. Despite its practical uses, chat sessions also have a fantasy element as well. Participants usually adopt chat names taken from movies and novels, or they use their imagination to create a new persona.

In this session, Mike (Bogart) is taking advantage of his instructor's e-office hour to discuss an upcoming essay assignment that requires an application of Morton Ritts' article "Portrait of the Arts" to a picture of a statue that Professor Lee (Mrs_Dalloway) had previously made available to the class. Professor Lee holds e-office hours, in addition to regular office hours, to make it easier for students who attend her classes on two distant campuses to confer with her.

François Rude: *Departure of the Volunteers of 1793 (Le Marseilleise)*, sculpture on the Arc du Triomphe, Paris, 1833–36.

"A Chat Session: Why No One Looks Where a Statue Points" is by George Byrnes of Humber College. Used by permission.

**You have just entered chat room: "Mrs_Dalloway"**

| | |
|---|---|
| **Mrs_Dalloway:** | Hi, Mike. How are you today? |
| **Bogart:** | Great, Prof. Lee. Has anyone else dropped in during your chat time? I see no one else is online with you right now. |
| **Mrs_Dalloway:** | No, you're the first today. What's on your mind? |
| **Bogart:** | I'm feeling a bit confused about our next assignment. I've gone over the list of essay topics but the one I keep returning to is the one that seems most confusing. I've never seen a topic like this one: *Why no one looks where a statue points, but should.* |
| **Mrs_Dalloway:** | Ok. Sometimes it's a good idea to choose a topic that really puzzles you. That's why it's there. Let's spend this session exploring it. First, the good news: it doesn't take a brain surgeon to figure out why no one looks where a statue points. What kind of society would we have if we all routinely stopped what we were doing and took orders from inanimate things? |
| **Bogart:** | But people do—when they drive and see a stoplight. A stoplight is inanimate, isn't it? |
| **Mrs_Dalloway:** | Well, yes, good point, but that's not my point. Let me think of another way to say this. I was trying to have you explore what concerns the special status of art, namely that we treat art differently than other things. |
| **Bogart:** | At those prices, I can see why. Remember that "stripe" painting the National Gallery of Art bought for millions? I read in the newspaper that some farmer duplicated the painting on the side of his barn and no one offered him millions. And they would have gotten a whole barn, not just some painted-up canvas. |
| **Mrs_Dalloway:** | The commercial valuation of art is another matter, and a confusing one for everyone really. I think you are referring to Barnett Newman's *Voice of Fire*. I didn't think much of it either, but then again I only saw a photograph of the painting in the newspaper. I might have a different opinion if I went to the gallery and took the time to view it and experience it. Abstract art asks for different things from us than traditional art. |
| **Bogart:** | That's just it. I don't know what this kind of art asks for, much less than what it says. I at least understand the statue even if I don't understand your essay topic. |

**Mrs_Dalloway:** Abstract art is less controversial today than it was in the early and middle part of the 20th century, but one of the reasons it continues to create controversy is that it challenges us to respond directly to it without the usual visual clues: human forms, realistic objects and scenery. Some of these paintings contain a wild splattering of colours and lines typical of Jackson Pollack's paintings. This was called Action Painting.

**Bogart:** There was a commercial that showed André Agassi in a warehouse hitting paint-soaked tennis balls against a canvas. That looked like fun. Was that action painting?

**Mrs_Dalloway:** Yes, that's the idea, though I doubt it resulted in a painting of any significance. Barnett Newman used a different approach call "colour-field" painting. Painters in this group used colour and geometric shapes. Both groups were concerned with how the artist was expressing himself/herself in a spontaneous way, and so the painters in this movement are called Abstract Expressionists. So we might say that the Agassi commercial was poking fun at abstract art just as *Time Magazine* was when in 1947 it called Jackson Pollack "Jack the Dripper." However, Agassi was just hitting the balls for the purposes of the commercial. He wasn't connected to the painting in the way Abstract Expressionists are connected. Pollock often painted with the canvas on the floor because "On the floor I am more at ease, I feel nearer, more a part of the painting, since this way I can walk around in it, work from the four sides and be literally 'in' the painting."

**Bogart:** Expressionism is about feeling then? That's funny because I don't get any feeling from most of this kind of art. It just leaves me cold.

**Mrs_Dalloway:** Some of it may. New things are often difficult to understand because we are always looking at them with eyes trained to look for and value something that seems to be missing. Newman wrote something about this many years ago. Hold on a second while I do a quick search of the Web to find it.

[Three minutes later]

**Mrs_Dalloway:** Yes, here it is: "To us art is an adventure into an unknown world, which can be explored only by those willing to take the risks. . . . We favour the simple expression of the complex thought. We are for the large shape because it has the impact of the unequivocal. We wish to reassert the picture plane. We are for flat forms because they destroy the illusion and reveal the truth." He wrote this in 1943. Open your browser and check out **home.sprynet.com/~mindweb/ page69.htm**.

**Bogart:**      Ok, give me a second. Hey, I actually like this painting. And I see he likes having a bit of fun too. He must have been thinking of me when he called this painting "Who's Afraid of Red Yellow & Blue."

**Mrs_Dalloway:**      Exactly. Think about what he is saying: the "impact of the unequivocal," flat forms "destroy the illusion and reveal the truth." That's pretty powerful language. It doesn't sound like Newman wants a painting of his to "leave you cold." Just the opposite. Remember, however, that *Voice of Fire* was controversial not just because it is abstract art. It was controversial because, as someone has said, it "mixed money, politics, and taste" in an explosive way.[1] In other words, people don't evaluate art only from one perspective, especially not if public money is being used to buy it. In any case, how art is priced and sold is not what we should talk about really. What I want you to see is that when we don't look where a statue points tells us something important about art and, by inference, about things that are not art. Are you with me?

**Bogart:**      Ok, but I don't know why yet this is important, except I assume this will be on a test.

**Mrs_Dalloway:**      The importance will come as we talk about it, and that's what will be on the test. I assume you have read "Portrait of the Arts."

**Bogart:**      Yes, I've read it.

**Mrs_Dalloway:**      Good. You'll remember that the author of that article begins by making a distinction between art and science, that science is "propositional" and art is "problematic." Did you understand this distinction?

**Bogart:**      More or less. It has to do with different kinds of truth that science and art deal with.

**Mrs_Dalloway:**      Right. We'll begin the same way. Let's put everything that has been created into two boxes. We'll name one box "Art" and the other box "Not Art."

**Bogart:**      I don't see how you can do that. Where would you put something like the CN Tower? Architecture is art, isn't it? But it's also a building that has restaurants and offices and washrooms and so on. It would have to go in both boxes, so what have we gained?

**Mrs_Dalloway:**      You're right. The names of these categories create confusion right away. Let's try something else. Let's not talk about "art" in its entirety but instead let's narrow art down a bit to just literature and try to distinguish between what is literary and what is not. In many ways, literature is a lot closer to us than other forms of art since it is created just with words, words we use every day in other ways.

**Bogart:** Ok, but are you sure you can get us back to why no one looks where a statue points? That's the point of this conversation, isn't it? I mean, I really want to know that, not being a brain surgeon and all.

**Mrs_Dalloway:** Very funny, Mike. Actually we will just be talking about this topic from a different vantage point, one that should be clearer for both of us, so I think we will be all right. First, I think we want to find some basis to distinguish between a literary use of language and non-literary use of language.

**Bogart:** You mean when Shakespeare says, "The lady protests too much, methinks." I never say "methinks" so that must be literary.

**Mrs_Dalloway:** You normally also don't say "parallax" either but this term is used all the time by astronomers to talk about the position of planets. I don't think we can just identify unusual words to determine what is literary and what is not. But here's a clue: it's not Shakespeare who "says" this, is it? It's one of his characters in one of his plays.

So what's the difference between what authors write in their own names and when they write literature? I mean, when an author signs a cheque or writes a letter to a friend, that's the author speaking. The author's account will be debited and the return letter will go to the author. But when an author creates a character, the words assigned to that character do not necessarily represent what the author believes or wants or understands to be true. There are lots of murders in Shakespeare's plays, but we shouldn't assume he was a murderer or advocated violence.

**Bogart:** But if I think something, isn't it true that it says something about me? In fact, when we studied Freud and the Psychoanalytic School, I learned that the subconscious was basically a huge dark force within us, that we really couldn't know the unconscious, but that it was always trying to break out. Maybe we're all murderers.

**Mrs_Dalloway:** Now you have me scared, Mike. Actually, the point is not that the author may not actually agree with what a character does or says. He or she may in fact believe or behave in exactly the same way. That doesn't really matter.

**Bogart:** It might matter to me.

**Mrs_Dalloway:** The point is that we do not have a reliable way of knowing whether this is true—at least not just from the text of the literary work and so it would be false to assume that this is so. More importantly, to do so is of little or no value since it will not help us to understand the literary work.

**Bogart:** So you're saying it's not important to know anything about the author.

**Mrs_Dalloway:** I didn't quite say that. What I am trying to say is that to understand a literary work, we need to understand how a character's words or behaviour fit in with the words and behaviour of all the other characters, how they fit into the big picture of the literary work itself. Think of the words of the literary work as the facts of the case, but the facts need to be organized if we are to be able to make sense of them, if we are to find the keys to unlock the story's meaning.

**Bogart:** So you're saying we should look at a literary work as a little world, a kind of parallel universe. But the stories I read always seem so real, so much like the way I live my life.

**Mrs_Dalloway:** Actually, that's another good point but if you think carefully, the worlds in the stories, while very similar to ours because they may be set in Toronto or New York or someplace we have visited, and may deal with teachers and students or a woman of Asian heritage like me or a man of Canadian heritage like you, the stories themselves are a bit different in one important way: they always deal with events that are either more wonderful or more disastrous than the events we normally experience.

**Bogart:** I see what you mean. I must have witnessed a thousand murders watching TV and movies and yet I've never actually seen anyone killed. I don't think I've even seen anyone who was dead.

**Mrs_Dalloway:** That doesn't sound much like someone with the name Bogart, Mike.

**Bogart:** No, I guess not.

**Mrs_Dalloway:** So what we are really noticing then is a correspondence between our world and the fictional world of the story. It's not exactly a one-to-one correspondence but it's close enough so you believe the two are the same. Of course there are many other kinds of stories, futuristic dramas like *Star Wars*, or animated films such as *Antz* or *Toy Story*, that do not resemble our worlds, at least not exactly. There is something that is similar though. What do you think it is?

**Bogart:** Well, in *Star Wars*, people and androids are still shooting at each other. I didn't see *Toy Story* but I remember in *Antz* Woody Allen was the voice of one of the main characters and he was just like himself, except he was an ant.

**Mrs_Dalloway:** So what's similar?

**Bogart:** I guess they're all about people even when people are not directly in the story.

| | |
|---|---|
| **Mrs_Dalloway:** | Exactly. Art is always about human values, explorations of these values in the highest works of art, demonstrations of these values in more conventional works of art. |
| **Bogart:** | I'm getting a bit lost. I don't see how all this relates to that statue you want us to write about. |
| **Mrs_Dalloway:** | Why don't you take a moment and look back over the transcript of our chat session and then tell me what you think we have established so far? I'm going to be marking some papers here in my office while you do this so take your time. I'll keep an eye on the screen for your message. |
| **Bogart:** | Ok. |
| | [Five minutes later] |
| **Bogart:** | I'm back. |
| **Mrs_Dalloway:** | Ok, what have you found? |
| **Bogart:** | So far I think you have said that the statue tells us something important about art. You then said we should limit the discussion to literature because it is made of the same language we normally use and this will help us to recognize what it is we are looking for. I thought the use of words that were not common like "methinks" was one way to recognize literature but you said this was not a reliable method. Instead, you pointed out that the words and behaviour of characters in a story are not the same as the author's, that a story is like a separate world. You said we should treat the words as the facts of the story and to use these facts to make keys to unlock the story's meaning. And then you pointed out that a story might not have real people in it but even then it was about people, about human values. |
| **Mrs_Dalloway:** | That's a good summary of what we said but what does it all mean? What did you learn? |
| **Bogart:** | Two things I guess: 1) I liked the idea about the words of a story being the facts that we need to collect to make them into keys to unlock the story's meaning. It kind of makes me into a detective, searching through the clues. 2) That all art is about human values. |
| **Mrs_Dalloway:** | Great. Now why don't you test these ideas on the essay topic. How do they apply? |
| **Bogart:** | The first idea tells me that I have to look closely at the statue, as though it were a separate universe. Oh, I see! If the statue is a separate universe, why would anyone look to where it points! The figure that is pointing is pointing from within its universe, not ours. The pointing only has meaning to the other figures that are part of the statue. |

**Mrs_Dalloway:** Excellent. Now how about the second idea?

**Bogart:** Well, the statue is about a war and the main figure is urging the people to go forward or to charge ahead. You can tell that by the expression in the main figure's face and the gestures. She seems very determined and yet some of the other characters seem almost confused or uncertain. I can see that the sculptor was trying to say something about dedication, maybe even sacrificing your life to win victory. At least that's what I see.

**Mrs_Dalloway:** That sounds pretty good. Remember, though, your essay is not about the statue; it's about what the statue tells us about art. Don't spend a lot of time describing the statue itself. I want you to explore the larger question, about art.

**Bogart:** I'm not sure how to do that.

**Mrs_Dalloway:** Let's go back to where we left off our discussion. Let me ask you this: what criteria do you think are appropriate to evaluate statements made by a scientist or a journalist?

**Bogart:** What they say has to be true, especially what a journalist says. Otherwise what is the point?

**Mrs_Dalloway:** Yes, in most cases, or at least statements that point to what is true. Some scientific ideas can't be tested, at least not at present, but the statements might still be true. Journalistic statements are usually more easily tested for their veracity. What else would you expect from these kinds of statements?

**Bogart:** I guess I would expect them to be clear. I mean, not to me. I probably wouldn't be able to read a real scientific article. I was never very good in math. But it should be clear to the experts in the field. I think I understand journalistic articles. These kinds of statements shouldn't be ambiguous or how else could it be tested or validated?

**Mrs_Dalloway:** That's a good beginning list: scientific and journalistic statements should try to say something that is true about the world and they should be unambiguous. Now, from your experience, do literary works measure up to these criteria?

**Bogart:** As I said before, some stories are very realistic but they're nothing like science. Even science fiction stories only use science as a kind of backdrop. They don't really discuss science. So they don't really make statements that are "true" like science does and they are far from being unambiguous. I mean, that's really what's frustrating about poetry—everything means everything. It's like the words refuse to sit still and just be words.

**Mrs_Dalloway:** Good, so what criteria do you think are appropriate to evaluate artistic statements? Mike, it doesn't matter whether we are talking about paintings, ballet or novels but let's keep things simple and continue to limit our discussion to literary works.

**Bogart:** Well, I'm tempted to say that the most important thing is that I understand it after one reading. Just kidding! I guess if science says something true about the world, then a story should say something that is true about people.

**Mrs_Dalloway:** Nice. Since you are matching things up, how would you apply the second criterion?

**Bogart:** Since science needs to be unambiguous, I guess I would expect stories to be ambiguous. You said words are the facts of a story and we need to use the facts to make keys to unlock the meaning of the story. Maybe literary works are ambiguous because that's how they work, that's how the keys are made.

**Mrs_Dalloway:** Some critics would say that science and journalism make statements whereas artistic works make pseudo-statements, statements that are not to be taken at their face value. If I write "it's raining," you would expect that I mean exactly that; get out the umbrellas. When Shania Twain sings, "It's raining on our love," however, you know intuitively that something else is meant, that the image of rain is being used figuratively to say something about a love relationship.

**Bogart:** Pseudo-statements, then, are another way of saying that literary works create a separate but parallel world.

**Mrs_Dalloway:** Yes, separate but parallel. That's it. The artistic world relates in some important way to our world even if it doesn't exactly resemble it. Here's one of my favourite passages from the poet William Carlos Williams that helps to say this:

> It is difficult
> to get the news from poems
> yet men die miserably every day
> for lack
> of what is found there.[2]

**Bogart:** Isn't that sexist?

**Mrs_Dalloway:** Williams was writing before gender equality was a language issue. If it were not a poem, we might want to change "men" to "humans." Maybe he would write it differently if he were writing it today … But let's not worry about that now. What do you think Williams is saying?

**Bogart:** He's saying that poetry really matters, that it gives us something, that it feeds us in some way. I don't know if he really means people will die if they don't read poetry, but it might mean this. The word could mean many things. I think the word "die" is one of those ambiguous words that are a key to the poem's meaning.

**Mrs_Dalloway:** That's right. Now compare what you just said with another quote, this one from a poem by Stephen Crane, the author of *The Red Badge of Courage*:

> *A newspaper is a symbol;*
> *It is feckless life's chronicle,*
> *A collection of loud tales*
> *Concentrating eternal stupidities,*
> *That in remote ages lived unhaltered,*
> *Roaming through a fenceless world.*[3]

**Bogart:** That's an interesting one but kind of depressing at the same time. I'm not sure I get it all but let me give it a try. Williams is saying there is something important for us in poetry, even though most of us don't read it, and yet Crane says that when we read newspapers, which we do every day, we think we are getting something important, something we need, but really it's just the same old story told over and over.

**Mrs_Dalloway:** That's pretty good.

**Bogart:** I think sometimes we do get something we need from newspapers. I mean we learn about our city or country. We learn about dangers, maybe there's a mad killer out there. But generally, what's in newspapers doesn't mean very much to me. It's even more confusing than poetry. I don't even know where half the places are that are mentioned. I like the sports section though.

**Mrs_Dalloway:** I don't think it's a question of reading one and not the other. It's a question of what is important to us and where we can find it. We have already established that art is always about human values, about creating a space where values can be explored and understood. Newspapers report what's going on but they don't provide the same shared experience as artistic works. In fact, I would think that many people use newspaper stories to harden their positions rather than opening themselves to explore why they believe or feel as they do.

**Bogart:** I think I have a good sense of what you are looking for now. We don't look where the statue points in an everyday sense, but, since the artistic experience it provides offers us something we need, we should. I get it, Professor Lee. Thanks for your help. I think I can work on my rough draft now.

**Mrs_Dalloway:** Remember, Mike, if you use anything I've written here in your paper you have to cite the source just as you would any other reference.

**Bogart:** I'll remember.

**Mrs_Dalloway:** I always save the transcripts of my e-office hour chat sessions. Make sure you save our chat in case you want to review what we have said.

**Bogart:** Ok. By the way, I've been meaning to ask you what your chat name means. Who's Mrs. Dalloway?

**Mrs_Dalloway:** Mrs. Dalloway is the main character in a novel by Virginia Woolf. If you're in my Modern Literature course next semester, you'll get a chance to read it. I use it as a screen name because Mrs. Dalloway represents something special to me, something I like to be reminded of every day. I assume your name is taken from Humphrey Bogart. Why do you use that name?

**Bogart:** It sounded good. I'm wondering if I should choose another one now. Maybe Brain_Surgeon.

**Mrs_Dalloway:** I told you—you don't have to be one of those! In any case, if you do change your chat name, make sure you e-mail me the new name so I know who you are when you sign in next time. See you in class.

**Bogart:** Thanks again. Bye.

# Notes

1  Robert Fulford, "The Uses of Controversy," Walter Gordon Forum in Public Policy, Massey College, March 4, 1997 <**www.robertfulford.com/gordon.html**>.

2  William Carlos Williams, "Asphodel, that Greeny Flower," *The Collected Poetry of William Carlos Williams: 1939–1962* (New York: New Directions, 1988).

3  Stephen Crane, "War Is Kind and Other Lines, XII," *The Collected Poems of Stephen Crane* (Ithaca, New York: Cornell University Press, 1972).

StudyDesk:
A Computerized
Guide for
*The Human Project*

# StudyDesk

To help you understand the many topics covered in *The Human Project*, we have included a computer study guide with the textbook. The StudyDesk program, which works on any Pentium-level PC, contains the following elements for each unit of the textbook:

- **Unit Overview:** a brief introduction to the main themes and issues of each unit;
- **Learning Outcomes:** a list of activities you will be able to complete at the end of each unit;
- **Key Concepts:** a quick way to review essential concepts you should understand, unit by unit;
- **Unit Review:** a complete list, on an article-by-article basis, of all terms and historical figures mentioned in each article;
- **Terms and Concepts:** definitions of and commentary on over 150 terms and concepts;
- **Biographical Sketches:** background information on over 80 historical figures mentioned in the textbook;
- **Summaries of Textbook Articles:** point-form summaries of each textbook article;
- **Reading Room:** a selection of representative works by authors cited in the textbook along with reference materials.

The StudyDesk program screen is split into two panes. An expandable table of contents appears on the left side of the screen. To view the topics contained in each unit, just click the **+** sign next to the unit number. Similarly, to hide the topics from view, click the **−** sign. To read the information contained in any topic, double-click the topic name. The topic information will then appear on the right side of the screen as demonstrated in the graphic below:

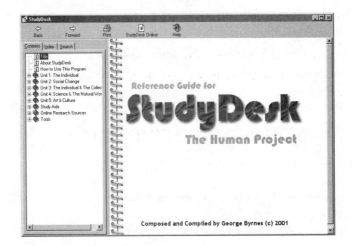

If you have ever used a Web browser to view pages on the Internet, you will be familiar with the basic format of StudyDesk: clicking hotlinks calls up new pages that contain additional information. StudyDesk, however, uses a special form of Web page. Most of the pages are contained in the program itself while others are available only when you are online. The online pages are clearly identified by a special graphic ⓘ.

Unlike the textbook, which has pages usually read in order, with StudyDesk you use the mouse to call information to the screen in the order that serves your needs. You control what you read simply by clicking with the mouse on a hot-word (words in **bold** or graphics that contain links) to activate a "jump" or a "popup" of a new page. When a jump occurs, new information replaces what you were reading. When a popup occurs, new information appears on top of what you are reading in a scrollable window.

StudyDesk also includes several function buttons at the top of the screen:

- **Back/Forward Buttons:** take you back or forward to pages you have viewed in the order that you viewed the pages;
- **Print:** allows you to print the selected topic or all topics in the current heading;
- **StudyDesk Online:** links you to online pages with links to articles that extend the scope of the articles in the textbook.

# How to Start StudyDesk

StudyDesk can be run directly from the disk that accompanies the textbook. For the program to run faster, you can download the **studydesk.chm** file to your hard drive. Please consult your computer manual to learn how to create a directory, copy files to it and create a desktop icon for the StudyDesk program.

## Running StudyDesk from a Floppy Disk

1. Insert the StudyDesk disk in the external 3.5″ floppy drive.
2. From the Windows Desktop, click the **Start Button** and choose **Run** from the menu.
3. In the dialog box, type the following: **a:\studydesk.chm**.
4. Click the **OK** button to start StudyDesk. (If StudyDesk does not start, see Note below.)

# Minimum System Requirements

**Computer:** Pentium-level PC
**RAM:** 32 MB
**Disk Space:** 1 MB (if loading StudyDesk on the hard drive)
**Operating System:** Windows 95 or higher
**Browser:** Microsoft Internet Explorer, Version 4.0 or later

**Note:** some older systems running Windows 95 may have to install a service package to run StudyDesk. The service package can be downloaded from the Internet at the following Web site:

**generaleducation.humberc.on.ca/humanities/studydesk/service.htm**.

# Contributors

**George Byrnes** (StudyDesk; "A Chat Session") teaches humanities at Humber College.

**Melanie Chaparian** (general editor; "Am I Free or Determined?") teaches philosophy and humanities at Humber College.

**Clive Cockerton** (general editor; "Serious Pleasure," "Stories: An Introduction," "Objectivity and Subjectivity," "The Search for Form") has been teaching film, literature and humanities since 1975.

**Brian Doyle** ("On Human Reproduction and the Limitations of Science") teaches sciences and humanities at Humber College, where he has been teaching since 1985.

**Scott Greer** ("Music as History") teaches psychology at Concordia University and has a passionate interest in classical music.

**William Hanna** (consulting editor) is the Dean of the School of Media Studies at Humber College, where he has been an administrator and teacher for more than 20 years.

**Michael Horwood** ("Music as History") teaches music and humanities at Humber College where he has been teaching for more than 25 years. Michael is also a distinguished composer.

**Mitchell Lerner** ("On Inhumanity") has taught sociology at York University and humanities at Humber College. While pursuing an active business career, he remains an articulate voice on contemporary issues.

**Jason MacLean** ("The New Capitalism—and What It Means for You") has taught sociology at Humber College, the University of Toronto and Ryerson Polytechnic University. He presently lives in Berlin, where he is working on a novel.

**Greg Narbey** ("Multiculturalism and Equity") teaches philosophy and humanities at Humber College. Greg has a keen interest in political philosophy and contemporary liberalism.

**Wendy O'Brien** ("From Biology to Biography," "Fashion Statements") teaches philosophy and humanities at Humber College. Wendy has also lectured on business ethics at Sir Wilfrid Laurier University, and delivered a number of conference papers on Simone de Beauvoir.

**Tom Olien** ("The Path of Scientific Development") teaches physics, astronomy and humanities at Humber College. Tom combines a practical and philosophical interest in science with a desire to bring that interest to the community.

**Earl G. Reidy** ("Being and Becoming"), who passed away in 1997, taught anthropology, sociology and religion at Humber College from 1971 to 1996.

**Morton Ritts** ("Politics in the Life of the Individual," "Soul Force versus Physical Force," "Portrait of the Arts") teaches humanities and history at Humber College. He is also a frequent contributor to a number of newspapers and magazines.

**John Steckley** ("Introduction" [Unit 2], "A Canadian Lament," "The Great Law of Peace") teaches anthropology, sociology and humanities at Humber College, where he has been a teacher for 14 years. He is a specialist in the Huron language and history. As well, John is an avid student of percussion.

# LITERARY CREDITS

[1] Ackerman, Diane, excerpt from *The Moon by Whalelight*, reprinted with permission from Random House, Inc.

[88] Auden, W.H., from *A Certain World*. "Work, Labor and Play," exerpted from W. H. Auden's *A Certain World, A Commonplace Book*. New York: Curtis Brown: 1970. Reprinted with permission.

[170] Barber, Benjamin. "Jihad vs. McWorld" from *The Atlantic Monthly*, March 1992. Reprinted with permission.

[256] Bernstein, Alan, "Secrets of the Human Genome" originally appeared as "The Human Genome. Balancing Act: Science and Society" in *The Globe and Mail*, February 14, 2001.

[312] Carlson, Ron. "The Disclaimer". Copyright © 1997 by Ron Carlson. Originally appeared in *Harper's*, May 1997. All rights reserved. Used by permission of Brandt & Hochman Literary Agents, Inc. Reprinted by permission of the author.

[46] Castell, Alburey and Donald M. Borchert, excerpt from *An Introduction to Modern Philosophy*, 5th edition. Reprinted with permission from MacMillan Publishing.

[259] Cronenberg, David, excerpt from "Cronenberg on Cronenberg," edited by Chris Rodley, reprinted with permission from Faber and Faber.

[230] Davies, Paul, from *The Fifth Miracle*. From Paul Davies' *The Fifth Miracle: The Search for the Origin and Meaning of Life*. New York: Simon & Schuster, 1999. Reprinted with permission.

[234] Dyson, Freeman, from *Imagined Worlds*. Cambridge, Mass.: Harvard University Press, 1997. Copyright © 1997 by the President and Fellows of Harvard College. Reprinted with permission.

[216] Futuyma, Douglas. "Scientific Knowledge" in *Science on Trial: The Case for Evolution*. New York: Sinauer Associates, 1995. Reprinted with permission.

[157] Gandhi, Mohandas, K. "Non-Violent Resistance". Reprinted by permission of Navajivan Trust and Mahatma Ghandhi Estate.

[327] Herr, Michael, excerpt from *Dispatches*, reprinted with permission from Alfred A. Knopf, Inc.

[184] Ignatieff, Michael. "A Cosmopolitan among True Believers" in *Blood and Belonging*. Toronto: Penguin Books Canada, 1993. Reprinted with permission.

[60] Kettle, Martin. "If It's in the US, It's News. If Not, Forget It." in *The Guardian*, Vol. 160, Number 20, week ending May 16, 1999.

[324] Lux, Thomas. Reprinted by permission of the *New Yorker*.

[152] Malcolm X, copyright © 1965, 1970, 1991 by Betty Shabazz and Pathfinder Press. Reprinted by permission.

[304] McEwan, Ian, from *The Daydreamer*, copyright © 1994. Reprinted by permission of Alfred A. Knopf Canada.

[29] Morea, Peter. "Personality and Science: The Assumptions of Materialism" in *In Search of Personality: Christianity and Modern Psychology*. London: SCM Press, 1997.

[314] Olds, Sharon. "I Go Back To May 1937." Reprinted with permission from the author.

[67] Postman, Neil, from *Technopoly*. Copyright © 1992 by Neil Postman. Reprinted by permission of Alfred A. Knopf, Inc.

[25] Restak, Richard. "My Brain and I Are One" in *The Brain Has a Mind of its Own*. New York: Random House, 1991.

[197] Ryan, Nigel. "In Rwanda, The Smell of Death Permeates the Air" from *The Spectator*, June 16, 1999. Reprinted with permission.

[113] Smith, Vivian. Reprinted with permission from *The Globe and Mail* and Vivian Smith.

[80] Ullman, Ellen, "The Museum of Me" from *Harper's*, May 2000. Reprinted with permission from the author.

# PHOTO CREDITS

# LICENSE AGREEMENT AND LIMITED WARRANTY

# DRAW 50 BOATS, SHIPS, TRUCKS, AND TRAINS

## Experience All That the Draw 50 Series Has to Offer!

With this proven, step-by-step method, Lee J. Ames has taught millions how to draw everything from amphibians to automobiles. Now it's your turn! Pick up the pencil, get out some paper, and learn how to draw everything under the sun with the Draw 50 series.

Also Available:

- *Draw 50 Aliens*
- *Draw 50 Animals*
- *Draw 50 Animal 'Toons*
- *Draw 50 Athletes*
- *Draw 50 Baby Animals*
- *Draw 50 Beasties*
- *Draw 50 Birds*
- *Draw 50 Buildings and Other Structures*
- *Draw 50 Cats*
- *Draw 50 Cars, Trucks, and Motorcycles*
- *Draw 50 Creepy Crawlies*
- *Draw 50 Dinosaurs and Other Prehistoric Animals*
- *Draw 50 Dogs*
- *Draw 50 Endangered Animals*
- *Draw 50 Famous Cartoons*
- *Draw 50 Flowers, Trees, and Other Plants*
- *Draw 50 Horses*
- *Draw 50 Magical Creatures*
- *Draw 50 Monsters*
- *Draw 50 People*
- *Draw 50 Princesses*
- *Draw 50 Sharks, Whales, and Other Sea Creatures*
- *Draw 50 Vehicles*
- *Draw the Draw 50 Way*

Lee J. Ames began his career at the Walt Disney Studios, working on films that included *Fantasia* and *Pinocchio*. He taught at the School of Visual Arts in Manhattan, and at Dowling College on Long Island, New York. An avid worker, Ames directed his own advertising agency, illustrated for several magazines, and illustrated approximately 150 books that range from picture books to postgraduate texts. He resided in Dix Hills, Long Island, with his wife, Jocelyn, until his death in June 2011.

**Diesel Streamliner**

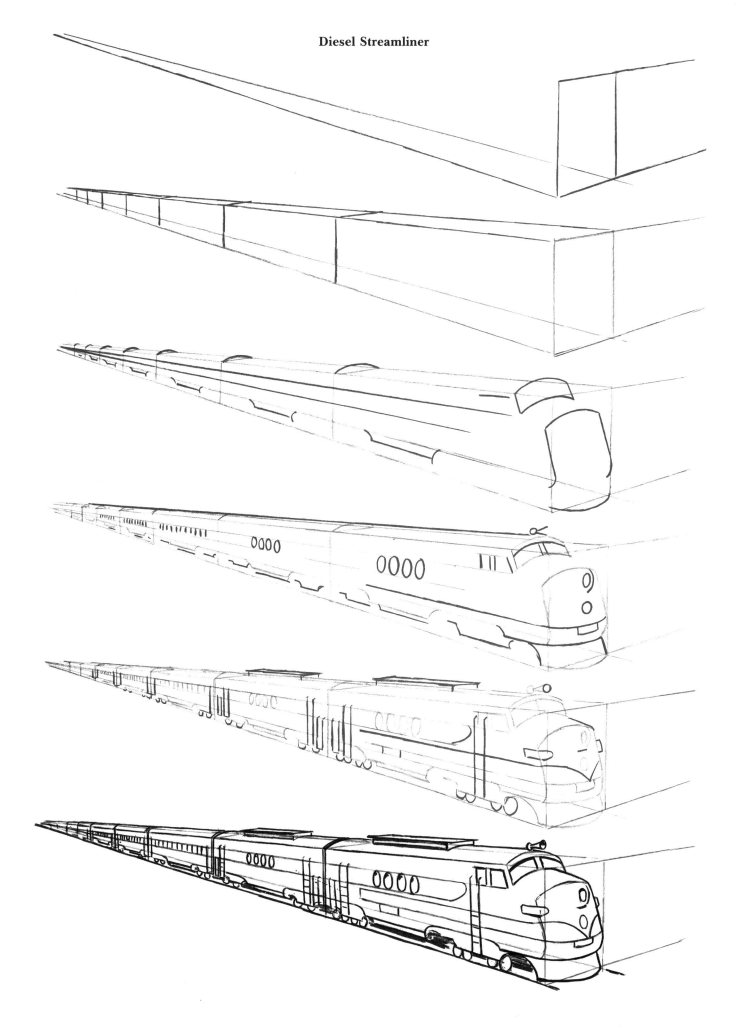

**Diesel Streamliner**

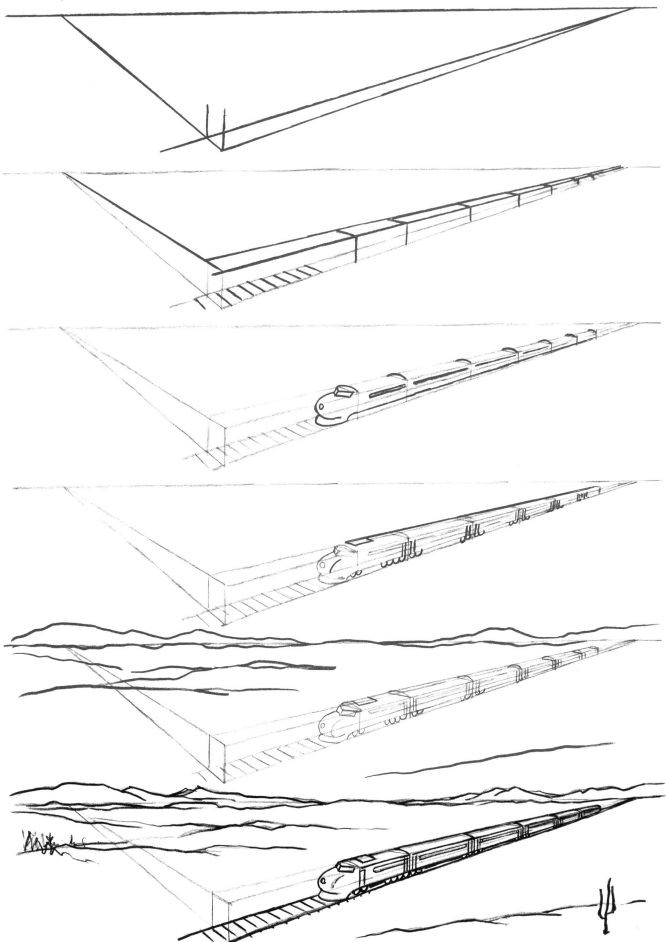

# Diesel Streamliner

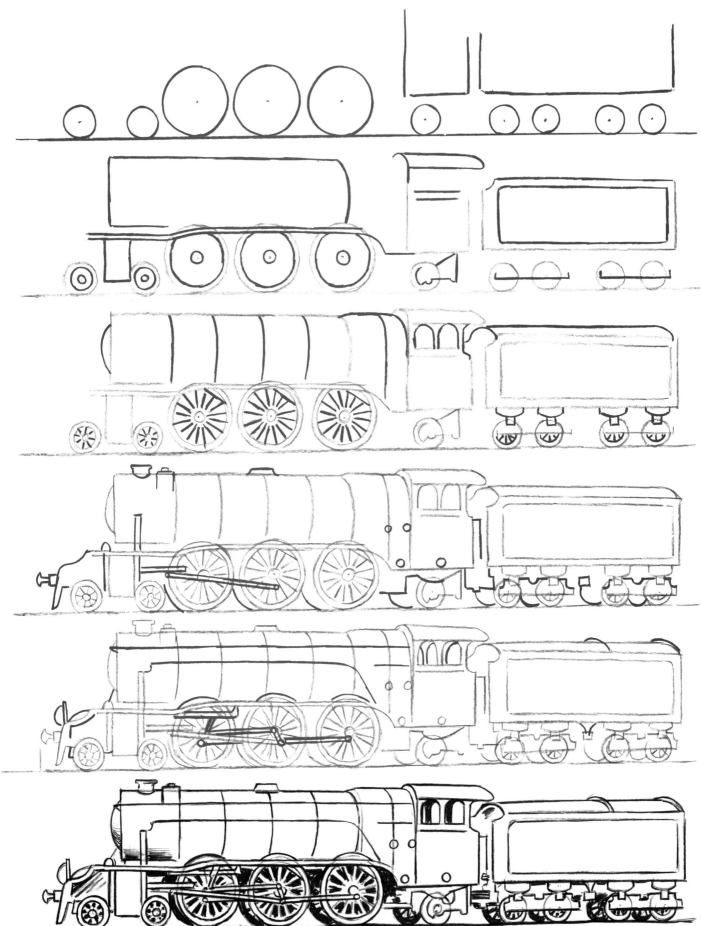

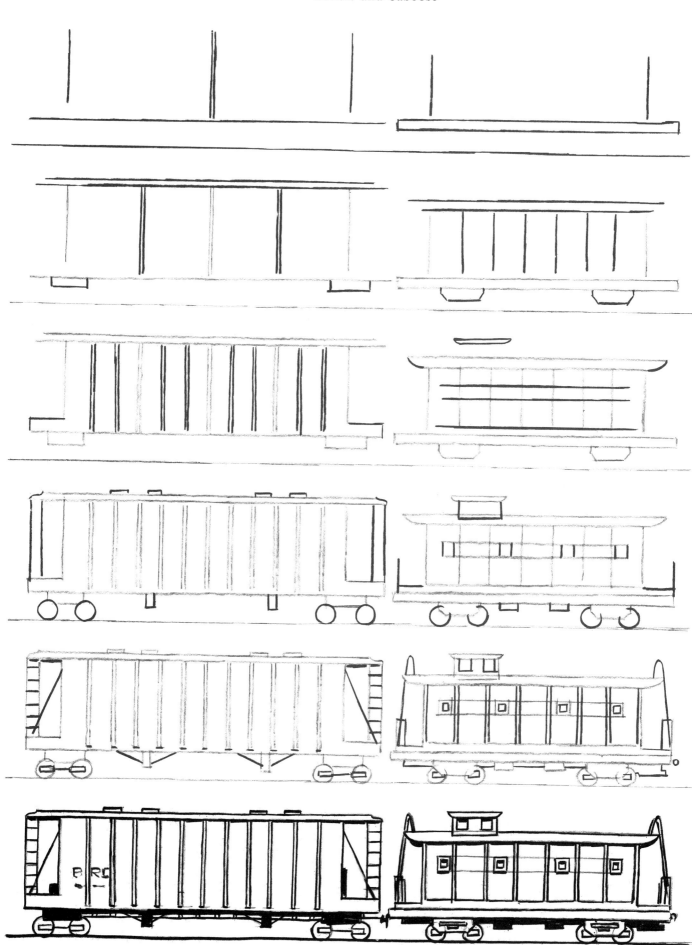

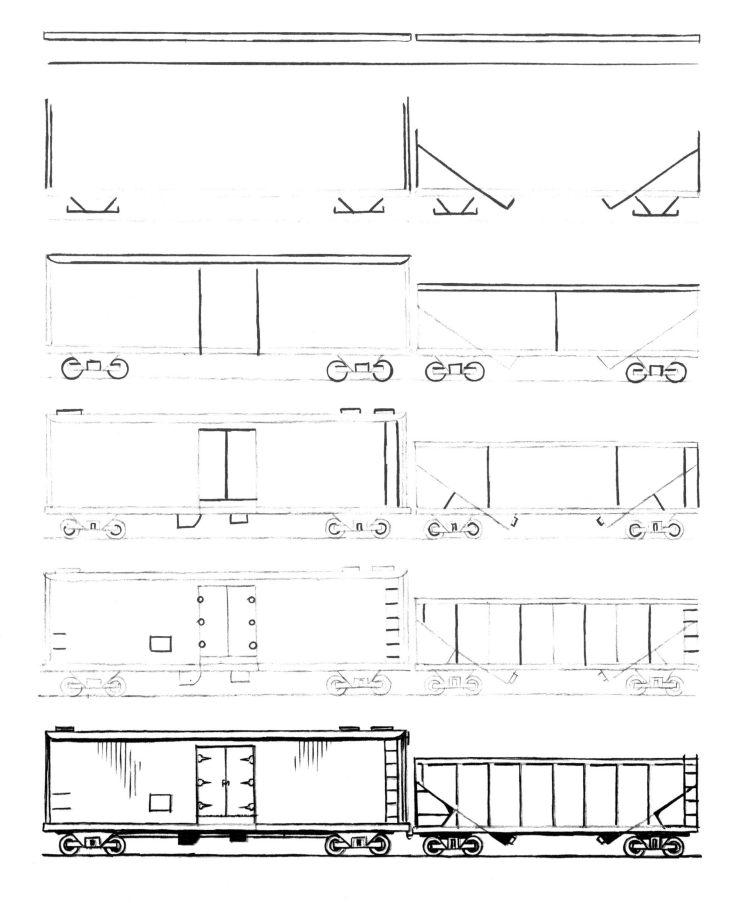

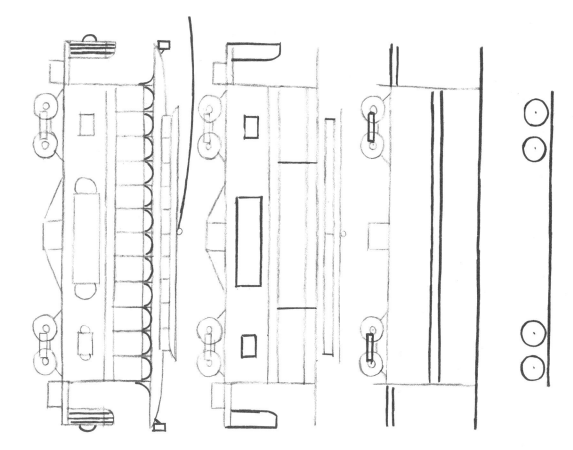

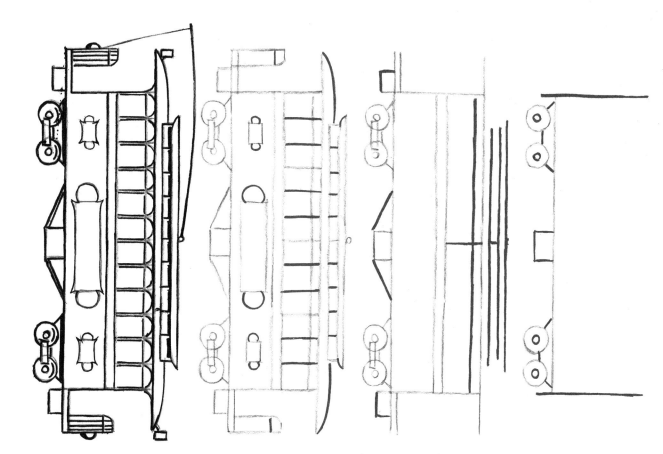

Trolley Car

**Locomotive (Circa 1893)**

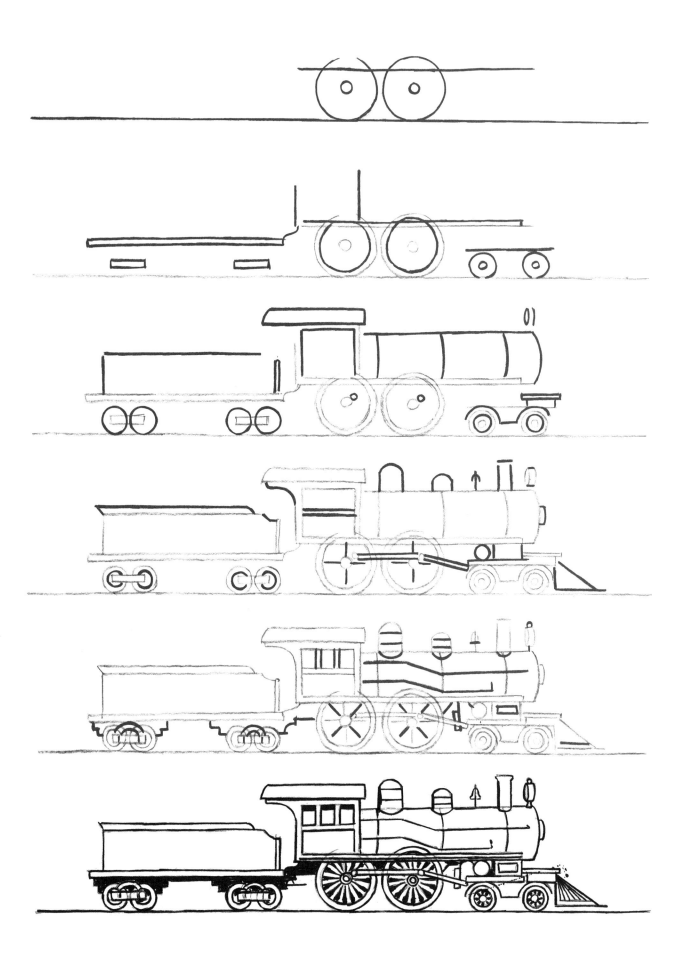

**Locomotive (Circa 1879)**

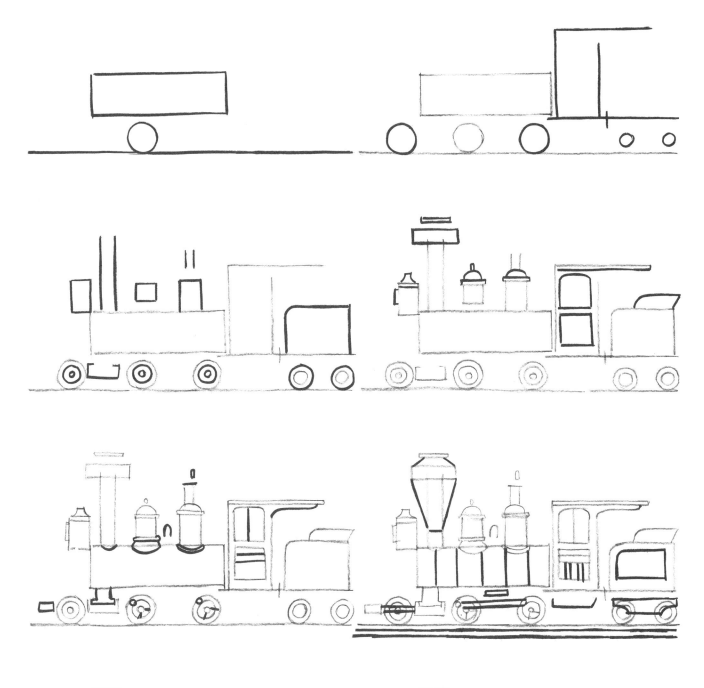

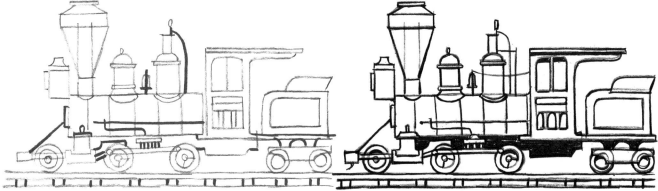

**Locomotive (Circa 1865)**

**Military Tank**

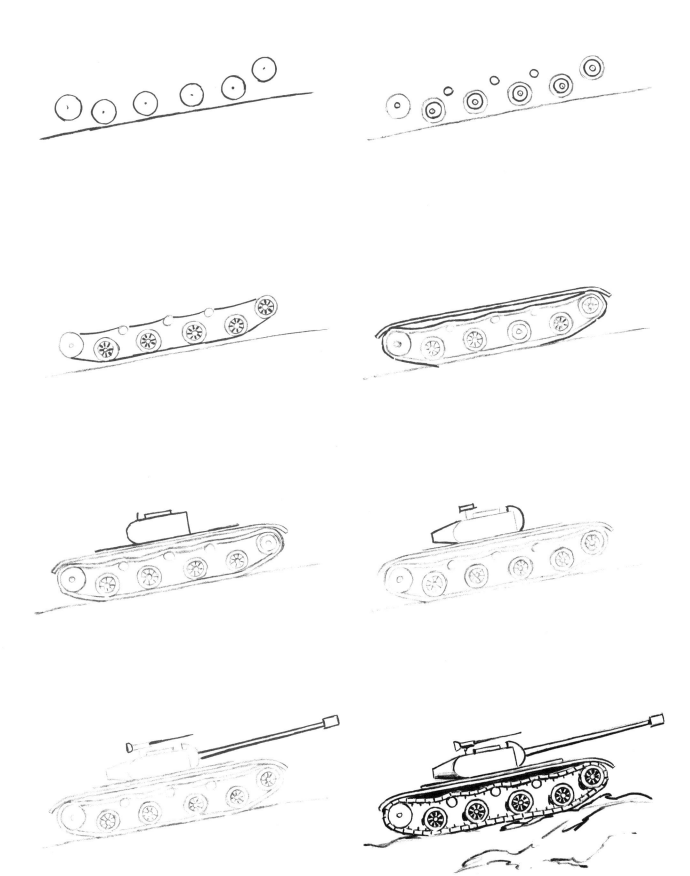

**Steam Shovel**

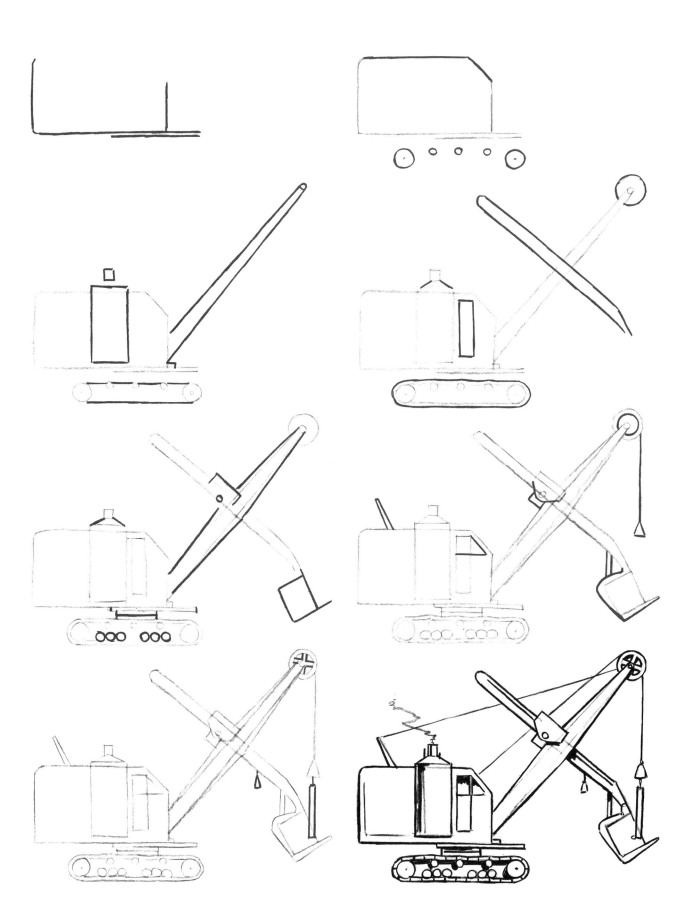

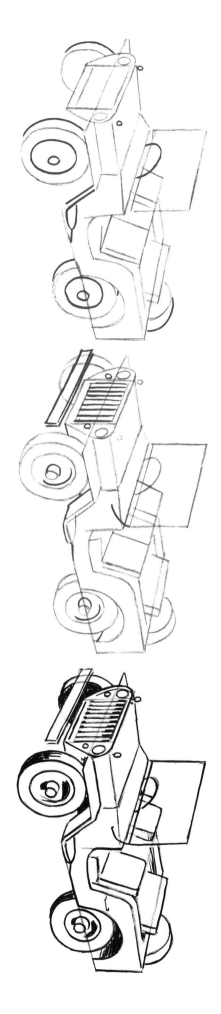
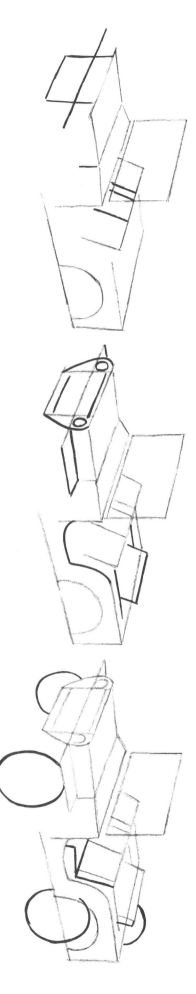

Jeep

**Moving Van**

**Moving Van**

**Tanker**

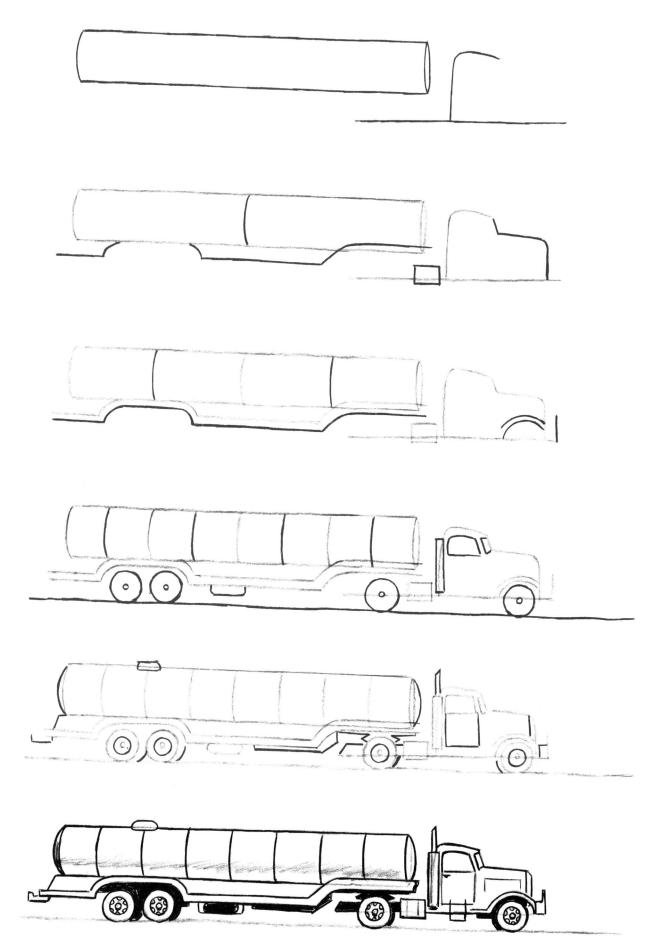

**Fire Truck**

**Tractor-trailer**

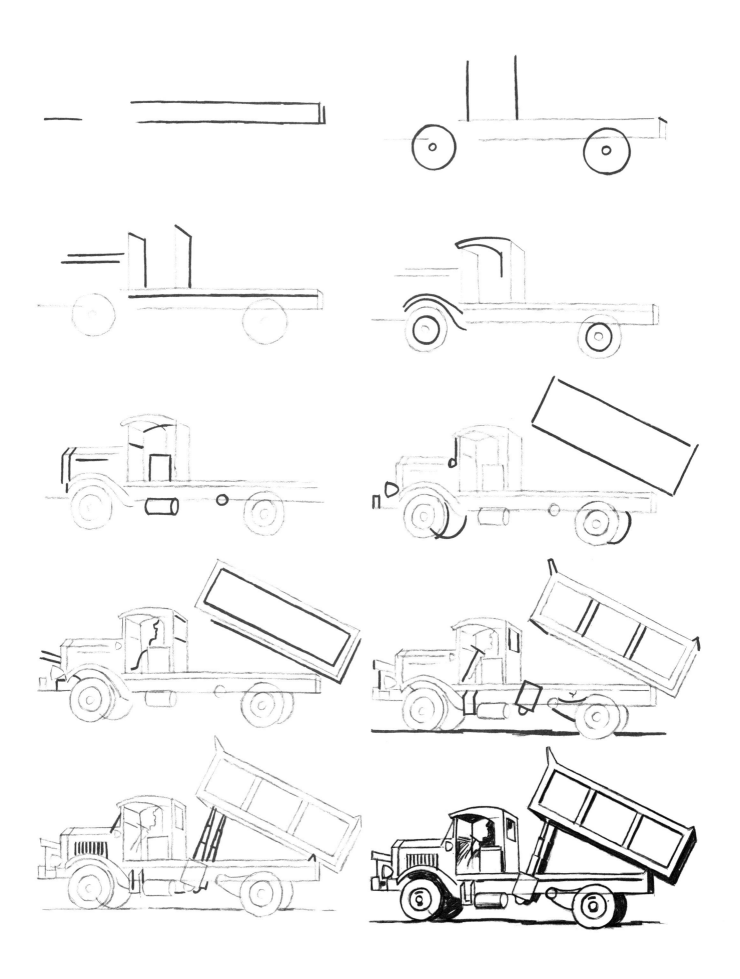

**Pickup Truck**

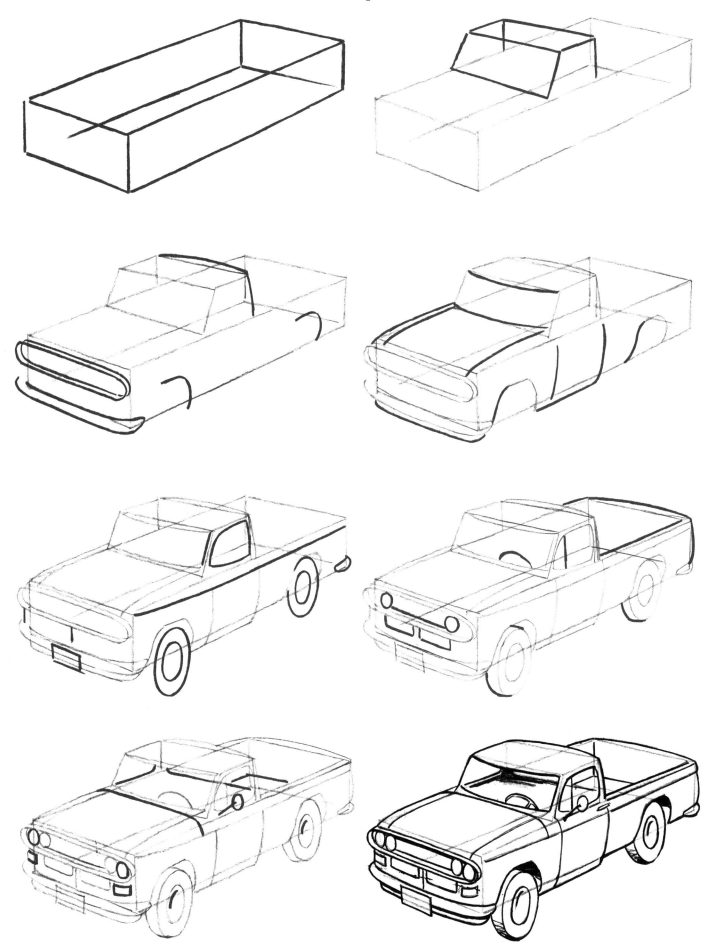

**Fifteenth-century Ship**

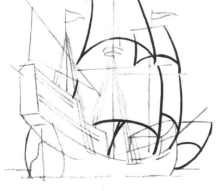

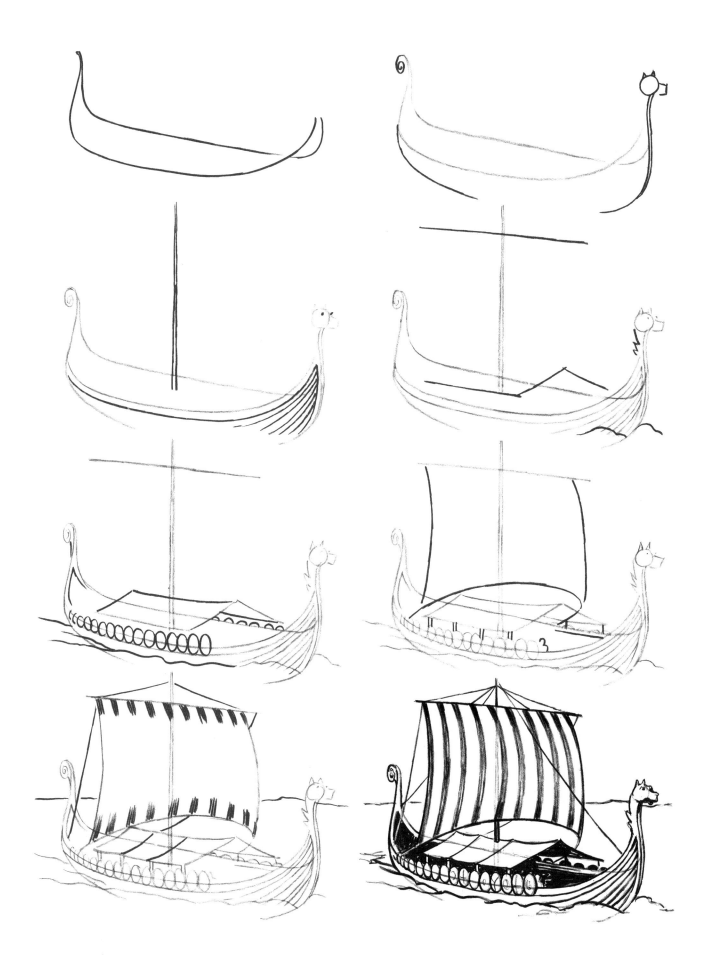

# Brigantine

**Three-masted Schooner**

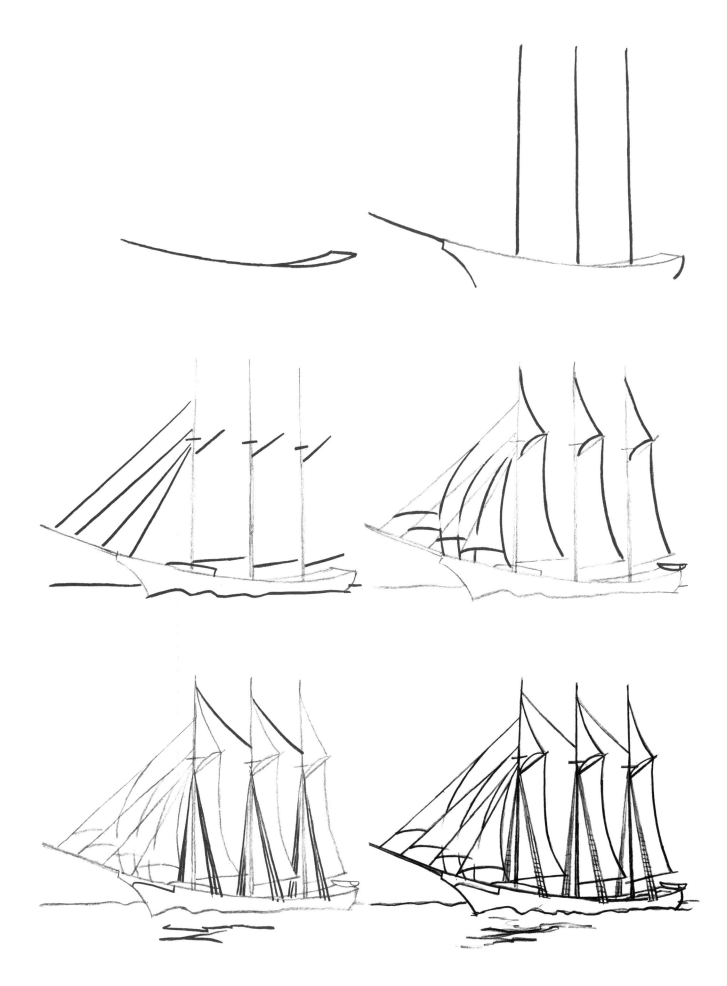

**Sloop with Spinnaker**

**Sloop**

**Kayak**

**Sampan**

**Dory**

**Rowboat**

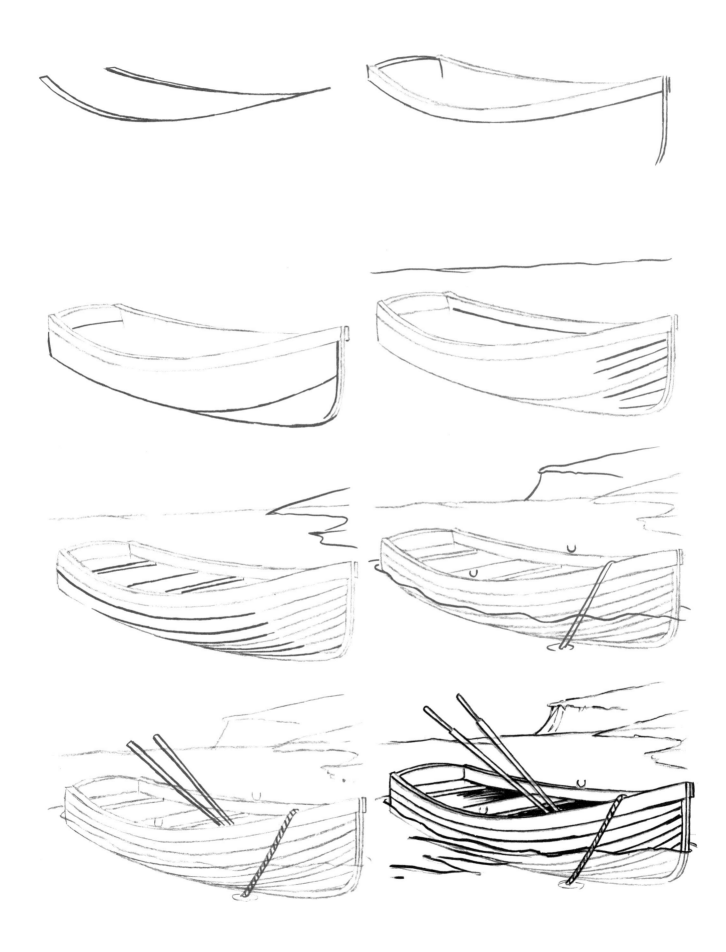

# Canoe

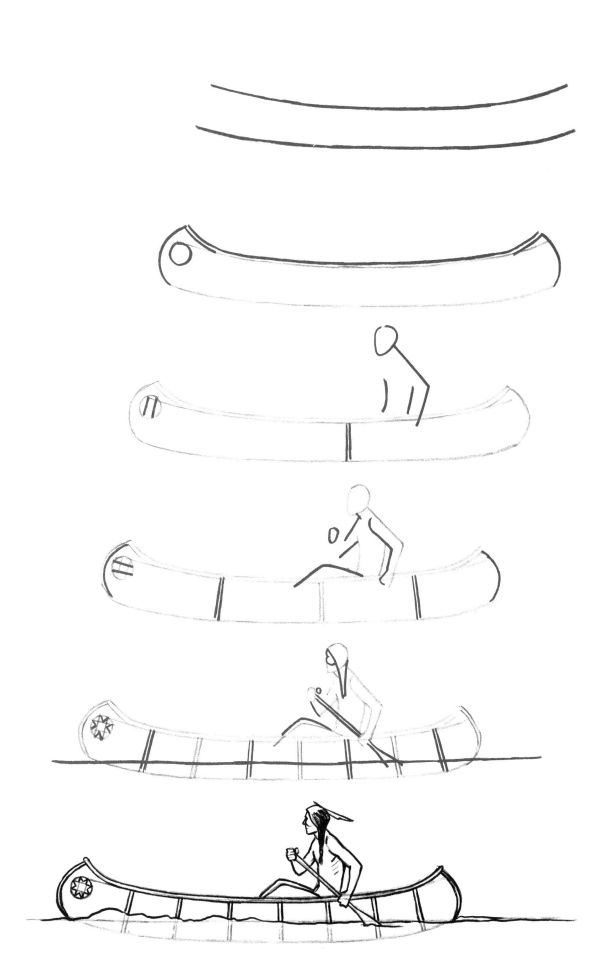

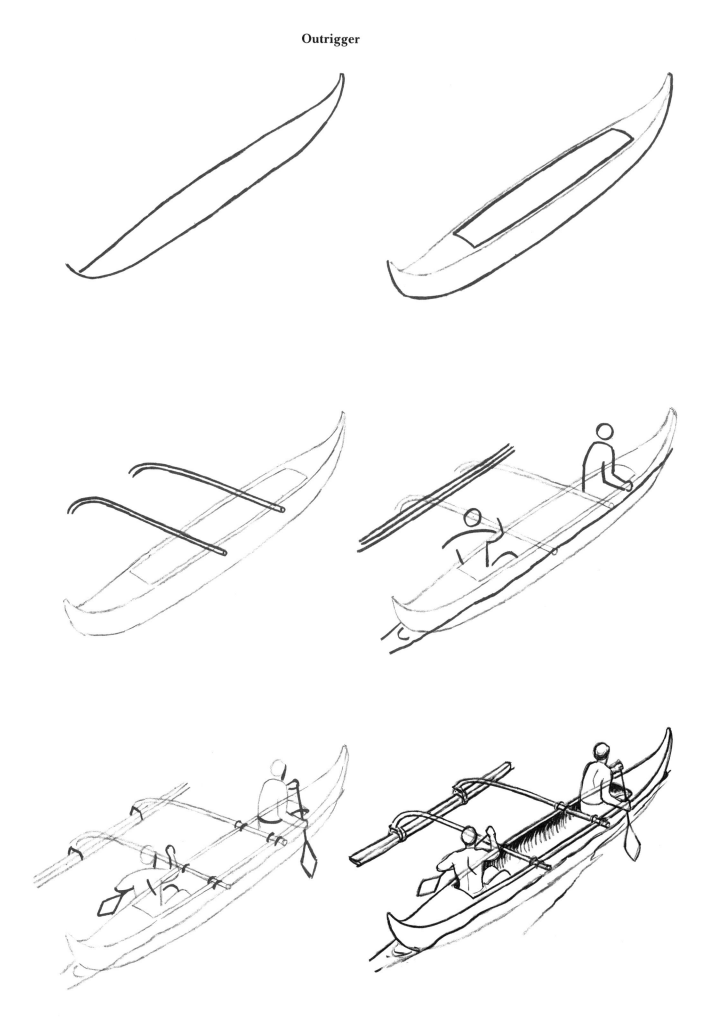

**Nuclear Submarine (U.S.S. *Nautilus*)**

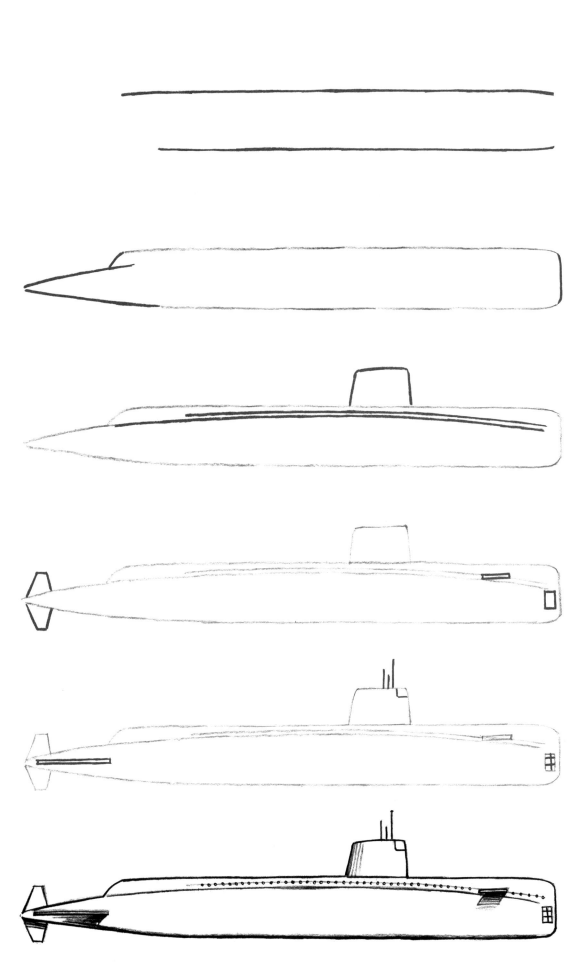

# World War II Destroyer

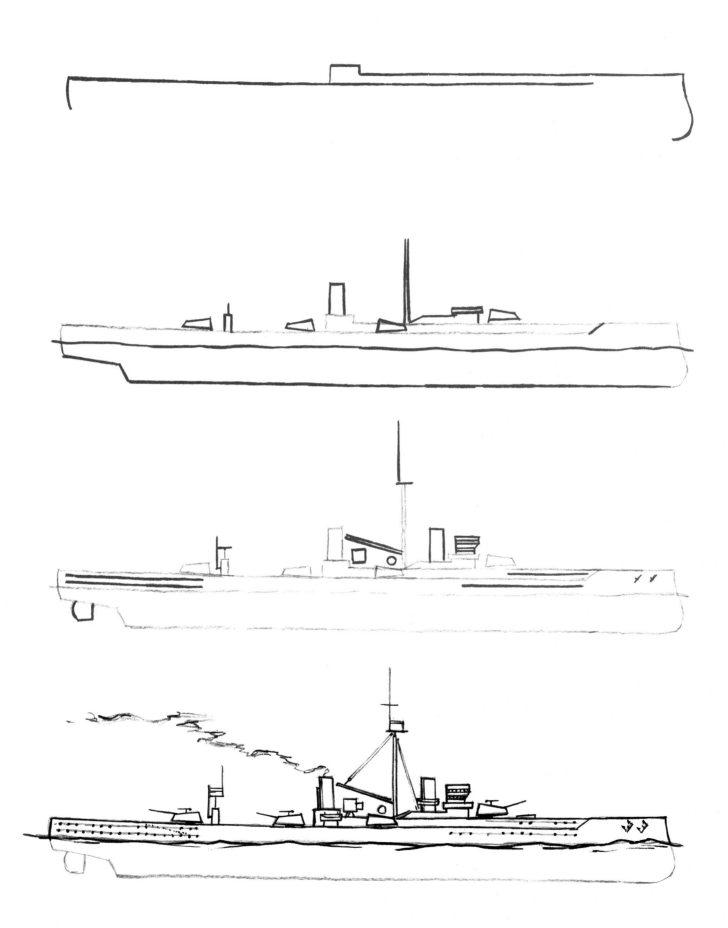

# Ocean Liner (Early Twentieth Century)

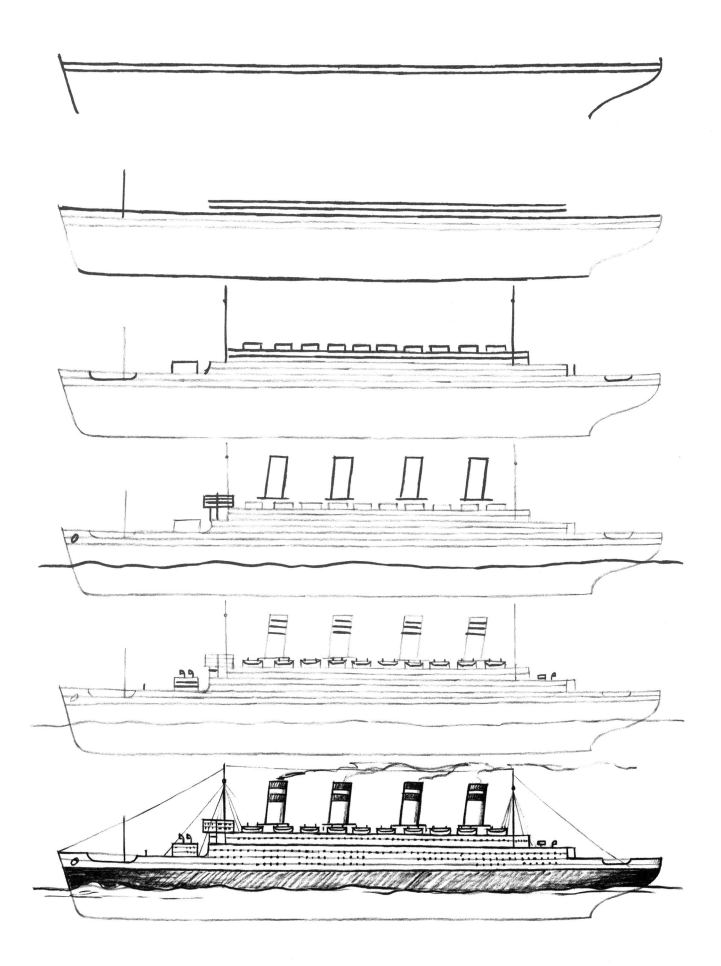

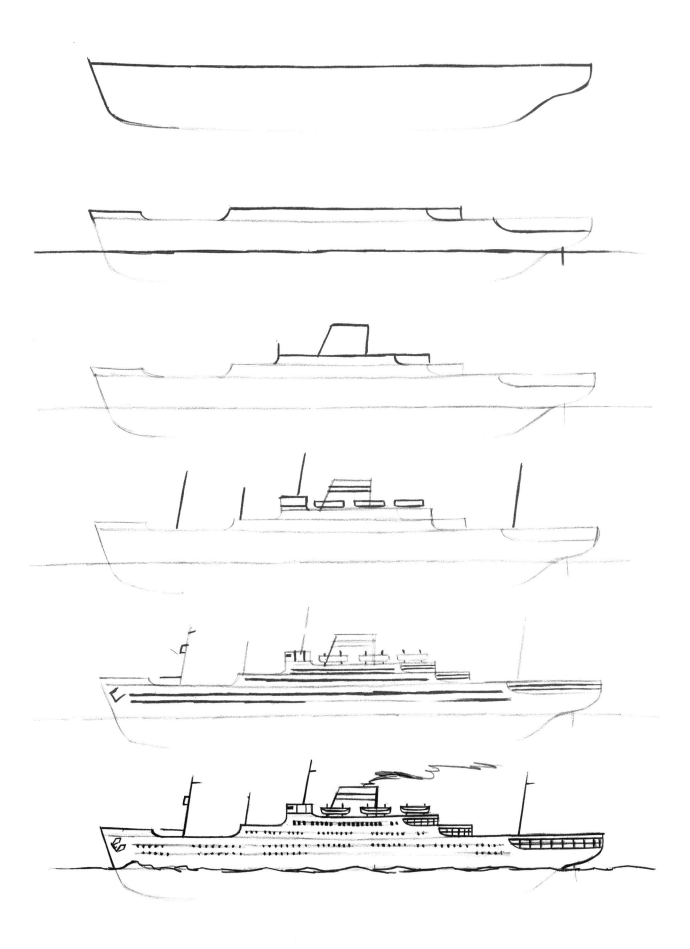

**Paddle-wheel Steamer**

**Tanker**

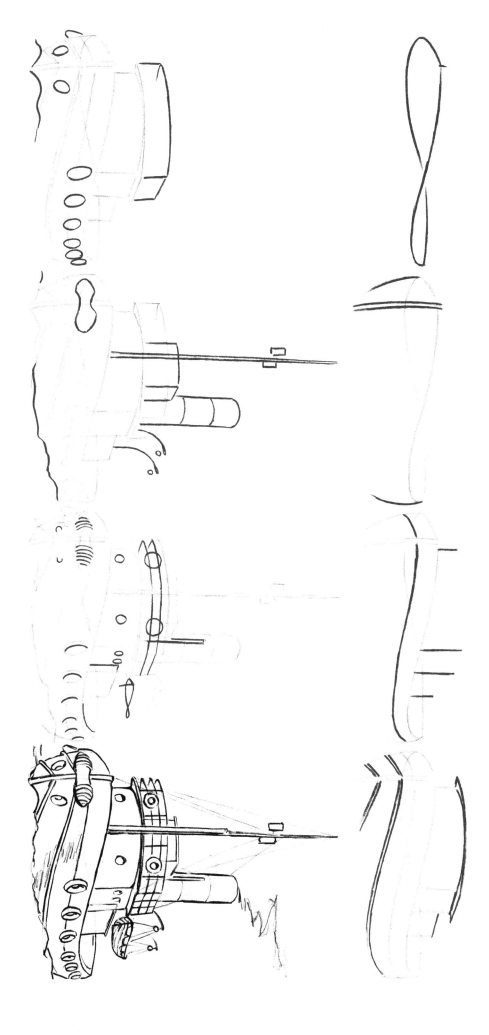

Tugboat

**Yacht**

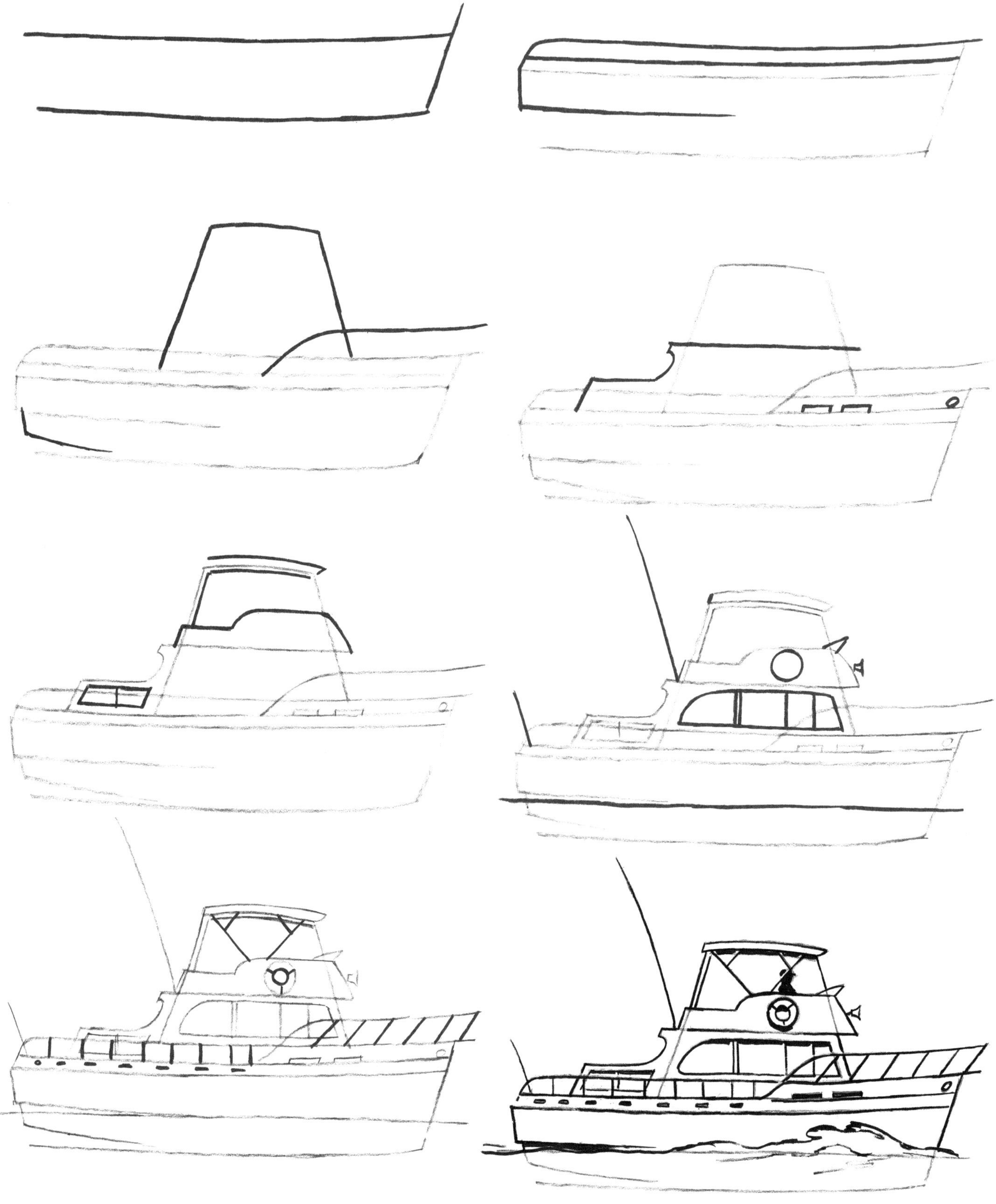

# Mini-tugboat

**Outboard Speedboat**

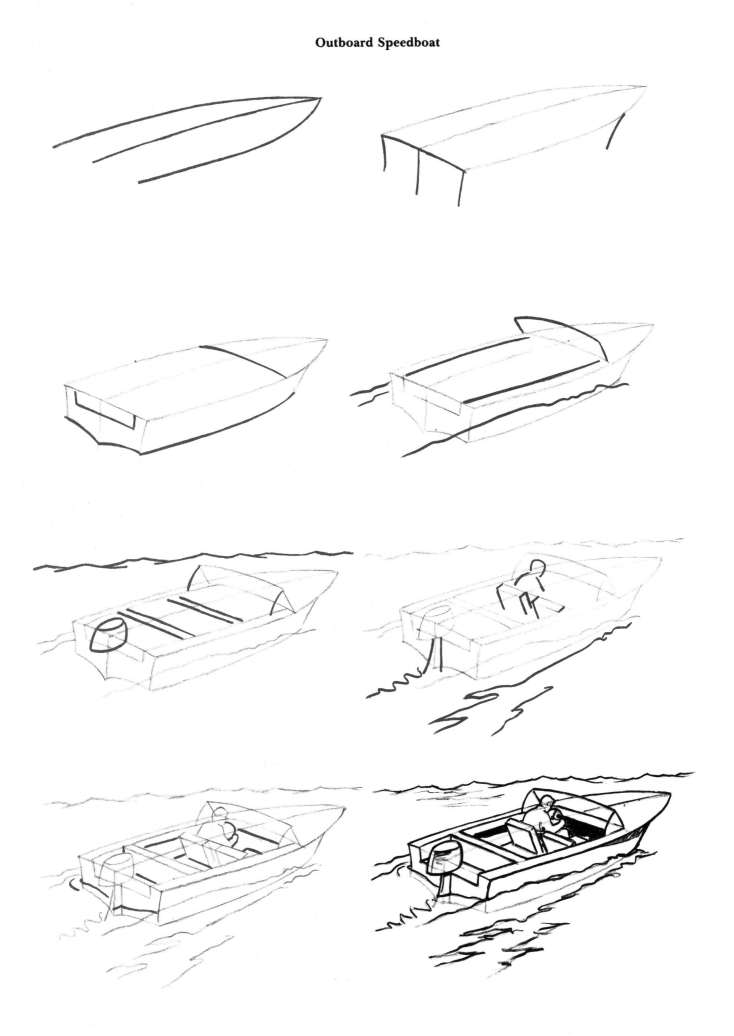

**Racing Craft**

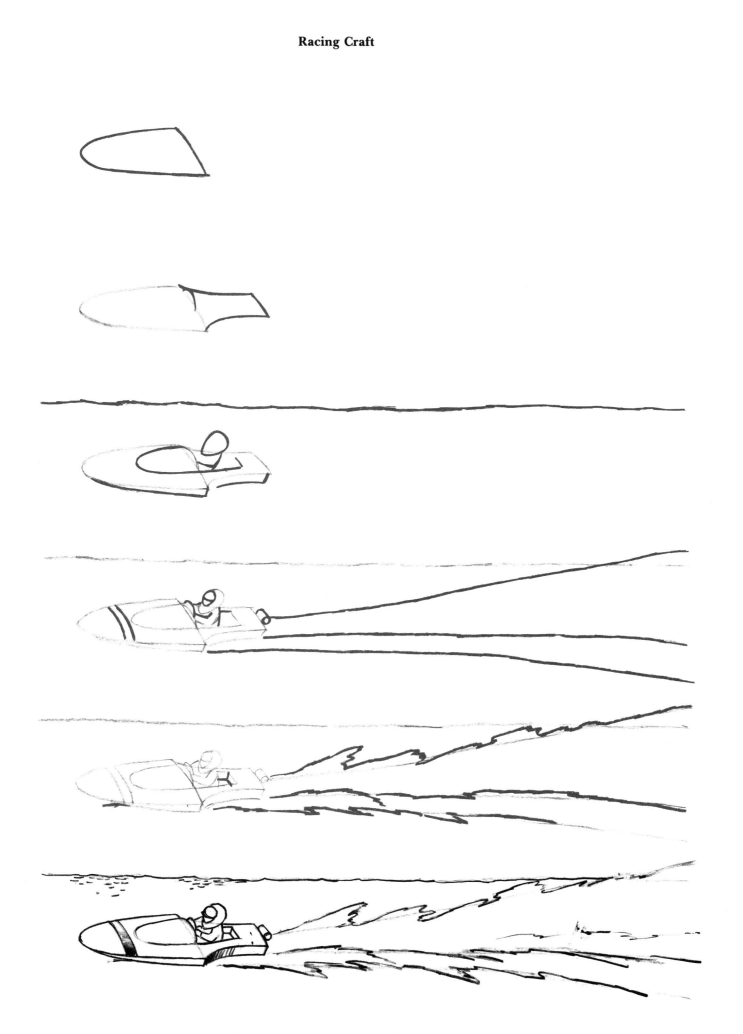

**Paddle-wheel Houseboat**

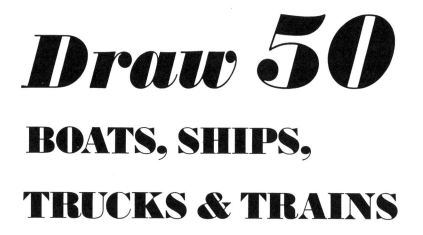

# *Draw 50*

## BOATS, SHIPS, TRUCKS & TRAINS

We learn the use of our tools by mimicry. Then we can use those tools for creativity. To this end I would offer the budding artist the opportunity to memorize or mimic (rotelike, if you wish) the making of "pictures." "Pictures" he has been anxious to be able to draw.

The use of this book should be available to anyone who *wants* to try another way of flapping his wings. Perhaps he will then get off the ground when his friend says, "David can draw a speedboat better than anybody else!"

LEE J. AMES

# *To the Parent or Teacher*

"David can draw a speedboat better than anybody else!" Such peer acclaim and encouragement generate incentive. Contemporary methods of art instruction (freedom of expression, experimentation, self-evaluation of competence and growth) provide a vigorous, fresh-air approach for which we must all be grateful.

New ideas need not, however, totally exclude the old. One such is the "follow me, step-by-step" approach. In my young learning days this method was so common, and frequently so exclusive, that the student became nothing more than a pantographic extension of the teacher. In those days it was excessively overworked.

This does not mean that the young hand is never to be guided. Rather, specific guiding is fundamental. Step-by-step guiding that produces satisfactory results is valuable even when the means of accomplishment are not fully understood by the student.

The novice with a musical instrument is frequently taught to play simple melodies as quickly as possible, well before he learns the most elemental scratchings at the surface of music theory. The resultant self-satisfaction, pride in accomplishment, can be a significant means of providing motivation. And all from mimicking an instructor's "Do-as-I-do . . ."

Mimicry is prerequisite for developing creativity.

where you wish. Don't be discouraged. The more you practice, the more you will develop control. Use a compass or a ruler if you wish; professional artists do! The only equipment you'll need will be a medium or soft pencil, paper, the kneaded eraser and, if you wish, a compass, ruler, pen or brush.

The first steps in this book are shown darker than necessary so that they can be clearly seen. (Keep your work very light.)

Remember, there are many other ways and methods to make drawings. This book shows just one method. Why don't you seek out other ways and methods to make drawings—from teachers, from libraries and, most importantly . . . from inside yourself?

LEE J. AMES

# *To the Reader*

This book will show you a way to draw boats, ships, trucks and trains. You need not start with the first illustration. Choose whichever you wish. When you have decided, follow the step-by-step method shown. *Very lightly* and *carefully,* sketch out step number one. However, this step, which is the easiest, should be done *most carefully.* Step number two is added right to step number one, also lightly and also very carefully. Step number three is sketched right on top of numbers one and two. Continue this way to the last step.

It may seem strange to ask you to be extra careful when you are drawing what seem to be the easiest first steps, but this is most important because a careless mistake at the beginning may spoil the whole picture at the end. As you sketch out each step, watch the spaces between the lines, as well as the lines, and see that they are the same. After each step, you may want to lighten your work by pressing it with a kneaded eraser (available at art supply stores).

When you have finished, you may want to redo the final step in India ink with a fine brush or pen. When the ink is dry, use the kneaded eraser to clean off the pencil lines. The eraser will not affect the India ink.

Here are some suggestions: In the first few steps, even when all seems quite correct, you might do well to hold your work up to a mirror. Sometimes the mirror shows that you've twisted the drawing off to one side without being aware of it. At first you may find it difficult to draw the boxes, triangles or circles, or to just make the pencil go

To *Mom* and *Toby* and most especially to the memory of
*Pop*

Originally published in hardcover in the United States by
Doubleday, a division of Random House Inc., New York, in 1976.

Library of Congress Cataloging-in-Publication Data
Ames, Lee J.
    Draw 50 boats, ships, trucks & trains
    Summary: Step-by-step instructions for drawing a variety of boats,
ships, trucks, and trains.
    1. Ships in art—Juvenile literature. 2. Boats in art—Juvenile
 literature. 3. Trucks in art—Juvenile literature. 4. Railroads in art—
Juvenile literature. 5. Drawing—Technique—Juvenile literature.
[1. Drawing—Technique] I. Title
NC825.S5A43     1987     743'89629046

Trade Paperback ISBN: 978-0-8230-8602-3
eBook ISBN: 978-0-8230-8603-0

Printed in the United States of America

10  9  8  7  6  5  4  3  2

2016 Watson-Guptill Edition

# DRAW 50

# Boats, Ships, Trucks, and Trains

THE STEP-BY-STEP WAY TO DRAW
*Submarines, Sailboats, Dump Trucks,*
*Locomotives, and Much More . . .*

## LEE J. AMES

WATSON-GUPTILL PUBLICATIONS
Berkeley

# BOOKS IN THIS SERIES

# DRAW 50

# Boats, Ships, Trucks, and Trains

THE STEP-BY-STEP WAY TO DRAW
*Submarines, Sailboats, Dump Trucks,
Locomotives, and Much More . . .*